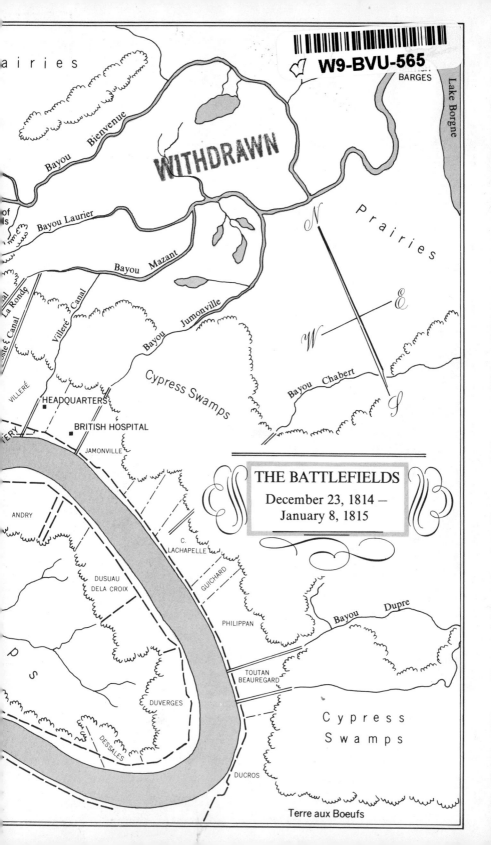

P r a i r i e s

BARGES

Lake Borgne

Bayou Bienvenue

WITHDRAWN

Bayou Laurier

Bayou Mazant

P r a i r i e s

N

E

W

S

Villeré Canal

La Ronde

Bayou Jumonville

Cypress Swamps

Bayou Chabert

VILLERÉ

HEADQUARTERS

BRITISH HOSPITAL

JAMONVILLE

ANDRY

C.
LACHAPELLE

| | **THE BATTLEFIELDS** |
| December 23, 1814 – |
| January 8, 1815 |

DUSUAU
DELA CROIX

GUICHARD

PHILIPPAN

Bayou   Dupre

TOUTAN
BEAUREGARD

P S

DUVERGES

Cypress
Swamps

DESSALES

DUCROS

Terre aux Boeufs

THE BRITISH AT THE GATES
The New Orleans Campaign
in the War of 1812

The British
at the Gates

THE NEW ORLEANS
CAMPAIGN
IN THE WAR OF 1812

by ROBIN REILLY

FOUNDED 1838

GPPS

G. P. Putnam's Sons, New York

Contents

Illustrations

(Following page 190)

Acknowledgments

Every effort has been made to trace owners of copyright in manuscript or other material and to obtain permission for the use of the extracts quoted. To any who may have eluded my searches I offer my apologies. Extracts from *Pakenham Letters 1800–1815* are quoted by kind permission of the Earl of Longford; from Lieutenant Gordon's Diary by courtesy of Brigadier A.. C. S. Boswell, colonel of the Argyll and Sutherland Highlanders Regiment; from the Dickson manuscripts by courtesy of the Royal Artillery Institution, Woolwich; from manuscripts in the Special Collections Division, Howard Tilton Memorial Library, Tulane University, by kind permission of the director; and from the Parsons collection of manuscripts by courtesy of the Humanities Research Center, the University of Texas at Austin. Transcripts of Crown-copyright records in the Public Record Office appear by permission of the Controller of H.M. Stationery Office. Extracts from *The Correspondence of Andrew Jackson* and quoted by courtesy of the Carnegie Institution; from Sir John Fortescue's *History of the British Army* by permission of Macmillan, London and Basingstoke; and from *The Autobiography of Lt.-Gen. Sir Harry Smith* (ed. G. C. Moore Smith) by permission of John Murray (Publishers) Ltd.

Permission to reproduce photographs of paintings or engravings was kindly granted by the Trustees of the British Museum; the Chicago Historical Society; the Chrysler Museum, Norfolk, Virginia; the Isaac Delgardo Museum of Art, New Orleans; the Ladies Hermitage Association; the Library of Congress; the Louisiana State Museum; the Metropolitan Museum of Art; the National Army Museum, London;

7

8 THE BRITISH AT THE GATES

the National Maritime Museum, London; the National Portrait Gallery, London; the Rifle Brigade Club; the Trustees of the Royal Fusiliers Museum, H. M. Tower of London; the National Collection of Fine Arts, Smithsonian Institution; the Tennessee State Museum; and the Warburg Institute.

To all who have generously contributed time, and expert knowledge and advice, to the preparation of this work I offer my sincere thanks. I am particularly indebted to Major R. G. Bartelot, Assistant Secretary of the Royal Artillery Institution; Mr. Robert D. Broussard; Dr. David L. Campbell; Mr. Boyd Cruise, Director of the Historic New Orleans Collection; Dr. G. Nañez Falcón; Mrs. Henrietta Gatehouse; Mrs. Connie G. Griffith, Director, Special Collections Division, Howard Tilton Memorial Library, Tulane University; Mrs. Arthur Hehr, Superintendent, Chalmette National Historical Park; Mrs. June Heyman; Mr. Victor L. Kirkpatrick; and Mrs. Edith Long, for personal assistance and encouragement which made five years of research both stimulating and rewarding.

Readers of the later chapters will have no difficulty in recognizing the warmth of my personal feelings for the city of New Orleans; but the character of a city is determined by its people, and it is to the people of New Orleans, who have made me welcome during ten years of frequent and prolonged visits, that I owe my most enduring debt of gratitude.

Introduction

The campaign misleadingly known as the Battle of New Orleans has always been the prerogative of American historians. For the United States it was a resounding and unexpected victory and is thus deservedly remembered; in Britain it was an astounding and catastrophic defeat which has been deliberately forgotten. Sir Winston Churchill accords it a brief paragraph in his *History of the English Speaking Peoples,* Sir Arthur Bryant does not mention it in *The Age of Elegance,* and no British historian has ever published a full account of the campaign. The nearest approach to such a work is Dr. Carson A. Ritchie's excellent study of the Dickson papers, published in the *Louisiana Historical Quarterly* in 1961.

It has been said that the British consult history and, when necessary, invent it. An examination of the accounts of the New Orleans campaign demonstrates that this custom is not exclusively British. The mythology of the campaign has grown to outweigh its history, and much of the invention is homegrown. To the historian, memoirs written for publication must always be suspect, and the battle recollections of generals in old age are notoriously unreliable. It is, therefore, in the private diaries and letters of the period that the truth is most likely to be found. These are not innocent of personal or national prejudice, or of judgments unsoundly based on inadequate information or understanding, but they are generally free from the flatteries, rationalizations, and justifications imposed on a chronicler of contemporary events by his audience.

There is no lack of memoirs of the campaign. So brilliant and so startling was the victory, and so great the personal glory attached to having played a part in it, that memorialists jostled one another into print, competing for ever more romantic or damning recollections like sinners at a disreputable public confession. While private journals and correspondence remained hidden, these writers laid a foundation of prejudice, misrepresentation, and invention which few historians have been able to resist as a basis for their own work. The uncritical use of the accounts given by Latour, Walker, and Gleig, in particular, has created a mythology of the campaign which is in the true sense romantic.

Such memoirs are nevertheless valuable. They contain many accurate details of the movements of troops, the conditions under which the battles were fought, and documented incidents which lend authentic color to the narrative. It is when they deal with matters affecting individual motives and reputations, or report conversations held among enemy commanders, or recount their own invariably blameless deeds that their authors must be challenged.

Of all the contemporary accounts so far discovered, the least questionable is the journal of the British artillery commander Lieutenant Colonel Alexander Dickson. Though later copied in manuscript for presentation to Lord Mulgrave, Master General of the Ordnance, it was never intended for publication, and its authenticity as a day-by-day record of events as they were known to him is beyond doubt. Dickson makes few judgments and fewer criticisms. Nor does he attempt to disguise the failures, including his own, which led to defeat. Dickson's is an uncompromisingly factual account of events, set down without elaboration and almost without comment. It is a bleak tribute to his integrity as a diarist that without his journal we would not know the extent of his own responsibility for defeat.

George Robert Gleig's diary, in its original manuscript, was manifestly truthful in intention. As a junior British regimental officer he had no part in command decisions and little understanding of the considerations which shaped them. His judgments are generally unsound, and parts of his account, presented as fact but based on hearsay or supposition, are inaccurate; but he provides a vivid and authentic picture of the conditions under which the men of Pakenham's army lived, fought, and died. The various published editions of Gleig's narrative are witness to a progressive submission to the weight of his literary pretensions and a desire, as a minister of the church,* to draw moral conclusions.

---

*Gleig later became chaplain-general to the army.

If Gleig's narrative is to be accepted, in its early form, with reservation, Benson Earle Hill's recollections must be regarded as dramatic entertainment. Buell appears to have taken him seriously and in his *Life of Andrew Jackson* writes of Hill as commander of the British artillery before New Orleans. Hill was a lieutenant and acting adjutant in an artillery force which included a lieutenant colonel, two majors, and five captains. He does not appear to have commanded a battery in action. His account is amusing but highly imaginative.

No detailed journal of any British officer senior in rank to Dickson has survived. Both Keane and Lambert left official reports of their actions in command of the army before Pakenham's arrival and after his death, but neither Sir Edward Pakenham nor Sir Alexander Cochrane, the two commanders who bore the chief responsibility, appears to have kept a diary of operations. Their motives, some of their actions, and the quality of their relationship during the campaign remain the subject of conjecture.

Of the American source materials the most detailed is Arsène Lacarrière Latour's *Historical Memoir,* which was rushed into print in 1816. Latour's prejudice was so strong, and his desire to please so great, that all pretense of historical integrity drowned beneath the flood of malice, distortion, and congratulation. But as chief engineer officer to Jackson's army, his expert and personal knowledge of events cannot be ignored. No significant part of his account may be accepted without corroboration, but no part of it should be discarded without authoritative evidence in refutation. There is much in Latour's *Historical Memoir* which is both accurate and truthful, and historians of the campaign will continue to consult his work, but with caution.

Alexander Walker's *Jackson and New Orleans,* published forty years later, wears a mantle of respectability skillfully woven from the threads of his presence in New Orleans during the campaign. His work is both useful and informative, but his admiration for Jackson and his desire to present as complete a history for which he had less than half the required evidence led him into elaborate inventions. The mythology of the campaign fathered by Latour was fed, clothed, and groomed by Walker.

An American journal of the campaign comparable to Dickson's has yet to be found, but there is a wealth of shorter journals and private correspondence which provide reliable evidence of the sequence of events and records of personal experience. Andrew Jackson's letters are particularly revealing of the man who, by extraordinary exertions, triumphed over the inertia of a people and the best endeavors of a superior army. With the single exception of Sir Isaac Brock, no general, from either side, matched Jackson for energy, skill, determination, or leadership. His presence on the northern frontier early in the war would have transformed the American campaigns for conquest and might have altered Canadian history. It was Britain's good fortune that the United States administration was as bungling as the generals it chose to appoint.

At New Orleans Jackson was given the opportunity, for the first and last time in his life, to display the full armory of his qualities as a general. To assume that the British commanders opposing him were incompetent is unjustly to underrate those qualities. Three generals —all young, courageous, and experienced—separately led the invading army during the campaign. Considering the extraordinary difficulties confronting them, they came remarkably close to success. Against a less vigilant opponent, their errors would not have led to failure. When, by a daring and even reckless landing, the British Army was brought to within eight miles of New Orleans, it was the flexibility of Jackson's defensive plan that enabled him to regain, that same night, the lost initiative, and it was Jackson's domination which converted a position favorable to victory into a dangerous trap from which even immediate withdrawal offered no certainty of escape. In the last analysis no military commander can succeed without a fair share of good fortune. Jackson had the luck he deserved.

The purpose of this book is twofold: to show the campaign in perspective against the War of 1812, of which it was a small part; and to present an account which is securely cast from evidence, making no concessions to romance. I make no apology, therefore, for including an outline of the war in America or for what may appear to be digressions into Europe. Without this background the New Orleans campaign is incomprehensible and the extent of Jackson's achievement impossible to measure. Nor should it be necessary to make excuse for the rejection of all dramatic incident or dialogue which cannot be substantiated by reliable evidence or documented events. The history of this campaign requires no additional mythographer.

As a British historian I make no claim to impartiality. If integrity of research demands that prejudice and preconception be cast aside to allow for the free assessment of evidence, involvement and partisanship are the inevitable consequences of honest research. In this connection it is the serious duty of the historian to differentiate between fact, so far as it may be ascertained from evidence, and opinion, which is a considered deduction. This division must be made clear.

National partiality is among the most difficult of prejudices to overcome, and its suppression often produces violent and irrational alienation. A common language and shared heritage may be as divisive as they are binding. By 1812 the enmity between the United States and Britain engendered by the Revolution had become a national tradition. A century passed before the breach was fully healed and another fifty years and two world wars were required to forge and temper an enduring friendship. It is not entirely fanciful to suppose that the seeds of that friendship were sown on the field of Chalmette, on January 8, 1815, when armies of the United States and Britain faced each other in battle for the last time.

I

War in Europe 1803–1807

On June 18, 1812, James Madison, fourth President of the United States of America, signed a declaration of war against Great Britain. The causes of the war were obscure, and the motives for Madison's decision inadequate. The timing of this declaration was, and has remained, incomprehensible. When the peace treaty was concluded, thirty months later, those Americans who had demanded war found that none of their stated objectives had been achieved. An unnecessary and costly war had ended in a draw.

The American aims are clear, and there is ample evidence of them in the speeches made in the House of Representatives:[1] the restoration of maritime rights; an end to impressment; the final destruction of the Indian threat to frontier lands; and the annexation of Canada. The first two arose directly from Britain's military commitment in Europe, and the fourth could not have been considered without it. The third was the consequence of understandable but exaggerated fear. The true causes of the war had been sown half a century earlier and germinated during the Revolution. They lay in the deeply rooted characteristics of a vigorous people, emerging as a nation and confronted by the continuing dominance of the country from which they came: affronted pride; territorial greed; and a bitter resentment which had been fed but not satisfied by revolution. The greatest single cause of war was nationalism, and it was nurtured by a lofty condescension, amounting at times to open contempt, explicit in British dealings with the American ex-colonists. The tacit refusal of the British to regard the Americans as anything more than immature and disaffected colonials was as much responsible for war as were the untiring efforts of the Hawks who promoted it.

In February, 1793, Britain embarked upon the longest war in its history. With one short period of uneasy peace, while the powers of Europe gathered strength for the renewal of the conflict on an ever more savage and destructive scale, the war lasted for 22 years. More than any other in 700 years, it threatened the existence of Britain as an independent nation. "We must now," said Pitt, "declare our firm resolution effectually to oppose those principles of ambition and aggrandisement which have for their object the destruction of England, of Europe and of the world." In 1793, when he made this stirring pronouncement in the House of Commons, he might have been accused of exaggeration, but 10 years later the war had become, for Britain and for much of Europe, a struggle for survival. Ruthless measures demanded countermeasures no less ruthless, and America gradually became trapped between the hinges of opposing European strategies. Washington, Adams, and Jefferson succeeded in shielding America from any direct engagement in the war in Europe. Madison had war thrust upon him, by his own people, in his own country.

During the first eight years of war against France, Britain was able to behave with moderation toward America. The Navigation Acts, frequently modified in detail but unchanged in principle since the first Act of 1651, had secured for Britain not only the greater part of the carrying trade of the world, but also a vast merchant marine from whose ranks trained seamen could be drawn in time of war. Although a liberal policy of free trade between the two countries had been advocated by Pitt and Lord Shelburne, it was no part of the British government's policy to relax the Navigation System in favor of America. As a concession American commerce with the West Indies was permitted, and even goods destined for France were, for a time, allowed to pass from the French colonies through American ports. Two factors determined the end of moderate attitudes: the necessity for an absolute blockade of France, and the growing strength of American competition in maritime trade.

The Treaty of Amiens in 1801, greeted with rapture and disarmament in Britain, was founded upon the false assumption that Napoleon wanted a permanent peace. Britain surrendered all its colonial conquests except Ceylon and Trinidad: Martinique and Guadeloupe were returned to France, Minorca to Spain, the Cape of Good Hope to the Dutch; and Malta was restored to the suzerainty of the Knights of St. John. France agreed to recognize the integrity of the Turkish Empire and Portugal, promised an indemnity to the House of Orange, and undertook to evacuate all troops from Egypt and Naples. While the militia was disbanded and British visitors jostled one another across the Channel to gape at Paris under the newly proclaimed First Consul, Napoleon annexed Piedmont and Parma. While tourists gazed in silent astonishment at the plundered wealth of Italian art reposing in the Louvre or exclaimed in admiration at the sight of the new Caesar at the head of his Guards, a French army entered and occupied Switzerland. When, to the feeble Henry Addington, the British Prime Minister, and his dotty old King, it appeared that Napoleon was planning a new invasion of Egypt, instructions were given to retain Malta as a base for the Mediterranean fleet. This was the first indication that Britain would not continue indefinitely to meet aggression with appeasement, and it came at an inconvenient moment for France. Toussaint L'Ouverture, leader of the blacks in Santo Domingo,* had set up a constitutional government, declaring himself president for life. Napoleon dispatched a strong army under his brother-in-law, General Charles Leclerc, to reestablish French rule. Toussaint L'Ouverture was captured by treachery and sent to France, where he died in prison in 1803, but the Haitian climate took an appalling revenge. While the natives hid in the mountains, the French force was decimated by disease: Leclerc and 25,000 of his troops died of yellow fever. A substantial part of Napoleon's naval strength was occupied in the Caribbean in support of Leclerc. It was no time to indulge in a war against the strongest naval power in the world.

As it became clear that Britain would fight, and if necessary alone, to prevent further French conquests, it was evident that Napoleon could no longer pursue dreams of empire in America. In 1800, by secret treaty with Spain, France had acquired the Louisiana Territory. By the spring of 1803, this great acquisition had become a liability. Napoleon's threat to control shipping on the Mississippi by occupying New Orleans had alarmed and alienated the Americans almost to the point of war. Without strong bases in the West Indies the territory would be indefensible against either the Americans on land or a British invasion protected by superior naval strength. On April 30, 1803, Napoleon solved the problem by selling the territory to America. It was a masterly strategic stroke which appeared to please everyone but the British.

*The island discovered by Columbus in 1492 and named Española (Hispaniola), now Haiti.

Nothing, it seemed, would please the British. Napoleon sought to gain time by diplomacy, but the minuet of negotiations lacked a necessary precision and stateliness. The British were intransigent, and the First Consul was unable to restrain his temper. While French troops remained in Switzerland and Holland, the British refused to leave Malta. Napoleon began his preparations for the invasion of England, and Ambassador Lord Whitworth packed his bags to leave Paris. A last-minute intervention by Russia, persuaded by France to mediate, appeared certain to procure for Napoleon the time he needed to regain his fleet and complete his invasion plans. It was inconceivable that the British would risk offending the one powerful nation able to help them in a war in Europe. But the British were not only intractable, but also unpredictable. Whitworth left for London, William Wordsworth composed for the *Morning Post* a patriotic sonnet[2] which remains a masterpiece of uninspired fervor, and five ships of the line under Sir William Cornwallis put out into the Channel, destined for Brest. On May 18 Britain declared war on France. Nelson rejoined the *Victory* at Portsmouth. Major General Arthur Wellesley was harrying the Mahrattas in India. The young officer who was to be his brother-in-law, Lieutenant Colonel Edward Pakenham, was with his regiment, the 64th Foot, on Barbados. British travelers in France were arrested and interned. French troops occupied the harbors of Taranto and Brindisi and took possession of the free towns of Bremen and Hamburg. The foundations of Napoleon's Continental System, the exclusion of Britons and their goods from the whole of Europe, were laid, but the real economic war was to come later.

Napoleon believed that Britain could be vanquished by invasion. His energies were directed toward the building and assembly of a vast fleet of troop-carrying boats and the erection of gun batteries along the coast to protect his shipping from the British fleet. The task was obviously formidable; in the event the problems proved to be insuperable. Throughout the golden summer of 1803 the British waited for the promised assault. The government's appeal for volunteers had succeeded beyond the most optimistic expectations, and the reconstituted militia acquired 350,000 recruits, for many of whom there were no arms. In the beleaguered island, resplendent uniforms clothed men whose only weapon was a pike; the fragile William Pitt was a colonel, and the corpulent Charles James Fox a private; and arrangements were made for the King to join his army while his Queen and the court removed to Worcester. The apprehension was not unfounded, nor were the precautions unnecessary. Napoleon planned to transport 120,000 men with horses, supplies, and artillery in 2,400 boats, some of which were armed. Through the summer he waited impatiently for the boats to be built. By July he was demanding more than 3,000 to transport 160,000 troops. As autumn came, and winter, the possibility of Channel fog intensified the task of the watching British fleets: Collingwood's, outside the Atlantic ports of Brest, L'Orient, and Rochefort; Keith's, watching the remainder of the Dutch fleet on the Texel; and Nelson's, off Toulon. Admiral the Earl of St. Vincent, First Lord of the Admiralty, remained confident: "I do not say the French cannot come. I only say they cannot come by water."[3] Napoleon's fleet, recalled from the West Indies, was unable to reach a home port. It was blockaded in neutral Spanish ports by Alexander Cochrane. The first year of the war's second and decisive phase passed. Napoleon's much-advertised invasion had not set out, but Britain had been forced onto the defensive. Unless the initiative could be regained, the threat of invasion would remain, and one day that threat must inevitably become a reality.

There was little hope of any British initiative while the government remained in the hands of the bloodless Addington and his sycophantic supporters, but in May, 1804, Pitt returned to office. Physically he was the enfeebled shadow of the great leader of 1798, his health no less precarious than his Parliamentary position; but his strength of purpose was undiminished, and his return to power provided a nice balance for Napoleon's elevation to the title of Emperor. Napoleon's impatient brilliance in tactical warfare was matched by Pitt's tenacious cunning in strategic diplomacy. For nearly two years, until Pitt's death in 1806, the struggle was as much one between two men of genius as between the great countries they led. While Napoleon attempted, by military maneuvering, to obtain the release of his fleet and the overthrow of Pitt's ministry, Pitt sought, by diplomacy, to gain the active support or the guaranteed neutrality of the European nations. That neither was successful in his efforts was due to the thwarting countermeasures of the other.

Throughout 1804 Napoleon strove to extricate his scattered naval squadrons from British blockades at Brest, Rochefort, Cádiz, Toulon, Texel and Ferrol, where a total of thirty-six ships was bottled up by the Royal Navy. No invasion force could cross the Channel without a strong escort, and every stratagem was employed to decoy the superior British blockading fleets from their stations. Cornwallis, Nelson, Pellew, and Thornborough were too experienced to be drawn away, but withdrew over the horizon occasionally in attempts to lure the enemy into the open where he must give battle. Napoleon's confidence in his maneuvers even extended to his having a medal struck to commemorate, prematurely, the *Descente en Angleterre*. Veracity was sacrificed to optimism in the inscription *"frappé à Londres en 1804."*

Pitt, despairing of help from Prussia or the smaller German states, or from Spain, negotiated with the young Czar Alexander of Russia and fed the fears of Austria. By the autumn the Russians were prepared to sign a treaty to enforce French withdrawal from Italy, Holland, and North Germany, but such an alliance could not be effective unless British lines of communication with the Mediterranean could be secured. Across this route lay the powerful Spanish fleet based in Ferrol, Cartagena, and Cádiz, officially neutral but liable at any moment to be driven into open and active alliance with France. Pitt determined to force the issue. The British ambassador was instructed to demand the demobilization of the Spanish fleet, and Cornwallis was ordered to send four frigates to intercept the returning Mexican treasure fleet and confiscate the silver destined for use in financing the equipment of Spanish warships. The fleet escorts fought, and 300 Spaniards were killed. Spain declared war on December 12. Meanwhile, the Austrians yielded to pressure from Russia and Britain and agreed to join them in imposing peace on France. Napoleon reacted with customary speed and lack of diplomacy. Early in the new year of 1805 he sent an ultimatum to Austria, demanding an immediate explanation and an end to all military preparations. To King George III he sent a personal message, addressed in the brotherly terms of one emperor to another, proposing conciliation and peace. The Austrians were cowed into temporary inactivity, but the old King, sufficiently restored in health to recognize impertinence and accustomed to the deviousness inseparable from absolute power, left it to his government to compose a freezing reply.

For several months Napoleon, unable to concentrate the French and Spanish fleets, planned to strike at British possessions in India and the West Indies, and a small force succeeded in slipping away to Martinique; but these were diversionary expeditions more than an essential part of his strategy. Britain could be defeated only by invasion, and the prerequisites for invasion were a substantial army at the Channel ports, sufficient transports, and the absence or destruction of the British fleet. While Pitt struggled to construct an offensive alliance on the continent of Europe, Napoleon issued a series of feverish instructions to his admirals. They were to break out of the blockades, put to sea without a fight, and concentrate in the West Indies. Their combined strengths would enable them to return, raise the blockades on any French and Spanish squadrons still trapped in port, and take control of the Channel. The failure of the design was due less to its impracticability in terms of naval strategy than to the differences in experience and command structure between the French and British navies. The French Navy took its instructions from the Emperor. Little opportunity existed for personal initiative or deviation from instructions, and the painful slowness of communications often nullified the effect of orders before they were received. British admirals, on the contrary, received information and instructions within which they were expected to act as experience and local circumstances dictated. A fighting squadron might give chase to the enemy—as Nelson's fleet pursued Villeneuve to the West Indies and back—but in time of danger to the British Isles the fleet gathered, it seemed by instinct, at the approaches to the Channel.

Napoleon's efforts to concentrate the French and Spanish fleets culminated in their destruction at Trafalgar on October 21, 1805. It was a crushing defeat but had little effect upon Napoleon's immediate plans, for he had already abandoned his design for invasion. The war at sea was lost. Britain should be isolated and ignored while France subdued the rest of Europe.

The news of Trafalgar was received in London with relief and gratitude but without jubilation. The death of Nelson cast a pall over public rejoicing. The government had even more gloomy events to endure. In September, Pitt's diplomatic overtures, sustained by the offer of military assistance in force, had brought both Russia and Austria into the field against France. This triumph was short-lived. Napoleon marched 200,000 troops 500 miles from the Channel to the Danube, encircled and routed 70,000 Austrians at Elchingen, and accepted the surrender of the remainder on October 20, before the Russian Army could cover a similar distance from Cracow. The Prussians, whose territory had been violated by the French armies in their march to Ulm, vacillated between the threats of Napoleon and the promise of a British expedition which landed at Cuxhaven in December. The Austrians were regrouping, and the Russians under Czar Alexander and General Mikhail Kutusov were reported to have defeated the French in Moravia. The truth was not known in London until the end of the year: the allied armies had been shattered on December 2 at Austerlitz, and the Austrians were preparing to make a separate peace. On January 9, 1806, Nelson's body was buried in St. Paul's Cathedral. Less than two weeks later Pitt died. Charles James

Fox, appointed Secretary of State for Foreign Affairs and Leader of the
Commons in William Grenville's new ministry, opened negotiations
for peace, but the events of the last seven months of his life convinced
him that it was unattainable on any but the most humiliating terms.
With his death from dropsy, on September 13, died also the last hope of
ending the war by diplomacy.

Two minor military sorties, faint and somewhat distant gleams of
hope in a year of almost unrelieved gloom, were greeted with satisfaction out of all proportion to their significance: Sir Home Popham, with
a regiment of Highlanders from the Cape of Good Hope and 400 men
from St. Helena, assaulted Buenos Aires and robbed the affronted
colonists (whom he had come to rescue from Spanish suppression) of
more than $1,000,000, and Sir John Stuart, temporary commander of
the British troops sent earlier by Pitt to defend Sicily, attacked the
Italian mainland with 6,000 troops and trounced a French army,
which outnumbered his by eight to one, before withdrawing.* Home
Popham's extraordinary exploit in September, reinforced by Samuel
Auchmuty's capture of Montevideo five months later, was nullified by
General John Whitelocke's disgraceful defeat and capitulation there in
October, 1807. Stuart's achievement was confined to an indication
that British troops, competently led, might be a match even for
Napoleon's veterans. Further eccentric attacks, aimed at Turkey and
Egypt, were as unsuccessful as they were ill-judged. They dissipated
the strength of the army and made certain that no effective force was
available in time to assist the Russians after they had beaten the
French in the carnage of Eylau.

In the thirteen months following Pitt's death the Grenville administration, for all its efforts to take the initiative, had shown no sign
of grasping the essentials for British survival: the preservation of the
alliance with Russia and the encouragement of European resistance to
Napoleon; the concentration of land forces, in concert with allies, to
strike an effective blow at the French; and the use of unchallenged
command of the sea. The government's single great achievement, the
abolition of the African slave trade, made a significant contribution to
humanity but none to the prosecution of the war. An attempt to extend
political rights to Irish Catholics was blocked by the King's prejudices,
and he dismissed his government. For England, Grenville's liberal
intentions were a happy accident: indirectly they were responsible for

---

*This engagement produced the only recorded example of a British regiment fighting stark
naked. The 27th Foot, surprised by an attack while bathing, snatched up their muskets and,
unconventionally stripped for action, repelled the charge of the French cavalry.

the formation of a ministry which, though led by the elderly Duke of Portland, included Canning, Castlereagh, Chatham, Mulgrave, and Perceval. It was a promising change of government, but it came too late to repair the errors and omissions of the previous administration. In June, 1807, the Russians were routed at Friedland, and two weeks later the Czar signed the Treaty of Tilsit. All French conquests were recognized and accepted; Russia secretly pledged support against Britain; and Denmark, Portugal, and Austria were to be compelled to join the alliance. Prussia, cowed and truncated, agreed to close its ports against England and subscribe to the Continental system. The new British government found itself exposed and friendless.

Disciples of Pitt, the new ministers acted with commendable speed and decision. An expeditionary force under Lord Cathcart, landed at Rügen too late to reinforce the Russians, was hastily withdrawn and redirected against Denmark. An ultimatum for its surrender having been rejected, the Danish fleet was captured, Copenhagen bombarded until it capitulated, and any possibility of Denmark's active participation in the war against Britain indefinitely postponed. Just five weeks elapsed between the issue of Castlereagh's orders and the Danish surrender. If the operation was morally indefensible, it was strategically essential. Moreover, it demonstrated a renewed ability to act, which impressed other neutral nations. At the end of November, less than two months after the surrender of Copenhagen, a French army under Andoche Junot, ignoring the terrified protestations of the Portuguese Regent that his country supported the Continental allies, entered Lisbon. Junot was disappointed: the British had again forestalled him by removing to safety both the Regent, Prince John, and the Portuguese fleet. Within three weeks Madeira had been occupied, and seven months later British troops landed in Portugal. They did not leave the European continent until the war was over.

By the time Castlereagh and Canning had taken over their ministries at the War Department and the Foreign Office in March, 1807, the danger to Britain was as much economic as military. Four months earlier, on November 21, 1806, Napoleon had issued the Berlin Decree. It was a beginning to a counterblockade, a bold attempt to exclude Britain from its most important markets by closing the ports of Europe to British goods and forbidding European commerce with Britain. This Continental System, a blockade by the denial of commerce in port, was an effective answer to the British naval blockade which relied on the seizure of ships at sea. British exports to northern Europe fell, in less than two years, by 80 percent. British Orders in Council intensified the naval blockade, closing all ports from which British commerce was excluded to neutral shipping which failed to call at a British port and pay duty on their cargoes. Napoleon replied with the Milan Decree, outlawing all neutral shipping which submitted to the British Orders in Council. By this series of retaliatory measures France and Britain embarked upon policies which came near to ruining both countries. Scarcely less important was their effect upon the industry and trade of colonial countries and neutrals. America, in particular, had just cause for resentment. At the moment when, as an emergent nation, it could look for expansion in competition with the two great European powers, it found its trade subject to the same British restrictions as had been imposed upon it as a colonial territory. There were many in America who, to protect their right to trade freely, were prepared to go to war. Nothing could be achieved without the support of the New England states, and this was not forthcoming. Moreover, as it was obviously unpractical to fight both France and Britain, it was necessary to decide against which of the great powers war should be declared. On this important question there appeared to be some doubt. It was the British, their eyes too firmly fixed on Europe and the immediate struggle for survival, who resolved that dilemma.

II

Blockade and Impressment

During the first phase of the war between Britain and France, which concluded with the Treaty of Amiens, American trade had prospered. Indeed, such advantage had the United States taken of its neutrality that, to the indignation of British shipping interests, it had become a serious rival for the carrying trade of the world. With other neutrals, the United States was barred from any direct traffic between the West Indies, or any colony of a belligerent, and any but its own or British ports. It was thus excluded from direct commerce with nations hostile to Britain and also from the carrying trade between neutrals. The right of absolute blockade against the hostile ports of Europe was asserted, at first unofficially but later with brazen clarity, by the British, regardless of their ability to enforce it at the entrances to those ports. In effect the British fleet was thus empowered to stop and search any ship on the high seas. This assertion did not go unchallenged, but it was an undeniable fact that American commerce had benefited by the war to an extent which made any alteration to the regulations, however desirable, an unrealistic aim. As late as November, 1804, Jefferson was satisfied with the undisturbed "friendship and intercourse" with the nations of Europe, and Monroe wrote from London "Our commerce was never so much favored in time of war."[4] Monroe's instructions were to negotiate for concessions. Any hopes he might have entertained were destroyed by the *Essex* case in May, 1805, and the commercial blockades which followed.

The case itself was trivial, but the principles it decided were significant. Previously it had been established that the landing of goods and the payment of duties in a neutral country constituted a "broken journey," enabling the reexport of those goods to a belligerent. The cost of the goods was inflated by these extra charges and British trade satisfactorily protected. The Americans found a way to evade these charges while, at the same time, observing the British regulations: duties paid by importers of goods into the United States were refunded, by "drawback," when the goods were reexported. It was ingenious but optimistic. The test case of the ship *Essex* redefined the conditions of importation by a neutral, and it was ruled that drawback of duties involved a failure to comply with the broken voyage principle and rendered the ships concerned liable to seizure. Once more Britain was imposing, by sole right of naval superiority, its policy of regulating the trade of a neutral in order to protect its own. At this period of the war the decision had little to do with the blockade of Europe, for the ultimate destination of the goods was not in question; the issue was the price at which American goods could be delivered and how this compared with the price of similar goods from British colonies carried in British ships. After Pitt's death, during the months while Fox was Secretary for Foreign Affairs, it appeared that some sensible compromise might be reached, but the chance was lost by Madison's insistence, as Secretary of State, on the establishment of an unacceptable principle: the right of American ships to trade direct between colonies and belligerents. His insistence on this principle was the more fatuous for his agreement, in instructions to Monroe in London, that it might be waived in practice. Monroe correctly assumed that no such concession could be obtained without pressure, and he advocated "invigorating the militia system and increasing the naval force."[5] His advice was not heeded.

This particular point of contention was thrust into the background by the British decision, in May, 1806, to order the commercial blockade of all European ports from the Elbe to Brest with the curious provision that the blockade would be absolute only between Ostend and the mouth of the Seine. Beyond these narrower limits, neutral ships would be seized only if they had been loaded in a hostile port, but within them, all trade was prohibited. In the context of the war of retaliatory blockade, this first British order assumed a special importance. The legitimacy of this blockade was later strenuously denied by the United States though no serious attempt was made to contest it at the time. It hinged on the precise definition of what constituted a blockade. Both countries—and in this they were in accord with French opinion—agreed that a lawful blockade required the presence of sufficient naval strength to prevent, or at least to make hazardous, a vessel's entry to or departure from the port. While the United States, however, contended that a legitimate blockade required ships to be stationed in the immediate vicinity of the port's entrance, the British argued that it was sufficient if they cruised close enough to the approaches to the port effectively to prevent entry or exit. Both were arguing to suit their own policies. The American argument, based strictly on a convenient interpretation of the law and having no recognizable connection with the practicalities of the situation as it existed, sought to reduce the blockade to the point where it would be ineffective. The British, holding command of the sea, found the argument unimpressive. But for the intervention of France, it is probable that the difference would have remained one of opinion which could have been settled by compromise; but Napoleon seized the opportunity simultaneously to retaliate and to foment discord between his enemy and the one country whose merchant fleet could supply goods needed from the Americas and the West Indies in sufficient quantity and under a neutral flag.

Whether or not the British blockade, as ordered in May, 1806, was legitimate has never been decided. That it made a direct contribution to war between Britain and America is beyond dispute. Loudly proclaiming the illegality of the blockade and his support for the American point of view, as yet but tentatively expressed, Napoleon issued, in November, the Berlin Decree. This was as ample in scope as it was ambiguous in wording. A long preamble condemning the British action was followed by the remarkable assertion that any country dealing in British goods in Europe was an accomplice. The British Isles being thenceforward in a state of blockade, all commerce with them was forbidden, and any ship carrying merchandise of British origin or manufacture, whether British-owned or not, would be liable to seizure.

It was left unstated whether such ships and goods would be seized only on entering French ports or whether they were liable to seizure anywhere on the high seas. Nor was it clear whether neutral ships bound for Britain could be detained anywhere at sea or only when trying to enter ports under effective blockade. These ambiguities were deliberate and ingenious. They made it possible for Napoleon to condemn the illegality of the British blockade while retaining the option to methods more obviously illegal and over a wider area. Finally, the Berlin Decree claimed that a legal blockade must be confined to a fortified place and required the investment of that place not only by sea but also by land. This claim struck at the heart of maritime power.

Although it was not a new concept, it had no basis in international law and was clearly unacceptable. The United States showed some inclination to support it.[6] That it was never recognized as a principle of international law must have been a substantial comfort to the Northern states during the Civil War.

British reaction to the Berlin Decree was not deferred or inhibited by any desire to find out, from experience, how far the practical application of the decree would clarify its more equivocal provisions. An Order in Council dated January 7, 1807, extended previous regulations to forbid the movement of neutral ships from port to port controlled by the enemy or closed to British shipping. In effect this order, which appeared to do little more than reiterate rules already declared, bore down particularly upon American traders who were accustomed to sailing freely among the Continental ports to collect cargoes for their homeward journeys. The arrogant and patronizing tone of the announcement to the United States government was sadly indicative of a British attitude, insensitive to American pride or honor and unaware of danger outside Europe, which contributed to a swift decline in Anglo-American relations and, in due course, to war.

The European war of blockade, a retaliatory war of commercial attrition, was not the worst of the serious disputes between Britain and the United States. Even more fundamental and more urgent was the quarrel over impressment. In a war against an apparently invincible French Army, Britain's survival depended on its navy. There was no shortage of ships, and after Trafalgar the supremacy of the fleet was not in doubt; but there was a continuing shortage of trained crews. Conditions in British warships were harsh and compared unfavorably with those aboard American merchantmen. When British ships put in to American ports, desertions were frequent, and the deserters were welcomed, sheltered, and reemployed by American shipowners. The problem was not new. The British solution—the search of neutral ships and the seizure of any of the crew considered to be British subjects—was never accepted by the United States, but there were marked differences of opinion about the measures to be taken against it. The dispute was greatly aggravated by a certain carelessness, among British captains, in the identification of British nationals. That American seamen were impressed in error is certain; that such mistakes were frequent and some deliberate is undisputable. A high-handed policy of arrest thus became an outrage against the freedom of neutral citizens.

Britain never claimed the right to the impressment of American nationals, but it did claim the absolute right to arrest British subjects, wherever they were to be found unless in foreign territory. Nor was it admitted that British-born subjects could change their nationality or their allegiance. It was recognized in law that British seamen serving aboard neutral ships could be arrested in British waters, but the extension of this principle to the high seas was a matter of necessity and recognized by the British alone. There were, nevertheless, those in America who sympathized with Britain's plight and with its actions, and their speeches were still being heard in the House of Representatives when America was in its second year of war.[7] British captains were, it is true, less than scrupulous in their identification of British-born seamen, particularly when their own ships' companies were depleted, but it was widely acknowledged that the "similarity of language, habits, and manners"[8] made the task extraordinarily difficult. Complaints about the illegal impressment of American seamen had been lodged as early as 1787, and negotiations had been almost continuous between the two governments to find a satisfactory solution to the problem. The provision of papers attesting the nationality of crew members was of little value, for these were easily exchanged, sold, and forged, and a thriving trade in them sprang up in American ports. In 1792, Jefferson, as Secretary of State, enunciated the homespun solution that "The simplest rule will be that the vessel being American shall be evidence that the seamen on board of her are such."[9] The unspoiled charm of this idea found little favor with the British, then or later, but it was, astonishingly, the principle which the United States finally insisted should govern the treatment of ships outside British waters. It does not seem that there was, at any time, a sincere desire or attempt by America to prevent or discourage the employment of British deserters aboard American ships.

There can be little doubt that the British action, however expedient, was both illegal in principle and unjust in practice. It was also grossly exaggerated in extent. Though the War Hawks of the South and frontier areas made much of the issue, the spokesmen of the New England states, from which the greater part of the maritime population was drawn, repeatedly denied that many of their seamen had been impressed. On the contrary, they affirmed that the British seamen employed in American ships greatly outnumbered the Americans taken from them. It was, in short, the principle that was in dispute, not its application in terms of the numbers of men involved.

The First Lord of the Admiralty, the Earl of St. Vincent, had offered, in 1803, to ensure that a sufficient crew was left or supplied aboard American ships from which British deserters had been taken to enable them to reach port, but this single concession was also his last. The discharge of about 40,000 sailors following the conclusion of the Peace of Amiens made recruitment and the maintenance of naval strength an urgent necessity. It has been estimated that nearly 400 more American seamen were impressed during the years 1803 to 1806 than in the previous ten years.[10] Trade, defense, and blockade created, in those years, a necessity which overrode all other conditions. Impressment became one of the major reasons for war.

As a temporary measure, Rufus King, the American minister in London, had suggested that Britain and the United States should agree not to impress seamen from each other. This principle should be accepted until some more formal and permanent agreement could be concluded. The proposal seemed logical enough and, considering that it offered an entirely one-sided exchange, came astonishingly near to being accepted. An exception was made for ships in each country's territorial waters, but Rufus King could not agree to making an exception of the Channel. St. Vincent, at the Admiralty, considered the Channel English—a belief shared by most Englishmen since the Norman conquest—and had no difficulty in persuading his Cabinet colleagues that the inclusion of British waters made the proposal unacceptable. At no other time during the long period of negotiations to end impressment was there any real indication that they were likely to succeed. It was impossible to find a solution Nhich would satisfy on the one hand the law and logic of America and on the other the power and necessity of Britain. The disgraceful *Chesapeake* affair put any possibility of successful negotiation out of the question.

On June 22, 1807, the United States frigate *Chesapeake,* which had been refitting in Hampton Roads, put to sea. The British ship *Leopard* intercepted her some 10 miles from shore and sent an officer on board to demand the return of deserters. Commodore James Barron of the *Chesapeake* refused. His ship was fired on by the *Leopard,* twenty-one of his crew were killed or wounded, and a full search was carried out. Four men, said to be British, were carried off. Five years later, after one had been hanged and a second had died, the two survivors were returned to the deck of the *Chesapeake.* The Americans, justifiably, considered this reparation both too little and too late.

The return of the crippled *Chesapeake* and her diminished crew to harbor provoked an outburst of indignation and belligerence out of all proportion to the damage suffered. Three lives had been lost; four seamen, possibly British deserters (at the time no one seemed to be certain of their nationality by birth and allegiance), had been arrested;

and an American frigate, defying an order to heave to and submit to search, had been fired on and obliged to strike her colors to a British warship. In the British defense it could be stated, and with supporting evidence, that the *Leopard* was part of a small squadron lying in wait for two French men-of-war harboring along the coast; that, while in harbor, a number of her crew had deserted and enlisted with American ships; and that there was ample reason to suppose that some of them were on board the *Chesapeake*. Vice Admiral George C. Berkeley, commander in chief at Halifax, had issued orders for the *Chesapeake* to be stopped and searched.

Two circumstances set this incident apart from any other: the *Chesapeake* had been attacked uncomfortably close to home waters, and she was a warship and thus not liable to search. Monroe, as American minister in London, made a formal complaint to the British government. Canning's reply was diplomatically soothing but evasive. It did, however, state without prevarication that "his Majesty neither does, nor has at any time maintained the pretension of a right to search ships of war, in the national service of any State, for deserters."[11] A warship represented the sovereignty of its country. An attack upon it was an insult to the national flag and thus to the nation itself. As Monroe's complaints to the British government, and Madison's instructions to him, made plain, a principle was at stake. The numbers of men arrested and the final proofs of their true nationality were matters of insignificance in comparison with the public affront to American national honor. Negotiations for reparation dragged on for five years, and by the end of this period America had declared war.

On July 2, 1807, Jefferson issued a proclamation listing grievances against Britain, describing the *Chesapeake* outrage, and banning all British armed vessels from the ports and harbors of the United States. Four days later, Madison's instructions to Monroe in London demanded, quite reasonably, apology and restitution, but also, as "an indispensable part of the satisfaction," the total abolition of impressment from ships flying the flag of the United States. This last demand, already rejected on every occasion when it had been raised, combined with the closing of American ports to British warships, weakened the case it was intended to strengthen. It confused an issue which might and should have been settled as a distinct grievance and enabled the British government, by emphasizing unacceptable demands and retaliatory measures, to postpone a just and necessary settlement. It was probably the last occasion when swift and conciliatory action by the British government would have prevented war with America. The repudiation of this opportunity displayed, once more, British insensitivity to American feelings of national pride and honor and a patronizing and dangerous disregard of the United States as a power of military consequence. The Americans, on the other hand, displayed an abysmal ignorance of diplomatic exchanges, perfunctorily dismissing practicalities in order to make a futile stand on unattainable principles and adopting an all-or-nothing policy which, since it could not achieve all, accomplished nothing.

The *Chesapeake* incident marked a watershed in Anglo-American affairs. It took place at a time when Napoleon's subjugation, by threat or conquest, of the greater part of Europe and the imposition of his Continental System threatened the continuing existence of Britain as powerfully as had his plans for invasion during the years before the Battle of Trafalgar. British maritime policy became necessarily more aggressive, more retaliatory, and more clearly illegal. It also bore down more powerfully upon the trade of neutrals, in particular upon that of the greatest trading neutral, the United States. Thenceforward relations between the two countries deteriorated. The Americans acquiesced in a British policy which they were unable to alter. Their objections lacked the conviction or urgency which stems from the wholehearted support of a nation united and prepared for war. America was, indeed, even less united in a desire for war than was Britain in support of the Orders in Council policy. While New England merchants required peace and neutrality at almost any price to continue their still profitable and expanding trade, Lady Bessborough spoke for many whose sympathies or business interests lay with America when she doubted the wisdom or morality of retaliation which, though aimed at France, struck so cruelly at America. "If a man who is fighting with me sets fire to one wing of my Neighbour's house, does it," she inquired, "give me a right to set fire to the other?"[12] It was a fair comparison.

The British government's reaction to the Berlin Decree had been swift but unremarkable. The order of January 7, 1807, preventing the movement of neutral ships among hostile ports to collect return cargoes, had little effect on French trade. The return to power of a Tory government in March ensured that popular demand for more strenuous measures would be satisfied. On November 11, Orders in Council prohibited, in principle, all trade with ports from which the British flag was excluded. There were exceptions which permitted trade with hostile colonies and also trade in British products or certain foreign goods destined for enemy ports, provided that heavy duties had been paid to Britain. Five weeks later, under the provisions of Napoleon's Milan Decree, all neutral ships submitting to British search or the levy of British duties or sailing to or from a British or British-occupied port were considered to have lost their nationality and were liable to seizure. The two orders could strangle American trade with Europe. Any American ship sailing to Britain might be seized by the French; any ship sailing to a Continental port might be seized by the British. On December 18, the same day that the Washington *National Intelligencer* published details of the British Orders in Council of November 11 and some weeks before news was received of the Milan Decree, Jefferson sent a message to Congress recommending "an inhibition of the departure" of American ships from home ports. The Senate passed an Embargo bill that day, and it was approved by the House, with amendments which had necessitated its return to the Senate, four days later.

This ugly rush to legislation produced from ill-digested information spawned a policy of ultimate fatuity. All American export was prohibited. The operation, from December 14, of the Non-Importation Act also banned imports from Britain. In spite of Madison's protestations to the contrary, the two bills in combination were undeniably hostile to Britain. Short of a formal treaty, America could have chosen no more offensive method of joining the European commercial blockade. By conquest or military pressure, Napoleon had bludgeoned Russia, Prussia, Austria, Portugal, Denmark, Naples, and the Papal States into supporting the Continental System. The last and most important market for British goods, the United States, was closed. The effects of this drastic measure, though entirely predictable, were not at all what Jefferson had anticipated. The bills, aimed in practice at Britain but in theory also at France, were an attempt to coerce the two great belligerents into the withdrawal of their sanctions against neutral trade. It was, however, American trade which faced extinction. Ships that had started to capture the carrying trade of the world rotted in harbor, and their crews starved or moved to Canada, where, in an ironic reversal of the situation before the embargo, they were glad to enlist for service in British ships. Others blatantly ignored the embargo. Jefferson wrote with pained astonishment of a "sudden and rank growth of fraud, and open opposition by force."[13] The great democrat had forgotten the people.

In America revolt against the embargo was widespread, but as the economy of the country was weakened so the one alternative, war, became less possible. In England the reaction was immediate and bitter. Any possibility of a relaxation of the Orders in Council, already remote, faded from sight. The arrest of deserters was still required; but the opportunity and the motive for desertion had been removed, and there was no need to impress American seamen who enlisted uninvited. British foreign trade, which should have been extinguished, was revived by Napoleon's attacks on Spain and Portugal and the subsequent realignment of both countries with Britain. This opened their ports and, more important, those of their colonies. The West Indies, which had been thought to rely on trade with the United States, turned from sugar to agriculture and found that they could support themselves. They were not discouraged by the number of American ships which found their way to them, in open disregard of the embargo and abetted and protected by the British Navy whenever they met. A thriving illicit trade sprang up across the Canadian border and through Canadian ports. Early in 1809 it was asserted that the port of Quebec had done more foreign business since the embargo than the entire United States,[14] and Sir George Prevost, governor of Nova Scotia, declared "the embargo has totally failed. . . . [It] is a measure well adapted to promote the true interests of his Majesty's American colonies."[15] British manufacture which relied on American raw materials was severely damaged, but the carrying trade, relieved of all competition, prospered.

For the rest of his life Jefferson remained convinced that embargo was preferable to war. His conviction was proved wrong in practice, but it also stemmed from a false premise. He calculated from the assumption that war could be fought only against Britain. A declaration of war against France, on the other hand, would have gained for America an unimpeded and expanded trade with Britain and its colonies and the protection of American ships trading, through British ports, with Europe. The benefits could have been enormous, and the attendant risks would have been negligible. With the French fleet defeated and blockaded in harbor there was little that Napoleon could have done to strike at America. That war with France would have found favor with the New England states, to which war with Britain could bring nothing but commercial disaster, there is little doubt. To those whose resentment of Britain bordered on hatred and blinded them to practical considerations, war with France had to be preferable in fact whatever the affront to cherished theory. The problems of trade and blockade would be solved at once, and the dispute over impressment would surely be settled among allies. Even the fears of an Indian uprising would be dispelled. One last factor remained: the hope of territorial gains in Canada and Florida. For the Northwestern and the Southern states this was at least as important as any of the other three reasons for war, and an ambition which would not be achieved by alignment with Britain and its recently acquired Spanish ally. For them the acquisition of the Louisiana Territory, more than 1,000,000 square miles of land, was not enough.

Under the mistaken impression that he was preserving peace, Jefferson chose a course which led unfalteringly toward war. Later he was to write of his loathing for Napoleon, "a moral monster" who had "inflicted more misery on mankind than any other"; but Napoleon represented the France of the "so beautiful revolution," and though the description was bizarre, Jefferson's sympathy for the original movement was sincere and representative of the majority of his countrymen. Britain he regarded as "rotted to the core," greedy and corrupt, and seeking by a mixture of brute force and the most devious diplomacy to secure permanent domination of the seas "and the monopoly of the trade of the world." Disillusioned and weary, unable to accept responsibility for the final decision which his policies had made inevitable, Jefferson refused the chance of a third term and retired. One of his last acts as President was the repeal of the Embargo Act. To James Madison, who succeeded him in March, 1809, he bequeathed a fixed course but no aids to navigation.

III

Drift to War

James Madison took office as fourth President of the United States at a time when war appeared to be the only alternative to commercial ruin. He was a man of considerable intellect who delighted in the clarity and narrow logic of legalistic argument. Like Jefferson, he was determined to maintain the neutrality of the United States, but he also shared Jefferson's inability to understand any but the American point of view or to accept the validity of both logical theory supported by established precedent and practical measures dictated by existing circumstances. Madison vacillated, negotiated, prevaricated, and at last allowed himself to be drawn into war. Throughout their exchanges Madison and Canning were candid but inflexible. Napoleon appeared more amenable. He made comforting promises. Madison believed in them.

Madison's reluctant but steady progress toward war with Britain had not the added impetus of Jefferson's often expressed hatred of the British.[16] Even Napoleon's Bayonne Decree of April, 1808, which announced the confiscation of all American ships entering ports controlled by France (on the principle that they were defying their own country's embargo and were thus trading illegally), had failed to weaken Jefferson's prejudice. Madison was still prepared to negotiate a settlement with Britain. He failed because he insisted, with dedicated myopia, on treating Britain and France as if they would be affected equally by the measures he proposed. By ignoring the widely divergent interests and circumstances of the two countries, he converted a logical impartiality into a policy of unintentional but obvious partisanship.

His intentions were not understood in Britain, and his apparent support of Napoleon was looked upon with disgust as treachery.

The heavy losses sustained by the United States during the period of the embargo had not been confined to trade. Many American merchantmen, at sea or in foreign ports at the time the embargo became effective, had failed to return home, preferring to trade illegally under British protection;[17] customs receipts had declined by half; and the opportunity of trading with Spain and Portugal, and their colonies, and of supplying the British armies in the Peninsula was lost. Some new method of coercion was needed, one which, unlike the embargo, would be more damaging to Britain and France than to America and which would not be so flagrantly flouted by Americans. Monroe had expressed the opinion that war with both Britain and France was the most likely outcome "unless some expedient consistent with the honor of the Government and Country is adopted to prevent it."[18] A month later, on February 27, 1809, the Non-Intercourse Act was approved by Congress, to become effective from May 20.

The British had watched the failure of the embargo with some complacency. The Non-Intercourse Act was a positive improvement. It closed American ports to all ships, whether warships or merchantmen, of both France and Britain, and banned trade with both countries and their colonies. If either country relaxed or abandoned its regulations of trade so that they ceased to violate American commerce, the President was authorized to proclaim the repeal of the act for that country. The improvement, from the British point of view, lay in two important changes from the embargo: the nonimportation legislation was extended to include French goods, and the opening of foreign ports not under British or French control to American goods exposed the opportunity for wholesale evasion by trading through neutral ports. Canning believed that a settlement could now be negotiated to embody the withdrawal of the Orders in Council. He sent instructions to David Erskine, the British minister in Washington, outlining the conditions for such an agreement. There were two of prime importance: that the withdrawal of the Orders in Council should be met with the simultaneous withdrawal of restrictions against British ships and goods while continuing those in force against France, and that the British Navy should be authorized to enforce the Non-Intercourse Act against France by arresting any American ships seeking to evade it. This second condition had in it the seeds of misunderstanding and dissension. Its implication—that the Americans were incapable of enforcing their own regulations—was clear and unflattering, but this was widely recognized as true and admitted by all but the most willfully blind. During the operation of the embargo, ships cleared for neutral ports had arrived in Britain. Nothing but the British Navy could prevent ships cleared for Britain from entering French ports. The condition was reasonable and essential, but it condemned the negotiations to abject failure.

Much blame has been heaped upon David Erskine for the ruin of the negotiations and the final destruction of the last hope of peace. His handling of the diplomatic exchanges was certainly inept and over optimistic, but his actions throughout were those of a man whose transparent sincerity in his desire to obtain a settlement was worthy of better treatment by the government he represented. Acting, perhaps foolishly, but from the best motives, he concluded an agreement which he was not empowered to conclude, based on false assumptions which could not be supported by fact. The agreement, which ignored Canning's conditions, leaving them to be incorporated in a formal treaty to be signed later, was repudiated by the British government, and Erskine was recalled. His successor, Francis Jackson, was invested with all the powers denied to Erskine to conclude a treaty. Faced by American dismay at his government's disavowal of an agreement entered into by his predecessor and by a somewhat aggressive demand for a formal explanation, Jackson adopted a haughty and intransigent attitude which did nothing to ease tension. Madison made his own unique contribution to the quarrel in a microscopic examination of every almost imperceptible detail in dispute, and in a predisposition to find fault and take offense which amounted to genius. Discord was further confused by discussion of the *Chesapeake* affair, for which the British government was at last prepared to offer some long-overdue reparation. Madison and Jackson found no obstacle to a rupture which was both open and final. Madison refused to have any further dealings with Jackson, who left Washington at the end of 1809. He was formally recalled in April, 1810. No successor was appointed.

Britain, meanwhile, had suffered a series of grave reverses, not the least of which was the disintegration of its government. The resignation of the Prime Minister, the elderly and inattentive Duke of Portland, who had suffered a stroke in August, 1809, could be borne with fortitude. He was succeeded by Spencer Perceval. The loss of both Canning and Castlereagh was more serious. A long-standing quarrel between them led to Castlereagh's resignation and his challenge to Canning to fight a duel in which he wounded the Foreign Secretary severely in the thigh. They were replaced by Lord Liverpool and Lord

Wellesley, elder brother of the commander of British troops in Portugal. To Canning's intractability Wellesley added a temperamental indolence unconducive to the speedy settlement of disputes with America. In January, 1809, Sir John Moore, Britain's most professional soldier since Wolfe, had been killed at La Coruña. At the end of the month, after a series of crushing French victories over the Spanish, Joseph Bonaparte was crowned in Madrid. The British clung precariously to the coast of the Peninsula, supplied, and when necessary transported, by the navy. One new factor gave reason for hope: behind Napoleon's armies, as they overran Spain, the people rose in vengeance. The first guerrillas* had taken to the hills.

There was hope, too, in the equivocal attitude of Austria, which was rearming. After Austerlitz, the Austrians had adopted a policy of patient self-preservation, subscribing to the Continental System and even declaring war against Britain, but preparing for a renewal of the fight against Napoleon. Their army of 300,000 well-trained and equipped men, commanded by the able and experienced Archduke Charles, was potentially a match for any in Europe. Sir Arthur Wellesley's plan for a campaign in Portugal, although modest in intent, offered the double advantage of requiring a comparatively small number of troops and yet pinning down a French army while the Austrians made their move. The escape of the French fleet from Brest provided a temporary complication. Pursued by the Channel fleet under Lord Gambier, the French anchored in the Aix Roads, close to the Spanish frontier and protected by shore batteries. On the night of April 11, they were driven from their moorings by fire ships,† personally commanded by Lord Cochrane, and all but two of the French ships were destroyed or run aground. Nothing but the irresolution of Gambier, whose gentlemanly code was outraged by the use of such irregular tactics, saved the enemy fleet from annihilation. Three days earlier the Archduke Charles had proclaimed his intention to liberate the German people from their oppressive masters, and on April 22, Sir Arthur Wellesley landed at Lisbon.

Everything seemed to promise well, and for a short time, the promise was fulfilled. On May 12, Wellesley crossed the Douro and heavily defeated Soult's army near Oporto. On the twenty-second the Arch-

---

*Adapted, in the English language, from the word meaning "a small war." The Spanish word for irregular forces engaged in such a war is *guerrilleros*.

† Ships filled between decks with gunpowder and combustible materials. These were set on fire and steered among the enemy fleet, the skeleton crews escaping in ships' boats. Fire ships were used against the Spanish Armada in 1588 and during the siege of Quebec in 1759. The Roman historian Livy records the use of fire rafts as early as the second century B.C.

duke Charles, routed with 30,000 casualties barely a month earlier,
crushed Napoleon's army as it tried to cross the Danube. Animated by
these encouraging events, the British government agreed that
Wellesley should extend his operations into Spain. On June 27 he
began to move against the French army under Marshal Claude Victor.
Two days later he joined up with a ragged Spanish army commanded
by Don Gregorio García de la Cuesta, "a fine stout rough-looking old
man,"[19] bedizened with tinsel and medals, who had been run down by
his own cavalry and could sit his horse only when supported by four
pages. Undeterred by the evident incompetence and indiscipline of his
allies, Wellesley continued his advance toward Madrid. Cuesta alternated between mulish inactivity and headlong, and unsupported, assault upon a superior enemy. The antics of this extraordinary old
gentleman eventually brought his army, in hasty retreat from an
ill-considered advance, to join Wellesley at Talavera, where, on July
28, Marshal Victor's attack was beaten off with 7,000 casualties.

Public rejoicing was not prolonged. A French fleet was building in

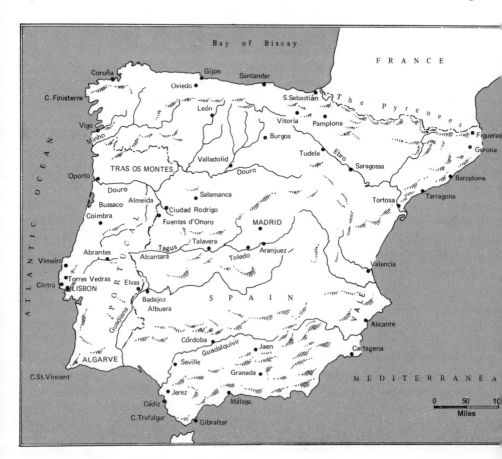

the Scheldt, and as early as March an attack on Walcheren and Flushing had been proposed. As the troops required for the expedition had not yet recovered from the La Coruña disaster, it was postponed, but the idea was revived in July. A respectable force was gathered— some 40,000 men, with transports and a vast fleet of more than 20 men-of-war—but it was assembled with such stately demonstration of military precision that when, at last, it set out, it was already too late. The capture of Antwerp, essential both to the destruction of the French warships already afloat and to the purpose of obliging Napoleon to withdraw troops from the Danube, was never clearly projected although no other objective could have justified so large an invasion. Nothing but brilliant leadership could have redeemed the expedition. The appointment of Pitt's elder brother, the second Earl of Chatham, to command, ensured that the lethargy which had distinguished the expedition's assembly would also guarantee its failure. Within six weeks of setting out, Chatham's army, trembling with fever and dysentery, was back in England. A small typhus-ridden garrison was left on the untenable island of Walcheren.

The Walcheren expedition had begun to embark on July 20. Three days later news was received in London of a battle fought outside Vienna. On July 6, Napoleon had smashed the Austrian Army under the Archduke Charles at Wagram. By the twenty-sixth it was known that Austria had signed an armistice. This was not considered sufficient reason to cancel Chatham's leisurely embarkation. He sailed at dawn on the twenty-eighth. In the Peninsula, Wellington, threatened by French armies numbering nearly 100,000, unable to coordinate the actions of Cuesta's army with his own tactics, and desperate for supplies of food, clothing, and ammunition, withdrew from Spain to save his army from destruction. By the first week of September, having lost a third of his force, he was back in Portugal.

For Britain the year 1809, which had shown such promise, died under the weight of misfortune and mismanagement. In March, 1810, Lord Collingwood, last of the great admirals of Nelson's era, died at sea, worn out in the service of his country. The power of the navy remained unchallenged, for it had been built to survive its architects, but the day of the great commanders was over. They had saved Britain from defeat. Victory could be won only on land, and no military commander of genius had been recognized. For all his plainness of speech and dress, Sir Arthur Wellesley enjoyed recognition. After Talavera, in spite of public dissent, he had been raised to the peerage as Viscount Wellington.

Even in the face of the repulses to British hopes in 1809, there were already signs, so faint and indefinite as to be discernible only in retrospect, that Napoleon's domination of Europe was weakening. His Continental System of blockade, though practical in theory with the wholehearted support of willing allies, could not be enforced without such cooperation or command of the sea. The British conquests of the last French possessions in the West Indies, of Cayenne and, later, of Mauritius, were a severe blow to French wealth and trade. British manufactured goods and the produce of its colonies were needed in Europe, and enterprising smugglers succeeded in increasing British exports to Europe in 1810 by 40 percent. Savage penalties and the collapse of industries dependent on imported materials produced resentment and hardship. Already, in Spain, a disorganized and largely peasant army had proved that the French armies were vulnerable to guerrilla attack across their lines of communication and supply. The oppressed peoples of French-dominated Europe grew increasingly restless. Napoleon's problems in Spain were aggravated by the presence of Wellington's small army in Portugal. Any attack in Spain was in danger from Wellington on the flank, and any attack on Portugal was vulnerable to Spanish attack in the rear. Two French armies had to be engaged, powerful enough to crush both enemies simultaneously or to contain one while the other was destroyed. Napoleon dispatched his most experienced general, André Masséna, to deal with Wellington. Nicolas Soult, Louis Suchet, and Pierre Augereau were left to prevent the Spanish from interfering. When Masséna began his campaign, the British army in Portugal had not seen any action for six months.

Outnumbered by two to one, Wellington's army depended on the Portuguese, whose reputation for flight from a numerically inferior enemy was second to none in Europe. Since March they had been commanded, under treaty, by General William Beresford, who had transformed them from a demoralized and undisciplined rabble into a potentially valuable army. Their training was completed. It remained to be seen how they would behave in battle. Masséna advanced with caution, securing his communications and hoping to draw Wellington into action. Wellington, who had ordered the construction of impregnable lines of defense at Tôrres Vedras to protect his supply from the sea and ensure the retention of a foothold which included Lisbon, refused to be drawn. He was, however, harassed by the political situation at home, where growing unrest at his inaction and the constant menace of a change of government threatened the continuance of the campaign. He determined to fight one battle, to restore public confidence, before he withdrew behind his mountain defenses. On September 27, 1810, he confronted Masséna at Busaco and flung him back with heavy casualties. By October 8 the British, with their Portuguese allies, who had behaved with calmness and courage in their first battle, were safely behind the lines of Tôrres Vedras.

Apart from their forbidding strength, the most extraordinary aspect of the Tôrres Vedras fortifications was the secrecy with which they had been built. Neither Masséna nor any of his generals had any idea that they existed, although thousands of Portuguese had labored over them for almost a year. After a short probing attack on October 14, Masséna realized the futility of an assault and settled down to wait for reinforcements. There was, he knew, the alternative possibility that the British army would be withdrawn if Spencer Perceval's government fell and was replaced by the Whig opposition. What Perceval's administration lacked in strength and support it made up in courage and tenacity. Against all the odds it clung to power. Nevertheless, it was well known, on both sides of the Channel, that the Prince of Wales favored the opposition led by the Grenvilles. The death or incurable derangement of the old King must bring the government down and, with it, Wellington's campaign in Portugal. Masséna waited before Tôrres Vedras for a month, his lines harassed by the Portuguese, his army suffering from shortage of supplies and the onset of winter, and then withdrew about 30 miles to a strong defensive position. Wellington followed him but declined to attack. Masséna waited for the British government to fall. Wellington waited for winter.

On November 2, 1810, the King's favorite daughter, Princess Amelia, died of erysipelas at the age of twenty-seven. George III lived for another ten years, but in darkness. Blind and demented, he was no longer capable of performing the duties of sovereign. Less than seven weeks after Princess Amelia's death a Regency bill was introduced, and the Grenvilles began to form their government. They were premature. The Prince Regent abandoned both his political principles and his friends, retained Perceval's government, and confirmed the decision to persevere with the Portuguese campaign.

In Portugal, winter came and Wellington continued his vigil. Masséna held on grimly, his army decimated by starvation and disease, hoping for Soult's arrival with reinforcements. On March 5, he began his long retreat to the north with Wellington in close pursuit. In bitter revenge for their treatment at the hands of the Portuguese and the privations they had suffered through the winter, the French destroyed and killed as they went. They left behind them a grotesque trail of murder, rape, mutilation, and wanton brutality, which appalled the most hardened British campaigners.[20] After giving battle at Sabugal on April 1, Masséna's defeated army struggled into Spain, reaching its base at Salamanca ten days later. Wellington's army had stretched its lines of supply to the utmost limit. In an advance of more than 300 miles in a month, 8,000 prisoners had been taken and 2,000 of Masséna's army killed. Some 20,000 more had died of wounds, starvation, and disease. Though it was not immediately apparent, Napoleon's empire was beginning to crumble. Britain had found its greatest general since Marlborough.

While Wellington was painstakingly establishing a strategy which would drive the French from Spain, Spencer Perceval and his ministers sought, with equal patience, to detach Napoleon's allies from their allegiance. Lacking the gifts of Pitt or Canning, they confined their efforts to the passive diplomacy of extreme caution. The countries subscribing to the Continental System were treated with punctilious 'courtesy. Britain alone represented European hopes of freedom, and it was made abundantly clear that those who joined it against Napoleon would be welcomed with money and arms. This policy was in marked contrast with Napoleon's treatment of his allies, to whom he used a hectoring and authoritarian manner which failed to win the friendship of hereditary princes. They considered him a dangerous vulgarian, but their fear was more powerful than their loathing. At the end of 1810 the Continental System, already weakened by widespread and successful smuggling, cracked open in Russia; the Czar opened his ports to British colonial goods. Napoleon's failure to conquer Spain and Portugal was watched with growing satisfaction and hope in Russia, Austria, Prussia, and Holland. As Wellington wrote in March, 1811, two days before his proclamation of the French evacuation of Portugal, "the war is now likely to take on a new shape."

Within a year the truth of Wellington's prediction was becoming clear. In the Peninsula, British victories at Fuentes de Oñoro and La Albuera, in May, 1811, and at Ciudad Rodrigo, in January, 1812, had broken Napoleon's grasp on Spain. The precarious foothold in Portugal was consolidated in such strength that Wellington's army, with the effective support of the Portuguese and rather less reliable assistance from the Spanish, presented a serious threat to the continued presence of the French in Spain. It did not require much imagination to forecast that this might grow into a threat to France itself. The Continental System was breaking up. In August a conspiracy to evade the Napoleonic Decrees had been discovered. It involved Russia, Austria, and Naples. Sweden was displaying a deplorable inclination to prefer trade to obedience. Even in his own country the Emperor's authority was weakening. A massive campaign of conquest would accomplish the two essential purposes of uniting France and intimidating its allies. During the autumn of 1811 Napoleon again began to assemble troops and transports for an invasion of England. This plan, which had no possibility of success, was intended to frighten the British into withdrawing their Peninsular army for defense and to divert attention from the grand design for which a vast army was being mobilized: the invasion of Russia.

As Napoleon prepared to extend the war to the east, there were disturbing signs that it was also spreading to the west. The American Non-Intercourse Act had, by general consent, failed in its purpose. American goods continued to be exported to Britain and its colonies, the bulk of them sailing from Canada in British ships, which, once more, monopolized the carrying trade of the world. The effect on France was, predictably, negligible, for American ships were seldom able to evade the British blockade of Europe whatever the regulations pronounced by their government. On May 1, 1810, the Non-Intercourse Act was repealed and replaced by a bill which reopened commerce with both Britain and France but with one important condition: if either country should agree to revoke its orders or decrees or so qualify them that they ceased to violate the neutral trade of the United States, the President should recognize this by proclamation, and if the other country should not, in return, similarly revoke or modify its orders or decrees within three months of the date of the President's proclamation, the provisions of the Non-Intercourse Act should be revived against it. Barely two weeks later, Napoleon caused to be published the Decree of Rambouillet, signed nearly two months earlier and with retroactive effect from May, 1809, a whole year prior to publication. This ruled that all American ships which had entered French ports or those under the control of France since May 20, 1809, should be confiscated and sold. It was estimated that at least 100 American merchantmen, which had been trading abroad at the time the Non-Intercourse Act was passed and which had not returned home, might be affected.

Napoleon appears to have received news of the new American legislation, obscurely named Macon's Bill No. 2 after a Congressman who had introduced it, early in August. He replied at once in a form which was not only ambiguous, but also misleading. Through Jean

Nompère de Champagny, his Minister of Foreign Affairs, he let it be known that the Berlin and Milan Decrees were revoked and would cease to be effective from November 1, it being understood that the British would, in consequence, revoke their Orders in Council or that the United States would revive the Non-Intercourse Act against them. That John Armstrong and William Pinkney, the American ministers in Paris and London, should have accepted Champagny's letter as revocation in form and in fact is less surprising than indicative of their honest desire to see negotiations succeed. The British refusal to accept Champagny's assurances was also predictable, testifying to long experience of Napoleon's devious methods and a deep distrust of them. It is Madison's acceptance of this informal announcement which remains unexplained, for it is inconsistent with his attitude to all previous negotiations. The decrees, enacted by proclamation, could be revoked only by similar proclamation in the Emperor's name. No such proclamation was forthcoming, and it was clear that there was no intention of issuing one. The decrees were to be withdrawn from operation against the United States, but not formally revoked. They were to lie dormant but capable of revival at any convenient time. Throughout his time as Secretary of State, Madison's narrow attitudes and preoccupation with minutely correct legal detail had introduced an undeviating formality into his diplomatic exchanges. His opinion, expressed in 1807, that reparation for the *Chesapeake* incident required the appointment of a special envoy from Britain to lend adequate dignity to the compensation was typical of his method. This caution and formality were now cast aside for a hasty and ill-judged conclusion based on a demonstrably unwarranted belief in Napoleon's good faith. For a man of Madison's intellect, experience, and rigidity it was an extraordinary exercise in self-deception.

Pinkney, in London, unavailingly urged on Wellesley the acceptance of Napoleon's withdrawal of the decrees, in form if not in fact, and the withdrawal of the British Orders in Council which should follow. There were two valid reasons why Napoleon's so-called revocation was unacceptable: it was not a public revocation in the Emperor's name but a private withdrawal appearing only in correspondence between Champagny and Armstrong, and it demanded not only the repeal of the Orders in Council, but also the renunciation of the British blockade of unfortified ports and harbors, a lawful act without which Britain's economic war against France would be ineffective. On November 2, Madison proclaimed Napoleon's revocation of the Berlin and Milan Decrees as a fact. In the absence of the

British repeal of the Orders in Council, the provisions of the Non-Intercourse Act would be revived against Britain alone on February 2, 1811.

It is undeniable that Wellesley, in all his negotiations with Pinkney, displayed an unfortunate and characteristic lack of any sense of urgency. He continued to repeat previous assurances, originally issued in instructions to Erskine, that the Orders in Council would be repealed if and when the French decrees were revoked. It was not until December 4 that he finally wrote to say that no evidence could be found of such a revocation. Pinkney made one last attempt, on December 10, to provide conclusive argument, but there was nothing in his letter adding any evidence which might be regarded as proof. On the day he wrote it an official complaint was being sent to Champagny with a demand for the release of an American ship seized in Bordeaux on December 1, precisely one month after the decree had been "revoked." In reply, Armstrong was informed that vessels seized under the terms of the decrees would be held until after February 2, when it could be seen that the United States had honored its pledge to act against Britain. Whether formal revocation was intended or not, it was already clear that no such revocation had taken place and the decrees were still in force. The President's proclamation was, therefore, clearly mistaken, if not invalid. Disregarding the evidence, the United States continued, nevertheless, to act as if revocation were a fact. On January 14, 1811, Pinkney informed Wellesley that the United States would no longer be represented in Britain by a minister plenipotentiary and began to make his arrangements to leave.

Pinkney's departure from London was postponed by the derangement of George III and the institution of the regency. These circumstances also contributed to the extraordinary delay in naming a successor to Jackson as British minister in Washington. Judging from previous experience, there is little reason to suppose that the presence of a minister in the American capital would have promoted understanding of the British point of view or prevented a diplomatic breach, but the absence of any obvious attempt to appoint Jackson's replacement gave offense as a public and continuing insult. On February 15, within ten days of officially assuming his responsibilities and authority, the Prince Regent appointed Augustus John Foster British minister to Washington. Pinkney, invited by Wellesley to reconsider his decision, embarked for the United States.

Augustus Foster was thirty-one years old and no stranger to the United States. As Secretary to the Legation in 1804 he had expressed his contempt and loathing for Americans in his letters to his mother.[21] "Corruption, Immorality, Irreligion, and above all, self-interest" had, he considered, "corroded the very pillars on which their Liberty rests," and as for the women, they were V'a spying, inquisitive, vulgar, and most ignorant race." Foster's mother was a good friend of the Prince Regent's, and Foster was a Whig; but his appointment at such a time of crisis was less than ideal and seemed unlikely to exert a soothing influence. "I know," wrote his mother consolingly, "how you dislike that country, but it is a wonderful opportunity for future advancement."[22]

Foster arrived in Washington in June, 1811. Whatever his qualifications for the task, and it must be admitted that they were such as might reasonably have been considered disqualifying, his mission was hopeless. Wellesley had given him long and precise instructions, including a summary of policy which was definitive. By military conquest or intimidation Napoleon had forced Europe to cooperate in a system which, if allowed to operate unchallenged, threatened Britain's survival. The British Orders in Council were retaliatory and protective. In their operation against the neutral trade of America they were admittedly illegal, but indisputably essential. They would be repealed when it could be demonstrated beyond doubt that the French decrees had been revoked. Meanwhile "the public safety of the nation" was "the primary object of all national councils, and the paramount duty of the Executive power," and it was urged that the United States should not, by the partial operation of the Non-Intercourse Act against Great Britain, support Napoleon's Continental System. Under conditions of free negotiation, Wellesley's lucid instructions to Foster might have formed a basis for constructive discussion, but the United States was already bound by Madison's proclamation of November 2. Napoleon continued to seize American ships. Twelve months after Champagny's letter had announced the withdrawal of the decrees, and eight months after the reintroduction of a Non-Intercourse Bill against Britain, Monroe was writing to the American minister in France complaining of the seizure of American vessels and the absence of any effective measures to prevent such action. It was clear that the United States had been duped and Britain outmaneuvered.

Even the conclusion of the *Chesapeake* affair was again postponed for several months. It was settled on November 11, 1811, nearly four and a half years after the incident, but not until a formal court of inquiry had examined the circumstances of an action on May 16, 1811, in which the United States frigate *President* had pursued and crippled the British sloop *Little Belt,* causing thirty-two casualties. The incident was trivial and unintentional, but it provided evidence of a new tide in American affairs. The United States had ceased to drift, helpless, toward a war which it was powerless to avoid; the course was set, and powerful forces had gathered in America to ensure that it was not altered. When Congress met, summoned a month early by the President, in November, 1811, the demands for war were strident and compelling. It was significant that little provision was made for increasing the navy, the essential ingredient of effective defense; but it was agreed that the regular army should be more than tripled in size and further augmented by the recruitment of 50,000 volunteers. The speeches made in Congress left no doubt about their intended employment: they were to be used for an invasion of Canada. In the absence of a British invasion of the United States, an eventuality neither apprehended nor at the time possible, there was no other field in which such an army might be actively employed.

IV

Territorial Ambition

The Twelfth Congress of the United States opened on November 4, 1811. In the great debate in the House the subject of the annexation of Canada was mentioned with such frequency and demanded with such vehemence that it appeared to be a new project. It has even been argued that no mention of territorial expansion northward appears before 1810 and that this new design was thrust upon the United States by defensive needs against the threat of a British invasion supported by savage Indians. This argument is now discredited. There is ample evidence that the ambition was forged out of the Revolution and tempered by the Napoleonic Wars in Europe. By 1807 what had been a distant purpose had become a practical intention canvassed by Lafayette and openly declared by Jefferson.[23] Whether the ambition was animated more by fear or by greed is not clear. That it was cherished for years before Britain's total commitment in Europe made its achievement possible is beyond doubt.

The Treaty of Paris, signed on September 3, 1783, set the terms of peace between Britain and its rebellious colonists in America. The terms were reasonable and binding. Both parties to the treaty violated them from the outset. Those colonists who, in fighting for Britain, had lost land and property were to have their possessions restored to them; but the central government of the newly created United States lacked the power to enforce obedience, and the obligation was not honored. The British continued to occupy forts on the southern banks of Lake Ontario and Lake Erie and at Detroit and the northwest corner of Lake Huron although they were built on United States territory. Some pretense was offered that this illegal retention of property surrendered by treaty was in retaliation for the American failure to restore property to the British Loyalists, but it was generally believed that Britain continued to occupy the forts for their value as trading posts with the Indians. Many of the dispossessed Loyalists left the United States to settle in Canada, where some compensation for their losses was available from the British government.

The situation of the Indians was a more serious problem. The British peace negotiators had ignored the claims of their Indian allies, and the new frontiers defined by the Treaty of Paris placed the greater part of the Indian hunting grounds in American territory. As the Americans moved westward, occupying and cultivating lands previously unexplored and traditionally Indian, British concern for their allies grew. Humanitarian motives and guilt for having failed to make adequate provision for them were insignificant beside the anxiety that, in fury at their betrayal by their allies and persecution by their enemies, the Indians might turn on the British as they had in 1763. There were still many who remembered Pontiac. Confronted by a problem which threatened to become dangerous, the British behaved to the Indians with a duplicity that was both dishonorable and short-sighted. Trade was welcomed, and hostility toward the Americans encouraged; but when the Indians, in defeat, called upon their white allies for help, they found themselves deserted and denied refuge.

In 1790 Washington had made temporary peace with the Creek nation in the South, entertaining the chiefs in New York and concluding a treaty protecting their hunting rights. While these negotiations were in progress, Brigadier General Josiah Harmar was on his way to a crushing defeat at the hands of the Miami in the northwest. His place was taken in 1791 by Major General Arthur St. Clair, Harmar's senior in rank and at least his equal in incompetence. On November 3 his army of 1,400 was attacked by the Miami, again under their leader Michikinikwa (Little Turtle). St. Clair was driven from the field, having lost his guns and most of his equipment and suffered 900 casualties. While a third army was being assembled, Washington turned his attention to the problem of the disputed frontier forts. By Jay's Treaty, signed in London on November 19, 1791, agreement was obtained to the British withdrawal from all the trading posts on American territory no later than June 1, 1796. In August, 1794, Major General "Mad Anthony" Wayne crushed the western tribes at Fallen Timbers.* Twelve months later the Western Indian chiefs signed the

*Close to the site of Toledo, Ohio.

Treaty of Greenville surrendering the whole of the area now defined as the state of Ohio and part of Indiana. Settlers streamed to the new territories It was not long before they began to encroach on the lands guaranteed by treaty to the Indians.

The settlement of the frontier posts dispute and the eviction of the Indians from much of their territory in the northwest might appear to have satisfied American demands for frontier security, but the British in Canada were uneasy. The war in Europe, renewed in 1803, stretched military resources to the limit and left Canada dangerously exposed. Few regular troops could be spared from Britain, and the vast North American colony relied for its land defense upon an inadequate regular force and the ill-trained militia, drafted by ballot and generally unarmed. Those regiments posted along the frontier of Upper Canada, the area bounded by the Ottawa River and the Great Lakes, were often divided into as many as eight sections, each one separated from another by several hundred miles of rough country which became impassable in winter. The inducements offered by Americans across the frontier included tempting offers of land and the promise of prosperity,[24] and it was not to be wondered at that the regiments were decimated by desertion.

The feeble condition of the American Army was not considered any serious obstacle to invasion. The difficulties to be encountered later with the American militia were not anticipated, and it was assumed that an army of such strength could be raised that Canada would be overwhelmed. It was agreed that in the event of an American invasion in sufficient strength the British troops would withdraw to the St. Lawrence and try to hold Montreal or Quebec until relieved by the navy and reinforcements.[25] The belligerent outcry evoked by the *Chesapeake* incident in 1807 renewed apprehension in Canada, and 10,000 militia were drafted to prepare to march. It was fortunate that they were not needed on that occasion, for the small numbers who answered the call were unarmed, untrained, and widely dispersed. Their services would have been of no military value whatever.

Under conditions of such disorganization, weakness, and potential danger a new approach to the Indians seemed necessary. In the autumn of 1807 Sir James Craig arrived as governor-in-chief and devised the policy which formed the basis for British relations with the Indians for the following three years. It was founded on the assumption that in case of war the Indians would fight on one side or the other. Its aim was to ensure that they did not fight for the United States. The operation of this policy required conciliation and the encouragement of informal alliance without incitement to premature action. It was a policy requiring great delicacy and skill. It was not difficult to persuade the Indians that the Americans intended to take their land—that much was obvious, and even the Americans scarcely troubled to deny it—but it was necessary to prevent unconcerted action which might provoke the United States to war. The most promising instrument of this policy was the great Shawnee warrior-leader Tecumseh.

Born about 1768 in Ohio, the son of the Shawnee chief Pucksinwa, Tecumseh achieved fame among his people and among white settlers as a warrior and as a leader whose moderation and ability amounted almost to statesmanship. His humane treatment of prisoners contrasted with the savage cruelties of other Indian leaders, and he gained respect among the settlers as a man whose word might be trusted. Tecumseh's brother, Lalawethika, known as the Prophet, claimed supernatural powers and set himself up as the religious leader of Indians in the northwest, preaching a return to the old traditional way of life. The Prophet was a fanatic, dedicated to the overthrow of white influence. Tecumseh was a leader, both in the political and the military sense, whose dream was the construction of an Indian confederacy stretching from the Lake of the Woods to the Gulf of Mexico, an area which followed one of the most important trading routes in the world, the Mississippi River.

Tecumseh believed that a confederacy could achieve the creation of a great buffer state between Canada and the eastern United States. He failed because he misunderstood the character and motives of the peoples concerned. The Indians were incapable of accepting the sort of discipline and organization inseparable from the establishment of an effective league; the Americans were greedy for land, adventurous, and determined to explore, occupy, and hold the country they had won; and the British cared nothing for the Indians except for trade and defense. The encouragement Tecumseh received from the British was misconstrued, as it was intended to be, as a pledge of support for his ambitions.

William Henry Harrison, governor of the Northwest Territory, had declared openly that he intended to challenge the Greenville Treaty under which all lands allocated to the Indians were held by them in community interest and could not, therefore, be sold or ceded without the approval of all the tribes. In September, 1809, Harrison purchased 3,000,000 acres along the Wabash for a cash price of $8,200 and annuities totaling $2,350 paid to the six tribes most closely concerned. The purchase was fraudulent and prohibited by treaty, but the central government made no attempt to have it rescinded. Tecumseh and the Prophet met Harrison in August, 1810, to lodge a formal complaint and offer their alliance to the United States if the land was returned, but nothing was done. Further complaints produced no result. Tecumseh had gathered about 1,000 warriors from the northwestern tribes at Tippecanoe. He went south to raise the Creek, Choctaw, and Chickasaw.

In September, 1811, Lieutenant General Sir George Prevost arrived to replace Sir James Craig as governor and commander in chief in Canada. On October 9, Major General Isaac Brock became administrator and military commander in Upper Canada.* The two appointments were clear evidence of the apprehension felt in London for the safety of Canada. The events of November, at Tippecanoe and in Congress, intensified that apprehension. William Henry Harrison led a mixed force of regulars and militia to Tecumseh's village headquarters, where, in the absence of Tecumseh, the Prophet was provoked into a disastrous attack. The Indians were beaten off with heavy losses, Tippecanoe burned, and the nucleus of the confederacy destroyed. Harrison claimed that he had not intended to fight, but if that was true, it was difficult to explain why he marched on Tippecanoe in such strength. Tecumseh, on the other hand, genuinely wished to avoid a premature battle and, had he been there, would not willingly have risked the dissolution of the alliance he had constructed with such care. On his return he led the remainder of his followers to Amherstburg and joined the British.

Reports of the speeches made at the Twelfth Congress convinced Prevost and Brock that an American declaration of war was imminent and that the invasion of Canada would be among the first acts of war. Strenuous efforts were made to put Canada into some state of defense, but it was an unrewarding task. In a war in which the enemy of America was also the enemy of France, the loyalty of French-speaking Canadians must be considered doubtful. Even less to be relied upon were many of the American settlers in Upper Canada. The regular troops in Canada numbered less than 10,000, of whom about 1,200 were in Upper Canada and more than half of the remainder in Nova Scotia, Newfoundland, New Brunswick, and Prince Edward Island. No reinforcements could be expected from Britain. Nor was Prevost

---

*Following the Constitutional Act of 1791, the Province of Quebec was divided along the line of the Ottawa River. Upper Canada (broadly defined as the territory south of the river) was settled by a small, predominantly English-speaking, population. About four-fifths of the population of Canada spoke French and lived north of the river (Lower Canada) and particularly around the growing cities of Montreal and Quebec.

confident of the effectiveness of the militia, which numbered 11,000 in Upper Canada "of which it might not be prudent to Arm more than 4,000," and 60,000 in Lower Canada, "a mere posse, ill arm'd, and without discipline, where of 2,000 are embodied for training."[26] Brock took a more positive view than Prevost. The Provincial Marine, though pathetically small, held control of the Great Lakes. If this could be maintained, an American attack on Upper Canada must be confined to attempts to cross the Niagara or St. Clair rivers. He advocated strengthening the inadequate naval force in the Lakes and attacking the American forts at Detroit and Michilimackinac before they could be strengthened and reinforced. On the assumption that war was inevitable and imminent, Brock's advice was sound, but the British government could not condone any act of provocation which might precipitate collision. Prevost's situation was critical. As governor and commander in chief he was responsible for the defense of a vast territory and a population whose loyalties were divided. His army was pitifully inadequate and poorly armed, and reinforcements, even if they became available, had to travel several thousand miles by sea to the mouth of the St. Lawrence River, which was blocked by ice through the months of winter. "Much," wrote Prevost with resignation, "must depend upon Contingencies in the event of Invasion."[27]

American territorial ambitions were not confined to Canada. Jefferson had made plain his interest in Spanish possessions in the New World, particularly in that part of them east of the Mississippi. The original instructions to Monroe and Livingston in 1803 had been to obtain New Orleans and the Floridas. The acquisition of the whole of the Louisiana Territory for a risible price did not satisfy the President's appetite. It was conveniently "discovered" that West Florida was also part of the transaction, "that France had actually bought West Florida without knowing it, and had sold it to the United States without being paid for it."[28] Jefferson maintained this extraordinary claim, with an engaging disregard for the facts and unsupported even by France, until the end of his Presidency, when it was inherited by Madison. While Spain was allied with France, Jefferson's desire for the Floridas even led him to suppose that Britain might, in return for American cooperation, agree not to make peace until he had achieved his objectives. It was not a supposition shared by Madison or by Britain. From May, 1808, when the Spanish rebellion overthrew the alliance with France, Britain had a vested interest in preserving the integrity of its new ally's possessions. No time was lost in making this clear to the American government, and nothing more was heard from Jefferson of an alliance with Britain. British warnings were ignored, and after a brief American-inspired revolution in September, 1810, West Florida was occupied by the United States. The American government also connived at illegal attempts to take over East Florida and left troops in the area even after all responsibility had been disclaimed by Madison in 1812.

There were already signs of a future schism between the North and South in their different views of these territorial claims. The Southern states looked with suspicion upon plans for the invasion and annexation of Canada which would greatly enhance the power of the North. The Northern states, for similar reasons, were less than enthusiastic about plans to annex the Floridas. There was a fundamental difference between the two ambitions which united all parties: the annexation of Canada would deal a direct blow to the common enemy. If it was later considered that this conquest could not be held, it could be used as a powerful counter in the inevitable bargaining for peace. In the absence of a navy strong enough to give battle at sea or to transport and convoy troops to attack British possessions in the West Indies, the invasion of Canada offered, in the meantime, the sole possible method of attacking British territory.

Whatever restraint might be exercised by the New England maritime interests, there was a new strength and determination in American attitudes. Diplomatic exchanges had been fruitless, and attempts at economic coercion damaging. The remaining alternative was war. Though the country was divided into two opposite factions, this solution to the continuing disputes appealed to an increasing number of Americans. The new defiance found an impassioned spokesman in Henry Clay, then in the Senate. In a speech on December 28, 1810, advocating the annexation of West Florida in spite of British warnings, he had castigated the submissiveness and lethargy of his countrymen. "Is the time never to arrive," he demanded, "when we may manage our affairs without the fear of insulting his Britannic Majesty? Is the rod of British power to be forever suspended over our heads?"[29] His voice was to be heard in Congress a year later, more powerful, more urgent, and commanding greater respect.

The British were also divided in their attitude to war with America. Tory policy, a stern refusal to compromise and an undeviating dedication to winning the war against Napoleon, found no favor with those whose financial interests lay in American trade or whose livelihood depended on the import of American raw materials. As early as 1808 Alexander Baring, head of the great financial house which had become general agents in Europe for the American government, wrote of trade with the United States: "It is impossible to conceive, upon the whole, a commercial intercourse more interesting and important in every point of view, or less deserving of being sacrificed to any other."[30] With the Whig politician Henry Brougham, Baring organized public opposition to the Orders in Council, and petitions were received by the government from ports and manufacturing centers. The opposition failed to bring about any reform of the orders for two reasons: the government held firm to the declared belief that the policy of blockade, however inequitable and injurious to neutrals, was vital to the survival of Britain so long as European trade was denied to it by Napoleon's Continental System, and the regeneration of trade with Spanish and Portuguese colonies, particularly with South America, bred hopes that trade with the United States would not be greatly missed. It was assumed, at the time correctly, that America would accept any measure but war, and the privations suffered by the American people during the period of embargo and nonintercourse were considered just retribution, and justly self-inflicted, for treacherous Francophile policies. These attitudes were sustained and promoted by the Tory press in articles, lampoons, and caricatures. The intention of the Whig opposition to rescind the Orders in Council savored too strongly of commercial self-interest and was too closely associated with a policy of conciliation and withdrawal from the war in Europe to command general support.

By 1810 British attitudes were showing signs of change. Forecasts of trade with South America had proved overoptimistic, and the renewal of nonintercourse against Britain alone coincided, unhappily, with a sharp commercial depression. The total value of exports declined by 30 percent in one year, and the value of exports to the United States fell from nearly 11,000,000 pounds to less than 2,000,000. The dire effects of opposing policies designed to strangle trade were no longer confined to vulnerable manufacturing cities; they were widespread throughout the country, causing the collapse of industries, the fall of respected financial houses, individual bankruptcies, and unemployment. The Tory government remained obstinate in support of the Orders in Council, but the rising tide of opposition to policies which deprived the people of work threatened, in turn, to drive the government from office. It was also becoming apparent, to the astonishment of Europe, that America was preparing for war. Spencer Perceval had survived powerful Whig opposition, temporary failure in the Peninsula, and "Prinny's" accession as Regent, with his policy intact. Recognition of the difference between the courageous preservation of principle against adversity and obstinate perseverance in error is a common human dilemma, and the reversal of a major political policy invites the charge that principle has been sacrificed to expediency. This was Perceval's most intricate problem, and one which he was not destined to solve. On May 11, 1812, as he entered the lobby of the House of Commons, Spencer Perceval was assassinated. The death of the author of the Orders in Council was greeted by public demonstrations of joy. Bells were rung and bonfires lit to celebrate the murder of Britain's Prime Minister. The way was clear for the withdrawal of the orders and a new approach, in friendship, to the United States. It was too late.

V

The Twelfth Congress

The Eleventh Congress, devoted to a nugatory policy of complaint and inaction, had accomplished little. Its one altogether singular achievement had been the confirmation of Madison's proclamation of November, 1810, accepting, in spite of ample evidence to the contrary, the revocation of the Berlin and Milan Decrees and renewing nonintercourse against Great Britain. The elections swept nearly half the members from the House. The new Congress made its spirit clear on the first day: Henry Clay, who at thirty-four had already served two terms in the Senate and switched to the House, was elected Speaker. Madison's message to Congress, delivered the following day, was typically judicial without pronouncing judgment. A long catalogue of grievances concluded with a tentative exhortation: "With this evidence of hostile inflexibility in trampling on rights which no independent nation can relinquish, Congress will feel the duty of putting the United States into an armor and an attitude demanded by the crisis, and corresponding with the national spirit and expectations."[31] The message was no clarion call to arms, but it indicated a readiness to give approval to stronger measures, and Clay carried it like a fiery cross.

The direction in which Congress was to be led was evident in the composition of the committees of the House, which Clay openly packed with War Hawks. The important nine-man Foreign Relations Committee included five Hawks: Peter B. Porter of New York, nominated chairman; John C. Calhoun of South Carolina; Felix Grundy of Tennessee; John Adams Harper of New Hampshire; and

Joseph Desha of Kentucky. Their report was submitted on November 29. The main recommendations consisted of six specific measures to increase military strength and prepare for war. Felix Grundy, a noted Anglophobe, had summed up the feeling of the committee in a private letter to Andrew Jackson written on the evening of the twenty-eighth. "If," he wrote, "the opinion of the Committee is to prevail, I may say the Rubicon is pass d." He made it plain that he wanted war, but realized the unpracticability of action without first raising the means. "Rely on one thing," he added, "we have War or Honorable peace before we adjourn or certain great personages have produced a state of things which will bring them down from their high places."[32] There can be no doubt that these sentiments appealed to Andrew Jackson, whose love of action matched his loathing of the British, but if he hoped for early employment, he was to be disappointed.

The debate in the Twelfth Congress was not one-sided. Powerful forces were mobilized against proposals for war, and the high, piping voice of John Randolph of Virginia, sharply sarcastic, cut swaths through the ranks of belligerent argument. Porter's opening speech adequately described the recommendations of the committee but lacked fire. War, he maintained, should be declared to assert and protect America's right to export its goods, unhindered and untaxed by any other country. It was not to be fought for the New England carrying trade or to defend the Northwest from Indians incited and supplied by the British. He was strongly supported in his call for war, but other members of the House revealed other motives. Felix Grundy referred briefly to impressment and the violation of maritime rights, but made much of the British alliance with the Indians: "If British gold has not been employed, their baubles and trinkets, and the promise of support and a place of refuge if necessary, have had their effect."[33] His reasons for advocating the conquest of Canada are significant: "When Louisiana shall be fully peopled, the Northern States will lose their power; they will be at the discretion of others; they can be depressed at pleasure, and then this Union might be endangered—I therefore feel anxious not only to add the Floridas to the South, but the Canadas to the North of this Empire."

John Randolph was quick to answer. He found Grundy's accusations of British incitement "destitute of any foundation." On the contrary, he believed that advantage had been taken of the spirit of the Indians, "broken by the war which ended in the Treaty of Greenville." They had been "pent up by subsequent treaties into nooks, straightened in their quarters by a blind cupidity, seeking to extinguish this title to immense wilderness, for which, (possessing, as we do already, more land than we can sell or use) we shall not have occasion, for half a century to come." He described the proposed attack on Canada as "This war of conquest, a war for the acquisition of territory and subjects." Referring to Felix Grundy's offer to "receive the Canadians as adopted brethren," Randolph reached his peak of scorn: "it seems," he declared bitterly, "this is to be a holiday campaign—there is to be no expense of blood, or treasure, on our part—Canada is to conquer herself—she is to be subdued by the principles of fraternity. The people of that country are first to be seduced from their allegiance, and converted into traitors, as preparatory to making them good citizens." Alliance with France roused him to passion. He believed that the United States was about to "abandon all reclamation for unparalleled outrages, insults and injuries." What reparation or atonement could they, he demanded, expect to obtain "in hours of future dalliance after they should have made a tender of their person to this great deflowerer of the virginity of republics"? It was a fine harangue, full of characteristic biting invective, but the eccentricities of speech and manner, later to degenerate into obvious mental abnormality, were already becoming apparent. He was not yet forty, but there were younger members of the House who found his views, and the extreme expression of them, outdated and even ludicrous.

Robert Wright of Maryland concentrated his attack on the evils of impressment, picturing the unhappy plight of American sailors, "thousands of whom, at this moment, are languishing under the ignominious scourge, on board the infernal floating castles of Great Britain." He was followed by John C. Calhoun of South Carolina, serving his first term in the House at the age of twenty-nine. Elected on a prowar platform he was contemptuous of Madison, who, he considered, lacked "those commanding talents, which are necessary to control those around him," and "reluctantly gives up the system of peace." Calhoun was "not prepared for that colonial state to which again that power [Great Britain] is endeavoring to reduce us." He appears to have found Napoleon's phantom revocation convincing: "We still have cause of complaint against France; but it is of a different character from those against England. She professes now to respect our rights, and there cannot be reasonable doubt but that the most objectionable parts of her decrees, as far as they respect us, are repealed." This was self-deception of a most dangerous kind.

William L. King of North Carolina, also serving his first term in Congress, at the age of twenty-four, repudiated Randolph's accusation that Canada was to be won by subornment with all the heat and indignation of youth: "Sir, I trust if our differences with Great Britain are not speedily adjusted (of which, indeed, I have no expectation) we shall take Canada. Yes, Sir, by force; by valor; not by seduction." He agreed with Porter that war should not be fought for the carrying trade but for the right to carry American goods wherever they might be sold.

A Federalist of the antiwar party, from Randolph's state of Virginia, Daniel Sheffey, made a powerful and carefully reasoned appeal for peace by negotiation. He stressed the right of Americans to be free from impressment, but vigorously denied that this right should be claimed for "every person who shall sail under our flag. . . . I confess I am not disposed to enter into a war for the security on the high seas of the latter class." He proposed the sensible compromise of demanding protection for genuine American nationals while taking active measures to prevent the employment of any others so long as the war in Europe continued. He accused the Hawks of advocating war for "the unmolested commerce to France and her dependencies. . . . This is the real object, disguise it how you will." He went on to discuss trade figures, deliberately choosing to quote those for 1807, the last year before the Orders in Council became effective. These showed that of a total for domestic exports of $48,000,000 no less than $28,000,000 were to Great Britain, its possessions or dependencies, while less than $2,750,000 were to France. Since that date Britain had acquired the French West Indies, the Isles of France and Bourbon, the Cape of Good Hope, and Dutch possessions in Asia and America, which had accounted for a further $4,000,000 worth of exports. His logic was difficult to refute: "Estimating our exports to Great Britain and her present possessions and dependencies as they stood in 1807, the amount would be about thirty-two millions—about two-thirds of the whole amount of our domestic exports to every part of the world. Thus, while we are about engaging in a war for commerce, we abandon the greater, absolutely, and *contend* for the lesser." He went on to warn Congress of the possible loss of all European commerce, pointing to the protective tariffs on tobacco and cotton, the Continental surplus of flour and other food staples, and the doubtful benefits to be gained from the reciprocal imports of French wines, silks, and brandies. "I believe," he concluded, "were the Orders in Council repealed tomorrow, our commerce to France would not be worth two millions and . . . we may expect that it will daily diminish." The speech was well argued, but it was out of time with the spirit of the new Congress.

Henry Clay's speech added little to the previous arguments about impressment, trade, or the British incitement of the Indians, but it contained, more than any other, the true sentiments of the young Hawks of whom he was the accepted leader. "What," he demanded, "are we not to lose by Peace?—commerce, character, a nation's best treasure, honor!" Britain, he declared, "sickens at your prosperity, and beholds in your growth—your sails spread on every ocean, and your numerous seamen—the foundations of a Power which, at no very distant day, is to make her tremble for naval superiority." It was a quaint and indifferently accurate picture, which paid little attention to the British blockade of Europe or the French confiscations of American merchantmen, but it expressed the deep resentment of the war party. Clay's demand for the defense of the national honor was repeated with a frequency and anger which were less evident in support of any other argument. It was gradually becoming clear that none of the logical reasons for war was, by itself, adequate to justify it. Moreover, each was vulnerable to contradictory argument, for in no case was the evidence either sufficient or irrefutable. The one reason for war which provoked no contradiction was the preservation and defense of the "nation's best treasure, honor." It was a stirring appeal to patriotism, but unlike so many appeals of its type, it was no politician's trick. It was the expression of an emotion which was genuine and widespread, and it evoked an emotional response.

Randolph's second speech was both long and acidulated. He spoke with disgust of those who considered America under an obligation to France, "Bound to France, as Sinbad the sailor was bound to the putrefying corpse of his deceased wife." He demanded to know what might be gained by such bondage: "Where is the mess of pottage, the miserable dish of French broth, of soup maigre, for which you have bartered away your birthright?" He derided those who accepted the revocation of Napoleon's decrees as fact: "We have unquestionable testimony that France has played us false. . . . And yet, with all this glaring testimony of French perfidy, injustice, injury, and insult, we hear of *pledges to France,* of designating our enemy, and that enemy *not* France." He complained of the endless cry "like the whip-poor-will, but one eternal monotonous tone—Canada! Canada! Canada!" It was a speech of great oratorical power: trenchant, vigorous, and convincing, but not moving. It held no appeal to the emotions, no call for patriotism, no urgent summons to the defense of the nation's honor. There was no glamor to be found in negotiation, no glory to be plundered from peace.

The final decision for war was not taken by vote of Congress until

June, 1812, but the outcome was predictable almost from the start of the session. The debate underlined the deep divisions between states and among representatives of the same state. It gave expression to passionate patriotism and equally passionate self-interest. It remains the best record of American reasons for going to war and also, but less conspicuously, the underlying causes. It also broadcast, for the first time, the doctrine which came later to be known as Manifest Destiny, propounded by Richard Mentor Johnson of Kentucky and John Adams Harper of New Hampshire. Johnson stated it without dissimulation: "The waters of the St. Lawrence and the Mississippi interlock in a number of places, and the great Disposer of Human Events intended those two rivers should belong to the same people." Harper's proposition was more picturesque but no less explicit: "To me, Sir, it appears that the Author of Nature has marked our limits in the south, by the Gulf of Mexico; and on the north, by the regions of eternal frost." The sword of righteousness, it seemed, was no longer to be a weapon exclusive to the British. The United States snatched it up as the only weapon immediately available.

Surely no nation ever contemplated making war from a position of such total unpreparedness as the United States in the winter of 1811–12. While the war in Europe continued, however, there was little to be feared from British action on land. The army in Canada was too small to offer any serious threat to the northern frontier, and it seemed unlikely that it could be reinforced. The deliberate and wide publication in Europe of the resolutions to prepare for war, recommended by the Foreign Relations Committee and passed by Congress by December 19, makes it hard to avoid the conclusion that they were as much intended to threaten and persuade as they were a genuine declaration of intent.

The major proposals of the Foreign Relations Committee called for the recruitment of 10,000 men on a three-year term of service to the regular army, a volunteer force of 50,000, the refitting of warships not in service, and the arming of merchantmen. The army bill passed backward and forward between the House and the Senate before being sent for Madison's signature on January 11 after amendment to provide for recruitment of 25,000 regulars to bring the total 35,000. It was clear from the start that the raising of such an army was likely to prove impossible. The militia bill nearly foundered on the old question of whether the volunteer force could be used outside United States territory. Both Henry Clay and Langdon Cheves of South Carolina insisted that the militia must be available to carry the war onto foreign soil—in fact for the invasion of Canada and Florida—but they were not supported by Porter, Grundy, or other members of the war party. The bill was finally approved and was signed by the President on February 6, with this vital problem unresolved. Madison, who was not noted for dynamic leadership, wrote critically to Jefferson of the delays in Congress: "With a view to enable the Executive to step at once into Canada they have provided after two months parlay for a regular force requiring twelve to raise it, and after three months for a volunteer force, on terms not likely to raise it at all for that object."[34] The delays in Congress were negligible compared with those experienced in recruiting the regular and volunteer forces required. The leaders of the war party soon understood that it was one thing to make resolutions but quite another to carry them into effect.

Attempts to create a navy were even less successful. Langdon Cheves introduced a bill in January to provide for the building of twelve ships of the line and twenty frigates, but he was opposed by many Republicans who, though members of the war party, were adherents of the traditional and Jeffersonian distrust of maritime adventure. Henry Clay abandoned his political prejudices to argue with passion for the creation of a navy which could defend New Orleans, through which the produce of the West was carried to market, protect American shipping, and continue the war at sea after the land conquests had been completed, but the bill was defeated by a margin of three votes. Political dogma, entrenched prejudices, and interstate jealousies were already making preparation so difficult that even Felix Grundy began to have doubts, as he reported to Andrew Jackson in February, whether Congress would vote for war: "Shall we have War? That is the question you want answered—*So do I*—I thought some time ago there was no doubt."[35]

More difficulties were encountered when bills were introduced to raise money to pay for the war. Heavy taxation and massive increases in duties were approved by Congress on March 4, but on condition that they should not become effective until war was declared. Later in the month Clay suggested to Monroe that a thirty-day embargo should be introduced, to be followed by a declaration of war. Amended by moderate opinion to allow more time for Britain to avoid war by conciliation, this measure, extended to ninety days, was passed by the House and the Senate and the bill was signed by Madison on April 4. The two objects of the embargo were of equal importance: to prevent the movement of supplies to the British army in the Peninsula and to secure in harbor the ships and seamen of the mercantile fleet. The action of Josiah Quincy of Massachusetts, abetted by Senator James Lloyd of Massachusetts and Congressman James Emott of New York, in leaking information of this measure two days before the bill was presented to Congress and five days before it received the President's signature, falls little short of treason. Expresses dispatched simultaneously to Boston, New York, and Philadelphia on March 31 produced a burst of activity in the Eastern ports which destroyed the effect of the embargo before it was enacted. *Niles' Register* reported: "Drays were working night and day, from Tuesday night, March 31, and continued their toil till Sunday morning, incessantly. In this hurly-burly to palsy the arm of the Government all parties united. On Sunday perhaps not twenty seamen, able to do duty, could be found in all Baltimore."[36] In New York, where forty-eight vessels were loaded and cleared for Europe, a newspaper declared: "The property could not have been moved off with greater expedition had the city been enveloped in flames."[37]

It was estimated that in those five days granted to the ports by Quincy and his fellow conspirators, not less than $15,000,000 worth of goods left the country. Jonathan Russell, transferred from Paris to London as chargé d'affaires, reported that supplies had reached the Peninsular army sufficient for two months, at the end of which the local harvest would be gathered. This action by the mercantile interests in America was significant, not only at the time, but also for the future. It provided clear evidence of widespread lack of unity in support of a war which effectively allied the greatest democratic nation with a hated and feared dictatorship, and a disconcerting willingness to put patriotism a poor second to personal gain. An almost total lack of recruits for the army seemed to reinforce this evidence. To a government intent on making war, whose only weapons were commercial coercion and an invasion of Canada, the prospects were hardly encouraging. Undaunted by such evidence and buoyed up by a totally unjustifiable optimism, the government of the United States, united in name alone, stumbled resolutely to war. It was a fair indication of the pardonable but blind resentment and belligerence felt by many Americans that this period of preparation for war against Britain was one of renewed demands for war also against France.

In April, 1812, events occurred in Europe which, had the British been less indolent and the Americans less obdurate, should have prevented war. Conditions in England were beginning to cause real concern to Perceval's government. Newspapers, including the influential London *Times,* demonstrated a belief in American preparations which was not shared by the administration, and Brougham's agitations among the northern manufacturers were producing a steady stream of protests against the damaging Orders in Council. Even Canning, one of the most loyal and persistent advocates of the orders, was in opposition, and the government was coming to depend for a majority on the unreliable attendance of country members. Early in March the Duc de Bassano, French Minister of Foreign Affairs, repeated to the Senate the doctrine of enforcement of the Berlin and Milan Decrees until such time as Britain should yield to the demands required by them. He reiterated that the decrees would be enforced against neutral nations allowing their flags to be denationalized by violation of those decrees. No exception for the United States was mentioned. The British government was unusually quick to take advantage of this situation. On April 21 a new Order in Council was issued. This recognized the French Foreign Minister's statement as unqualified proof of the continued application, without exception, of the Berlin and Milan Decrees and declared that if, at any time, they should be revoked by an authentic and publicly promulgated act of the French government, the British Orders in Council should, from that date and without the issue of any further order, stand "wholly and absolutely revoked." There was no doubt of the official standing or legality of this order, and its provisions were admirably explicit.

The British Order in Council of April 21, 1812, was a masterly piece of diplomacy, constructed with a precision and timed with an accuracy worthy of British experience and opportunism. It neatly combined three essential objectives: a demand, which could not be ignored, for a public and binding declaration by France that the Berlin and Milan Decrees were or were not revoked; the embarrassment of the American government, shown to have accepted and acted rashly upon information which was unsupported by adequate evidence; and the temporary satisfaction of rapidly growing protest at home. The order was countered by a piece of French chicanery of such shamelessness that, although both Britain and America accepted it as providing a convenient excuse for conciliation, neither made any pretense of believing in it. In reply to a letter from Joel Barlow, the United States minister to France in succession to Armstrong, demanding, as America should have demanded eighteen months earlier, the publication of an authentic act showing the decrees to have been revoked (as they affected the United States) in November, 1810, the Duc de Bassano presented him with a decree dated April 28, 1811. This decree, apparently issued a full year earlier than it was produced, declared the

Decrees of Berlin and Milan "definitively, and to date from the first day of November last [1810], considered as not having existed in regard to American vessels." According to Bassano, this document had been shown to Russell and sent to the French minister at Washington with instructions to show it to the American government. All the parties concerned denied ever having seen it. When Barlow reasonably inquired whether the document had been published, the predictable but no less remarkable answer was that it had not.

Barlow acted with commendable speed and a lack of fastidiousness which Madison would never have contemplated. He sent a copy of the French decree to Russell in London, where it was handed to the Foreign Secretary on May 20. The assassination of Perceval on the eleventh and the consequent reconstitution of the British government delayed an immediate reaction. It has been suggested that the necessary delay was welcomed by ministers, who extended it deliberately, but there seems to be no evidence to support this theory.[38] On the contrary there is ample reason to believe that Castlereagh, who remained Foreign Secretary in the government formed by Lord Liverpool, was eager to grasp the excuse to revoke the Orders in Council. American goods were essential to much of British industry and also to the army in the Peninsula, and the avoidance of war with America could be considered a major triumph for British diplomacy, following directly from the initiative of the Order in Council of April 21.

Russell's correspondence with Monroe provides significant evidence of the British government's change of attitude toward war with America. During the first three months of 1812 there was no sign that American preparations were considered any cause for apprehension. As late as March 12, Castlereagh told Russell that he believed the display of belligerence in the United States to be no more than party maneuvering, but two months later Russell reported that he believed the British would "endeavor to avoid the calamity of war with the United States by every means which can save their pride and their consistency. The scarcity of bread in this country, the distress of the manufacturing towns, and the absolute dependency of the allied troops in the Peninsular on our supplies, form a check on their conduct which they can scarcely have the hardihood to disregard."[39]

Russell's report to Monroe had not arrived on June 1, when Madison sent his war message to Congress. The President summarized the grievances against Great Britain, and much significance has been attached to the order in which he chose to list them. He was, however, submitting a historical survey, and it is evident that his intention was to list the grievances as nearly as possible in chronological order. For this reason impressment, which was the oldest but by no means the most serious, was considered first, leading logically to the connected complaint against British warships cruising off the American coast to stop and search merchantmen leaving harbor. Madison went on to deal with illegal blockades and the Orders in Council, making the plausible charge "that the commerce of the United States is to be sacrificed, not as interfering with the belligerent rights of Great Britain; not as supplying the wants of her enemies, which she herself supplies; but as interfering with the monopoly which she covets for her own commerce and navigation."[40] Last of the complaints, he mentioned, with a brevity which indicated his personal estimation of its value, the problem of recent Indian uprisings as possibly attributable to British influence and support. In conclusion, Madison reverted to maritime affairs and the continuing seizure of American ships, goods, and men, amounting to "on the side of Great Britain a state of war against the United States, and on the side of the United States a state of peace toward Great Britain."

Prolonged debate in Congress was superfluous. Every aspect of the situation had already been discussed at length. On June 4 the House voted for war by a majority of 79 to 49, and the bill was passed to the Senate. On June 16, in London, Castlereagh agreed in debate that the Orders in Council should be withdrawn. The American declaration of war was approved by the Senate by 19 votes to 13 on the following day and signed by Madison on the eighteenth. Five days later the British Orders in Council were officially revoked.

The War of 1812 is often presented as having been forced upon an unwilling America by Britain's continuous and provocative violation of neutral rights. It is an attractive theory for those who like to believe that American intentions were invariably peaceable, but there is little evidence to support it. On the contrary, although American opinion was divided, a powerful majority wanted and demanded war. It is evident that the votes of many of the Hawks would have been unchanged by the revocation of the Orders in Council. Nevertheless, it is undeniable that the provocations were many and damaging and that the government of the United States had tried, over a period of many years, every method short of war to obtain the freedom of trade and movement to which a neutral was entitled. All these efforts had been without effect. The growth of the war party was gradual, gaining impetus from the *Chesapeake* affair but lacking essential authority or substantial political power until 1811. Had the British made any sincere attempt at conciliation prior to the opening of the Twelfth Congress, there is good reason to suppose that war would have been prevented.

The British did not want war with America. The struggle against Napoleon's legions and the Continental System of commercial warfare was a desperate and ruinous fight for survival. Nothing could be spared for another, unnecessary, war at a distance of 3,000 miles from which, moreoever, there was nothing to be gained. The war in Europe made demands on British money, arms, and supplies which stretched resources to the limit. The continuation of the battle required the supply of American goods to Britain and, at the same time, their denial to the countries of Europe occupied by or in alliance with the French. The British regarded their fight as a crusade: their country was the last bastion of freedom against the tide of a fearful dictatorship which had overwhelmed the rest of Europe. It seemed inconceivable that the Americans, many of whom were of the same blood and who had already demonstrated their independence, would not both understand and sympathize with this struggle. When America failed to respond with the brotherly support expected, British requirements, which were often neither reasonable nor legal, became demands and, finally, regulations which were enforced.

The prolonged negotiations between Britain and America during the period 1803 to 1812 cannot be considered in a vacuum. They arose directly from the war in Europe, and no settlement could be made except in the context of it. It was the failure, or refusal, of successive American administrations to understand and accept this fact, and to make allowance for it, that led, as much as any other single factor, to war. The Revolution had left a legacy of bitter and fundamental distrust which made all British actions or proposals objects of profound suspicion. Madison's obsession with minutiae, sometimes ludicrous in retrospect, has to be considered in perspective with this inherited distrust which it reflected. Of all the senior American statesmen of the period, Monroe, alone, appears to have comprehended fully the motives underlying British policies and the measures required to defend America against them.

Above all, perhaps, among the hidden causes of the war was the abject failure in genuine communication. British ministers appointed to Washington were, without exception, unsuitable, hostile, incompetent, or lacking the plenipotentiary powers essential to the conclusion of any settlement. American ministers to London were treated with correctitude, but coolly and without concern. Compared with the complications of European diplomacy and the continuous efforts required to erode Napoleon's alliances, American grievances and attitudes were of little consequence. It was not possible to persuade the British government that America would go to war, effectively allying itself to the French, whose violations of United States neutrality were as offensive as those of the British. A not totally unjustified belief in American weakness, maladministration, and military incapacity encouraged the British to treat the threat of war with fatal indifference.

The American distrust of the British and the lack of realistic communication between the two countries led to refusals on both sides to believe clear evidence. The British refused to believe in the American intention to go to war, and the Americans refused to believe in the British intention to revoke the Orders in Council. The American refusal is all the less comprehensible for Madison's public acceptance, although he admitted privately to Russell that he did not believe it,[41] of Napoleon's spurious revocation of the Berlin and Milan Decrees. It was upon this that Madison's move to war against Britain was founded. Ironically, the British move to prevent war, the belated revocation of the Orders in Council, was founded upon the French decree dated April, 1811, a document no more authentic or credible than the revocation. The American declaration of war against Britain was in fact a triumph for French diplomacy.

Of all the arguments for war produced during the long debates in the Twelfth Congress, the most cogent and influential was the defense of the nation's honor. Daniel Sheffey spoke against it with gloomy prophecy: "Are we," he asked, "to draw upon us all the miseries that attend war . . . without any practical good in prospect, when perhaps at the end of seven years we shall be compelled to sit down and acquiesce under the system against which the war is waged, merely to have it to say—that we acted like men of spirit?"[42] Congress had responded by sounding a trumpet call to arms. It remained to be seen how many Americans would answer it.

VI

1812

America had not entered upon the war lightly or without sufficient debate, but its leaders displayed a lamentable ignorance of what it was likely to entail. Ten days before the declaration, the Secretary of War, William Eustis, reported without any evident concern that the regular army was more than 30 percent under strength. He was unable to give any account of the progress of the recruitment of 25,000 men but confidently produced an uninformed guess that 5,000 had joined. Nor was there any obvious profusion of military leaders. The senior general officer was James Wilkinson, whose twenty years of service had done nothing to endear him to his fellow officers. His complicity in Aaron Burr's conspiracy to split the Union and separate Louisiana from the United States had not affected his military rank, but his attempted treachery and subsequent betrayal of Burr in order to save himself had made him the object of suspicion and contempt. Henry Dearborn, Eustis' predecessor as Secretary of War, was hastily promoted to major general to outrank Wilkinson. William Hull, governor of the Michigan Territory, reluctantly accepted a regular commission as brigadier general and the command of an army in the Northwest. Andrew Jackson's immediate offer of 2,500 Tennessee militia, which he proposed to lead at once against Quebec, was politely accepted and filed without any orders being issued to implement it.

The navy, on the other hand, consisting of some 16 small warships and about 200 scattered gunboats, many of them requiring extensive repairs, was commanded by a cadre of well-trained and efficient officers. The names of Commodore John Rodgers, Stephen Decatur,

Oliver Hazard Perry, Isaac Chauncey, Thomas Macdonough, and Daniel T. Patterson were to find a permanent place in naval history. Their ships, the three largest of which were the 44-gun frigates *United States, Constitution,* and *President,* were equal to any of their class and temporarily outnumbered the small British naval force operating along the east coast, though powerful squadrons were stationed in the West Indies and Newfoundland.

There was a marked difference of opinion between the administration and the naval officers about how the small American Navy should be used. The government tended toward the view that it must be preserved at all cost and should therefore be concentrated in a safe harbor. The precise purpose of such a policy was never clear, but it was soon pointed out that a force thus concentrated could be blockaded in port, leaving the entire coastline and all merchant shipping at the mercy of the enemy. Commodore Rodgers favored offensive operations in squadrons in the West Indies and along British trade and supply routes. Captains William Bainbridge and Stephen Decatur, on the other hand, urged that the offensive should be left to the individual enterprise of ships' commanders. The orders issued by the Navy Department on June 22, 1812, showed a preference for defense. The two squadrons commanded by Rodgers were to separate and cruise near the coast to protect returning merchantmen. The declaration of war arrived on the twenty-first, enabling Rodgers and Decatur to put to sea before the orders restraining them to defensive operations were dispatched. In debate in the Twelfth Congress Josiah Quincy had prophesied that the glorious exploits of a navy unprejudiced by divisive state politics would unite the country as no military action or government exhortation could. His opinion was to be vindicated sooner than he could have anticipated.

While America prepared for war, events occurred in Europe which were to make the timing of the declaration even less favorable than it already appeared. In February the British army in the Peninsula had left their winter quarters and, two months later, after a bloody siege, had captured the fortress of Badajoz. Early in May Napoleon had joined his army to begin his assault on Russia. The Grande Armée assembled in Prussia numbered more than half a million men, drawn from France, Austria, Prussia, Spain, Italy, Denmark, Holland, and the Duchy of Warsaw. Alone among the countries of Europe and Scandinavia, Sweden refused to subscribe troops or money, allying itself irrevocably with Russia and with Britain. In Napoleon's eyes there was no neutrality in Europe: those who were not for him were against him. The crushing results of Napoleon's invasion of Russia were not generally anticipated. Both in Europe and in America the invincibility of his armies had become legendary, and it is not surprising that the news of his march eastward was greeted with jubilation in America. When it was known, in November, that Napoleon had reached Moscow, *Niles' Register* declared, with evident gratification, "All Europe, the British Islands excepted, will soon be at the feet of Bonaparte." It was an opinion shared also throughout Europe during the summer of 1812. Few people could imagine the defeat of Napoleon. For this reason the consequences of such a defeat were not examined. They were of vital interest to the United States.

To Wellington, who had been elevated to an earldom early in the year, Napoleon's march into Russia meant the certainty that the French armies in the Peninsula could not be reinforced to an extent which would make British defeat inevitable. The reprieve, however short, would enable Wellington, once more, to consolidate his position by a victory. At Badajoz he had broken down and wept for his 5,000 dead and wounded, but plans were already in his mind for the defeat of Marmont, whom Napoleon had sent against him. By the time Napoleon began his advance into Russia, Wellington was already across the frontier into Spain. By a series of tactical maneuvers in advance and withdrawal, Wellington tempted Marmont into overextending his line of pursuit. At the Battle of Salamanca, on July 22, he seized the opportunity to strike down Marmont's army while it was divided, inflicting 15,000 casualties and taking 7,000 prisoners. On August 12 Wellington entered Madrid in triumph.

There was a particular significance in Wellington's victory at Salamanca which did not escape the notice of the French. For the first time in his career in Europe he had attacked and defeated an enemy army in the open. His reputation as a purely defensive fighter was obliterated, and his presence in the Peninsula, previously considered an irritant which could be contained until it could be cured without inconvenience, had become a positive threat to French occupation of Spain. Although the British were obliged to fall back to the frontier for the winter, the initiative was never again lost. The destruction of the Grande Armée before the end of the year made certain the final withdrawal of French armies from the Peninsula.

By the end of 1812, within six months of America's declaration of war, Britain's double vulnerability on which the declaration largely depended was already lessening. Napoleon's stranglehold was broken;

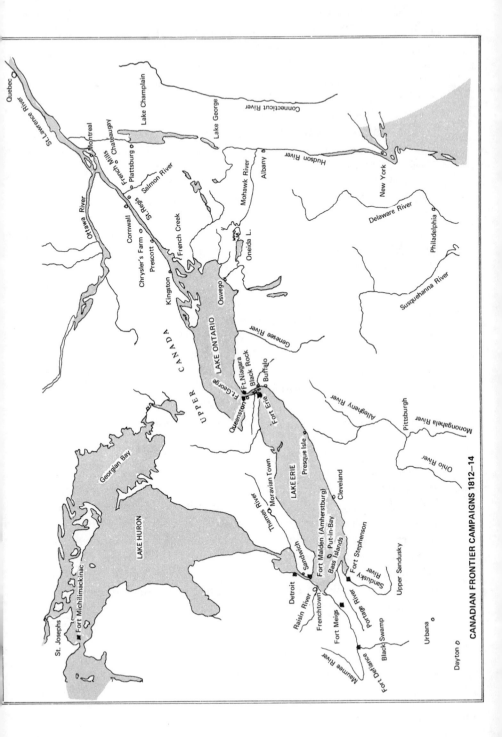

CANADIAN FRONTIER CAMPAIGNS 1812–14

Russia and Sweden had entered the war against France, at the same time opening their ports to British trade; and the paltry little army with a defensive foothold in Portugal had become a fast-moving and deadly striking force which either eluded or destroyed the French armies sent against it. So sweeping were the changes in the state of the war in Europe that even the reinforcement of the army in Canada seemed a practical possibility.

The American war strategy was uncomplicated by alternatives. Offensive action against Britain was necessarily confined to the invasion of Canada, and if this was to be accomplished, it had to be attempted without delay. The weakness of the army in Canada, the extent of the frontier to be defended, and the uncertain loyalty of the Canadians of French descent were encouraging factors which provoked great optimism in American forecasts of the course of the war. More damaging was the effect of this optimism on planning. American success depended on a correct strategic assessment and the military capability to convert it into action. Madison believed rightly that the key to Canada lay in possession of Montreal. The territory was dependent for arms and supplies on two sources: goods from Europe and the West Indies following the route of the St. Lawrence River, and the American frontier trade, which, it was incorrectly assumed, would cease for the duration of the war. The capture of Montreal or of Kingston would inevitably lead to control of the Lakes and the fall of Upper Canada. The theory was sound, but its practical application served only to underline the fundamental weaknesses of the United States as a nation at war.

Congress had voted for a regular force of 35,000 men at a time when the army was some 3,300 below its authorized strength of 10,000. At the time war was declared even the most optimistic estimates put the total strength, including all recent recruits, at less than 12,000. The failure of Congress to decide upon the use of the militia resulted in a flat refusal by the governors of Massachusetts and Connecticut to allow their well-trained forces to be used for invasion. Under the Constitution the President could call for the use of militia to suppress insurrection or repel invasion. Neither of these emergencies was apprehended, and the New Englanders, who had generally voted against the war, had no enthusiasm for an invasion which would destroy profitable trade. Kentucky and Ohio had no such inhibitions, and an attack from the Northwest Territory seemed to offer some prospects of success. Madison therefore accepted a revised plan, submitted by Major General Henry Dearborn, for a main thrust toward

Montreal supported by secondary thrusts from Detroit, Niagara, and Sackets Harbor, 30 miles from Kingston.

The attack through Detroit was entrusted to Brigadier General William Hull. Subsequent events branded Hull as a commander whose ineffectiveness was matched by his incompetence, but his ludicrous failure was in part the fault of the government. He was fifty-nine, and his military experience was confined to service, as a subordinate, thirty years earlier in the Revolution. He had accepted his commission with great reluctance and, in March, had submitted to the War Department a memorandum drawing particular attention to the absolute necessity of naval control of Lake Huron and Lake Erie. Without such support he believed Detroit to be untenable. On a subsequent visit to Washington he appears to have abandoned this view, giving Madison an opportunity, which he was not slow to grasp, of planting the blame for the lack of naval support on Hull's shoulders.[43]

Hull arrived at Dayton, Ohio, to take up his command on May 25, more than three weeks before war was declared. With three regiments of militia he began his advance, reaching Urbana, where he was joined by the 4th U.S. Infantry, on June 10. The route from there to the Maumee River, which they reached three weeks later, was hacked through forest and laid over swamp, often under heavy rain which made the movement of baggage and stores laborious and slow. Finding the schooner *Cuyahoga* at the Maumee, Hull relieved his army of a large part of the military stores, medical supplies, and baggage, which he loaded onto the schooner for transportation by water. With his own baggage was included, inadvertently, a trunkful of confidential correspondence. No desire, however estimable, to increase the speed of march, can excuse Hull's folly in entrusting his stores to a schooner upon Lake Erie controlled by the British. Nor can it be argued that the risk was justified by his ignorance of the declaration of war, news of which had not reached him. If war had not been declared, it was at least imminent, as his own presence at the head of 2,000 troops marching to Detroit amply proclaimed.

News of the declaration of war had reached Montreal on June 24, and Sir George Prevost immediately put into effect his plans for the defense of Canada. The difference of opinion between Prevost, who favored defense, and Brock, who intended to adopt a policy of limited offensive, was temporarily disguised by difficulties in communication between Lower and Upper Canada, and Brock was therefore left free to deal with the first American assaults in his own way. One of his first actions had been to send instructions to Captain Charles Roberts, commander of the small garrison at Fort St. Joseph, the most westerly of all British military posts, to attack Fort Michilimackinac. The importance of this American fort lay, in combination with Detroit, in the control of transit through Lake Huron, and thus of a large part of the fur trade of the Northwest Territory. Free use of this waterway was vital to Indian interests, and it followed that whoever controlled it would gain the alliance of the tribes in that region. Despite later orders from Brock which first canceled and then repeated his original instruction and a letter from Prevost urging vigilance and caution in defense of his post, Roberts set out on July 26. His force consisted of 45 troops of the 10th Royal Veterans, less than 200 fur traders, and about 400 Indians, embarked in the North West Company's schooner *Caledonia* and numerous canoes. This ill-assorted band completed their 50-mile journey early the following morning and, landing a 6-pounder gun which was manhandled to a hill overlooking the fort, called upon the American garrison to surrender. Lieutenant Porter Hanks and his 61 regular soldiers had no alternative but to obey or risk the massacre by Indians of any survivors of the attack. Roberts succeeded in controlling the excited Indians and no lives were lost. He took possession of the fort with his Royal Veterans, whom he described as "worn down by unconquerable drunkenness," relying on the Chippewa and a band of untrustworthy Ottawa for support in case of counterattack.

Two weeks before the British capture of Fort Michilimackinac General Hull crossed the Detroit River and took possession of the Canadian village of Sandwich. This put him within 15 miles of the Provincial Marine's dockyard at Amherstburg, covered to the north by Fort Malden. The Amherstburg garrison was commanded by Colonel Henry Procter of the 41st Foot, Brock's most professional subordinate, and the fort defenses had recently been strengthened. It therefore represented a formidable objective to any but seasoned troops. Hull's force at Sandwich was reduced to about 1,200 m 1, the Michigan militia having been left at Detroit and about 100 of the Ohio militia having refused to serve in Canada. The capture by the Provincial Marine's brig *General Hunter* of Hull's stores and correspondence aboard the *Cuyahoga* on July 2 had alerted Brock to the danger to Amherstburg, and Fort Malden was in a fair state of defense.

Hull was paralyzed by indecision. His reports dithered between almost bombastic optimism and a catalogue of excuses for delaying any action. He fell back on the last resort of the vacillating commander, the council of war. His first council, summoned on July 14, voted to postpone an assault until heavy guns could be brought across from Detroit. The guns were obtained and, after much delay, mounted on rafts. At another council of war on August 6 the vote for an immediate assault on Fort Malden was carried by a majority and approved by Hull, but new intelligence was received that Brock was on his way to relieve Amherstburg. Hull packed up and withdrew across the Detroit River on the eighth. Five days later Brock arrived at Amherstburg with 50 regulars, 250 militia, and a 6-pounder gun. He wasted no time in organizing his total strength of 300 regulars and 400 militia into three brigades, and on the fifteenth he sent his aide to Detroit to demand Hull's surrender. Hull was, once more, undecided. Two of his colonels, Lewis Cass and Duncan McArthur, both of whom had intrigued to replace Hull as commander, were absent with 400 picked men meeting a supply column. On the sixteenth Brock's three brigades crossed the river, joining about 600 Indians under Tecumseh, who had crossed during the night. Fearing for the safety of the women and children in his camp, Brigadier General William Hull surrendered his entire force, including the absent colonels and their detachments. Sixteen hundred militia troops were paroled and sent home. Hull and nearly 600 regulars were sent as prisoners of war to Quebec. Thirty-three guns, 2,500 muskets, the brig *Adams,* and quantities of military stores fell into British hands. By proclamation on August 16, Brock declared the territory of Michigan reannexed to Britain. His brigades had not suffered a single casualty.

Once more the Indians had behaved with restraint, but the little garrison of Fort Dearborn, evacuated on Hull's orders, was caught by 400 Potawatomi Indians. Twenty-six regulars, 12 militia, 2 women, and 12 children were massacred. The remainder escaped or were later ransomed by the British.

Two years after Hull's surrender he was tried by court-martial and sentenced to be hanged for cowardice. Through the personal intervention of Madison his life was spared, but even the attempts of the most compassionate historians have been unable to mitigate his disgrace. His defense that he was short of ammunition and food is not borne out by Brock's records of supplies captured. His concern for the women and children in his camp was genuine, but there can be no doubt that Brock would have agreed to an arrangement to ensure their safety. Since he had failed to achieve the conquest of Amherstburg, the first objective of his expedition, it was his plain duty to prevent at all costs the loss of Detroit. Failure might have been blameworthy; such abject surrender was contemptible.

While Hull was fumbling his way toward disgrace in the West, Dearborn was presumed to be directing the attacks through Niagara and Sackets Harbor and the main thrust along Lake Champlain to Montreal. In fact, he had made little progress. After setting up his headquarters at Albany in May, Dearborn had spent two full months in Boston, where, for some reason apparent only to himself, he had been occupied in strengthening the coastal defenses. He confessed himself "at a loss to determine" whether or not he should leave the coast and ignorant of the extent of his command. Ironically, as Dearborn floundered around in his morass of confusion and indecision, it was Prevost who flung him a lifeline. Hearing from Augustus Foster, in July, that the Orders in Council were about to be revoked, Prevost sent his adjutant general, Colonel Edward Baynes, to Dearborn's headquarters proposing an armistice until the state of war between their two countries should be confirmed. Dearborn agreed to an informal cessation of all offensive action, hostilities to be resumed only after four days' notice had been given. This understanding was signed on August 9.

Prevost's agreement with Dearborn was not at all to the taste of Brock, who had hurried from his success at Detroit to take command of the small garrisons concentrated at Fort Erie and Chippewa above the Falls and Fort George by the mouth of the Niagara, and he heard with relief of Madison's unhesitating repudiation of the armistice. The President had replied to Dearborn instructing him to "proceed with the utmost vigor" with his operations, which were to include the capture at least of Kingston and the Niagara Peninsula if not of Montreal. Hostilities were resumed on September 4, and Dearborn returned to the examination of his overwhelming anxieties.

Command of the considerable American force assembled at Niagara had been given to Major General Stephen Van Rensselaer. He was a leading Federalist, whose knowledge of military affairs was confined to his recent appointment as commander in chief of the New York militia, experience which the War Department apparently considered sufficient to equip him for this key command. His task was made no easier by the arrival, toward the end of September, of Brigadier General Alexander Smyth, a regular soldier who refused to take orders from a general of militia although his own service dated only from 1808 and he had never seen a shot fired in anger. Disapproving of Van Rensselaer's plan to attack at Queenston, below the Falls, Smyth refused to have any part in it and sulked in his tent. Van Rensselaer, with some 6,000 militia and regulars at his disposal against Brock's

1,600 and acting on the advice of his kinsman Colonel Solomon Van Rensselaer, who was a veteran of the Revolution, persevered with his plan. On the morning of October 11 an abortive attempt was made to cross the river. The lack of practice boat drills produced a scene of the utmost confusion, compounded by a heavy rainstorm and the loss of oars, many of which had been taken inexplicably to the opposite shore. Brock remained at Fort George. Before dawn on the thirteenth a second attempt was made, under cover of a heavy bombardment. The first wave of 600 regulars and militia made a landing under fire, and although Colonel Solomon Van Rensselaer was wounded, a company of the 13th U.S. Infantry succeeded in gaining the heights above Queenston. Brock, who had ridden from Fort George as soon as the direction of the attack was known, led an assault on the hillside to recapture a British gun position and the commanding heights above it. He was killed almost immediately. Lieutenant Colonel John Macdonell, Brock's aide, was mortally wounded leading a second attempt on the American position and the British retreated to wait for reinforcements. On the heights, Captain Alexander Wool, who had led a successful American attack, had been wounded, but a strong body of reinforcements had arrived under a twenty-six-year-old Virginian, Lieutenant Colonel Winfield Scott. When Van Rensselaer visited the position, he left Brigadier General William Wadsworth in command. By noon about 1,300 Americans had landed, some 600 of whom were established on the heights above Queenston.

This was the crucial situation when Major General Roger Schaeffe, following Brock's death the commander of the British force, arrived from Fort George. Had the remainder of Van Rensselaer's force crossed to Queenston the British would have been defeated; but the American militia refused to move, and they were even rejoined by some of their comrades who had crossed earlier. With the help of Indians, Schaeffe gained the heights by a circuitous route unknown to the defenders and forced the Americans to surrender. The remainder in the village either fled across the river or were captured. American casualties were more than 300 killed and wounded, nearly three times the British total, and 958 men were taken prisoner. After a three-day armistice the captured militia were paroled and the regulars sent to Quebec. Van Rensselaer resigned. His command at Niagara was given to Brigadier General Smyth.

If Hull's performance at Detroit had been pathetic and Van Rensselaer's at Queenston tragic, Smyth's at Fort Erie was farcical. His preparations were well publicized by a series of bombastic statements of a "conquer or die" resonance, though whether these were intended to fortify the spirit of his own men or strike terror into the hearts of his enemies is not clear. Early on the morning of November 28 he made his attempt. A first assault party made a landing above the Falls some two and a half miles below Fort Erie, but this, with a second party which landed near Frenchman's Creek, was driven back across the river by a British counterattack. By midday Smyth had failed to embark his main force, and the inevitable council of war voted against continuing with the operation. Two days later he succeeded in embarking some 1,500 men for a second attempt, but once more, a council of war voted to abandon the attack. General Smyth applied to Dearborn for leave to visit his family, a request which was readily granted. He did not return. Without court-martial or inquiry, his name disappeared from the army lists.

In the northeast, where Dearborn himself commanded the main thrust to Montreal, more than 6,000 troops had been assembled. In November he moved his army up Lake Champlain to Plattsburg. Early on the morning of the twentieth his advance guard crossed the border from the village of Champlain and attacked the Canadian outposts, capturing a blockhouse. Confused by this unusual success, different sections of the assault party fired upon one another and retreated. Dearborn's militia having refused to cross the frontier, he withdrew the entire army. The regulars went into winter quarters. The militia went home. The military campaign of 1812 was over.

When Colonel Edward Baynes visited Dearborn's headquarters to propose an armistice, he took careful note of all he saw. His observations were subsequently reported to Prevost,[44] and they revealed many of the fundamental weaknesses in the American Army. The war was unpopular and, in spite of generous pay and bounties, recruitment slow; the regulars were mostly raw recruits; the militia, distinguished in dress from the civil population only by a cockade, expressed a firm resolve not to serve beyond the frontier; and the majority, like the Canadians, were anxious to return to their homes. Dearborn appeared to be over sixty and, although strong and healthy, seemed to lack the energy of mind or activity of body necessary to a command of such importance. Baynes did not consider there was any serious danger of invasion.

This report adequately summarizes the obvious reasons for the humiliating failure of the American campaign on land in 1812, but there were other and more significant causes. Prevost and Brock experienced many of the same difficulties as Dearborn and Hull: a necessary reliance on untrained militia; the general unpopularity of the war and the doubtful loyalty of a substantial part of the population; and slow recruitment. In addition, they were dangerously outnumbered and required to defend a frontier of enormous length without any sure guide to the point of attack. For three vital reasons the American campaign was doomed to failure before it began: the army lacked the experienced and vigorous leadership provided, on the British side, by Brock and a small number of subordinates; the limited but adequate resources were frittered away in separate campaigns when they should have been concentrated in one powerful assault; and the prejudice and dilatory behavior of successive administrations had allowed the Canadian Provincial Marine to take control of the Lakes. Success in an invasion of Canada required speed, an early victory, and good communications. Speed and good communications were essential if the advantages of numerical superiority and the first initiative were not to be lost. An early victory would have done much, as Brock proved in Canada, to overcome divided loyalties, lack of enthusiasm for war, and the scruples of the militia. It would also have cooled Indian ardor for the British cause.

The solitary success of the American campaigns in the north was gained on Lake Erie. On September 3, after Hull's disgraceful capitulation, Captain Isaac Chauncey received orders to take command of the naval force on Lakes Erie and Ontario and to "use every exertion to obtain control of them this fall." The method and means to be employed were left entirely to his discretion. Chauncey was just forty and an officer of ability, energy, and experience. There was little but his personal qualifications in his favor, for the lack of naval preparedness was equal to that of the army, but he attacked his task with a knowledge and sense of urgency altogether different from the languid hesitancy of the military commanders. Within two months he had completed all his preparations, dispatching ships' carpenters, seamen and marines, cannon and small arms, and ammunition to Sackets Harbor on Lake Ontario, where he took over the 18-gun brig *Oneida* and five schooners which he purchased and armed. Two 24-gun vessels were under construction in the builders' yard. On Lake Erie there were no American ships or an organization for equipping any. Chauncey sent Lieutenant Jesse D. Elliott to Buffalo to select a site for shipbuilding, and ninety seamen were dispatched from New York on September 22 to man any vessels he might purchase. On October 8 two

British armed brigs, *Detroit* and *Caledonia,** anchored off Fort Erie. Elliott's preparations were not complete, and his seamen did not arrive until noon that day, having marched 500 miles. Undeterred, Elliott piled 100 men into two boats, surprised the British brigs, and, after a brief struggle, captured them. The *Caledonia* was beached at his temporary navy yard, and the *Detroit,* swept by the current within range of the British shore batteries, ran aground and was destroyed.

The approach of winter made operations on Lake Erie impossible, but ships were being assembled there for use in the following spring. By November 13, after two successful excursions in the *Oneida,* driving British ships into the safety of Kingston Harbor and capturing a couple of lake vessels, Chauncey was able to report that control of Lake Ontario was in his hands. At the beginning of December all ships were laid up for the winter.

The importance of control of the Great Lakes and of Lake Champlain was paramount. They provided interior lines of communication for either army along the frontier and a swift and easy route for reinforcements and supplies throughout the spring and summer months. Isaac Brock had understood their value and had made full use of their waters to compensate for his shortage of troops. Brock's death was a double loss to the British, for it robbed them of their most capable field commander and of the one senior officer who appreciated fully the tactical use of the inland waters. By the end of the year there were already signs that the British were allowing their great asset, naval control of the Lakes, to slip from their grasp.

At sea, too, Quincy's prophecy was being fulfilled. Rodgers and Decatur, with five ships, put to sea in pursuit of a British convoy which had sailed from Jamaica on May 21. Diverted by giving chase to the 32-gun *Belvidera,* which escaped after inflicting some damage on the larger *President,* Rodgers continued the pursuit of the convoy almost to the Channel, returning by Madeira and the Azores and capturing seven merchant vessels. Materially the voyage was no great success, but the knowledge that a powerful American squadron was at sea had forced the British to concentrate their naval forces and had severely hampered the blockade of American ports.

While Rodgers was cruising the Atlantic, Captain Isaac Hull, nephew of the disgraced general, was in Annapolis signing on a crew for the 44-gun frigate *Constitution.* On July 12 he sailed and, five days later, sighted a British squadron of two small ships of the line and three

Detroit was the *Adams,* renamed after being surrendered by Hull. *Caledonia* had played an important part in the capture of Michilimackinac (see p. 78).

frigates commanded by Captain Philip Bowes Vere Broke in the *Shannon*. Broke had already captured the 14-gun brig-sloop *Nautilus* and immediately gave chase. The pursuit lasted for more than two days, much of it in a dead calm, and demonstrated the seamanship for which the United States Navy was soon to be noted. Broke was an officer of considerable experience and ability, and his superiority in numbers enabled him to man every boat in the squadron to tow the *Shannon*. Hull mounted guns in the stern of the *Constitution* and pulled his ship forward on kedge anchors.* When a light breeze blew up, he sent men aloft with water to wet the sails. As a last resort he jettisoned much of his drinking water to lessen the ship's draft. At last, on the twentieth, he slipped away in a rainstorm, and on the twenty-sixth he entered the harbor of Boston. Hull's escape was a genuine victory for American seamanship, and to a nation starved of success, it seemed almost equal to a victory in battle. Hull wasted no time in showing that he could fight as well as run. On August 2, in the absence of any orders to the contrary, he sailed again. On the nineteenth, some 750 miles east of Boston, he sighted HMS *Guerrière*, a 38-gun frigate captured from the French and commanded by Captain James Dacres. The *Constitution*'s broadside was considerably heavier than the *Guerrière*'s, and Hull also had an advantage in commanding a crew which outnumbered his adversary's by more than 200 men. In a hard-fought engagement lasting from late afternoon until dusk, the *Guerrière* was battered to a helpless hulk, too crippled even to be towed into port. At dawn on the following day she was set on fire and, soon afterward, blew up.

Emboldened by such welcome news of activity and success, the Navy Department threw caution to the winds and issued new orders. Since most of the navy happened to be in harbor at the time, these instructions were received and acted upon. Three squadrons, each of two or three ships led by a 44-gun frigate, were to be commanded by Rodgers, Bainbridge, and Decatur. They were commissioned to cruise over the Atlantic trade routes, using whatever means they thought fit to disrupt British shipping and protect United States commerce. Decatur detached his brig-sloop *Argus* to operate separately and was cruising alone when he encountered, on October 25, the British frigate *Macedonian*, commanded by Captain John Carden. Decatur's frigate, the *United States*, was the stronger in weight of broadside by at least 50 percent, but the *Macedonian* had the advantage of greater speed. Deca-

---

*Small ship's anchors dropped ahead by cutters. The cable or hawser attached to the anchor was hauled in by the crew until the ship was abreast of the anchor. The maneuver was then repeated.

tur's heavier guns outranged Carden's, and the British captain attempted to bring on a close action; but he delayed his decision until too
late, and the *Macedonian* was already crippled when he was able to
bring her alongside the enemy. After a short, brisk action at close
quarters, the *Macedonian* was surrendered, and after some necessary
repairs had been effected, she was sailed into Newport.

Other single-ship engagements before the end of the year substantiated the impression that the American Navy was a force to be respected. In October the sloop *Wasp* defeated the *Frolic,* and at the end
of December Bainbridge in the *Constitution* defeated and destroyed the
frigate *Java* off Bahia. The American frigates, though rated as 32-, 38-,
or 44-gun vessels, generally carried as many as 10 guns more than their
rated capacity and therefore enjoyed a substantial advantage in weight
of broadside, and often in range, over British ships of equivalent size. It
was also becoming plain that the American ships were better built than
the British, that the seamanship of their captains was in no way
inferior, and that their gunnery was generally of a high standard. The
actions of the past six months of the war should have been sufficient
warning to Prevost as commander in chief in Canada that British
control of the Great Lakes was to be challenged. Had successive administrations of the United States not neglected the navy so
shamefully, the challenge could have been extended successfully, later
in the war, to the whole of the Atlantic seaboard.

British reaction to these defeats at sea was one of angry disbelief.
When news of the defeat of the *Guerrière* reached London, the *Times*
pointed out with disgust that never before had a British frigate struck
to an American. If such shocking episodes were allowed to be repeated,
the Americans would become "insolent and confident." Both Dacres
and Carden were tried by court-martial. The newspapers consoled
themselves by discovering that the American frigates were carrying
guns substantially above their rating and were therefore battleships
artfully disguised as frigates. It was comforting to believe that the
Americans could win only by cheating.

VII

The Burning of York

At the end of 1812, after six months of war, American achievements on land were one degree worse than nonexistent; they were measurably negative. A few hundred American soldiers remained on Canadian soil, but they were prisoners. Attempts at invasion had resulted in the loss of Detroit and Michilimackinac and, even more serious, had allowed the British to demonstrate to a doubtful and divided nation the feasibility of a defense of Canada. Nothing of importance could be attempted before the spring thaw, and with the reopening of the St. Lawrence River to navigation, the possibility that Prevost's small army might be reinforced from England became a relevant factor. No less disheartening was the certainty that the British Navy would send officers and crews to supplement the meager forces of the Provincial Marine on the Lakes. From the American point of view the war was not lost, but there were disturbing signs that whatever opportunity might have existed for winning it had already been forfeited.

For Britain the prospect, though still daunting, showed some improvement. Wellington's army in the Peninsula, the pivot of British diplomacy to separate Napoleon from his allies, had achieved some spectacular successes and consolidated them with resolution and caution. Prevost's inadequate and overextended army had profited by Brock's energetic leadership and the incompetence of the American commanders and held the Canadian frontier. Neither of these favorable situations, however, could compare in importance with Napoleon's disastrous defeat in Russia. The Grande Armée was all but annihilated by winter and the avenging Russian armies, and the typhus-ridden remnants were deserted by the Emperor. Napoleon's long history of victories was not yet closed, but his years of conquest were at an end. If, by subsidy and diplomacy, Czar Alexander could be persuaded to keep his army in the field, and the Prussians and Austrians would join a new alliance, Napoleon's final destruction was assured.

By the beginning of the year it was known that Napoleon was gathering another great army, withdrawing seasoned troops from Spain and replacing them with untried adolescents. In response, the army in Britain was stripped to 25,000, every regiment which could be spared being sent to the Peninsula or placed under orders for Canada. Meanwhile, Admiral Sir John Borlase Warren, commander in chief of British naval forces on the American station, was ordered to blockade Delaware and Chesapeake bays. At the same time, he assumed responsibility for operations on the Lakes. Later in the year the blockade was extended to cover the coast as far south as the Florida boundary, but significantly, the ports and harbors of New England were excluded.

The result of these moves was to reduce the American Navy at sea to impotence. Decatur, with the *United States* and *Macedonian,* was bottled up in New York from December, 1812, and Captain Charles Stewart, with the *Constellation,* was trapped in Norfolk from February, 1813. None of these ships was able to put to sea again during the war. Rodgers, with the *President* and *Congress,* was held in Boston for the first four months of the year, and Bainbridge, with the *Constitution,* was unable to escape from the same port until December. Captain James Lawrence, who had commanded the sloop *Hornet* in a bloody victory over the *Peacock* in February, slipped out of Boston in command of the *Chesapeake*[15] on June 1, but was intercepted by the *Shannon,* whose captain, still Philip Vere Broke, had been watching for him. After a desperate engagement, in which Lawrence was mortally wounded, the *Chesapeake* was boarded and captured. The overwhelming superiority of the British in American waters not only shackled the greater part of the small American Navy to anchors in safe harbors but also strangled American commerce. During the first four months of the year the only frigates at sea were the *Chesapeake* and the *Essex,* and both were lost within twelve months.

The responsibility for offensive operations at sea thus devolved largely upon American privateers outside their home waters. Privateers—armed vessels privately owned and officered but commissioned by the government—enjoyed substantial advantages over warships of the navy. Their shallow draft enabled them to make use of waters prohibited to larger and heavier vessels, and their primary object was profit by capture. They avoided fighting whenever it was possible to do so and preyed on unarmed merchant shipping. As the war continued, the British blockade of the American coast forced the privateers away from coastlines patrolled by the Royal Navy, and the convoy system reduced the chances of success along the Atlantic trade routes. The privateers soon found that the approaches to the British Isles yielded rich prizes, for merchantmen entering their own home waters broke away from the warships screening the convoy from attack. During the first six months of the war the total number of prizes falling to the American Navy and privateers was 305. Between January and June, 1813, after the beginning of Warren's blockade, this figure fell to 159, of which more than half were captured far from American shores. In the twelve months from September, 1813, however, when the indiscipline and vulnerability of convoys approaching their destination had become known to the Americans, 639 prizes were taken, of which more than 400 fell to American ships cruising far from home.[46]

There can be no doubt that the depredations of American privateers were the subject of serious concern. Wellington had cause to complain that supplies for his Peninsular army were delayed, and occasionally captured, by American ships in the Channel, and British manufacturers and newspapers were indignant at the failure of the navy to protect rich convoys into safe harbor. These criticisms were popular, following the bitter defeats of the first few months of the war, but they were uninformed. Convoys from Canada and the West Indies often numbered more than 200 ships whose captains held individual views about collective discipline and security. Often they invited capture by abandoning the convoy before it was safe to do so. The number of British merchantmen taken as prizes is a fair measure of the Royal Navy's ability to keep the seas open for commerce; it represented a substantial financial loss, but a meager fraction of the number of ships at sea. British captures, on the other hand, numbering some 300 before May, 1813, and a mere 30 from September of that year to September, 1814, underline the plain fact that legitimate American overseas trade had been eliminated. What survived was the coasting trade between states and the withered remains of commerce carried in neutral ships from the unblockaded New England ports.

The Eastern states had shown no sympathy for the war and continued to display an altogether unwarlike impartiality in their attitude to trade. The lack of a commercial blockade against their ports was of some advantage, but their trade was dependent on the products of others and thus particularly vulnerable to the restrictions imposed on the country as a whole. Reexports of foreign goods sank from nearly $6,000,000 in 1811 to little over $300,000 in 1813. Prices in the United States came to be ruled by the costs of overland transport. In the sugar-producing area of New Orleans, sugar was quoted at $9 a hundredweight, while in Baltimore it fetched more than double that price; but flour in Baltimore at $6 a barrel was $25 in New Orleans.

Admiral Warren's operations against the American coast had been limited in 1812 by lack of sufficient strength and the British government's hope that the repeal of Orders in Council might induce the United States to make an early peace. At the end of the year his fleet was reinforced by the arrival of Rear Admiral George Cockburn, a distinguished and experienced officer whose energy was not inhibited by any niceties of behavior or feelings of compassion toward his country's enemies, and several ships of the line. By February, 1813, Warren's command comprised nearly 100 armed vessels including 17 ships of the line, and he was under pressure from the government to destroy the remaining ships of the American Navy and to carry the war into the harbors which sheltered them and supported the coastal carrying trade. The Chesapeake and Delaware offered obvious opportunities for the achievement of both objects.

At the beginning of April, Warren, with Cockburn as second-in-command, led a strong detachment of his fleet into Chesapeake Bay. On the third a privateer and three letters of marque,* at anchor in the Rappahannock, were attacked and captured. The fleet moved northward, landing at several points to harass the local population and alarm the militia, until it reached the mouth of the Patapsco. There Warren anchored with the main body, threatening an attack on Baltimore, some 12 miles away, while Cockburn took a small squadron with marines and a detachment of artillery to the head of the bay. Cockburn's repeated offers to pay with British government bonds for goods given over to him without resistance were ignored, and he determined to make clear to the population the gravity of their error. At Frenchtown he captured or destroyed five schooners and quantities of flour and army equipment; at Havre de Grace he overcame the resistance offered, captured the guns of a defending battery, and burned the greater part of the town as punishment; early in May he

---

*Letters of marque were privately owned armed vessels commissioned by the government. In contrast with privateers, which were similarly owned and commissioned, they carried cargo, and their object was trade. Their armament was light and intended for defense.

sailed up the Susquehanna, destroying five more vessels and quantities of provisions; and on the fifth he entered the Sassafras River and, in return for local resistance which cost five wounded, burned the villages of Georgetown and Frederickstown. By the thirteenth Cockburn had rejoined Warren and the whole fleet had withdrawn down the bay to Cape Henry. Little had been achieved by this brief show of force, though there may have been some comfort to the British government in the thought that the navy could molest so freely the state of Virginia, home of America's President and a leading representative of the group most hostile to Britain.

To the surprise of the Americans, Warren withdrew his fleet from Chesapeake, leaving Cockburn with five ships to keep the bay closed. Warren had returned to Bermuda to take on troops, and he returned in June with 2,650 ready to attack Norfolk where the frigate *Constellation* was sheltering. The only other American Navy ship in the Chesapeake was the *Adams* in the Potomac. The initiative was grasped by the Americans, who sent fifteen gunboats to attack the British frigate *Junon,* becalmed without escort in Hampton Roads; but a fortunate breeze enabled *Junon's* sister ships to come to her aid, and the engagement was broken off without serious loss on either side. Warren's first attack on Craney Island, at the approaches to Norfolk, was a ludicrous failure, abandoned almost before it was begun and at the loss of 3 killed, 16 wounded, and no less than 62 missing. The last figure is less surprising when the American accounts of British desertions are considered.[47] On the morning of the twenty-sixth Warren's troops landed at Hampton. Seven field guns and a quantity of ammunition were captured and the town defenses destroyed, but the troops were then withdrawn. It was later alleged that several women had been raped, and the Canadian Chasseurs, who were not Canadian but French prisoners serving in the British Army, were blamed and dismissed from the service.

Warren's fleet occupied the Chesapeake until the end of the year, making marauding sorties of uneven success against various villages in the bay, but his lack of enterprise was apparent and his single achievement, the spreading of fear and disorder among the population, insignificant. In April, 1814, he was replaced by Vice Admiral Sir Alexander Cochrane.

The campaign of 1812 on the Canadian frontier had revealed three fundamental requirements for American success: control of the Lakes; resolute leadership; and a firm strategic plan which provided for the concentration of maximum force against essential objectives. The British forces in Canada were inadequate and could be brushed aside by a powerful breakthrough on a narrow front. Much depended, on both sides, on the use of militia. Attempts to employ militia in attacks across the frontier had produced serious and unnecessary defeats. While the problem of their employment abroad remained unresolved, they should have been used to hold the frontier while the regular army units were concentrated in a main assault.

On the Lakes some useful progress had already been made. Chauncey claimed to have seized control of Lake Ontario before the end of the year, and in March, 1813, he sent Oliver Hazard Perry to command on Lake Erie and speed the building of a fleet. The British commanders, delayed by greater distances and inferior communications, were later to arrive. Captain Sir James Lucas Yeo, a thirty-year-old veteran of many sea fights who had been knighted for his part in the capture of Cayenne in 1809, arrived at Kingston on May 15 and took command on Lake Ontario. He had brought with him more than 400 officers and men to provide a nucleus for the Lake fleets and immediately dispatched Captain Robert Barclay to Lake Erie. Three vital months had been lost, and the advantage was already with the Americans. The importance of Lake Champlain, which provided a natural highway toward Montreal, escaped the notice of both sides.

Chauncey had proposed, as early as January, to attack Kingston. The capture of this harbor and the destruction of its defenses was the key to control of Lake Ontario and thus also of Lake Erie and communications with the armies in the Northwest. Failing a successful assault on Montreal, no other plan offered such rewards. John Armstrong, who had replaced the ineffective William Eustis at the War Department (an appointment insanely offered again to General Dearborn), approved the plan and communicated the President's orders to this effect to Dearborn who remained in command on the New York frontier. Using Sackets Harbor as a base, Kingston and York* were to be attacked and taken. With the cooperation of a second army assembled at Buffalo, the campaign would then be extended to the British positions on the Niagara frontier, Fort George and Fort Erie. The plan was sound, and its objectives were attainable; but it took no account of the commander to whom it would be entrusted. Dearborn had given ample proof of his ability to discover prodigious reasons for caution, and he lost no time in finding incapacitating evidence of

*Now Toronto.

British strength at Kingston, based apparently on the intelligence that Sir George Prevost was making a brief visit to the town to inspect the defenses and examine the progress in shipbuilding.

Dearborn's timidity and gloomy acceptance of false intelligence appear to have affected Chauncey's judgment. He proposed a second plan, a version of which was subsequently put into operation, which turned the essential strategy on its head and effectively disposed of any probability of success. By changing the main objective to York and then turning the offensive westward, Chauncey hoped to ensure victory in the Northwest, but this was employing unnecessary means to achieve a limited end. Shortly before the end of the war he was to revert to his original opinion, likening Canada to a tree whose taproot was the St. Lawrence. Lopping off the branches, he asserted, would have the effect of strengthening the tree by reducing the demands on its resources.[48] Success in the Northwest would force the British to concentrate their strength at Kingston and Montreal, precisely those points which America must take in order to win Canada. Their capture would gain control of the Lakes and, by destroying communications with the Northwest, make American victory in that region a foregone conclusion. Chauncey's subsequent, and wholly accurate, opinion was based on bitter experience.

The first blow was struck in April. The ice in Sackets Harbor had broken up during the second week, and by the nineteenth the dangerous floes in the lake had melted. Eighteen hundred troops were embarked on the twenty-fourth and, after delays caused by rough weather, were landed west of York. The town was lightly defended, and the small number of British troops soon retired after inflicting, with the unforeseen help of a magazine explosion, some 300 casualties. The 20-gun *Prince Regent* had left for Kingston three days earlier; but the 16-gun schooner *Duke of Gloucester* was captured, and a 30-gun vessel nearing completion on the stocks was burned. Although the American troops, and the sailors landed with them, behaved with some restraint, generally looting only those houses left empty, the Parliament Buildings, Government House, and a number of military garrison buildings were set on fire and burned to the ground. This wanton destruction of the capital of Upper Canada was to be remembered when, seventeen months later, the British found an opportunity for revenge. Large quantities of naval stores were seized or destroyed. York being untenable, the troops were reembarked on May 1, and the squadron stood off to sail to the second objective, Fort George. Heavy gales prevented a landing until the eighth, by which time the overcrowded troops were sick from exposure and all chance of surprise was lost. The squadron returned to Sackets Harbor. On the twenty-seventh an attack was made on Fort George. The small British garrison was driven to retire on Beaver Dam and then, joined by the garrisons of Fort Erie and Chippewa, to Burlington Heights.* In the fortunate absence of Dearborn, who was too infirm to land with his troops, the attack was conducted by Colonel Winfield Scott and Captain Perry, whose ships at Black Rock would be released if the British withdrew from the area of Fort Erie. The plan succeeded, but the success was not exploited. The Niagara had been retaken and Perry's ships released, but while General John Vincent and his consolidated forces remained at Burlington Heights, the area could not be considered secure.

Yeo, the new British commander who had arrived at Kingston on May 15, lost no time in attempting to redress the balance. Taking advantage of Chauncey's absence at Fort George, Yeo launched an attack, which he subsequently described as a diversion, against Sackets Harbor. The troops, under Colonel Edward Baynes, were landed on the twenty-ninth and routed the screen of militia sent forward to the beaches. The defense, organized by a young militia officer, Jacob Brown, was spirited and strongly posted in fortified positions supported by artillery. When Prevost arrived to take command in person, he found a failed assault deteriorating toward costly defeat. He ordered an immediate withdrawal. The minimal achievement of the raid was enhanced by the action of an American navy lieutenant who burned his own stores and came close to destroying the *General Pike* which was near completion on the stocks. Brown was rewarded with a brigadier's commission in the army.

On June 1, Dearborn gathered sufficient energy to make a foolish error, sending General William Winder with 1,000 men to attack Vincent's 1,600 on Burlington Heights. After four days it occurred to Winder that his force was inadequate, and he was joined by General John Chandler, who assumed command of the two brigades, then strengthened to about 3,000. Vincent's unfortified position was too precarious to allow a setpiece battle. He dispatched Lieutenant Colonel John Harvey with 750 regulars to attack the Americans at night. The British force, greatly outnumbered, suffered heavy casualties, but the Americans broke before Harvey withdrew, taking with him both Generals Winder and Chandler. Dearborn, a prey to his usual fears of disaster, ordered a general retreat to the Niagara. Vincent followed to within 10 miles of Fort George and settled down to

*Now the city of Hamilton.

wait for Dearborn's next mistake. On the twenty-fourth he was rewarded by the surrender of Colonel C. G. Boerstler and 600 men sent to dislodge the British from their new position. Dearborn attributed these misfortunes to a temporary loss of control of Lake Ontario but declared himself "so reduced in strength as to be incapable of any command" and wisely asked to be removed to a place where his mind might be "more properly at ease." His request was granted with a promptitude as unflattering as it was characteristic of the new Secretary of War. Dearborn had served with gallantry in the Revolution, and his retirement from active command was viewed with sympathy. At the War Department his successor had been known for several months. Major General James Wilkinson, commander at New Orleans, arrived to take command of the army in August.

On July 20 the heavily armed *General Pike,* so nearly destroyed on the stocks in May, was ready for service. It outgunned any British vessel on the Lakes, and Yeo prudently decided to keep it at a distance. There followed a duel between Chauncey and Yeo which was as intricate as it was intelligent. Yeo, with a fleet which was outnumbered by the enemy, was also at a disadvantage unless he could bring his fleet into close combat; Chauncey relied on range and weight of shot. Both understood clearly that a single defeat would be decisive. Each therefore looked for action, but on his own terms. Yeo's command was the more efficient as a fighting unit, but Chauncey's, handled with skill and discretion, was the more likely to reap victory from the seeds of shipbuilding and the harvest of an engagement. After several desultory meetings without loss, the two fleets met in a three-day engagement —or maneuver—during which Yeo succeeded in detaching two schooners from Chauncey's line and forcing them to surrender. It was a minor victory, demonstrating Yeo's superior handling of his squadron, but it was indecisive. Chauncey continued to invite a more general engagement. Yeo wisely continued to avoid it. Throughout the summer they played for advantage without reaching a conclusion.

On Lake Erie, Captain Oliver Hazard Perry was less cautious. He believed in treating his enemy with respect, but not with reverence, and he was not hampered by the strategic considerations which all but incapacitated Chauncey. Defeat on Lake Ontario would result, almost inevitably, in the loss of control of the Lakes. An American defeat on Lake Erie would be a severe setback but not conclusive to the campaign. Perry did not share Chauncey's responsibilities, but his added freedom does not detract from his achievement. Chauncey, who had command in chief of the American naval forces on the Lakes, had sent his subordinate a letter which, ill-judged in terms, was nevertheless sound in advice. Perry, twenty-eight years old and quick to resent any implied criticism, asked to be relieved of his command. It was fortunate for America that his request was received by the government too late to be accepted at its face value. His actions on Lake Erie were of some significance in the war on the northwestern frontier.

On September 17, 1812, after Hull's calamitous surrender, Madison had appointed William Henry Harrison, victor of Tippecanoe, commander in chief of the army in the Northwest with the regular rank of brigadier general. The thirty-nine-year-old general was undismayed by the onset of winter and indeed planned to make use of the ice to ease the transport of artillery and supplies across the great swamp which barred his path. Harrison's plan was to assemble his army at the Maumee rapids and concentrate his strength in an assault on Detroit. By the end of December he had gathered some 6,500 troops and felt ready to order his left wing, under Brigadier General James Winchester, forward to the Maumee River. With 1,200 men the elderly general struggled through snow 2 feet deep to reach the river on January 10 and began to fortify a camp on the north bank. There he received urgent requests for help from American settlers at Frenchtown* some 35 miles to the northeast on the Raisin River. The settlement was held by a small garrison of Canadian militia and Indians, and in spite of its proximity to Malden, Winchester decided to attack. He sent forward a detachment of about half his total strength under Colonel William Lewis, and on January 18, after a brisk engagement, the town was captured. Too late Winchester realized that by dividing his force within striking distance of a powerful enemy force at Fort Malden he had jeopardized both divisions. He hastened with 300 men to Lewis' aid.

At Malden, Colonel Henry Procter had also realized Winchester's error. On January 21 he crossed the ice-covered Detroit River with 1,200 men, about half of whom were Indians led by Roundhead and Walk-in-the-Water, and several 3-pounder guns on sleighs. Winchester later admitted that he had not ordered night pickets or patrols, and had Procter not forfeited surprise by the use of his guns before he made his attack on the twenty-second, the Americans would have been defeated before they could offer any resistance. Nevertheless, the British were greatly assisted by Winchester's deployment of his outnumbered force with its back to the river instead of using it as a natural line

---

*Now Monroe, Michigan.

of defense. Procter's premature and unnecessary use of artillery gave sufficient warning of his attack for Winchester's regulars to form up in good order and inflict nearly 200 casualties; but the militia were outflanked by the Indians, and those who were not hacked to pieces were taken prisoner. Among those captured was Winchester, who immediately surrendered his entire force, but Major George Madison refused to surrender the regular detachment without guarantees of safety for all prisoners. This demand was granted by Procter, but it was beyond his power to honor his promise. The immediate withdrawal of his mauled force to the security of Fort Malden across the river was imperative, and he was obliged to take with him almost as many prisoners as he had troops. The wounded, the number of whom is uncertain but was probably about thirty, were left in Frenchtown attended by American doctors. When Procter's regulars left, his Indians, drunk with looted whiskey, scalped most of the wounded and burned the rest alive. In the American army of the Northwest "Remember the River Raisin" became both a battle cry and a strident warning against defeat and surrender.

Harrison, who had hurried to the Maumee rapids, heard news of the disaster on the twenty-third. He had no alternative but to postpone his campaign against Detroit until the spring, but he decided to retain a forward position on the south bank of the river and built there a well-constructed defensive stronghold which he named Fort Meigs. Prevost, in relief at the destruction of the immediate threat to Detroit, granted Procter the local rank of brigadier general.

When spring came, Harrison found himself still too weak to take the initiative. Twelve hundred Kentuckians were on their way under General Green Clay, but before they could arrive, Procter had again crossed the Detroit and laid siege to Fort Meigs. He had established batteries on both sides of the river and was preparing for a general assault with about 1,000 regulars and militia and 1,200 Indians under Tecumseh, who had returned from raising support for the Indian confederacy along the Wabash. On May 4, Clay arrived with his Kentuckians, and Harrison sent a strong detachment of 800 under Lieutenant Colonel William Dudley to spike the British guns on the north bank of the river while his own troops destroyed the battery on the south and the remainder of Clay's force cut through the besiegers to relieve the fort. Dudley was under strict orders to withdraw and rejoin the main body as soon as the British guns had been put out of action to avoid being cut off by a counterattack, but he disobeyed them. His attack succeeded in part, the guns being seized and spiked; but the work was not properly carried out, and the batteries were brought into action again after they were recaptured. Dudley then led his men in an insane advance on the main enemy camp. He was counterattacked, and 600 men were killed or captured. The Indans at once began to massacre their prisoners, even killing a soldier of the 41st Foot who tried to prevent them, and only the presence of Tecumseh averted a repetition of the Raisin River disaster on a larger scale. On the south bank the British battery was taken and the fort reinforced, but the cost had been high. More than 1,000 Americans were killed or taken prisoner against British losses of 15 killed and 46 wounded. Procter had won a substantial victory, but he was unable to take advantage of it. His militia regiments announced their intention to return home to plant their crops, and even Tecumseh was powerless to prevent the wholesale desertion of the Indians. The siege was lifted, and Procter withdrew his withered army into Canada. The problems inherent in campaigning with an army composed largely of militia were becoming dispiritingly apparent to the military commanders on both sides.

Procter's troops and their Indian allies were short of supplies, and he favored an attack on Harrison's supply depot near Fort Stephenson on the Sandusky River. Tecumseh and his Indians preferred another assault on Fort Meigs. By July Procter had assembled sufficient troops for an expedition and unwisely allowed himself to be persuaded to move against Fort Meigs. An attempt to trick the American garrison into leaving the fort failed, and Procter, deciding against a costly assault, reembarked his men and sailed down the lake to the mouth of the Sandusky. As usual in any campaign without the early inspiration of bloodshed, most of the Indians had drifted home in frustrated boredom, and Procter's force was reduced to about 600, of which half were Indians. Fort Stephenson was defended by fewer than 200 United States regulars under Major George Croghan, a twenty-three-year-old Kentuckian who had been ordered by Harrison to evacuate the fort. Croghan hurried to Harrison's headquarters at Seneca Town, obtained permission to defend his post, returned to Fort Stephenson, and on August 1 flung back a determined attack, inflicting nearly 100 casualties. Procter withdrew, and the British offensive was ended. The motive behind his promotion, shortly afterward, to the rank of major general is not immediately clear.

The shortage of supplies at Amherstburg and Fort Malden was becoming critical, and it was a shortage which could be made good only by the movement of stores by Barclay's ships on Lake Erie from supplies accumulated at Long Point. Procter feared the widespread defection of his Indian allies, who, with their wives and children, depended entirely on the British for food. Further delays, he reported to Prevost, would be attended by "the most frightful Consequences." Under pressure from the army, Barclay was forced to act before he was ready. The stage was set for the first major engagement in the crucial struggle for control of the Great Lakes.

VIII

The 1813 Campaigns

Control of the Lakes depended primarily upon shipbuilding and the ability to man and arm the ships completed. The withdrawal of the British garrison at Fort Erie had released the ships then building at Black Rock to join the squadron Perry was assembling on the lake. Chauncey had had the forethought to send carpenters to Black Rock to put the ships into a state of repair which would enable them to be moved to Presque Isle as soon as the British guns at Fort Erie, on the opposite shore, had been taken. With the help of oxen and troops from Dearborn's army, the ships were dragged against the Niagara current and made ready to sail, but Barclay had brought out the British squadron and cruised between Black Rock and Presque Isle to prevent their escape. Sailing dangerously close to the beaches, the Americans slipped past the British blockade in thick fog and reached their new harbor, safe behind a great sandbar, on June 18. Procter, who was not devoid of tactical sense, understood the danger and pleaded with Prevost for reinforcements to enable him to attack the harbor at Presque Isle and destroy the ships on the stocks, but none arrived. Barclay, who was urging on the completion of the 20-gun *Detroit* at Amherstburg, was, as he wrote to Prevost in the middle of July, critically short of seamen and guns. The sandbar across the mouth of the main harbor at Presque Isle prevented his sailing in to destroy the American ships before they were completed. It has been asserted[49] that he should have sent in his ships' boats, which could have been rowed across the bar without difficulty at night; but his crews were under strength, and he had no troops or marines to carry out such a raid. The best he could hope to achieve was the blockade of Presque Isle, preventing the American squadron, once ready to sail, from putting out into the lake.

Oliver Hazard Perry's problems were similar to Barclay's, with the added disadvantage that his adversary was already in control of Lake Erie. Like Barclay, he depended on his superior officer on Lake Ontario for reinforcements of men. Support from the army comprised a regiment of Pennsylvania militia whose ineffective colonel was unable even to persuade his men to guard Perry's ships at night. While Barclay cruised off Presque Isle he would retain control of the lake, but so long as he remained there in sufficient strength he could offer no assistance to the army. Unless both Harrison's and Procter's troops were to be reduced to inactivity, the stalemate on the lake could not continue. It was broken on August 1, when Barclay relaxed his blockade. His reason for doing so has never been explained, but it is probable that he was personally involved in assisting in Procter's withdrawal after the abortive attack on Fort Stephenson.

Whatever the cause of Barclay's apparent negligence, the way was clear for the completed American squadron to sail. The obstacle of the sandbar was surmounted by the use of camels,* and after three anxious days and nights, the squadron of ten vessels came safely over the bar. Barclay had returned before the operation was completed, but noticed the three long 12-pounders mounted on the beach to cover approaches to the harbor and held off. The American excursion into the lake reversed the previous situation and transferred control to Perry. Barclay, still waiting for the *Detroit* to be completed, dared not risk an engagement without her and retired to Malden.

On August 10, Perry received reinforcements of about 100 experienced seamen, including a new second-in-command, Commander Jesse D. Elliott, who took charge of the *Niagara*. Perry's squadron was still 250 men short of its complement, even when the soldiers aboard the vessels were included; but his assistance was urgently required by Harrison's army, and a brief but brilliant opportunity existed to gain permanent control of Lake Erie. The risks involved in provoking a major engagement were formidable, but while Chauncey continued to contest Lake Ontario, Perry considered them justified. On August 12 he sailed westward and, after a conference with Harrison in Sandusky Bay, established a new naval headquarters at Put-in-Bay in the Bass Islands some 30 miles southeast of Malden.

---

*Floats filled with water and attached to the sides of the ships so that, as the water was pumped out, the floats raised the vessels.

Barclay was determined not to fight until he received reinforcements of men and guns. Of his total of 450 men only 50 were regular seamen. The rest were soldiers from Procter's army and Canadian boatmen. The *Detroit* was completed, the largest vessel on the lake, but the armament intended for her had been captured or destroyed at York in the previous April. To arm the new ship, Barclay was obliged to ransack the ramparts of Malden for a curious assortment of elderly guns, many of which could be discharged only by firing a pistol into the vents. Spurred on by a ludicrously optimistic exhortation from Sir George Prevost and the desperate need of Procter's army and some 14,000 Indians for food, Barclay sailed from Amherstburg on the morning of September 9.

Comparisons between the two squadrons are not particularly illuminating. Stripped to arithmetic, Perry's squadron outnumbered Barclay's by nine ships to six and enjoyed substantial superiority in firepower at short range. The *Detroit*, with Barclay in command, out-ranged any ship in either squadron, but at close quarters both the *Lawrence* and the *Niagara* of Perry's squadron threw a greater weight of shot. The tactics of each commander were thus clear before the battle. Barclay would stand off and try to destroy his enemy in detail. Perry would hope to oppose vessel to vessel at close quarters, a plan which would enable him to exploit his superiority of 50 percent in weight of broadside. The outcome depended on the skill of the two commanders, the training and discipline of their officers and crews, and, as always at sea, the behavior of the weather.

The Americans sighted the British squadron at five o'clock on the morning of September 10. By noon the British had opened fire with their long guns. Perry, in the *Lawrence*, made sail and closed with the enemy, taking station in the center of his squadron behind the schooners *Scorpion* and *Ariel*. Behind him were the *Caledonia*, the *Niagara* under Jesse Elliott, and the remaining four schooners. The British squadron hove to in column in the order *Chippewa, Detroit, Hunter, Queen Charlotte, Lady Prevost, Little Belt*, so that the two most powerful ships, *Detroit* and *Queen Charlotte*, were each escorted by two smaller vessels. Perry had previously designated the target for each of his own ships and, under galling fire, crammed on sail to bring the *Lawrence* within range of the *Detroit*. Behind him the *Caledonia* and *Niagara* should have been in close support to engage the *Hunter* and *Queen Charlotte*, but the *Caledonia* was slow and clumsy to handle and lagged far behind. Elliott, in the *Niagara*, maintained his position behind her, leaving the *Lawrence* exposed to the concentrated fire of the *Detroit, Queen Charlotte*, and *Hunter* and supported only by the little schooners *Ariel* and *Scorpion*.

After two hours of continuous battering the *Lawrence* was still afloat; but more than half her crew were killed or wounded, and she had only one gun in action. The *Detroit* was severely damaged. Barclay, who had lost an arm at Trafalgar, had been wounded twice and was forced to go below, and his first lieutenant was dying. Aboard the *Queen Charlotte* the captain had been killed and the first lieutenant knocked unconscious. At this critical stage of the battle the British ships which could influence its outcome were commanded by third officers of little experience. Perry was miraculously unscathed. With his thirteen-year-old brother, Alexander, and four seamen he leaped into a boat and rowed across to the *Niagara,* which had at last come to his assistance. Sending Elliott to bring up the schooners in the rear, Perry took command of the *Niagara* and broke through the British line, distributing port broadsides among the *Chippewa, Little Belt,* and *Lady Prevost* and raking the *Detroit, Queen Charlotte,* and *Hunter* on the starboard side. The *Detroit,* attempting to wear, fouled the *Queen Charlotte,* and while the two ships were helplessly locked, Perry concentrated the fire of the *Niagara, Caledonia, Ariel,* and *Scorpion* against them. The *Detroit,* already fought to a standstill in the first battle with the *Lawrence,* was reduced to a pitiful hulk, her shattered decks piled with dead and wounded and the wreckage of masts and rigging. The *Queen Charlotte* was in no better condition, and by three o'clock that afternoon both ships had struck their colors. The *Chippewa* and *Little Belt* tried unsuccessfully to escape, and by evening the battle was over.

Perry's dispatch to General Harrison was admirably succinct: "We have met the enemy and they are ours: two ships, two brigs, one schooner, and one sloop." His message to the President was less sober, and he was rewarded, by return of post, by promotion to the rank of captain in the United States Navy. Jesse Elliott, blamed by Perry for neglect to engage his assigned target, the *Queen Charlotte,* a dereliction of duty which nearly lost the battle, was acquitted of misconduct by the court of inquiry convened in 1815 at his request; but the verdict of the court, which failed to call Perry and heard no firsthand evidence from senior officers engaged in the battle, is open to doubt. Barclay, captured with his remaining crews, was returned to England in the summer of 1814 to face a court-martial. Eight times wounded in battle, he appeared before the court wearing one empty sleeve and with his other shattered arm still in bandages. He was honorably acquitted.

The battle was decisive, not only for control of Lake Erie, but in the military campaign in the Northwest, and the influence of Perry's victory spread later to the peace negotiations at Ghent.

The immediate consequences were local. Procter, realizing that his position at Amherstburg and Fort Malden had become untenable, proposed to retire on Niagara, but Tecumseh, who had paddled out into Lake Erie in a canoe to get a close look at the battle, refused to contemplate abandoning the lands which he considered belonged to his people. The small British garrison was in peril of being massacred unless the Indians could be pacified, and Procter at length agreed to a compromise withdrawal to the Thames, where the army would make a stand.

Procter's retreat, delayed until September 18, was altogether too leisurely. Perry had both his own and the captured British squadron, with the exceptions of the *Lawrence, Detroit,* and *Queen Charlotte,* repaired within a week of the battle, and on the twenty-seventh Harrison's army was transported to Malden. Three days later he took possession of Detroit and Sandwich. On October 5 he met the British and their Indian allies at Moravian Town, where Procter had chosen a defensive position guarded on the flanks by the Thames and a large swamp. It was not ideal, but it offered the advantage of forcing Harrison's army, which outnumbered Procter's, to attack on a narrow front and into thickly wooded country. Colonel Richard Johnson, who had raised a mounted regiment of backwoodsmen to join Harrison, persuaded him to abandon an orthodox frontal attack by infantry in favor of a cavalry charge. The results were even more spectacular than Johnson had anticipated, the two lines of British regulars being broken and scattered at the first impact. On the American left, Tecumseh's Indians fought with savage desperation inspired by the personal example of their leader, but when Tecumseh fell, the survivors fled in despair. A body was later found which the victorious Kentuckians believed to be his, and strips of skin were cut from it as souvenirs; but the Indians maintained that Tecumseh's body had been recovered from the battlefield at night. Whatever the fate of his body, the spirit of the great Shawnee chief remained with his people and the tribes which he had tried to organize into an Indian confederacy. He left behind him a legacy of hatred which bred new leaders, more violence, and renewed terror along the American frontiers of the South and West.

In the Battle of the Thames more than 600 British officers and men were killed, wounded, or captured. Harrison reported his own casualties as 29, of whom 7 were killed. Procter escaped with 246 survivors and made an orderly but hasty retreat to Burlington Heights to join Vincent, who had withdrawn to his old defensive position as soon as he heard the result of the battle. There being no other British force to contest Harrison's occupation of the Northwest or American control of

Lake Erie, the war in that sector was considered ended. Detroit, Sandwich, and Amherstburg were garrisoned, an armistice was signed with the Indians, and the Kentucky volunteers were discharged to their homes. Deciding that it was too late in the season to try to recapture Michilimackinac, which remained in British hands until the end of the war, Harrison transported 1,200 regulars down the lake to Buffalo to join the army in the Niagara Peninsula. By the victories on Lake Erie and at the Battle of the Thames, the Americans had secured free communications all the way from Detroit to Sackets Harbor. The season for military operations was closing, but there was still time for a series of incredible blunders which robbed the achievement of much of its importance.

Secretary Armstrong was determined to put into operation his original plan for an assault on Kingston or Montreal. No longer, as he believed, hamstrung by the incompetence of his commanding general, he communicated his instructions to General Wilkinson.* There was some confusion in these instructions, as there was apparently in his mind, about the relative importance of the two objectives, and his plan included attacks on both. The orders concluded, however, in a triumphant burst of clarity and decision: "in conducting the present campaign, you will make Kingston your *primary object,* and . . . you will *choose* (as circumstances may warrant), between a *direct* and *indirect* attack upon that post." Ten weeks later he had again changed his mind.

Command of the army at Plattsburg was given to Major General Wade Hampton, Wilkinson's army was reinforced to 7,000 men assembled at Sackets Harbor, and Armstrong moved there himself in September to keep the peace between his two generals. The resulting confusion was indescribable and made a more direct contribution to the subsequent failure of the campaign than any action of the British. After interminable discussion it was finally determined that Wilkinson's main force should be carried down the St. Lawrence, bypassing Kingston, where Yeo would be blockaded by Chauncey, and that Hampton should simultaneously cross the Canadian border where it met the Châteauguay River. The two armies, totaling some 12,000 men, would converge on Montreal. While Wilkinson gathered his army at Sackets, and even after he entered the St. Lawrence, it would be impossible for the British to guess whether his objective was Mon-

*Later described by General Winfield Scott in his *Memoirs* as "this unprincipled imbecile."

treal or Kingston. The plan had much to recommend it, and the forces available were adequate to the task. The fundamental weakness lay, as usual, in the leadership of the army, but by the time the armies moved the season was already too advanced to leave much hope of their success.

Prevost appreciated the danger and rightly considered that Hampton's army must be stopped as close as possible to the Canadian frontier to prevent a junction of the two invading forces. Both armies set out toward the end of October. Wilkinson's, delayed by rough weather, began to enter the St. Lawrence River on November 1. Hampton ran into 1,500 Canadians 15 miles from the mouth of the Châteauguay, suffered about 50 casualties, and withdrew. Ordered by Wilkinson to join the advance at St. Regis, on the far bank facing Cornwall which the main force had reached, Hampton marched in the opposite direction and settled into winter quarters at Plattsburg.

Wilkinson's army, though it had been transported into the St. Lawrence without interference from Yeo on Lake Ontario, was not alone as it moved downriver. Following instructions issued previously by Prevost, who had anticipated the circumstances, more than 600 British regulars under Lieutenant Colonel Joseph Morrison had embarked in two schooners and a number of smaller craft commanded by Captain William Howe Mulcaster and slipped out of Kingston. They followed behind Wilkinson's force, waiting to fall upon any detachment of comparable strength. On November 11, Morrison had taken up a strong defensive position at Chrysler's farm, about 20 miles from the Long Sault Rapids, when the American rear guard under Brigadier General John Parke Boyd turned and attacked in strength. Although outnumbered by more than two to one, Morrison's troops drove back the Americans with 350 casualties and took more than 100 prisoners. While this British engagement was in progress, Captain Mulcaster's small squadron shelled the American headquarters. Wilkinson, having received a letter informing him of Hampton's withdrawal to Plattsburg, abandoned the campaign and retreated across the river to French Mills, inside the New York boundary. The threat to Montreal remained, but no operations could be undertaken until the spring of the following year.

While Wilkinson and Hampton were resigning from their abortive campaign against Montreal, the British took advantage of their absence to launch a counterattack in the Niagara Peninsula. The term of service for which the militia at Fort George were engaged expired on December 9, and on the tenth the commander, Brigadier General

George McClure, found his garrison reduced to "sixty effective regulars and probably forty volunteers." Hearing that the British were advancing from Burlington Heights, he wisely retired to Fort Niagara. Less prudently he burned to the ground the adjacent Canadian village of Newark, an act which was taken to justify retaliation in kind. On the nineteenth the British, under General Phineas Riall, who had succeeded Vincent, surprised and captured Fort Niagara, and the villages of Lewiston, Youngstown, and Manchester were burned. On the thirtieth Riall took and burned Buffalo and destroyed at Black Rock the *Ariel, Trippe,* and *Little Belt** of the Erie squadron. In a three-week campaign the British had regained control of the entire Niagara Peninsula and cut communications between the American armies in the East and their garrisons in the Northwest.

The military campaigns of 1813 along the Canadian frontier ended with the American loss of Niagara. The total result of the war in the Northwest had been to restore the territorial situation which had existed before the war began, and in the East there had been no progress whatsoever. The misdirection of American strategy, in which Armstrong had yielded to the commanders concerned, and the appointment of broken-down and tremulous generals to positions requiring active enterprise robbed the United States of its last chance of victory in Canada. With the ending of the war in Europe the most America could hope for was a swiftly negotiated peace.

The first overtures to peace had already been made. In March, 1813, President Madison had received from John Quincy Adams, United States minister to Russia, an offer from Czar Alexander to act as mediator in the war between Britain and America. The series of military fiascos which had followed the proud boast that the conquest of Canada required nothing more than marching impelled the normally cautious President to accept the offer without even taking the natural preliminary step of discovering whether such mediation would be acceptable to Britain. Albert Gallatin, Secretary of the Treasury, and the Federalist James Bayard were hurriedly named as peace commissioners and dispatched in May to join Adams at St. Petersburg. The renunciation of impressment was to be a *sine qua non* of any agreement, and in June, exultant at the news of the fall of York and successes in the Niagara district, Madison was pointing to the advantages to both countries of the "transfer of the upper parts and even the whole of Canada to the U.S." The Americans arrived in the Russian capital in

---

*Captured from the British in the Battle of Lake Erie. See p. 103.

July to find the Czar absent at the front and neither inclined nor available even to meet the commissioners, far less to assist them in their deliberations. More disconcerting even than the absence of the mediator was the absence of the third party to the negotiations. The British did not reply to the invitation until November 4 and then only to decline the Czar's offer and propose direct negotiation instead. Madison, buoyed up by Monroe's extraordinary belief that the British refusal and counterproposal were made from fear, accepted. Henry Clay, Speaker of the House of Representatives, and Jonathan Russell, former chargé d'affaires in London and the new minister to Sweden, were appointed to the peace commission and set out to join the other members at Gothenburg. Gallatin, who was thought to be on his way home, was not included, but his name was added in January. When the first suggestion of mediation was made in March, the United States had suffered a series of humiliating defeats which made it anxious to obtain peace, although both Madison and Monroe held curiously optimistic views about the terms they were likely to obtain. In November, when the proposal for direct negotiation was accepted, America had in fact already failed to win the war, but the results of the 1813 campaigns, though disappointing, were at least not so derisory as those of 1812. By the time the commissioners of both countries finally met, nine months later, the American negotiating position had been drastically weakened.

In the autumn of 1813 America's frontier problems were not confined to the North. A year earlier Andrew Jackson had offered to lead 1,000 mounted riflemen from Tennessee to recapture Detroit, but his request for active employment was not even acknowledged. In October, 1812, it was Governor William Blount of Tennessee who was asked to raise 1,500 men to reinforce Wilkinson at New Orleans. They were to be used for a descent on West Florida, a venture originally proposed by Jackson but not entrusted to him. Militia officers of field rank were generally elected by their men, a method which Jackson rightly considered more democratic than effective. He believed that senior officers should be appointed, on merit, by their commander. It was a belief that he was soon called upon to justify. At the personal request of his old friend Willie Blount, Jackson agreed to accept an appointment subordinate to his old enemy, James Wilkinson, and received from the governor his commission as major general of United States volunteers.

Twenty-five hundred volunteers answered Jackson's call for 1,500, and they brought rifles, knowing their commander's opinion that smoothbore muskets might be good enough for regular soldiers but not for his Tennesseans. Many of the rifles had been paid for by Jackson himself, and his promissory notes were honored as currency in the state for much of his life. In January, in freezing weather, he took two infantry regiments down the Cumberland and Ohio rivers and into the Mississippi, while Colonel John Coffee led his regiment of cavalry down the Natchez Trace. To his friend George Campbell, Jackson admitted, "It is a bitter pill to have to serve with . . . Wilkinson,"[50] but

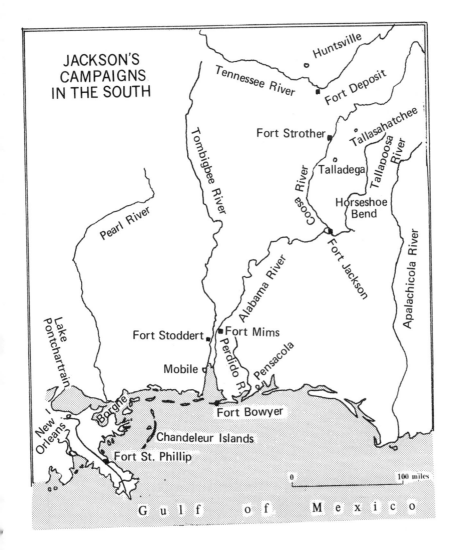

JACKSON'S
CAMPAIGNS
IN THE SOUTH

even he had underestimated the ability of his superior officer to make it unpalatable. In spite of floating ice and the loss of a boat, he covered the 2,000 miles by water to Natchez in thirty-nine days. He was met by Major William Carroll with orders from Wilkinson to halt and make camp where he was. For a month he waited, fuming, for instructions to bring his men into action, but the dispatches, when they arrived, contained orders of a very different kind. Wilkinson, he learned with astonishment, was transferred to command the army destined for Montreal, succeeding Dearborn, and Jackson's brigade was to be disbanded, where it stood. The swift current of the Mississippi precluded any possibility of the troops returning to their homes by water, and the land route along the Natchez Trace was a march of 800 miles. In a letter of saccharine hypocrisy Wilkinson deprecated the dissolution of their partnership in arms and suggested that Jackson's most acceptable service would be to encourage his volunteers to enlist in the regular army. He concluded by wishing him pleasant weather on his journey home. Without transport or rations it seemed that the Tennesseans had little choice.

Jackson's reaction was characteristic of his unfailing concern for his men and an unyielding contempt for bungling or corrupt authority. He flatly refused to demobilize his troops until he had personally led them home to Tennessee. Fulminating against "the wicked machinations of Armstrong and W---n,"[51] he obtained twenty days' rations for his troops and hired, at his own expense of $3,000, eleven wagons for the sick. Horses, including Jackson's own, were provided for others too weak to walk. The general marched with his men. "Tough as hickory" was how he was described by one of them, and as "Old Hickory" he continued to command the affectionate respect of the people of Tennessee for the rest of his life.

In May Jackson became involved in a feud between William Carroll and the brother of another of his officers, and on September 4 he was severely wounded in an affray resulting from it. His left shoulder was shattered, and a ball lodged in the upper part of the arm. Ignoring the advice of his doctors, he refused to allow his arm to be amputated. The news of the Fort Mims massacre contributed more to Jackson's recovery than all the skill of the medical profession. Governor Blount had ordered an expedition of 2,500 men to set out on October 2. On September 24, less than three weeks after he had been wounded, Jackson issued a general order from his bed: "The health of your general is restored. He will command in person."

Fort Mims was the stockaded home of a prosperous Creek half-breed, Samuel Mims, erected close to the Alabama River about 40 miles north of Mobile. It was occupied by fewer than 200 militia and about 400 civilians, including many women and children. On August 30 it had been attacked by Creek Indians. Seventeen white people escaped, and a few blacks were spared as slaves; but the rest of the garrison were butchered without regard for age or sex.

The Creek rising stemmed largely from Tecumseh's visits in 1811. Before his arrival the Creek, primarily interested in the peaceful cultivation of their lands, which extended through the greater part of the present state of Alabama, gave little trouble. They trusted the government agent, Benjamin Hawkins, and were content to negotiate the satisfaction of grievances through him. Tecumseh's inspiring oratory divided the tribe. The elders wished to maintain their lands in peace, but the young warriors, the Red Sticks, were excited by Tecumseh's stories of their past and the promise of a great future in a united stand by all the tribes against white encroachment and domination. Among them was William Weatherford, nephew of the extraordinary Alexander McGillivray.* Weatherford's ancestry was French, Scottish, English, and, through his great-grandmother, Creek. Their mixed blood had given William Weatherford and his brother a choice of races. John Weatherford chose to be white. William Weatherford chose to be a Creek Indian and, as Red Eagle, became the leader under whom the disaffected young warriors gathered. The war was also, in part, a civil war within the Creek nation. A band of warriors had taken part in the Raisin River massacre and, on their way home, had murdered some white families in Chickasaw country. In response to a demand from the Chickasaw, who feared they would be blamed for this outrage, the Creek murderers were hunted down and killed by their own tribe. The young militant Creek, particularly those who lived in the higher valleys of the Gulf Coast streams from whose families the offenders came, rose in vengeance against their fellow Creek and the white settlers in their territory. This already dangerous situation was inflamed by the killing by white settlers of a number of Creek returning from a visit to the Spanish governor at Pensacola, where they had been supplied with powder and shot "for hunting

*The son of a Scottish trader and Sehoy, daughter of a French captain and his Creek mistress, Alexander McGillivray (1759?–1793) was educated at Charleston, as a white man. While retaining the chieftainship of the Creek and control of the Seminole, he was successively a colonel in the British Army during the Revolution, a Spanish civil servant under Esteban Miró, and a brigadier general in the United States Army. On his death his fortune amounted to $100,000, and he was buried, with all the honors of a Masonic funeral, in a Spanish gentleman's garden at Pensacola, Florida. His attempts to form a confederacy of the Southern tribes against the whites failed, and he signed a peace treaty in New York in 1790 which he repudiated shortly before his death.

purposes." With the settlers, on this occasion, were two half-breeds, Major Daniel Beasley and Captain Dixon Bailey, who commanded the militia at Fort Mims when it was attacked on August 30.

Jackson had ordered his Tennessee volunteers, among whom were Ensign Sam Houston and the frontiersman Davy Crockett, to assemble at Fayetteville on October 4. When Jackson, haggard and obviously suffering great pain from his arm, which was in a sling, arrived on the seventh, John Coffee had already ridden ahead with the cavalry. Hearing that Coffee was in danger, a rumor later discovered to be false, Jackson broke camp on the eleventh and marched 39 miles in nine hours to go to his assistance. Whatever faults he might share with the American commanders in the North, indecisiveness was not one of them.

Jackson's plan, which characteristically bore little relation to his orders and also ignored the existence of the elderly Major General Thomas Pinckney, who commanded the entire Department of the South, envisaged a powerful thrust south to the Gulf at Mobile, destroying the Creek war parties as they were encountered, and opening up a new highway from Tennessee. From Mobile Jackson intended to invade Florida and capture Pensacola, cutting out at its root the cancer of Spanish influence and support for the Creek. He did not feel obliged to consult his superior officers or the government, for he required the support of neither, but he was relying on the continuing loyalty of his own troops and a junction with 2,500 East Tennesseans under Major General John Cocke. Supplies and further reinforcements could reach him down the Tennessee River, at the southernmost bend of which he built Fort Deposit. Pushing on across the Raccoon Mountain, a formidable barrier but not, as some had naïvely supposed, as high as the Alps, Jackson built his advance supply base, Fort Strother, on the Coosa River.

Two hundred Red Sticks had gathered at Tallassahatchee, 13 miles from Fort Strother, and Jackson sent Coffee ahead with 1,000 troops. The battle was fought on November 3, and not a single Creek warrior escaped. Coffee was evidently a student of military history, for he employed tactics similar to those first recorded as used more than 2,000 years earlier by Hannibal at Cannae, tempting the enemy to attack the center of a line which retreated into horseshoe formation and closed on the attackers.* This maneuver depends for success on the sides of the horseshoe holding firm and preventing a breakout as the center

---

*These tactics were used with great success by the Russians against German tank assaults before Stalingrad in 1943.

withdraws. At Talladega, six days later, Jackson tried the same tactics, but his flank militia gave way, allowing the Indians to break out of the trap. Two hundred and ninety Creek had been killed, but about 700 fled into the woods.

Weatherford's situation was critical. Creek casualties had been serious enough in the two defeats they had suffered, but the defeats had also tarnished his reputation and dissuaded warriors from joining him. Jackson's position, in spite of his minor successes, had become desperate. His urgent order to the advance division of Cocke's East Tennessee division to occupy and defend Fort Strother, had been countermanded by Cocke, leaving Jackson's army stores, lines of communication, and 200 sick dangerously exposed. He was obliged to turn back to the fort, which he reached on the eleventh, to find that the food had been exhausted and no fresh supplies had arrived. The starving troops petitioned to return to the supply depot at Fort Deposit, and attempts by the militia and volunteer brigades to depart had to be prevented by force. On November 17, Jackson agreed to move; but 12 miles from the fort a supply train of flour and beef on the hoof was encountered, and he ordered his men back to Fort Strother. A company of infantry moved out, but toward Tennessee. Jackson and Coffee formed cavalry across the road and threatened to shoot any men who tried to pass. Returning to the main body, Jackson found a brigade about to desert and, snatching up a musket, faced them, supported only by Coffee and Major John Reid.

For three weeks Jackson had been racked by dysentery, and he was still in great pain from his wounds. When he discovered that Hall's brigade, enlisted for one year on December 10, 1812, intended to count time spent at home after their return from Natchez toward their service and therefore to disband within a week of returning to Fort Strother, he paraded them under the muzzles of his two small cannon until they agreed to wait until replacements arrived. On the twelfth, Cocke's division of 1,450 troops arrived, but Hall's brigade having left, Jackson discovered that his reinforcements had only ten days to serve. Worse followed when Coffee's cavalry deserted. The final blow came from an unexpected quarter: Governor Blount wrote advising the evacuation of Fort Strother and an immediate retreat to Tennessee. Jackson had declared that he would hold the fort if only two men stayed with him, and for a precarious few hours the garrison was reduced to 130. On December 29 he refused to accept the humiliating fate being forced upon him. He wrote to Blount in his curious antique and oratorical style, reminding him of the state legislature's pledge to keep 3,500 men in the field until the Creek should be annihilated: "And are you my Dear friend sitting with yr. arms folded ... recommending me to retrograde to please the whims of the populace? ... Let me tell you it imperiously lies upon both you and me to do our duty regardless of consequences or the opinion of these fireside patriots, those fawning sycophants or cowardly poltroons." He pictured the consequences of retreat—the secession to the Creek cause of the remainder of their tribe with the certain addition of the Choctaw and Cherokee—and ended in fine form with a clarion call which Blount might have done well to forward to the President: "Arouse from yr. lethargy—despise fawning smiles or snarling frowns—with energy exercise yr. functions—the campaign must rapidly progress or ... yr. country ruined ... let popularity perish for the president. ... Save Mobile—save the Territory—save yr. frontier from becoming drenched in blood. ... What retrograde under these circumstances? I will perish first."[52]

IX

America Secures Its Frontiers

Andrew Jackson's demand for help, for it could scarcely be described as a cry, stirred Governor Willie Blount to action, and he received unexpected support from the War Department. As the last of the militia at Fort Strother went home, 800 green recruits arrived to take their place. Jackson, who had recovered his health and part of his temper, was as usual spoiling for a fight and was undeterred by the indiscipline and lack of training of most of his troops. He knew, moreover, that there was no time to be lost if other Indian tribes, impressed by Creek strength and American weakness, were to be prevented from joining the insurrection. He pressed forward toward Horseshoe Bend on the Tallapoosa River, where Weatherford had established a well-sited stronghold. Three miles from his objective his troops were attacked at night by the Red Sticks, but Jackson was ready for them. The fighting was savage but indecisive. Coffee, who was wounded, had reconnoitered the stronghold at Horseshoe Bend and reported that an assault on it without reinforcements of seasoned troops was out of the question.

Jackson's impatience had led him into a position of considerable danger. The 200 Indians who had joined him had done well in the battle on the twenty-second, but the new militia companies had shown disquieting signs of fear and instability. This was scarcely surprising, but even to Jackson's impetuous temperament, the message was clear: with untried troops, 70 miles from their nearest secure base and surrounded by an experienced and numerically superior enemy of whom they were afraid, he would need all his cunning and a fair

measure of luck to survive for another campaign. He retreated, carrying the wounded on litters of skins cut from dead horses and taking
every precaution against attack by the Indians who hunted the army
day and night. On the morning of January 24 the army began to cross
the Enotachopco Creek, steep-banked, broad, and cold. This, Jackson
knew, was the moment of supreme peril in a long and dangerous
march, and he had laid a trap. He assumed that the attack would come
when his army was divided on both banks, and he had given orders
that the rear guard should contain it while the flank companies
recrossed the water and encircled the enemy. It was a variant of the
horseshoe formation, using the arms as twin pincers. His assumption
was correct and his tactics shrewd, but his troops lacked the essential
steadiness to carry out their orders.

The attack came, as expected, when about half the army had crossed
the creek; but both flanks of the rear guard crumbled under the first
assault, and accompanied by their officers, the troops fled in disorder
into the water. The center, exposed on three sides, disintegrated,
abandoning the commander, William Carroll, and a handful of men to
stand between the Indians and the terrified troops struggling across the
creek. Jackson raged up and down his line, restoring it by the physical
strength of his presence, rallying his raw troops with a mixture of curses
and the inspiration of his own courage. John Coffee, weak from the
wound he had received forty-eight hours earlier, stumbled from his
litter to lead a company across the creek to save Carroll. The remainder
of the army was brought across the water, and the Indians withdrew.
The engagement was reported by the American newspapers as a victory, but those who were present knew that only Jackson's titanic
leadership and the gallantry of the few had saved the entire force from
annihilation.

At Fort Strother Jackson waited for reinforcements in such might
that Weatherford's stronghold at Horseshoe Bend could be destroyed
with certainty. In the south and west, where thrusts into Creek country
were being made by Brigadier General F. L. Claiborne, brother of the
governor of Louisiana, and Brigadier General John Floyd, little
progress had been made though Claiborne had burned Weatherford's
hometown, Econochaca, and narrowly missed capturing the Creek
leader. Both campaigns, like Jackson's, had been paralyzed by the
short-term engagement of militia troops. At Jackson's home, the Hermitage, his devoted wife, Rachel, received news of his safety with
tremulous joy:

My Dearest Life, I received your Letter by Express. . . . I Cryed aloud and praised my god For your safety . . . how long o Lord will I remain so unhappy. no rest no Ease I cannot sleepe. all can come hom but you . . . you have done now more than aney other man did before you have served your Country Long Enough . . . you have been gon six monthes . . . oh Lord of heaven how Can I beare it.[53]

Governor Blount's continued appeals to the people of Tennessee had raised five thousand men. Most of them were untrained, ill-equipped, and far from willing volunteers for the arduous and frightening duty thrust upon them, but the arrival of the 39th U.S. Infantry Regiment gave the army a backbone which would hold it together. Officers and men who disputed Jackson's authority received summary treatment: Major General John Cocke, the second-in-command, and Brigadier General Isaac Roberts were sent home under arrest, and John Wood, a seventeen-year-old boy, who had been in the army less than a month, was sentenced by court-martial and shot for mutinous conduct. The last was a bitter decision which cost Jackson two nights' sleep,[54] but his determination to root out all sources of indiscipline before he took his army into action again was inflexible.

Weatherford's position at Horseshoe Bend was a peninsula covering an area of about 100 acres, the neck closed by a tall breastwork of logs arranged in an unbroken zigzag. Portholes in the angled defenses provided crossfire at every possible point of attack. Hundreds of canoes lined the river to provide for retreat if it became necessary. At dawn on March 27, Jackson's field army, 2,000 strong, faced about 900 Indians behind their stockade. While Coffee's Indian scouts swam the river under fire and removed the canoes, Jackson surrounded the peninsula. Coffee took the cavalry to the high ground along the river to cut off the last avenue of escape, and at ten thirty the 6-pounders opened fire on the palisade. No breach was made; but the Creek sent out their women and children, and Jackson delayed his assault until they were safely across the river. At twelve thirty the 39th U.S. Infantry stormed the defenses. The first man to reach the works was shot down, but the second, Sam Houston, scaled them. The Creek, urged on by their prophets, fought with desperate courage; but they were greatly out-numbered, and tomahawks were no match for steel bayonets. During a short lull in the fighting Jackson offered to spare any who would surrender, but the offer was scornfully refused. The carnage remained forever in the memories of the victors. At the end of the day 557 Creek warriors lay dead on the peninsula, and the blood of 200 more reddened the waters of the river. Jackson had exacted a terrible retribution for Fort Mims, and he had ended the war; but Weatherford was still at large. He had not expected Jackson's attack, and on the day of the battle he was rallying support elsewhere.

On the sacred Hickory Ground at the junction of the Coosa and Tallapoosa rivers the last remnants of the Red Sticks gathered for a final struggle, but on the approach of Jackson's army they fled. Some took refuge in Florida under Spanish protection, but Weatherford chose to surrender. He walked alone and unarmed into Jackson's camp and offered his life in return for food and safety for the survivors of his nation. Jackson undertook to help the women and children and set him free in return for a promise that he would use his influence to keep the remaining Creek at peace. They shook hands to seal the bargain, and Weatherford, in his worn buckskins and moccasins, strode past the astonished guards and out of the camp. He was, wrote Jackson's young aide John Reid, "the greatest of the Barbarian world."[55]

In August the Indians were summoned to a parley at which Jackson outlined the harsh terms of a new treaty of peace. Twenty-three million acres, about one-half of all Creek territory,* were to be ceded to the American government. Those Creek who had fought with Jackson against their own nation received no compensation; they suffered with those who had fought against him. On the ninth the treaty was signed, for the chiefs had no alternative. Peace for the future was assured. The lands ceded to the government effectively isolated the Creek from contact with the Chickasaw and Choctaw and from the influence of Spain through Florida. What Jackson described as "the path that Tecumseh trod" was barred forever.

Jackson's campaign, culminating in the Battles of Horseshoe Bend, put down a potentially dangerous local rebellion, but its effects were far-reaching. Of all the Indian tribes in the South, the Creek alone might have been counted upon to give active and powerful assistance to a British invasion, and such assistance might have proved decisive. Jackson's ability as a commander could no longer be ignored. He was appointed brigadier general with the regular army, and on May 28 promoted major general and commander of the 7th Military District, which included his home state of Tennessee with the Louisiana and Mississippi Territory. Finally, the war had proved the courage and ability of a number of younger officers whose services he was to need and depend upon. Most notable among them were John Coffee and

---

*About three-fifths of the present state of Alabama and one-fifth of Georgia.

William Carroll. Within the year they were to find themselves serving together in a desperate defense of one of the most important cities in the United States and against an army vastly superior in quality and numbers to any put into the field by Weatherford.

Jackson's victories in the South were achieved none too soon. For the Americans time was running out. The invasion of Canada could be accomplished only while British strength was concentrated in Europe. The end of the war against Napoleon released formidable reinforcements for the chastisement of the treacherous former colonies, and it was clear that the inadequate and poorly led American Army would soon be obliged to defend not only the vast Canadian frontier but also the entire eastern coastline against invasion. It was a prospect which was unlikely to provoke feelings of confidence and optimism in the hearts of the peace commissioners. They could not be said to be bargaining from strength.

On October 7, 1812, General the Earl of Mulgrave, Master General of the Ordnance, had written to the Secretary for War, "Bonaparte has conquered the greatest part of Europe by doing but one thing at a time, and doing that with all his heart, with all his soul, and with all his strength. If you succeed in the Peninsular, nothing of yours will go on ill elsewhere; if you fail, nothing will go on at all anywhere else."[56] This pithy and altogether accurate statement summarizes the deliberation behind British strategy in 1813. Everything was subordinated to the Peninsular campaign, and with massive government support securing supplies and reinforcements, Wellington's years of defensive maneuvering were at an end. The time had come to take and hold the initiative and to use victory to create and consolidate a new coalition. The Prussians and Russians concluded an alliance, and on March 16, Prussia declared war on France; but Napoleon had raised another great army and was on his way to join it. Wellington's offensive was delayed by a late spring, which denied his army fresh forage, and the belated arrival of a pontoon bridge essential to his plans. By the time his army marched through the Trás-os-Montes to cross the frontier into Spain, Napoleon had smashed the Russo-Prussian army at Lützen, entered Dresden, and won a second victory at Bautzen.

Victory in the Peninsula was urgent if the new alliance was to survive. Even as Wellington turned in his stirrups and waved farewell to Portugal, the Prussians had signed a five-week armistice. He concentrated his army, 81,000 strong, north of the Douro and struck fast and hard toward the Pyrenees. The French, taken by surprise, evacuated Valladolid and Burgos to avoid being cut off, enabling Wellington to open his right flank and turn north to encircle the enemy in the Ebro Valley. By June 14 his army had marched 300 miles without opposition, and though the men were footsore and ached in every muscle from manhandling guns through hills and valleys which had never before seen artillery, they were in good spirits. "It was," wrote Harry Smith, "a most wonderful march, the army in great fighting order, and every man in better wind than a trained pugilist."[57]

On the twentieth the French army of 58,000, with guns and a vast train of useless baggage and camp followers, poured into the valley of Vitoria, where Joseph Bonaparte drew them up into three lines behind the Zadorra River. He erected spectator stands in the town, from which the civilians were encouraged to watch the British being routed, but neglected to destroy the bridge across the river. Wellington launched his attack on the twenty-first in three columns, breaking the French center and threatening encirclement from the flanks. The gallantry of General Honoré Reille's division prevented the French army from being surrounded, but the defeat was decisive. King Joseph was swept up in the pandemonium of his fleeing army. Troops and civilians fought for horses to escape through the rapidly closing gap to the east. They left behind them the King's baggage train, guns and arms, food, clothing, and the large number of women who had caused a French officer to describe Joseph's army as *un bordel ambulant*.

The sun was going down, preventing successful pursuit; the streets of the town were jammed with overturned carriages; and the incredible wealth of the booty proved too much for the discipline even of Wellington's army. Exhausted after five weeks of continuous marching and a day's battle they might be, but they fell on the abandoned trunks and treasure chests with enthusiasm. One officer reported that "the whole wealth of Spain and the Indies seemed to be here" and helped himself to a silver brandy cup. The 14th Light Dragoons acquired a spectacular piece of royal silver, used ever since as a regimental toasting goblet. It holds an agreeable quantity of champagne, having been designed for a more basic use as Joseph's *pot de chambre*. Wellington received Marshal Jean Jourdan's gold-ornamented baton, which he later presented to the Prince Regent. Casualties on both sides had been heavy—5,000 British, Portuguese, and Spanish against 8,000 French —and the French had, in addition, lost 151 cannon and enormous quantities of ammunition. The French army in Spain was broken, and the route to the Pyrenees and, later, to the invasion of France laid open; but Joseph's army, which Wellington had hoped to capture, had escaped. Napoleon received the news at the end of the month and agreed to an extension of the armistice with Prussia and Russia. It gave him time to reorganize his armies to meet the new threat from the south, but it also enabled the Austrians to mobilize their army.

Wellington's victory at Vitoria was a strategic triumph and one of the most significant battles of the war. In disgust at the looting he described his army as "the scum of the earth," but he knew it to be the finest fighting machine in Europe and later admitted that he "could have done anything" with it. In honor of the occasion Beethoven composed *Wellington's Victory,* an impressive, if extravagant, piece replete with trumpets, cannon fire, and the sounds of battle mingled with the patriotic strains of "God Save the King," "Rule Britannia," and "Malbrouck s'en va-t-en guerre."

The Peninsular army reached the Pyrenees and took up defensive positions guarding the frontier passes. The French still held the Spanish fortresses of Pamplona and San Sebastián, and Wellington would not continue the advance until they had been reduced. Meanwhile, the veteran Marshal Nicolas Soult had taken command of the demoralized French army at Bayonne and, within two weeks, had re-formed it. He set out with 35,000 men to the relief of Pamplona. Wellington's line was dangerously extended, and it caved in under Soult's powerful thrust; but the main assault was delayed, and Soult lost the opportunity to break through. Wellington rushed reserves to the point of attack, and on July 28 the French were flung back. Two days later Wellington regained the initiative and struck a deadly blow at Soult's rear guard. Little more than half the French army survived to retreat in disorder into France. At the end of August San Sebastián fell, but the gallant garrison of Pamplona held out until October 31. The British had crossed the Bidassoa into France on October 7, but Wellington would not risk an assault on the mountain entrenchments above the Nivelle until the last pocket of resistance in Spain was destroyed.

On November 10 the hills were stormed, and Soult's chain of fortresses was broken. Wellington's regiments were invincible that day, the famous Light Division in particular performing prodigies of valor. Though Soult's army regrouped under his indomitable leadership along the Nive River, the way was open to Bordeaux. Wellington's Spanish allies had begun to plunder the captured French villages, and while Pakenham, as head of the reorganized military police, stormed about "like a raving lion" trying to prevent pillaging, Wellington decided to accept the numerical disadvantage and send them home.

The tightened discipline of the army, as it moved into France, was so unlike the brutal behavior of Napoleon's troops that the French welcomed the invaders as liberators. One of the greatest dangers inherent in operating inside a hostile country was avoided.

Even before the British and their allies entered France, Napoleon had suffered a crushing defeat at Leipzig. His army of 190,000 was overwhelmed by 300,000 Russians, Austrians, Swedes, and Prussians on October 16. Early in November allied troops reached the Rhine, and Holland was liberated. Offered the frontiers of the Rhine, the Alps, and the Pyrenees, Napoleon furiously rejected peace, pinning his hopes on his ability to foment the distrust and animosity already existing among the allies. To cement the alliance and remind its members that their troops were being paid by British subsidies, Castlereagh set out for Germany.

Wellington's advance, a risky operation involving the division of his army into two spearheads, each of which was greatly inferior to Soult's force, was delayed by torrential rain which made the roads impassable, but it began on December 9. Soult in fact attacked both divisions, the second of which under Lieutenant General Sir Rowland "Daddy" Hill was outnumbered by more than three to one; but both held firm, and the French were forced to retreat to Bayonne. The way was open for a British breakthrough to the east, and Wellington took it, leaving part of his army to contain the French at Bayonne. On February 27, 1814, Bayonne was invested, and Wellington struck simultaneously at Soult's riverline defenses based on Orthez. Once more risking the division of his force, the British commander drove the French from a position of natural strength which, with greater resolution and the effective use of reserves, might have been held. Soult retreated to the east, leaving the road to the north open. Sending William Beresford to Bordeaux, which was given up on March 12 without resistance, Wellington pressed forward to Toulouse. His lines of communication were stretched, unprotected, over 200 miles, but he had little to fear from any counterattack in that area and the capture of Bordeaux had opened the Gironde estuary for the transport of troops and supplies. As always in his campaigns, Wellington kept one foot firmly planted on the coast, using the Royal Navy to hold open and secure communications with his supply base, England.

Napoleon's belief that the resuscitated coalition of uncongenial allies could be destroyed for the fourth time in the war was realistic, but it required the impetus of a French victory. He lost no time in providing this essential impulse. On February 25, two days before

Wellington's assault on Orthez, Castlereagh, Czar Alexander, Prince Metternich, Prince Hardenberg of Prussia, and the Austrian commander in chief, Prince Schwarzenberg, met to consider a situation which threatened the survival of the alliance. After his crushing defeat at Leipzig in October, Napoleon had been powerless to hinder the triumphant advance of the allies as they swept into France, overrunning 250 miles in a single month. Two great armies—Gebhard Blücher's with 60,000 Prussians and Russians down the Marne; Felix Schwarzenberg's 100,000 down the Seine—bore down on Paris, and in the north a third under Count Bernadotte had taken Laon, Rheims, and Soissons, while Wellington's apparently irresistible Peninsular veterans moved into the south of France. Antwerp was under siege, an ill-fated British expedition under Sir Thomas Graham invested Bergen op Zoom, and the surviving French garrisons in Germany faced starvation. On February 10, Napoleon struck back. Moving swiftly against Blücher's mixed army, which had lost formation in the advance, Napoleon severed four columns in four days, crushing each individually and inflicting 20,000 casualties. On the seventeenth and eighteenth he turned on Schwarzenberg, who was within 50 miles of Paris, and flung him back with heavy losses. By the twenty-fourth the allied armies were once more in retreat and their leaders ready to make peace. Castlereagh's threat to withdraw British subsidies and his implacable refusal to discuss any terms which did not include the independence of Holland and the abandonment of all French claims in Germany, Italy, and Spain finally persuaded the allies to use their overwhelming strength to achieve total victory. By the Treaty of Chaumont, signed on March 9 but backdated to March 1, each of the four powers contracted to maintain an army of 150,000 men in the field until Napoleon was overthrown. The new Quadruple Alliance, firmly constructed by Castlereagh, lasted for twenty years.

Napoleon continued to harass the invading columns, but his own army was outnumbered, exhausted, and demoralized. On March 28, Blücher and Schwarzenberg joined forces at Meaux, forming an army of 180,000, and two days later they fought their way into the French capital. On April 6, Napoleon abdicated. He left Paris at midnight on the following day on his way to exile on the island of Elba.

News of Napoleon's overthrow was slow to reach Wellington 600 miles away in the south. On April 10, Easter Day, Toulouse was stormed and taken. Soult's last defensive position, founded as usual upon a river, the Garonne, was impregnable on three sides and heavily fortified on the fourth. The assault cost 4,500 of Wellington's finest troops, and he described it as "a very severe affair." Two days later he rode into Toulouse. That night, as he was dressing for dinner he was interrupted by Colonel Frederick Ponsonby, who told him of Napoleon's abdication. Field Marshal the Marquess of Wellington, more familiarly "old Nosey" to his troops, spun around on his heel, snapping his fingers in delight: "You don't say so, upon my honor! Hurrah!"[58]

Among the glittering array of gold lace and fur, stars, orders, medals, and brightly colored uniforms of the allied sovereigns and commanders who rode in ceremony through Paris on May 5, the thin figure in top hat, plain blue frockcoat and white neckcloth drew as much attention as any gilded peacock. Created Duke of Wellington the previous day, he knew that he was to be British ambassador in Paris and had no desire to enter the capital in martial splendor as a conqueror.

The war in Europe was ended, though the respite of peace proved temporary, and Britain was able to turn its attention to the war in America. For eighteen months Sir George Prevost had followed his instructions and his own inclinations and concentrated on the defense of Canada. The British Navy had initiated a successful blockade of the American coast, annihilating all commerce except some coastal trade and the trade with Canada which the New England states conspired to maintain. In 1813 naval operations had also included the limited offensive landings in Chesapeake Bay. They had accomplished little, but they had proved the vulnerability of the eastern coastline. The need for defense had passed. When the weather permitted the shipment of troops across the Atlantic, the British strategy would be offensive. The American territory was so vast that there could be no expectation of conquest, but a blow might be struck so damaging that the government would be forced by urgent public demand to seek peace on any terms. The problem was to decide how this might be accomplished. Wellington wrote to Bathurst in February: "I do not know where you could carry on . . . an operation which would be so injurious to the Americans as to force them to sue for peace, which is what one would wish to see." He added soberly, ". . . the prospect in regard to America is not consoling."[59]

President Madison and Secretary Armstrong would, no doubt, have agreed with him. They were, nevertheless, determined to persevere with the attempt to invade Canada in the hope of taking territory which could be held and used in the negotiations for peace. On February 28, Madison issued two sets of instructions to Major General

Jacob Brown, in command at Sackets Harbor. The first, apparently intended to fall into British hands, directed Brown to join Winfield Scott in an attack to recapture Fort Niagara. The second reverted to the project for the capture of Kingston, giving Brown full discretion in his choice of method and timing. Armstrong's capacity for penning directives open to misconstruction was a deadly counterbalance to his anxiety to inject new vigor into the prosecution of the war. Jacob Brown, in accord with Chauncey, decided that his force of 2,000 was inadequate for any attempt on Kingston, which he believed to be garrisoned by double that number. Thinking that Armstrong's Niagara plan provided an alternative intended to be put into operation at his own discretion, he set out from Sackets on March 13. He had covered less than 100 miles when he was persuaded by a subordinate that he had misconstrued his instructions. He returned in haste to Sackets, where Chauncey persuaded him that his original intention was correct. Setting out again, he reached Batavia on April 1.

Wilkinson, it appears, was not informed of either of the plans communicated to Brown, although he was the senior officer in the Eastern theater of operations. Hearing of Brown's march and fearing, as he explained later, that British reinforcements would be sent to Niagara, he embarked upon a diversionary attack. With 3,000 men he made a timid jab at Lacolle, a few miles from Plattsburg but across the Canadian frontier. The stone mill in which the small garrison was established was found to be proof against the fire of Wilkinson's guns, and he withdrew with 70 casualties. In April he was removed from his command and replaced by Major General George Izard. By degrees, and accepting the bitter lessons of experience, the War Department was cutting out the deadwood in the military hierarchy. At the start of the war the combined ages of the eight generals in the army totaled four hundred and eighty. By the summer of 1814 nine new generals had been appointed—Jackson, Brown, Izard, Daniel Bissell, Edmund P. Gaines, Alexander Macomb, Winfield Scott, Eleazar W. Ripley, and T. A. Smith—whose average age was thirty-six.

In the Niagara Peninsula the British force numbered about 2,600, spread thinly among garrisons from Burlington Heights to Fort Erie, under the command of Major General Phineas Riall. Brown, at Buffalo, mustered an army of nearly 1,000 more, but their numbers were less significant than their quality. Though lack of the regulation blue uniforms had obliged Scott to dress his brigade in militia gray, his men were regulars, and he had spent the winter months drilling them to a peak of physical fitness and disciplined efficiency. With Ripley's brigade of regulars, a third brigade of militia, and four veteran artillery companies, Brown's army was as formidable as any the Americans had put into the field. On July 3 he forced the garrison of Fort Erie to surrender and the following day advanced north to Street's Creek, one mile short of Chippewa, where Riall had gathered a force of 2,000 to oppose him. Riall attacked at once to prevent Brown from deploying his superior numbers to outflank him. Brown's militia were routed, but Scott's brigade, withstanding and returning a volley at 70 yards, went in with the bayonet and the British line splintered.* Brown advanced, turning Riall's flank at Chippewa and forcing him to withdraw to Fort George and Burlington Heights.

Brown made camp at Queenston and dispatched a note to Chauncey urgently requesting guns and supplies to enable him to lay siege to Riall's entrenched defenses, but Chauncey refused to move from Sackets Harbor. On July 24, Brown withdrew to Chippewa. The new commander in Upper Canada, Lieutenant General Gordon Drummond, an energetic Canadian-born officer with international experience of war, was considered a worthy successor to Brock. He sent reinforcements to Riall and followed with more troops to take command himself. Brown's situation was desperate. Riall, with a force increased to 3,000, followed his withdrawal, and a second British detachment threatened Fort Schlosser on the New York side of Niagara. Delay could only increase the danger. Brown ordered Scott's brigade to attack Riall's forward defensive position on a hill overlooking Lundy's Lane. Starting as an engagement between about 1,000 troops on each side, the battle rapidly involved both armies, including Drummond and the reinforcements he had brought to Fort George that day, and lasted from early evening until nightfall. Casualties were roughly even: Drummond, Riall, Brown, and Winfi'eld Scott were all severely wounded, and total losses on each side numbered between 850 and 900, but the tactical advantage lay with Drummond. The Americans, with Brigadier General Ripley in temporary command, retreated to Fort Erie, where they set to work to strengthen the already-substantial fortifications built by army engineers since its capture early in the month.

Drummond, reinforced by De Watteville's regiment of mercenaries, which had fought in the Peninsula, and the 41st Foot invested Fort Erie, where Major General Edmund P. Gaines, hurriedly transferred from Sackets Harbor, had taken command of the garrison. From

*Riall is reported to have exclaimed in astonishment, "Those are regulars, by God." The gray uniforms of cadets at the Military Academy at West Point commemorate this battle.

August 13, when the British guns opened the bombardment of Fort Erie, until September 21, Drummond made repeated and costly attempts to storm the fort but without success. When Gaines was wounded, Jacob Brown rose from his bed in bandages to resume command and on September 17 organized a sally from the fort which temporarily took possession of the British siege works and spiked a number of guns. Disheartened and short of supplies, Drummond lifted the siege and withdrew to garrison forts along the Niagara frontier. On October 5, Major General George Izard arrived with 4,000 American troops, but concluding that nothing of any value could be accomplished without the support of Chauncey's naval squadron, blockaded by Yeo in Sackets Harbor for the rest of the war, he blew up Fort Erie and retired across the frontier.

From a series of campaigns in which losses were heavier than on any other front, no territorial gains whatsoever had accrued to either side. The American Army, which had found little glory elsewhere during the war, had added the names of Chippewa, Lundy's Lane, and Fort Erie to a short military tradition. The British were denied even that doubtful consolation.

In June, 1814, Sir George Prevost received firm instructions from Lord Bathurst to invade the United States. Substantial reinforcements were to be made available to enable him to seize one of the two strong American bases at Sackets Harbor or Plattsburg. Lacking naval command of Lake Ontario until Yeo's great 104-gun three-decker, the *St. Lawrence*, was ready for action in October, Prevost chose Plattsburg as his objective. He had a particular reason for confining his operations to the west side of Lake Champlain. As he explained in his dispatch of August 5 to Bathurst, the people of Vermont had demonstrated "a decided opposition to the War" by providing all the cattle required to feed British troops in Canada. It would be a pity to repay such cooperation with invasion.

Armstrong's removal of Izard and 4,000 men from Plattsburg to go to the assistance of Jacob Brown on the Niagara frontier had left the American base particularly vulnerable. Brigadier General Alexander Macomb, left in command of four companies of infantry and three companies of artillery, reported that he had only 1,500 effectives and as many recruits and convalescents. Against this paltry garrison Prevost could muster an army of at least 11,000, of whom the greater number were veterans of Wellington's Peninsular campaign. For reasons which he never succeeded in making clear, Prevost believed that his immense superiority on land would be insufficient without naval control of Lake Champlain. This depended on the building of the *Confiance,* which was launched on August 25, but there was much work to be done before she could be ready for action. Meanwhile, the American squadron under Thomas Macdonough commanded the lake. The new British naval commander on Lake Champlain, Captain George Downie, did not arrive until September 2. Prevost was aware, as he had reported on August 14 in his dispatches, that the *Confiance* could not be ready before September 15, but from the seventh onward he badgered Downie with a succession of ever more irritable letters pressing him to provide effective support for his forthcoming attack. His impatience was ill-judged, creating resentment and manufacturing, without enemy help, the framework of unnecessary defeat.

Prevost began his advance into American territory on August 31. His army met with little opposition. Macomb had felled trees across the route and put out screens of skirmishers, but he was wisely content to use these delaying tactics while he strengthened his defenses. His call to the New York militia had been answered with an unexpected enthusiasm, but his garrison was still outnumbered by about three to one and he relied on Macdonough to ensure that the land attack received no effective support from the lake. Macomb reported that Prevost's veterans advanced in column, never even bothering to deploy as they brushed his skirmishers aside. They entered Plattsburg on the evening of September 6, and the Americans withdrew across the Saranac River, which ran through the center of the town, destroying the bridges as they went. Macomb's position, previously prepared by Izard, who had long expected the British attack, was strongly en- trenched on the hills above the river and overlooking the bay. Mac- donough had stationed his squadron of four vessels about a mile from the shore, within range of long guns mounted on the shore but effec- tively screening the defenses from any possibility of bombardment from the lake.

From the seventh until the eleventh, Prevost prepared for his assault, but his preparations, based on a total misjudgment of the tactical situation, were both inadequate and misdirected. While he assailed Downie with urgent demands that he come to his aid, he failed to ensure that the approaches to Macomb's position were thoroughly reconnoitered. Though he must have been aware that Macdonough's squadron was anchored defensively at a distance at which he could give no assistance to Macomb, Prevost not only waited for Downie to attack Macdonough, but built his own plan on the foundation of that attack's being successful. Most damaging of all, he made the coordination of attacks from the land and the lake the indispensable factor for victory and failed to make certain of that coordination in his own command.

Early on September 11, Downie's squadron sailed for Plattsburg Bay. At about five o'clock in the morning, approaching Cumberland Head, he fired the guns of the *Confiance** as arranged, to signal his arrival to Prevost. After a brief personal reconnaissance of Macdonough's position, Downie brought his squadron around the headland to attack. At this moment Prevost's land assault should have gone in. The wind dropped as Downie tried to close with Macdonough, and the British ships were obliged to anchor. After about fifteen minutes of a general engagement in which all the vessels received a severe battering, Downie was killed. The American ships succeeded in turning on their anchorages to present undamaged broadsides to the enemy. At the end of two hours the British ships, all of which were so mutilated that, with Macdonough's *Saratoga,* they were subsequently scuttled, struck their colors.

On land, Prevost's assault was a fiasco. The two brigades ordered to ford the Saranac and flank the Plattsburg defenses lost their way, and a third, ordered to cross a reconstructed bridge, never reached the river. Prevost decided that the loss of Downie's squadron precluded the possibility of any further action and retreated with his army into Canada.

At subsequent courts-martial it became clear that Downie had made his attack before the *Confiance* was fully prepared for action in response to Prevost's demands; that he had expected Prevost's assault to be made in coordination with his own, and at his signal; that one purpose of the land assault was to capture the defensive batteries and to use them to force Macdonough from his anchorage and into the lake, where Downie's superior firepower could be used to full effect; and that Prevost had delayed his land assault until after ten o'clock, when the lake battle had been in progress for more than an hour.

Prevost was ordered home, but he died before his court-martial could be convened. The Battle of Lake Champlain may be considered one of the decisive battles of the war, for, with Prevost's retreat, the war on the Canadian frontier ended. His campaign was, however, a part of a much larger design which threatened the centers of American government and trade: Washington and New Orleans.

---

*The guns were "scaled"—firing cartridges without shot—a method often used to clear them of dirt or rust.

X

Mission for Peace

As the British prepared a massive seaborne assault against the United States, the American peace commissioners were assembling in Ghent. Twelve months after they had set out to join John Quincy Adams at St. Petersburg, Gallatin and Bayard had been given no opportunity to exercise their limited powers of negotiation. Their stay in Russia had served only to develop and magnify their own mutual differences. Even if the British had accepted Czar Alexander's offer of mediation and sent commissioners to St. Petersburg, the terms imposed by Madison and Monroe must have proved so unrealistic as to make the meeting a waste of time.

The American President and his Secretary of State persisted in a ludicrous belief that they were in a position to dictate terms, as a victorious nation to the vanquished. This belief, the more extraordinary for being transparently sincere, ignored all the facts and appears to have been founded upon an indestructible optimism. With the benefit of hindsight over nearly two centuries of American history, it is possible now to understand the mainspring of this optimism: a belief, not shared by European countries, that justice is the most potent force in the conduct of war or diplomacy. Madison and Monroe had faith in the virtue of their cause and the rectitude of their terms; it was therefore manifest that their cause would triumph and their terms be accepted. Monroe composed a stream of instructions to the American commissioners, all emphasizing the prime condition of peace, the termination of impressment. When this essential condition had been accepted, the British were to be acquainted with the rest of the terms.

These included the prohibition of British trade with Indians under United States jurisdiction and the maintenance of American naval control of the Great Lakes. In return the British were to be offered restitution of Canadian territory captured by the United States, an indulgence which assumed a triumph for American arms which previous events had provided no reason to anticipate. That the British would not consider abandoning the right of impressment under any circumstances was a possibility which does not appear to have been considered. In June, 1813, the radiant but evanescent vision of the conquest of Canada inspired Monroe to expound the advantages, to both countries, of the British cession of Upper Canada, or even of the entire territory, to the United States. By the time this stupefying flight of fancy had been communicated to St. Petersburg the commissioners already knew that the prospect of mediation had vanished. The destruction of his high hopes of military conquest and the dismal retreat of Wilkinson and Wade Hampton into winter quarters at the end of the year did not dissuade Madison from assuring Congress, in his message of December 7, that the vicissitudes of war were illustrating "the capacity and destiny of the United States to be a great, a flourishing, and a powerful nation."

Gallatin and Bayard arrived in St. Petersburg on Wednesday, July 21, 1813, after a journey which had deprived them of three consecutive nights' sleep. After an hour exchanging news with Adams, they retired to bed. Adams had already confirmed the rumor they had heard in Copenhagen that the British had refused the offer of mediation. The day after their arrival, therefore, the American peace commissioners began to make preparations for their return home. To their embarrassment, however, they found that diplomatic form obliged them to stay. As commissioners accredited to the Court of St. Petersburg, they had be received by the Czar and present their credentials. Thereafter it was for him to decide when his efforts at mediation might be considered at an end. Until such a decision was made, the commissioners could not, without creating a diplomatic incident, return to America. Meanwhile, the Czar showed no sign of leaving his army to return to St. Petersburg, and the Americans were forced to wait for official acknowledgment of their presence in Russia.

Count Nicolas Romanzov, Chancellor of the Empire and Russian Minister for Foreign Affairs, did his best to keep them happy by conjuring from contrary evidence false hopes of a British agreement to the mediation proposal. Indeed, the confusion which had characterized American efforts to prosecute the war on land soon became an integral part of their strivings for peace. For nearly nine months Gallatin and Bayard, unlike Adams who was occupied with his ambassadorial duties, were involuntary tourists.

For Albert Gallatin, the sallow, long-nosed Secretary of the Treasury, the sight-seeing and formal entertainments were no great hardship. As head of the mission and a senior minister in Madison's government, he felt keenly the burden of his responsibility, but he adapted himself better than either Adams or Bayard to life at court. By birth Genevan, he was sophisticated and cosmopolitan in outlook, and he spoke French, the language of the court, fluently. With Bayard, he enjoyed the visits, conducted by Levett Harris, the American consul, to the Hermitage and the Winter Palace, the Peterhof, and Tsarskoe Selo, summer palace of the Empress. The magnificent amber room, presented by Frederick William of Prussia to Peter the Great and removed to Tsarskoe Selo by the Empress Elizabeth,* the gold-plated ceilings of the Winter Palace, and the great collection of masterpieces of European painting formed by Catherine II were as far away from the simplicity of Washington as the lavish and lengthy evening entertainments of St. Petersburg society were from the dinners given by Dolley Madison.

For Gallatin the role of tourist, though it at length became wearisome, was an esthetic and social experience which made a welcome diversion from years of Jeffersonian austerity. For James Bayard it was intolerable. The handsome Senator from Delaware had spent his political life in opposition to the Republicans, and he had voted against the war. His early misgivings about the mission were in no way mitigated by his increasing dislike of Gallatin and Adams, and he lacked the discretion to disguise his feelings. A lawyer of considerable ability, he was nevertheless provincial and homesick. His French was inaccurate and spoken with an execrable accent, his ignorance of social conduct exposed him to humiliating correction, and the drinking water drawn from the Neva, which poisoned all but the hardiest visitors, prostrated him with a bowel infection which the consumption of quantities of tincture of rhubarb failed to dispel. Spasmodic but frequent attacks of diarrhea intensified his exasperation as they weakened his body. Having little but their cause in common, Gallatin and Bayard occupied separate apartments in the same houses, used separate carriages, and led separate lives.

John Quincy Adams, whose puritanical principles were a match for

*Dismantled and looted by the Germans in 1942. Although known to have been at Königsberg Castle in 1942, it has never been recovered.

his relentless pessimism, viewed both his colleagues with the deepest suspicion. Before their arrival he had confided to Romanzoff that the appointments were unsuitable: Gallatin, he believed, could not and should not be spared from the Treasury, and Bayard would naturally have no incentive to contribute to the success of negotiations conducted by a Republican government. As the months passed, he found no reason to revise his opinions. He disapproved of Gallatin and disliked Bayard.

Gallatin was in correspondence with Alexander Baring, head of the great banking house which served American interests in Europe. Baring had married the daughter of an ex-Senator of the United States and, at thirty-eight, was a Member of Parliament. His own family and commercial interests were indissolubly tied to America and, moreover, to British friendship with America. He had campaigned against war and for the repeal of the damaging Orders in Council, and he maintained close links with the government and the people, which made his opinions—for his integrity was scarcely questioned—exceptionally sound and valuable. He wrote to Gallatin that mediation, which was generally believed to invoke foreign interference in a quarrel considered to be domestic, would never be accepted. Direct negotiation, on the other hand, either at Gothenburg in Sweden, or in London, would be welcomed. He regarded the discussion of impressment as possible but profitless. Britain, he declared, could never accept the American demands without losing its navy, and he warned Gallatin that it was both unrealistic and useless to discuss the subject as an "abstract question of right when it is one of necessity." Had either Madison or Monroe appreciated the wisdom of this judgment the war would have been significantly shortened if, indeed, it had been fought at all.

In October Gallatin decided that the failure of the British government to reply to a renewed offer of mediation warranted the sending of an unofficial observer to London. He chose George M. Dallas,* a twenty-one-year-old secretary, and instructed him to report, both to him and to Washington, any definite and final rejection of the mediation offer and to verify the British government's disposition to open direct negotiation.

On October 12 the Americans were at last permitted to present their credentials. The Czar was not present, having authorized Romanzov to receive the commissioners on his behalf. Within a week they were again stiffly dressed in their uniforms, this time at the Winter Palace, where they were received by the Empress. After three months of wait-

*Later Vice President of the United States of America (1845–1849).

ing they were finally recognized as commissioners to negotiate for peace under the mediation of Czar Alexander I, whose services had already been refused by the third party to the negotiations.

Eight days after Gallatin presented his credentials to Romanzov, securing his recognition by the Czar as minister plenipotentiary and extraordinary of the United States, he received unofficial news that his appointment had been rejected by the American Senate. Neither Adams nor Bayard, both of whom had received the information the previous day, had had the courage to tell him.

The Senate vote had been taken on July 19, two days before Gallatin arrived in St. Petersburg, and followed a demand by Federalist Senator Rufus King, a colleague of Bayard's, for an inquiry into the manner in which exchequer business was to be conducted in the absence of the Secretary of the Treasury. It came as no great surprise to Gallatin, who had sought the appointment against the President's wishes and was aware of his enemies in the Federalist Party. His continuing presence in St. Petersburg became increasingly an embarrassment and an irritation to Adams and Bayard, who appeared to want neither his cooperation, which they treated as interference, nor his withdrawal from affairs, which they interpreted as dereliction of duty. But Gallatin could not go home until he received official notification from Madison or formal release from the Czar. Through the following months, trapped by an iron Russian winter in a country they longed to leave, the three Americans were saved from open mutual animosity by the timely arrival of an object of their united loathing, the British ambassador, Lord Walpole. He was a man of brutish behavior, negligible intellect, and doubtful veracity, whose inattention to his duties was almost total. He brought with him the official and final rejection of mediation, but no offer of direct negotiation, nor was there any news of such an offer from George Dallas in London. Bayard, to whom everything in the freezing country had become detestable, noted in disgust that even Christmas Day, as celebrated in the Western world, was in Russia only the thirteenth day of the month.*

On January 3, 1814, Gallatin and Bayard informed Adams that they had decided to leave and, furthermore, that they intended to go to London. A furious argument ensued in which Adams alternately accused Bayard of desertion and of trying to assume the whole responsibility for bringing the mission to an end; but Gallatin's patience and

*Unlike the countries of Western Europe, Russia had retained the Julian calendar. Britain, its dominions and colonies (including the American Colonies) adopted the Gregorian correction in 1751, when, overnight, September 3 became September 15.

temperance resolved the quarrel and, after a week of composition, a much-edited note of explanation was dispatched to Romanzov. The Chancellor, acting for the Czar, gave his assent to their departure, confessing that he was disappointed at their treatment by Alexander but offering the unaccountable opinion that the Americans had shown "rather too much ardor in pursuing peace." Late on January 25, Bayard and Gallatin set out, in separate carriages, for Berlin. Adams, who had visited their house earlier in the day, bade them farewell without regret. When he learned, after their departure, some of the complaints and criticisms made by Bayard against both Gallatin and himself, he expressed a fervent desire to be spared the necessity of working with him again. In this he was to be disappointed.

Unknown to the commissioners in St. Petersburg, Castlereagh had signed, on November 4, a dispatch to Monroe in which he proposed direct negotiation either in London or Gothenburg. With a lack of regard for the truth surprising even in a statesman of such reputation and experience, he added that this proposal had already been communicated to the American commissioners in St. Petersburg, who had replied that they had no objection to London as the venue for the negotiations. This enterprising piece of fiction was followed by a neat example of his most precise composition. Britain, he concluded, would negotiate with an earnest desire to adjust the differences between the two countries "upon principles of perfect reciprocity, not inconsistent with the established maxims of Public Law, and with the maritime rights of the British Empire." It remained to be seen whether Monroe would interpret this correctly as an offer to negotiate on terms which excluded the surrender of the right of impressment.

On January 5, Monroe wrote his reply to Castlereagh, accepting the proposal of direct negotiation at Gothenburg. The reference to Britain's maritime rights was ignored, and the reply contained no indication of Monroe's interpretation of this condition. The Americans were prepared, he wrote, to negotiate on conditions of reciprocity "consistent with the rights of both parties as sovereign and independent nations" in an endeavor to make peace and to guard, as far as possible, against "future collisions" which might destroy it. A new commission composed of Adams, as leader, Bayard, Henry Clay,* and Jonathan Russell was approved by the Senate. Shortly afterward, Madison appointed George W. Campbell to the Treasury, releasing Gallatin, who at last achieved formal status as a peace commissioner.

*Speaker of the House of Representatives. See p. 59.

Gallatin and Bayard survived an appalling journey from St. Petersburg to Berlin. Traveling in separate carriages, they reached Riga after nine tortured days, spending several nights on the road and others in filthy posthouses. Their carriages frequently stuck fast in the snow and on several occasions overturned into deep drifts. Bayard was suffering from a severe feverish chill which threatened to develop into pneumonia, and he believed himself to be dying. On February 21 the exhausted party reached the comfort of the Prussian capital, where they heard from the American consul in Amsterdam of their nomination to the new peace commission at Gothenburg. Arriving in Amsterdam on March 4, they were able to obtain, for the first time in nearly a year, authoritative and fairly up-to-date news of events in their own country. The depression created by accounts of the military campaigns of 1813 was intensified, for Gallatin, by the first official list of peace commissioners, which did not, as he had been led to believe, include his name. Though there was no lack of unofficial information and Gallatin's replacement at the Treasury was published in the *Times* a month earlier, his official credentials did not arrive until the first week of May.

Bayard, who had recovered his health and spirits in the three weeks spent with Gallatin in Amsterdam, determined to accompany him to London to find out for himself the attitude of the British government to the forthcoming negotiations. Everything they heard in Amsterdam indicated to the Americans that the British would not negotiate on impressment and that the suggestion, still nurtured by Monroe, that part or the whole of Canada might be ceded to the United States was preposterous. Reuben Beasley, as agent for American prisoners of war the sole official representative of his country in Britain, wrote that there was no sign of any attempt to appoint a British commission. There seemed, also, to be some preference for The Hague as a meeting place. On the evening of April 6, Gallatin and his son joined Bayard and some of their staff at Hellevoetsluis, and two days later, they landed at Harwich.

Toward the end of February Henry Clay and Jonathan Russell had set sail from New York. They arrived in Gothenburg on April 13, filled with anxiety that the negotiations would have begun without them. To their astonishment they found neither the British nor the American commission in the city, and no one there seemed to know anything about the proposed negotiations. Clay addressed hasty letters to Amsterdam, where he supposed Gallatin and Bayard to be, only to discover to his fury that they were in London. His worst forebodings were confirmed when he received, at the end of the month, a letter urgently requesting his views about a proposed change of site for the negotiations from Gothenburg to Ghent.* Russell had left for Stockholm to present his credentials as minister to Sweden, and news had arrived of the entry of the allies into Paris and Napoleon's exile to Elba. Clay rather myopically described these as "wonderful events." He believed that the victorious countries of Europe, fearing an overwhelmingly powerful Britain, would join to oppose its further aggrandizement in America. He was to be sadly disillusioned.

Clay agreed to the change of site to Ghent, although he feared that it would be seen as a victory for the British, provided that it could be made without giving offense to Sweden. After a warm reception, he had noticed a distinct cooling of Swedish friendship, and he began to have doubts about the ability or inclination of the Swedish government to influence British action against America.

In London, Gallatin and Bayard, their somewhat unorthodox visit underwritten by Alexander Baring, had been well received in private circles, and they succeeded in opening unofficial channels of communication with the British government through Baring, Reuben Beasley, and the Russian ambassador, Count Lieven. They saw the grotesque figure of Louis XVIII passing on the way to his assumption of the creaking French throne; they visited Westminster Abbey and the British Museum; they attended, as spectators, sessions of the House of Commons; they dined with Madame de Staël, who remarked of the British Prime Minister, Lord Liverpool, that he had a talent for silence; they were presented to the widowed Grand Duchess Catherine, sister of Czar Alexander, who had come to England to reinforce the Russo-British alliance by marriage but had found the Prince Regent handsome, licentious, and obscene. Yet wherever they went, they were oppressed by visible evidence of British triumph and strength. Surrounded by a jubilant population glorying in victory, they became increasingly despondent about the negotiations. These were clearly to be delayed, for no decisions would be taken in Castlereagh's absence at the European peace conferences. Even more disturbing were the stories of British troop concentrations at the French Channel ports. It was rumored that 25,000 Peninsular veterans were being assembled for a punitive assault on America.

Early in May the two commissioners sent Monroe a detailed

---

*The port and capital of East Flanders, incorporated in the Kingdom of the United Netherlands under the Peace of Paris, 1814. The city passed to Belgium on the establishment of that kingdom in 1830.

description of the transformation in European affairs. Under the new circumstances, they declared, there was no possibility of negotiating an end to impressment. Unless this condition was surrendered, there was no alternative but to continue the war. Gallatin was aware that he was proposing the surrender of the American assertion of right on "the principal remaining object of the war," but if the rumors of the proposed invasion of America were true, the alternative threatened to produce far more damaging consequences. On May 23, Bayard set out for Ghent, traveling via Paris. Gallatin, knowing that nothing could be done until the British commissioners were appointed, remained in London, hoping to learn something of British demands and to find some way of influencing the British government to hasten its nominations to the commission.

On the afternoon of June 6 the beaches, piers, and streets of Dover were thronged with excited crowds. The route from the quay was lined by the Scots Greys and the three great light infantry regiments, the 43d, 52d, and 95th, heroes of Wellington's army. At six o'clock the passengers of HMS *Impregnable* disembarked. Through the ranks of the guard of honor walked a procession of the rulers, statesmen, and military commanders of the Quadruple Alliance: the Czar of Russia, in a tight bottle-green uniform heavily laced with gold; the King of Prussia, his white breeches strained across a massive rump, and the young flaxen-haired princes, already veterans of war; Prince Metternich, Chancellor of the Austrian Empire; Field Marshal von Blücher, Chancellor of Prussia; Prince Hardenberg; and a train of rulers and generals from the German kingdoms and principalities, conducted by the Duke of Clarence, the king's younger brother,* who had been sent to Boulogne in the *Impregnable* to bring them to England. The next morning the glittering cavalcade set out for London, but warned of the excitement of the crowds in the capital, they prudently dispersed and approached the city by several different routes. Thomas de Quincey chanced to be walking in Piccadilly when the Czar alighted from his carriage at the Pulteney Hotel, rented by the Grand Duchess Catherine as her residence in England, and noted Alexander's eagerness as he ran up the steps to greet his sister. He stayed for more than two weeks, cheered wherever he went by enthusiastic crowds, his obvious popularity a constant humiliation to the despised Prince Regent, whom he had taken an early opportunity of snubbing in public. For much of the period all London was in carnival mood: fireworks and

*Later William IV.

bonfires illuminated the streets and parks at night, and drunken mobs roamed the city. No comparable celebration had been seen in the British capital since the Treaty of Aix-la-Chapelle in 1748.

Albert Gallatin found little cause for rejoicing. A visitor without diplomatic status from a hostile nation, he was excluded from all official receptions, and although William Harris Crawford, the American minister in Paris, had succeeded, with the help of Lafayette, in putting a statement of the American case before the Czar, he believed that no help should be expected from the Russians. On June 13, Gallatin wrote a report of deliberate and profound gloom to Monroe. The Madison administration, weaving fantasies of military glory and of negotiation from the invincible strength of unquestionable rectitude, had to be awakened to the dark and perilous realities before it was too late. Gallatin wrote of the 25,000 troops rumored to be sailing to America—troops which he foresaw would be used to attack Washington, Baltimore, and New York. He predicted that, far from yielding any of its maritime rights, Britain would demand the cession of American territory and the emasculation of American mercantile power. He supported Crawford's belief that no help should be expected from the Czar and doubted that whatever attempt he might make would be effective. In conclusion he gave it as his considered opinion that the most favorable terms to be anticipated from a peace treaty would be those of the *status quo ante bellum.*

Gallatin remained in London long enough to make one last personal effort. He wrote a statement of the American arguments to be presented to the Czar and, on June 17, succeeded in obtaining an audience with him. Alexander received him with courtesy and listened with attention, but modestly doubted his ability to be of any assistance. Gallatin's exertions had justified his much-criticized visit to London. He had gauged accurately British strength and intentions and reported them, with unusual candor, to his government. The warning he had sent Monroe gave him cause to hope that the negotiations would not be made futile by absurd and extravagant demands. He had presented his country's case, with all the persuasion at his command, to the ruler of the one nation capable of exerting any influence on behalf of the United States. There was no more to do in London. On July 6 he joined his fellow commissioners in Ghent.

John Quincy Adams, head of the new American peace commission, was the last to be informed of it. It was typical of the man that he was, nevertheless, the first commissioner to arrive in Ghent. He had spent much of his exasperating and uncomfortable journey in a state of impotent fury. Pursued in St. Petersburg by the mendacious and repulsive Lord Walpole, baffled and frustrated by the misleading and contradictory information conveyed to him by Romanzoff, and enraged by the perfidy of Gallatin and Bayard as retailed to him by Levett Harris (presumably in revenge for Gallatin's having cast aspersions against his masculinity), Adams had barely recovered from a debilitating attack of jaundice when he heard, on April 1, of his appointment to lead the commission. During the week before his departure, he contemplated with mixed feelings the festivities celebrating the fall of Paris and Napoleon's abdication. The deafening cannon fire, convulsive rockets, and continuous clamor of bells were to him oppressive symbols of a nation's rejoicing. They filled him with apprehension and gloom.

On April 28, Adams left St. Petersburg and, after three days and nights of discomfort, filthy beds, and disgusting food, reached Revel* on the south coast of the Gulf of Finland. There he was forced to wait for nearly three weeks, with mounting impatience and irritation, for ice to leave the habor. On the twenty-fifth he reached Stockholm, where he was greeted by Russell. Adams had hoped to travel at once to Gothenburg, there to take charge of negotiations which he expected to start within a few days. Instead, he discovered that the members of the commission were dispersed, with Gallatin and Bayard in London inexcusably meddling in the commission's affairs and supporting the change of site to Ghent. Nor was there any sign of the British commissioners either in Gothenburg or in Ghent. It was clear that the British government was delaying its nominations while it mounted military and diplomatic offensives. On June 2 he left for Gothenburg, pausing on the way to receive dispatches informing him that three British commissioners had been appointed and confirming that the negotiations were to take place in Ghent. In cold fury at the change of arrangements without reference to him, Adams made a wild dash to Gothenburg, his driver falling asleep at the reins. He reached his destination on the night of April 6 and, arousing the suspicions of the police by his late arrival, was promptly arrested. At midnight, exhausted and trembling with rage, his passport confiscated, Adams was permitted to retire to his bed. It seemed that the world conspired against him, but he was slightly mollified when, on June 12, he began his journey to Amsterdam, in brilliant sunshine and aboard the *John Adams,* named after his father, second President of the United States.

*Now Tallin (Danish Town), capital of Estonia.

By June 28, Adams, Clay, Bayard, and Russell were assembled in Ghent, lacking only the presence of Gallatin to complete the commission, and Adams called the first meeting. The decisions made were little affected by Gallatin's absence—it was unlikely that he would have argued against a subscription to English newspapers or the motion to hold regular meetings—and his arrival on July 6 made no difference to the triviality of these sessions. They were held more to satisfy Adams' dislike of inactivity than in any hope of achievement. The British commissioners, though appointed, were in no hurry to arrive, and with the single exception of Henry Clay, who retained an impregnable faith in his country's military capacity, all the Americans believed their mission to be doomed. Adams described the negotiations as "absolutely hopeless." Meanwhile, they rented a house, the Hôtel d'Alcantara on the Rue des Champs, and tried to preserve harmony among themselves while they enjoyed the entertainments and hospitality offered to them.

American suspicions of deliberate delay in the nomination of the British commissioners were not without foundation, but it was also true that Liverpool's government, when, intermittently, it found time to give the matter any thought, found it difficult to arrive at a decision. The Colonial Secretary, Lord Bathurst, combined all the qualities required for the assignment, but though Liverpool described him to Castlereagh as "exactly the man for such a business," he added that there was "some objection" to appointing a minister of full Cabinet rank for "such a negotiation." It was clear he did not consider the "business" worthy of the time of a senior member of the government. In a sense he was right; it was obvious to all that decisions of any significance would be referred to Castlereagh.

At last, in May, three men of distressing mediocrity were appointed. Vice Admiral Lord Gambier, leader of the mission, had led the fleet at the bombardment of Copenhagen in 1807 and commanded the Channel fleet from 1808 to 1811. A competent, if uninspired, sailor, he could be relied upon not to exceed his instructions, and it was doubtless hoped that his rank, title, and gold-laced uniform would act as a suitable reminder of British power while disguising the remarkable lack of distinction of the other commissioners. He was to be assisted by William Adams, an obscure forty-two-year-old lawyer whose brief excursion into diplomacy was followed by a swift return to obscurity, and Henry Goulburn, variously described by the Americans as "Mr. Gouldsbourn" and "Mr. Goldsby," at thirty an undistinguished Under Secretary for War, though he was twenty years later to be Home

Secretary in Peel's administration and, from 1841 to 1846, an unusually successful Chancellor of the Exchequer. As a final gesture of indifference, Anthony St. John Baker, who had made himself loathed in Washington during a period of service as attaché to the British legation, was appointed secretary to the commission. In this capacity, as official courier and liaison officer, he would have ample opportunities for the display of the personality which Americans had found so disagreeable.

The British commissioners made their belated appearance in Ghent on the evening of August 6, nearly three months after their appointment, and settled into the Hôtel du Lion d'Or. The following day Baker was dispatched to invite the American commissioners to meet at the Lion d'Or on the eighth. Adams insisted that this amounted to a command and a dangerous assumption of authority. With the assent of his colleagues he replied agreeing to meet on neutral ground and proposing the Hôtel du Pays Bas in the Place d'Armes. At one o'clock on the eighth the two commissions met for the first time. After brief formal speeches expressing pious intentions, Goulburn opened the negotiations for Britain. With some condescension he explained that he would recite the points for discussion, after which the American commissioners would have an opportunity to state whether they were prepared to debate them and to add further subjects of their own. The British, he announced, would be prepared to talk about the matter of impressment, if this was insisted upon, but he made it plain that conversation did not postulate negotiation; the frontier between America and Canada needed to be modified, and unless some equivalent concession were offered, the privilege to dry fish on the Canadian coast would not be renewed; and finally, it was the prerequisite of any negotiations that the treaty should define peace terms and agree on boundaries for the Indians who were regarded as Britain's allies. In reply to Bayard, he stated that these boundaries would not be expected to entail acquisition of American territory.

After a silence, Goulburn inquired whether the American commissioners had been instructed on any of the matters he had raised. When Adams said that a considered reply would be made at their next meeting, Goulburn declared that he was instructed to require an immediate answer. Ignoring this demand, Adams accurately repeated the British points and asked if it was to be understood that the British wished to discuss impressment. Receiving an emphatic denial from all three commissioners, he repeated that a full answer would be made at the next session, which, it was agreed, should be held at the Hôtel d'Alcantara the following morning. After a meeting lasting little more than an hour the commissioners withdrew to their respective houses.

The Americans were at a loss to know how they might reply to the British terms which were far from explicit. Until they were revealed as detailed proposals, it was all but impossible to decide whether or not they could be discussed. Their latest instructions from Monroe, written on April 4, merely confirmed all those which had gone before, demanding an end to impressment, prohibition of British trade with the Indians, American naval control of the Lakes, and compensation for loss and damage and advising the cession of Canadian territory under threat of conquest. The commissioners had no authority to deviate from these instructions which, it was plain, would destroy any possibility of negotiation. That night as they discussed the situation with growing desperation, a courier arrived from Paris with dispatches from Monroe. Adams, Gallatin, and the secretary, Christopher Hughes, sat up into the early hours of the morning decoding the instructions which contained their reprieve. Monroe was writing after he had received Gallatin's and Bayard's report of May 6. He acknowledged the changed circumstances in Europe but insisted that the commissioners stand firm on all terms except impressment. If it was found "indispensably necessary" to the achievement of a satisfactory agreement, they might use their own judgment in deciding whether to insist on this condition. What many regarded as the principal cause for which America fought the war had been abandoned.

At the meeting on the ninth, Adams, disregarding his instructions, recited the American points for discussion: a definition of blockade and the rights of neutrals, and claims of indemnity to individuals "for captures and seizures preceding and subsequent to the war." That was all. After more than two years of war, America, for all the fantasies woven by Madison and Monroe, presented a request for definitions and a claim for damages. Conscious of the meager appearance of these subjects for discussion, Adams added that there were supplementary points which would be raised after the treaty was signed, but these were not to be allowed to obstruct a settlement. This was a brave attempt to disguise weakness as moderation, but it deceived no one. The British commissioners were aware that they were bargaining from strength, and although they wished for the personal prestige to be gained from an early settlement, they also believed that any delay sought by America would increase Britain's power in the negotiations.

There followed a long wrangle about the British demands for their Indian "allies." The Americans contended that since this had not been mentioned previously by Castlereagh as a matter for negotiation, it could not properly be included, and Bayard demanded to know, in more precise terms, what was proposed. Goulburn at length admitted that an Indian barrier-territory was to be created between America and Canada with the condition that neither Britain nor the United States should be permitted to purchase Indian lands. This, not altogether surprisingly, did not strike the Americans as an attractive proposition. The vast Indian territories recently acquired in the South were, it seemed, to be counterbalanced by the permanent loss of a similar opportunity in the North. The conference was suspended, and the commissioners parted with mutual, if strained, expressions of goodwill.

When they met again on the tenth, the discussions became heated, and the argument reached a stalemate which could not be resolved without instructions from their respective governments. Both missions therefore retired to compose their reports. The Americans, after much drafting, redrafting, and editing, finally reached some measure of agreement on the report they submitted, but each commissioner wrote privately to Monroe so that he should be made aware of the "true" situation. The British report was the subject of less dissension and contained a cold and fairly accurate account, unfortified by detail or emotional opinion, of the course of the discussions. Goulburn, however, wrote a private report to Lord Bathurst,[60] stating his opinion that the Americans were sincere in their desire to make peace and praising their candor. He added that their resistance to the proposal for neutral Indian territories was unlikely to weaken without new instructions from the American government, and he believed that no progress would be made unless this condition could be, at least temporarily, set aside. That the Treaty of 1783 had been, as Castlereagh declared, "hastily and improvidently framed" might well be true, but it was going to be no simple matter to change it. The two commissions continued to meet socially, establishing an atmosphere of less reserve and even of some cordiality, but formal discussions were adjourned pending the receipt of instructions from their respective governments.

Castlereagh received Gambier's report at a time when he was preparing to leave for the preliminary sessions prior to the Congress of Vienna, and his mood was not conciliatory. He decided to deliver his new instructions in person, and at a meeting of the commissioners convened on the afternoon of August 19, Goulburn recited them to the Americans. A provisional, but in substance irrevocable, agreement must be reached on the Indian question. The inclusion of the Indians in any peace treaty and the establishment of a buffer state were conditions of further negotiation, and as earnest of their moderation, the British would accept the boundaries of the Treaty of Greenville, concluded between the United States and the Indians in 1795, subject, of course, to certain essential modifications. These boundaries had long since been eroded by successive agreements, imposed or fraudulent, which had carved out great tracts of Indian territory. Although it may be doubted that anyone in Ghent remembered the precise area covered by the Treaty of 1795, the Americans, and certainly Goulburn, must have been aware that reversion to the frontiers defined twenty years earlier would deprive the United States of substantial dominion. The vulnerable Canadian frontier was to be further strengthened by British control of the Great Lakes. The United States would not be permitted to maintain warships on their waters or forts upon their shores. The British right of navigation of the Mississippi River, agreed in 1783, would be retained, though some boundary adjustment would be necessary to allow the British access to the river from Lake Superior, and the northern part of Maine would have to be ceded to provide more direct communication between Quebec and Halifax.

The Americans were stunned by these conditions. Their questions were received coldly, and no prospect was offered of negotiation upon any of the terms. John Quincy Adams finally obtained a reluctant promise that the terms should be delivered in writing, and the meeting was again adjourned. Castlereagh remained in Ghent long enough to reaffirm the terms, delivered in writing to the Hôtel d'Alcantara on August 20, and then continued his journey.

During the following four days the members of both commissions met twice, at social occasions where dinner and the presence of others do not appear to have precluded informal discussion of their problems. To both parties these seemed insoluble, and Goulburn reported to Lord Bathurst that the negotiations would soon be broken off by the Americans. Adams, Gallatin, Bayard, Clay, and Russell struggled, meanwhile, with a report, the drafting of which served to underline their many personal differences. Their reply to the formal British demands, a firm rejection of the provisional article propounding the principle of Indian reservations in the northern territories, was easier to compose, and it was delivered to the British on the twenty-fifth. The previous day, although it was not to be known in Ghent until five weeks later, a British army under Major General Robert Ross had captured and burned the American capital.

XI

The Destruction of Washington

On April 14, two days after Wellington rode into Toulouse, Frederick, Duke of York, brother of the Prince Regent and Commander in Chief of the British Army, wrote him a long letter[61] detailing the three powerful divisions of Peninsular veterans required for service in America. His Royal Highness also expressed a wish that Wellington's brother-in-law, Major General Sir Edward Pakenham, should be "employed upon this service, provided an acceptable command could be procured for him." Two months later Wellington claimed not to know "the nature of the service expected from each of these divisions,"[62] but he was aware that two divisions were to reinforce Prevost in Canada, and the third, commanded by Major General Robert Ross,[63] was ordered to join Sir Alexander Cochrane's fleet "employed upon the coasts of the United States."[64] On June 6, Pakenham, still Wellington's adjutant general and without a command, listed the general officers and their staffs already embarked and appended a "State of the Troops" in the divisions, the number of which had been increased, by an order of May 26, to four.[65] The total strength of the force was 16,300 officers and men. It was less than Gallatin had heard rumored in London but, if competently employed, quite large enough to persuade the Americans to accept unfavorable terms for peace.

The British strategy provided for two separate and contrasting assaults. The main offensive was entrusted to Prevost. Stiffened by three divisions of seasoned regulars, his army, which had held a vast frontier for two years against a numerically superior enemy, should have no difficulty in sweeping the same enemy aside in a swift advance down Lake Champlain and the Hudson River to New York, severing the dissident New England states from the Union. While this campaign engaged the greater part of the American Army, Cochrane would transport and assist the fourth division under Ross in diversionary attacks on the east coast. Britain's absolute command of the seas gave this force a maneuverability denied to troops on land and would enable it to make the maximum use of surprise. The precise objectives were to be left to Cochrane and Ross to decide together, but it was clear that Chesapeake Bay, where a British squadron under Cockburn was already operating, offered exceptional opportunities for the disruption of American government. Baltimore's shipping provided the lure of prize money, a consideration seldom far from the minds of naval officers, but Washington and Alexandria, with the addition of the navy yards and some small ships in the Potomac, presented the unusual attraction of a chance to strike at the heart of the administration. Ross sailed with his division from the Garonne on the evening of June 2.

Pakenham, who had evidently been given a strong hint of a new command, wrote on June 6, "The change will be rather an experiment to me, but I shall relish the Trial."[66] Later in the month he added, "I think I have escaped America, and shall consider myself vastly fortunate to have been spared such a service."[67] His good fortune was to be short-lived.

Pakenham's official report[68] of the troops embarked for America shows that Ross' division, comprising the 4th, 44th, and 85th regiments, totaled 2,501 officers and men, excluding a brigade of artillery and a detachment of sappers and miners, with commissariat and medical services. The division was embarked in "dirty little transports" which ferried the troops down the Garonne to the waiting men-of-war in the lower waters of the river. The fleet was commanded by Rear Admiral Pulteney Malcolm in the *Royal Oak,* and General Ross embarked in the admiral's flagship with his staff.

On board the *Diadem,* with the 85th Light Infantry Regiment, was a young lieutenant, George Robert Gleig, who kept a detailed journal of the events of the following ten months. That journal, later published as a narrative,[69] forms one of the most important accounts of the campaigns kept by any officer, British or American, who took part in them; but it is the journal of a junior regimental officer, who was not in touch with commanders or informed about the background to command decisions and is thus more valuable for vivid incidental detail than for the author's judgments, which are often unsound, or for his statements of numbers of troops engaged or casualties in battle, which were the inaccurate conclusions of guesswork. Gleig, at eighteen already a veteran of twelve months' fighting in the Peninsula, had served at the siege of San Sebastián, the passage of the Bidassoa, the Battle of the Nivelle, and the investment of Bayonne and had been wounded three times. A sensitive and observant young man, who was later to be ordained in the Church of England, Gleig had been appalled, as had been many older and tougher soldiers, by his experiences in the brutalizing conditions of the war in the Peninsula. He had witnessed bloody slaughter and the maiming and death of friends, he had followed the monstrous trail of devastation, rape, and pillage left by the retreating French army, he had known hunger, exhaustion, and the miseries of bitter weather without shelter, and he had endured the painful shortcomings of military surgery; but he had also found the exhilaration of comradeship in victory, and his youthful resilience enabled him to look back in satisfaction and forward with excitement. The prospect of a long period of service in England on half pay was not attractive, and the expectation of active service in America, "chastising an enemy," stimulated enthusiasm among all but the most disillusioned or fainthearted of Wellington's army. Gleig and his friend Captain Charles Grey had become "enthusiastically attached" to their profession. Their sentiments were not invariably shared by their men.

The regiments under Ross' command were seasoned troops. The 4th, the King's Own Regiment, had fought in the Peninsula for a full five years, and there were men among them who remembered earlier campaigns in India. Gleig's regiment, the 85th, Buck Volunteers, had been with Wellington's army in many of the most hotly contested engagements since April, 1813, and the 44th, East Essex Regiment, had served with Skerrett's brigade under Sir Thomas Graham in the expedition to support the Dutch revolution against French rule in November, 1813. In the subsequent failure of the assault on Bergen op Zoom the 44th had been severely mauled, losing more than half its number killed and wounded.

Ross was a commander of considerable experience, with a reputation for courage and strict discipline. Forty-eight years old and by birth an Irishman, he had not joined the army until he was twenty-three, preferring to complete his education at Trinity College, Dublin, before starting his professional career. He served under the Duke of York in Holland in 1799, distinguished himself at Maida in 1806,* and, as

---

*"The true heroes of Maida were Kempt, Acland, Ross of the 20th Regiment, Haviland Smith, O'Callaghan, and Lowry Cole." (Sir F. Maurice, *Diary of Sir John Moore*, Vol. II, p. 112.)

commander of the 20th, the Lancashire Fusiliers, had fought with Sir John Moore in the first Peninsular campaign and helped to cover the retreat to La Coruña. After taking part in the ill-conducted Walcheren expedition in 1809, he returned to the Peninsula in 1812 and remained with Wellington for the rest of the war. He was even-tempered but energetic, and having had some experience of cooperation with the navy, he could be relied upon to work in partnership with Cochrane. His division, which was to receive reinforcements at Bermuda, was small, but it was both professional and mobile. His instructions left no doubt that this force was not to be risked unnecessarily. Its object was to surprise the enemy, strike hard at naval and military stores and installations, and withdraw. Ross was specifically ordered not to undertake "any extended operation at a distance from the coast,"[70] nor was he to attempt to hold any captured territory. His communications, and in an emergency his survival, depended on maintaining contact with Cochrane's fleet.

On June 20 the fleet put in at the island of São Miguel, the largest of the Azores group, for fresh meat, fruit, and water, but by the twenty-seventh it had set sail again for the four weeks' voyage to Bermuda. From Gleig's journal it would appear that life aboard a man-of-war was not dull. "Balls and other public entertainments" were held through the fleet, and one of these he describes in lively detail:[71]

> On the 19th July, at an early hour in the morning, a signal was made from the Royal Oak, that the Admiral would be happy to see the officers of the fleet on board his ship that evening. Boats were accordingly sent off from the different vessels, loaded with visitors; and on mounting the gangway, a stage, with a green curtain before it, was discovered upon the quarterdeck. The whole of the deck, from the poop to the mainmast, was hung round with flags, so as to form a moderate-sized theatre; and the carronades* were removed from their port-holes, in order to make room for the company. Lamps were suspended from all parts of the rigging and shrouds, casting a brilliant light upon this singular playhouse; and the crew, arrayed in their best attire, crowded the booms, yards, and fore part of the deck; whilst the space from the mainmast to the foot of the stage was set with benches for the more genteel part of the audience.
>
> At seven o'clock the curtain drew up, and discovered a scene painted with such taste as would not have disgraced any theatre in London. The play was the "Apprentice," with the "Mayor of Garret" as an afterpiece, performed by the officers of the ship and of the artillery, and went off in high style, applauded, as it deserved to be applauded with the loudest acclamations. The quarter-deck of a

*Short-barreled, short-range cast-iron guns invented in 1752 and made at Carron for naval use.

British line-of-battle ship has often enough been a stage for the exhibition of bloody tragedies; but to witness a comedy and a farce upon that stage, and in the middle of the Atlantic Ocean, was delightful from its very singularity. When the performance came to an end, the stage was knocked down, the seats removed, and everything cleared for dancing. The music was excellent, being composed of the band of the Royal Oak; and the ball was opened by Admiral Malcolm and the Honourable Mrs. Mullens, in a country dance, followed by as many couples as the space would permit; the greater number of officers dancing, as necessity required, with one another. In this amusement every person, from the Admiral and General, down to the youngest ensign and midshipman, joined, laying aside for the time all restraint or form of discipline; and having kept it up with great spirit till considerably beyond midnight, a blue light was hoisted as a signal for the different boats to come off for strangers, and each returned to his own ship highly gratified with the evening's entertainment.

Time between such elegant diversions was spent in "parties of pleasure to the different ships," when weather permitted, or in browsing through books from the libraries kept by the ships' captains. Gleig spent much of his time watching the changing colors of the Atlantic and admiring flying fish or a dolphin, which the soldiers with help from the crew tried to harpoon. The officers appear to have amused themselves well enough. How the rank and file whiled away the long voyage is not explained. Their quarters were cramped, and except as spectators in their own ships, they had no part in the "more genteel" entertainments enjoyed by the officers. By the time the fleet sighted Bermuda on July 24, even the officers were beginning to feel "the encroachments of ennui" in spite of squalls and thunderstorms which increased in frequency and vigor as the fleet approached the island.

Gleig writes with enthusiasm of the beauty of Bermuda's beaches and the "delicious perfume" wafted across the island at sunrise and after sunset from the forests of cedar and comments on the huge water tanks, built to preserve rainwater for the exclusive use of British troops and ships' crews of the Royal Navy. The climate he found oppressive. The troops were landed for exercise and recreation, and in common with many of the officers, Gleig spent much of his time between his arrival on July 24 and departure on August 3 onshore, exploring the beaches and caves of the island. Ross' division had been augmented by the arrival of the 21st Regiment, the Royal North Britain Fusiliers, increasing his strength to 3,400, and, as soon as supplies of food, fresh water, clothing, and ammunition had been taken on board, the fleet

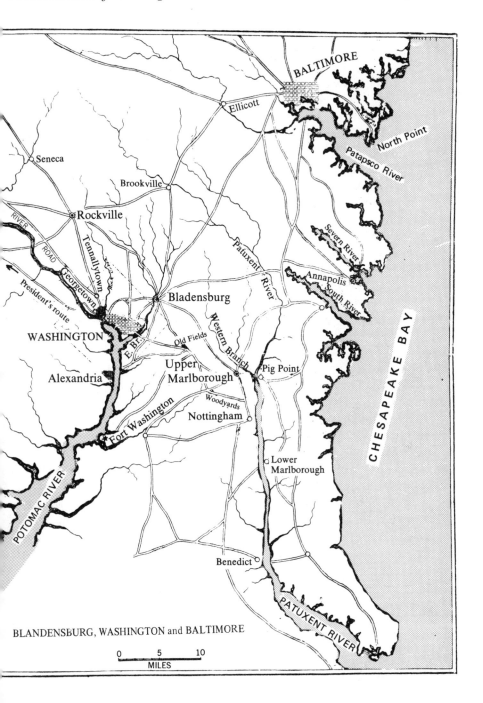

BLANDENSBURG, WASHINGTON and BALTIMORE

0   5   10
MILES

sailed for Chesapeake Bay. Cochrane, in his flagship, the *Tonnant,* an impressive 80-gun battleship captured by Nelson from the French in the Battle of the Nile in 1798, had sailed ahead after conferring with Ross.

There was already some difference of opinion between the two commanders about the object and handling of the expedition. Cochrane had received a letter from Prevost reporting the destruction by American troops of private property at Long Point on May 15 and urging him to take retaliatory action to "deter the enemy from a repetition of such outrages."[72] His new chief of staff, Rear Admiral Edward Codrington, wrote home that President Madison "by letting his generals burn villages in Canada again, has been trying to excite terror; but as you may shortly see by the public exposition of the Admiral's orders, the terror and the suffering will probably be brought home to the doors of his own fellow citizens. I am fully convinced that this is the true way to end this Yankee war, whatever may be said in parliament against it."[73] It is likely that this view was shared by the majority of senior officers at the time.

Ross, on the other hand, was uneasy that the expedition might be reduced to the sort of marauding sorties carried out in Chesapeake Bay during the previous year, a use of his force which would achieve nothing of military value and might have the effect of strengthening American determination to resist and take further reprisals in the North.

Cochrane had already issued a general directive to all the blockading squadrons under his command[74] "to destroy and lay waste such towns and cities upon the coast as you may find assailable" and to "spare merely the lives of the unarmed inhabitants of the United States." As senior officer of an independent command, subject only to the orders and instructions of his government, he was not obliged to take any action on the requests of the governor-general of Canada, and this order for general retaliation was both inhuman and ill-judged. It is significant as a measure of the bitterness which two years of war had bred between the two nations. With the exception of the Chesapeake raids in 1813, the incidents involving wanton killing or destruction of property on either side had been the result of incompetence or a failure in discipline. Cochrane's order made them a matter of policy. He exceeded his instructions. The army was not under his orders and took no notice of them. On the contrary, when Ross' troops were first landed, they showed an admirable consideration for private property and possessions.

Rear Admiral George Cockburn, who had been left in charge of operations in Chesapeake Bay in Cochrane's absence, had seized and fortified Tangier Island as an advanced base controlling the approaches to the six great rivers—Patapsco, Patuxent, Potomac, Rappahannock, York, and James—between Baltimore and Cape Henry. All sea communication was denied to Washington, and the small American flotilla of gunboats commanded by Commodore Joshua Barney was trapped in the Patuxent. Ross arrived in the bay on August 15 and joined Cochrane, who had preceded him by several days, at Tangier Island. With Cochrane's battalion of marines, Ross had a force of more than 4,000. There was nothing to be lost by making the destruction of Barney's flotilla the first action of the campaign. From his position at Pig Point, near Upper Marlborough, both Baltimore and Washington could be attacked from the land, or, if this appeared impracticable, the troops could be taken up the Patapsco to Baltimore. While the army was transported up the Patuxent as far as Benedict, where it was disembarked on the nineteenth, Cochrane sent squadrons up the Potomac and to the head of the Chesapeake above Baltimore to disguise, for as long as possible, the intention to attack Washington.

Organized into three brigades under Lieutenant Colonels Francis Brooke, William Thornton, and William Paterson, the army advanced northward, flanked by the river and a powerful squadron from Cochrane's fleet. On the twenty-second Ross and his force reached Upper Marlborough, above Pig Point, and the naval squadron came within sight of Barney's flotilla. Realizing that escape was impossible, Barney set fire to his boats and withdrew the crews.

Ross' advance had been painfully slow although he had met no opposition apart from a few skirmishers. It is true that his troops were unfit after their long periods at sea, and they were carrying loads to which they were no longer accustomed; but their real problem was the climate. Gleig reports that his men were "relaxed and enervated to a degree altogether unnatural" and mentions "the extreme sultriness of the day, which exceeded anything we had experienced." Ross evidently understood something about acclimatization, for he marched his men to Marlborough in easy stages which would have seemed ludicrous in the Peninsula, always looking for shelter and shade and at the same time exercising every precaution against attack. Guides were pressed into service from among the local population, and heavy guards protected the flanks.

At Marlborough Ross was faced by a decision which he had

deliberately left open: he could march north 30 miles and attack Baltimore, or he could march east 16 miles and strike at the heart of the United States by an assault on Washington. On August 23, after spending most of the day in thought, he marched toward Washington. In the late afternoon the British forward patrols struck some lightly defended outposts about 9 miles from the city. As the army formed to attack, the Americans dispersed and the British made camp for the night.

News of the British arrival in the Patuxent had reached Madison in Washington on the morning of the eighteenth. Incredibly, the city was almost totally unprepared. In spite of British activity in the bay during the previous year, Secretary of War Armstrong had taken no measures to defend the capital. Not until May, 1814, did the President start to press for action, and it was July 2 before the Cabinet created a new military district drawing upon the militia of Washington and the neighboring states of Maryland and Virginia. Overruling Armstrong, whose choice was Brigadier General Moses Porter, Madison made another of his politico-military blunders and appointed Brigadier General William H. Winder* of Maryland to command of the Potomac District. Armstrong, who had already made up his mind that no enemy within striking distance of Baltimore would waste time attacking Washington, resented the encroachment on his authority and adopted an attitude of indifference, leaving the unfortunate Winder to make what progress he might.[75]

Winder took up his appointment on July 5 and spent the following six weeks galloping about the countryside, exhausting himself and his horses, and achieving little more than a thorough knowledge of the terrain. Although he reported to Madison on July 9 that Washington could be captured by 1,000 determined men within thirty-six hours of landing, he made no attempt to strengthen Fort Washington, on the left bank of the Potomac below the city, or to erect breastworks or batteries along the easily defensible Eastern Branch which covered approaches to the capital from a point northwest of Bladensburg to the junction with the Potomac. The lack of substantial military fortification was the result of Armstrong's lethargy and neglect, but there was still time, as Andrew Jackson was to show four months later, for a determined commander to take full advantage of a natural defensive line behind which even a comparatively small force of militia, stiffened by a few regulars and resolutely led, might withstand an army more powerful than any sent against Washington.

---

*Captured at Stoney Creek in June, 1813, but exchanged early the following year.

By August 18, when the British were known to have landed, no ditch or trench had been dug, no breastwork thrown up, no tree felled or obstacle erected to impede the enemy's advance, and the call for 3,000 militia had yielded 250 men. This was the extent of Winder's achievement in six weeks of command and responsibility for the defense of his capital. Part of his failure must be attributed to the absence among the people of any sense of emergency, but it is impossible to escape the conclusion, which his own account confirms, that Winder's energetic and interminable reconnaissances were a thin disguise for bovine incomprehension. Devoid of constructive ideas, he charged about the district in a lather of activity carrying out his own opaque orders.[76]

The news of the British landing at Benedict at last aroused the city to some understanding of the imminent danger. Madison sent frenzied requisitions for militia to neighboring states and called out all regular troops and the militia of Washington. Monroe, finding little to do as Secretary of State, turned scout, riding to Benedict and remaining there all day on the twentieth and for most of the following night observing the British movements. Although Ross' division did not break camp until the afternoon, Monroe appears to have learned nothing he did not know before he set out.[77] Winder, according to his own report, abandoned his reckless rides and spent four whole days at his headquarters engrossed in paper work. His one constructive action was to accept an offer from a party of citizens to erect, at their own expense, breastworks at Bladensburg. An engineer officer, Colonel Decius Wadsworth, was hastily found and instructed by Armstrong to supervise the work.

Amid the confusion of the city, and in spite of Armstrong's and Winder's inaction, a force began to assemble. On the twenty-first, 300 regular infantrymen, with 150 light dragoons, 250 militia from Maryland, and about 1,200 district volunteers assembled at the Woodyard, a crossroads some 12 miles from the capital and covering the approach to Fort Washington. They brought with them twelve 6-pound field guns and were joined by Winder and Monroe. Winder rode forward with the dragoons and watched as Ross' division made a leisurely advance along the road running north to Marlborough. This would take the British to Washington, either through Old Fields and across the navy yard bridge over the Eastern Branch or by Old Fields to Bladensburg and thence to the capital. Winder was faced by a critical decision: either he had to fall back toward the navy yard bridge, leaving open the route through Bladensburg, or he could unite his force with other militia corps assembling at Bladensburg. The solution was simple: by arranging to destroy the bridge if the British tried to cross, Winder could cut one route to Washington, and by concentrating his total strength at Bladensburg, he could hope to block the other. This choice, however, exposed Fort Washington, and Winder seems to have been obsessed by this old building although he knew, from a military survey of July 25, that it was untenable.[78] He was afraid that Cochrane's fleet might sail up the Potomac and attack the city from the river, but he never explained how he proposed to prevent this.

Unable to make a decision, Winder postponed it. On the twenty-second he withdrew to Old Fields, and the following afternoon, the twenty-third, the British advanced. Winder, who had been on his way to Bladensburg to bring up a brigade of militia, galloped back to the American position and ordered a retreat. With a decision forced upon him, he made the choice which finally destroyed any remaining illusions of his competence: he withdrew to the navy yard. "In order to guard a bridge a quarter of a mile long over an impassable river covered by the guns of war-vessels and the navy yard, he left un-guarded the open high-road which led through Bladensburg directly to the Capitol and the White House."[79] From Gleig's account it appears that Ross feinted toward the Fort Washington road, but if Winder was deceived by this maneuver, it makes his withdrawal to the navy yard even less explicable. The previous day, Monroe had informed the French minister in Washington that the battle would be fought at Bladensburg, but if he communicated this information to Winder, the general showed no sign of acting upon the theories of the Secretary of State.

The British army made camp about eight miles short of Bladens-burg and spent another undisturbed night, although the outposts were kept alert by small parties of Americans who "hovered about." Winder, whose retreat had been made at his usual breakneck speed, spent a busy night personally supervising arrangements to blow up the navy yard bridge if this became necessary. On the morning of the twenty-fourth there was still time to retrieve the situation, for the American position at the navy yard was only five miles from Bladens-burg, but Winder wrote to Armstrong declaring his intention "to remain stationary as much as possible" but soliciting "the assistance of counsel" from the government and expressing readiness to "make an exertion" to go to the Secretary of War. When this extraordinary document was shown to the President, he rode at once to Winder's headquarters, followed by a retinue of ministers, including Monroe and Armstrong. Shortly afterward he was joined by a scout who

reported that the British had marched at first light toward Bladensburg. Preceded by scout Monroe, hotly pursued by the President and
his Cabinet, and followed at a brisk pace by his troops, Winder
galloped to Bladensburg.

The race to the battlefield was won by Monroe. He found there a
brigade of Baltimore militia, 2,000 strong and commanded by
Brigadier General Tobias Stansbury, already in defensive positions,
which, having no military authority, he immediately altered without
reference to the general. About 1,000 Maryland militia marched in at
about the same time, and Winder arrived to take command. As the first
British brigade under Thornton appeared, the President and his
Cabinet made an involuntary and unsupported cavalry charge toward
the advancing enemy, of whose presence they were unaware, and
narrowly escaped capture. Winder's troops came in from the navy yard
and were disposed about the ground by a confusion of generals and
military-minded politicians.

The American army, at last assembled, numbered about 7,000.
Competently commanded, this force, although composed largely of
inexperienced militia, should have been capable of inflicting crippling
casualties on a veteran division little more than half as numerous and
sweltering under the unaccustomed steam heat of the Potomac
summer. Gleig writes of dust rising in thick masses into the eyes and
lungs of the marching troops and adds, "I do not recollect a period of
my military life during which I suffered more severely from heat and
fatigue." Even the tough, well-disciplined Peninsular soldiers began to
break ranks and fall out by the roadside in exhaustion.

Winder's army, with twenty-six field guns, of which twenty were
only 6-pounders, was roughly drawn up in three lines on the high
ground overlooking the river which the British had to cross to attack
Washington. Colonel William Thornton led his brigade of light infantry in a reckless dash across the bridge and was sharply checked by
well-directed and accurate fire; but the arrival of two more brigades
and the terrifying spectacle of rockets fired by the British company of
artillery destroyed the resolution of the already-confused American
militia, and they fled. As they stumbled down the road to Washington,
they passed a field containing a battery of two 18-pounders and three
12-pounders served and defended by 400 sailors and marines. Commodore Barney, left without orders at the navy yard, had followed his
President to Bladensburg, where, still without orders, he determined to
make a stand. Twice during the following hour, his guns cleared the
road of advancing enemy infantry, and they were not surrendered until

the position had been flanked and Barney wounded. Gleig, who was also wounded, wrote that not only did the sailors "serve their guns with a quickness and precision which astonished their assailants, but they stood till some of them were actually bayoneted, with fuzes in their hands." His admiration for their brave effort was shared by the whole army. Barney later reported that he had been treated "with the most marked attention, respect, and politeness as if I was a brother."[80]

Ross halted his division to rest and regroup. He had lost 64 killed and 185 wounded,[81] and the extreme heat of the afternoon had exhausted his men. Colonel William Thornton, commanding the first division, and Lieutenant Colonel William Wood, commanding the 85th Regiment, were among the wounded, and Ross' horse had been shot under him. The Americans reported 26 killed and 51 prisoners, and the speed of their retreat prevented the British from taking many prisoners. Gleig considered Thornton's attack on the bridge rashly impetuous; but it was an objective essential to the attack, and it is difficult to see how it could have been taken by any other method without considerable delay.

After the army had rested for two hours, Ross led the advance to Washington, reaching the capital about eight o'clock that evening. The streets were dark and deserted, and camp was made a quarter of a mile to the east of the Capitol. As the British approached, the commander of the navy yard, acting on orders from the Secretary of the Navy, set fire to the yard and to the ships in the Eastern Branch, including a newly completed frigate and sloop. All day the citizens had streamed out of Washington, escaping to the west. Among them was America's First Lady, Dolley Madison, much encumbered by silver, pictures, and other portable valuables from the White House.

As Ross and Cockburn entered the center of the city, they were fired upon from a house, formerly Gallatin's, at the northeast corner of Capitol Square. For the second time that day, Ross' horse was shot under him. During the following twenty-four hours, interrupted only by a violent storm which moderated the flames and the need for sleep, the British set fire to part of the American capital. This was not the result of accident or a breakdown of discipline, but a deliberate and systematic act of wanton destruction, in which both Ross and Cockburn took a personal share. The published reports of this action were exaggerated and inventive, provoking a widespread and lasting sense of outrage which aggravated the bitterness already poisoning relations between the United States and Britain. Cockburn and Ross personally directed the destruction of the White House, the Capitol, the main bridge over the Potomac, the Treasury, the War Office, the National Archives, the offices of the *National Intelligencer,* barracks, stores, and powder magazines. Private property was generally respected, though the explosions from powder magazines demolished or wrecked a number of houses in the vicinity and also cost the British about 100 casualties. The French minister, Jean Matthièu Philikert Sérurier, described the scene as frightful and magnificent. Ross set a guard on Sérurier's house to ensure his protection, and it is evident from private accounts of citizens who remained in the capital that the British troops behaved to them with unexpected courtesy and even paid for provisions. In the light of the many published reports of Cockburn's unbridled ferocity, it is surprising to find him praised for his own good conduct and the discipline of his marines.

The destruction of Washington's public buildings, though not of its military stores and arsenals which were legitimate targets, was disgraceful and unwarranted. Nevertheless, it is reasonable to recall that American troops meted out much the same treatment to York, capital of Upper Canada, in April, 1813, when Government House, the Parliament, and all military buildings were burned, and, according to a resident, "every house they found deserted was completely sacked." The British, and more particularly the Canadians, could not be blamed if they considered the burning of government buildings in Washington no more than just retribution.

It is interesting that this view was not shared by British officers serving in Ross' division. Gleig, while praising the "forbearance and humanity" of the troops in spite of their justifiable irritation, was plainly saddened by the destruction, most particularly of "a fine library . . . and all the national archives." Captain Harry Smith of the 95th Regiment (Rifle Brigade), serving on Ross' staff, was even more forthright in his disapproval:

> We entered Washington for the barbarous purpose of destroying the city. Admiral Cockburn would have burnt the whole, but Ross would only consent to the burning of public buildings. I had no objection to burn arsenals, dockyards, frigates building, stores, barracks, etc., but well do I recollect that, fresh from the Duke's humane warfare in the South of France, we were horrified at the order to burn the elegant Houses of Parliament and the President's house. . . . Neither our Admirals nor the Government at home were satisfied that we had not allowed the work of destruction to progress, as it was considered the total annihilation of Washington would have removed the seat of government to New York, and the Northern and Federal States were adverse to the war with England.[82]

Smith added that the President's dinner table was found with dinner laid and food ready cooked, "which many of us speedily consumed." Gleig was evidently informed of this unexpected party, though not one of the uninvited guests:

> When the detachment sent out to destroy Mr. Maddison's [sic] house entered his dining parlour, they found a dinner-table spread, and covers laid for forty guests. Several kinds of wine in handsome cut-glass decanters were cooling on the sideboard; plate holders stood by the fire-place, filled with dishes and plates; knives, forks, and spoons, were arranged for immediate use. . . . Such were the arrangements in the dining-room, whilst in the kitchen were others answerable to them in every respect. Spits loaded with joints of various sorts turned before the grate.

The soldiers settled down to a satisfying meal accompanied by fine wine, and then set fire to "the house which had so liberally entertained them."

About midday on the twenty-fifth, a hurricane struck the city. Gales of wind ripped roofs off houses, whirling them into the air "like sheets of paper"; deluges of rain extinguished the fires; flashes of lightning briefly illuminated the dark streets; and the crash of thunder vied with the sound of falling masonry. The British troops were scattered in disorder, thirty of them being buried in the ruins of houses wrecked by the storm. It lasted for two hours, and as soon as it passed, Ross made preparations to withdraw. With the light brigade acting as rear guard, the division left the mutilated city, slipping silently away into the night, leaving campfires burning to deceive the watching Americans. They marched through the site of the previous day's battle where the bodies of the dead, stripped naked by their own countrymen, lay bleached white in the moonlight where they had fallen. The British wounded had been entrusted to the care of Commodore Barney, who was paroled until those who recovered should be returned, "a trust which," as Gleig recorded, "he received with the utmost willingness, and discharged with the most praiseworthy exactness."

Ross lost no time in disengaging his force. He halted for an hour at Bladensburg to allow stragglers to rejoin their regiments and again at seven o'clock to give his tired troops five hours' sleep. By nightfall they were at Marlborough. At Nottingham the walking wounded were embarked on a gun brig which had been brought upriver, and on the evening of the twenty-ninth the division reached Benedict, where it was reembarked next day.

While the British set fire to his government buildings, President Madison was jolting about in a carriage on his way into Virginia. Leaving the battlefield as the British attack began, he had trotted back to the White House, crossing the Potomac in a boat from the grounds at about six o'clock as the enemy began their advance on the city. He had arranged to meet his Cabinet members at Frederick, 50 miles away in Maryland, but made no attempt to go there himself. Accompanied by two of his ministers, he remained in Virginia, spending part of the night of the twenty-fifth uncomfortably hiding in the woods as the British, 20 miles away, crept off in the opposite direction. He was followed by Monroe, who had joined Armstrong and Winder at the Capitol. Winder, who had arrived first, rejected Armstrong's suggestion that a stand should be made in the city and led his disordered and exhausted army in headlong flight to Rockville, 16 miles from the capital. Armstrong and Campbell, Secretary of the Treasury, rode, as instructed, to Frederick. They were the only members of the Cabinet to do so.

On Saturday morning, the twenty-seventh, the President sent orders to his scattered colleagues to join him in Washington. As he and Monroe, amid the ashes of their records, grappled with the tasks of government, Captain James Gordon, commanding the British frigate *Seahorse,* sailed calmly up the Potomac to Fort Washington, which immediately capitulated. Gordon's squadron of two frigates and five smaller vessels sailed on to Alexandria, Virginia, which had been left undefended. In return for leaving the town unharmed, except for military installations, which were destroyed, Gordon took possession of twenty-one small vessels in the harbor and quantities of naval stores, flour, tobacco, and cotton, which were loaded on board. Gordon's return downriver was more exciting. A formidable collection of distinguished naval officers, temporarily shore-bound, erected gun batteries covering the river. Commodore John Rodgers, with Captains David Porter and Oliver Hazard Perry, directed a spirited fire from the shore which delayed Gordon until September 6 and cost him seven killed and thirty-five wounded.

The attack on Washington was over, but the danger remained. Cochrane's fleet, with Ross' division aboard, was still in Chesapeake Bay. Brigadier General Winder, his energy undiminished by the experiences which had annihilated his reputation, galloped ahead of his regrouping army to Baltimore, which he believed would be the target for the next British attack. For the first time in two months he was going in the right direction.

XII

The Threat to the South

Although most of Madison's Cabinet were present at Bladensburg when the battle began, there was only one casualty among the United States government. Secretary of War Armstrong escaped unhurt from Bladensburg and from Washington before its capture, but he was, nevertheless, a battle casualty. He waited, as instructed, for the President to arrive at Frederick. He followed the later instructions to join the President in Washington. When, early in the afternoon of August 29, he rode into the city, he found that he had lost his job. Profiting by the fears of the citizens of Washington and Georgetown, the numbed prostration of the President, and Armstrong's absence, Monroe had persuaded Madison to appoint him temporary Secretary of War and, for so long as Winder was at Baltimore, also commander of the military district of Washington. Within hours of achieving this coup he had succeeded in removing from his command a colonel who failed to accept his authority. Armstrong accepted Madison's suggestion that he should retire temporarily from the capital and, shortly afterward, sent in his resignation. Monroe was confirmed three weeks later as Secretary of War, retained his appointment of Secretary of State, and, during the period of the President's shocked incapacity, was the *de facto* head of government.

Brigadier General Winder retained his appointment but lost his most important command. He had left Washington on August 26, ahead of his army, which he had ordered to follow him to Baltimore. Arriving in that city to take over the troops already assembled and direct its defense, he found Senator Samuel Smith, a sixty-three-year-old major general of militia, in full control of the situation and disinclined to relinquish his command to a regular soldier of inferior rank and ludicrous reputation. Winder appealed in vain to the President and to his cousin, the governor of Maryland, whose political power had influenced Madison to appoint Winder in July. Under Smith's direction, the defenses of Baltimore were augmented and strengthened until the city was in a state of fortification capable of withstanding an army much larger than any likely to be sent against it. Earthworks were thrown up, artillery was mounted along the ramparts and in shore batteries, and reinforcements of militia poured into the city to join the Bladensburg army. On September 10, Smith's army numbered 13,000, and the gunboats and shore artillery were manned by sailors under the command of Rodgers, Perry, and Porter.

On September 11, Cochrane's fleet anchored off North Point at the mouth of the Patapsco. Ross' division made an unopposed landing at daylight on the following day and began the 14-mile march to Baltimore as the fleet moored upriver toward Fort McHenry, which commanded the narrow entrance to the harbor. Cockburn, with about 600 marines, accompanied Ross, increasing his force to about 4,200. The plan remained flexible. As in the advance on Washington, it was the intention to make a demonstration, probing the defenses, which would be enlarged into an assault "should circumstances appear to warrant it."[83] Smith detached a brigade of Baltimore militia under Brigadier General John Stricker to check the British advance at the narrowest part of the Patapsco Peninsula, where Rear Creek came within half a mile of Back River, and there on the morning of the twelfth Stricker formed his troops in three widely spaced lines which left open both flanks. As the British advanced, Stricker sent forward riflemen into the woods, where they soon made contact with the scouts of the 85th Regiment, at the head of the light infantry brigade.

Ross and Cockburn were with the leading brigade, and as firing broke out in the woods, Ross went forward to reconnoiter. As he joined the skirmishers, he received a musket ball in the chest. He was carried to the road and laid down under a canopy of blankets. A surgeon was rushed to attend him, but there was nothing to be done. Ross died as he was being carried to the boats. Command of the division fell to Colonel Francis Brooke of the 44th Regiment, Thornton having been severely wounded at Bladensburg, and the advance continued. Stricker's militia, soon flanked by the 85th, broke and fled under a setpiece attack of the entire British force, but succeeded in inflicting heavier casualties on the enemy than the whole of Winder's army had achieved at Bladensburg. Stricker has been criticized for the badly chosen dispositions and exposed flanks of his brigade, but the plain fact remains that his force of 3,000 inexperienced militia challenged and halted 4,000 regular British soldiers and marines and withdrew with little more than half the number of casualties suffered by the enemy. The death of Ross was an unexpected blow to the British, the effects of which reached far beyond the Baltimore campaign.

Brooke halted the advance and made camp on the battlefield. The next morning he halted the division again, about a mile and a half from Baltimore, to conduct a reconnaissance of the defenses. He agreed with Cockburn that an attempt should be made to storm the outer fortifications at night. Cochrane, meanwhile, attempted to bring his fleet within range of the shore defenses; but the Americans had sunk twenty-four small vessels across the entrance to the harbor, and the river was not deep enough to permit the passage of the larger warships. All through the day of the thirteenth, until after midnight, the British fleet bombarded Fort McHenry and Fort Covington guarding the river approaches to the town; but little damage was done, and the Americans suffered only 28 casualties. In pouring rain, Brooke, who had not maintained communications with the fleet, waited for news from Cochrane. In the early hours of the fourteenth he received the admiral's report. Bombardment of the forts had been ineffective, and there was no possibility of the fleet being able to give any significant support to a land assault. Brooke conferred with his brigade commanders and Admiral Cockburn, and all agreed that there was nothing to be gained by continuing the attempt. At three o'clock on the morning of the fourteenth the British division began its retreat. By the afternoon of the following day all troops had been reembarked.

On board one of Cochrane's ships during the bombardment of Fort McHenry had been a young American lawyer, Francis Scott Key, sent on a mission to obtain the release of Dr. William Beanes, an army surgeon captured at Washington. Seeing his country's flag still flying over the fort in the morning, Key scribbled on an envelope a piece of patriotic verse describing the scene he had witnessed. Published in Baltimore as broadsheets and later set to music by an English composer, John Stafford Smith, it was officially recognized, in 1931, as the national anthem of the United States.

Gleig had some highly critical remarks to make about the conduct of both armies, evidently believing that a British attack on Baltimore might have succeeded, if led with determination, and describing the blunders of the Americans as comparable with their incompetence at Washington. In common with the majority of his military opinions, which were evidently added long after the events, these remarks have little validity. Smith's defense was conducted with skill and determination, and after comprehensive preparation. Any attempt by Brooke to assault fortifications defended by a force more than three times as numerous as his division, and without close support from the fleet, must have ended in disaster. It was an essential part of Ross' orders, which were binding on his successor, that he should not hazard his division unnecessarily. Brooke rightly concluded that the risks involved in a frontal assault against such heavy odds would be unjustifiable.

Brooke sent his wounded to England, and Captain Harry Smith went home with dispatches, reaching Spithead in just twenty-one days; but the rest of the division remained with the fleet in Chesapeake Bay until the middle of October. Several landings were made, but Brooke seems to have had no particular objective in mind. The naval officers tended to treat raids onshore with more caution after the death of one of their most respected commanders in August. Captain Sir Peter Parker had been ordered to take a small squadron into the upper Chesapeake to distract attention from movements in the Potomac. Learning that a body of American militia was encamped near the beach, Parker had led a party of 124 sailors to attack them. Unwisely he allowed his guides to draw him several miles inland, where the militia were drawn up ready for an attack. Parker led an assault by moonlight. He and 12 of his party were killed, and another 27 were wounded.

Cochrane had left the fleet soon after the attack on Baltimore was abandoned, dividing the remaining ships into two squadrons under Malcolm and Cockburn. Early in the second week of October dispatches arrived for Admiral Malcolm, and on the eighteenth the fleet concentrated and sailed for Jamaica. It was already rumored among the officers that the division would be joined in the West Indies by strong reinforcements and "proceed upon a secret expedition against some place on the southern borders of the United States."[84]

The British "diversionary attacks" were significantly more successful than the main offensive from Canada, but their effect on the Americans was surprisingly similar. Both convinced the American people that their danger was real and near; both stiffened American determination to resist; and both contributed to the bankruptcy of the United States. While citizens flocked to join the militia to defend their homes, the Treasury found itself unable to meet the interest due on government loans.

The financial crisis was hardly more serious than the political dis-

sensions. The country was faced by the imminent collapse of government. At a time when the administration had recognized the danger of
relying on militia, the enlistment figures for regulars decreased, and
there was no money to pay recruits. At the moment when the unity of
the nation was a paramount necessity, the New England states were
displaying ominous signs of separatism. The northern frontier was
successfully defended against Prevost's powerful army, but the central
government, driven from the capital, was unable to exercise its powers.
It was not altogether surprising that the New England states, which
had resisted the war and indulged, throughout the previous two years,
in acts of cooperation with the enemy which were clearly treasonable,
should choose the time of government collapse to assert their
independence. There was little incentive to remain under the control of
a central administration which was bankrupt and powerless to provide
for defense.

Monroe's proposal, in October, to introduce conscription, merely
added fuel to the flames. Governor Caleb Strong* called the legislature
of Massachusetts into special session and, within a few days, obtained
agreement to call a convention of states of shared interest to discuss
defense and to provide for a later convention to revise the Federal
Constitution. The convention was summoned to meet at Hartford,
Connecticut, in December, but although Massachusetts, Connecticut,
and Rhode Island agreed to send delegates, there was some opposition
from New Hampshire and Vermont. The Hartford Convention met on
December 15 and remained in secret session until January 5, but the
resolutions passed were more querulous than rebellious. The extremists
failed to obtain support for secession. By the time Caleb Strong was
ready to send commissioners to Washington events in the South and at
Ghent had made their journey irrelevant.

The news of the capture and burning of Washington, which reached
London on September 27, caused great satisfaction, though Lord
Bathurst expressed his government's doubts about the wisdom of Ross'
treatment of the capital and its citizens, which he considered unduly
lenient. Unaware of the failure of the attack on Baltimore, Bathurst
wrote[85] to Ross on September 29:

> You and your troops have gained great credit in the discipline you
> observed at Washington. It is no disparagement of your merit to say
> that it was prudent as well as merciful to show such forbearance. If,

*In 1812, Caleb Strong had proclaimed a public fast as a penance for the declaration of war
against "the nation from which we are descended."

however, you should attack Baltimore, and could, consistent with that discipline *which it is essential for you not to relax,* make its inhabitants *feel* a little more of the effects of your visit than what has been experienced at Washington, you would make that portion of the American people experience the consequences of war who have most contributed to its existence.

Instructions had been sent to Ross, and to Cochrane, some six weeks earlier designating their next task and informing them of reinforcements which would increase the division to nearly 6,000. These reinforcements were augmented by a further brigade, more than 2,000 strong, on receipt of Ross' report of the capture of Washington. By the time the news of the reverse at Baltimore and Ross' death reached England the first reinforcements had sailed.

Prevost's failure at Plattsburg more than counterbalanced victory at Washington. It was clear that even the addition of 10,000 Peninsular troops could not compensate for overcautious leadership, and although Prevost had been recalled and replaced by General Sir George Murray, it was doubtful if any imperishable achievement could be expected from that arena of the war. The government decided on one last effort to gain a significant victory. Unlike Ross' expedition, Prevost's campaign had been launched with the intention of annexing territory which could be held and used in the negotiations for peace. This object might still be attained in time to influence the American government to submit to the British terms, but it was attainable only in the South.

In Ghent, Gallatin had already guessed British intentions. As he reported to Monroe in August, he believed the British object to be territorial conquest, and he warned the Secretary of State to expect a powerful offensive in the area of Lakes Erie and Ontario, but "the true and immediate object is New Orleans." Whether this statement was the result of deduction or of intelligence received from London is not clear, but it is remarkable that Gallatin was aware of the British plan in advance of the commanders who were intended to execute it.

After numerous and noisy quarrels the American commissioners decided on a reply to the British terms recited on August 19. Weary, despondent, and as little united as the country they represented, they nevertheless displayed more courage, more determination, and more dignity than any of their colleagues at home. Late at night on the twenty-fourth they agreed upon a note rejecting the terms. The British commissioners swiftly composed a reply, which they submitted to Castlereagh in Paris for his approval. They confidently supposed that the government would act on their advice and bring the negotiations to an end without delay, but Liverpool, Castlereagh, and Bathurst were all agreed that this would be a disastrous error. The abrupt conclusion of talks at that stage would merely reinforce American determination to fight. An adjournment, on the other hand, until the successful outcome of Prevost's offensive was known to both sides, would bring the Americans back to the conference table in a more docile mood. Bathurst's final draft, though it did not depart from the substance of the original conditions, showed a disposition to retreat from ultimatum toward discussion. Unfortunately he also gave the commissioners a free hand to alter the style of the message. By the time Goulburn had finished with it the ultimatum was back in place. The short expressions of willingness to discuss other propositions or modifications were almost invisible among the lengthy repetitions of former arguments and demands and the hectoring assertions that the British terms could not be altered.

On September 9 the Americans sent an equally lengthy and highly emotional rejection of the British proposals, refusing to refer them to their government but offering to continue discussions on the "points of difference." It was a remarkable situation. Neither side wished to accept responsibility for the breakdown of negotiations, and each presented to the other a front of inflexible resolution which neither of their governments could afford. The Americans were working alone. Even if their government had been capable of making any decisions, their instructions would have taken four or five weeks to reach Ghent. The British suffered under no such disadvantage and could consult Castlereagh in Paris or the Cabinet in London in a matter of days. If America's generals had been of the caliber of its peace commissioners, the war would have taken a very different course.

Liverpool and Bathurst began to have grave fears about the negotiations in Ghent. The war was not popular at home, and if it was prolonged unduly, the continuing blockade of the entire American coast would make it equally unpopular among Britain's Continental allies. If the American commissioners were obliged to return to their country having rejected terms which they considered dishonorable, any hopes for peace would be indefinitely postponed. On September 4, still hoping to hear news of victory on the Canadian frontier, Bathurst wrote, "We are certainly anxious to make Peace before this next Campaign."[86] As preparations were advanced for a new assault, against the South, the government yet believed that it might prove unnecessary. Bathurst declared that the object must be "to make a good Peace now." To this end the government would be prepared to withdraw the demands concerning the Indian reservation and the sole command of the Lakes as a *sine qua non* for negotiation. In a later set of instructions it was made clear that the Indians must, nevertheless, be included in the treaty and restored to the lands they possessed in 1811. The question of control of the Lakes could be included in discussions on revision of the Canadian border. The silkiness of Goulburn's reply, thanking Bathurst for "so clearly explaining what are the views and objects of the government," did not disguise his cold fury at finding that the most important of British demands had been abandoned. It was clear that the negotiations were to be kept alive at any cost.

Goulburn, Admiral Gambier, and Dr. Adams composed another note. The Americans replied with another rejection of the modified terms. The United States would not include the Indians in the treaty; they would not preserve "a perpetual desert for savages"; they would not, either, go home. In an atmosphere of ill-concealed hostility the negotiations continued.

The British government, having achieved its object of keeping the Ghent negotiations alive, continued with preparations for a campaign in the South while waiting expectantly for good news from Prevost. A new proposal to solve the Indian question, described as a final ultimatum, was delivered to the American commissioners on October 8, a week after they had received the appalling news of the burning of Washington. The demand for a permanent Indian buffer state was withdrawn. A treaty of peace had to be signed between the United States and the Indians, immediately after ratification of the treaty between the United States and Britain, restoring to the Indians all rights, privileges, and possessions held by them in 1811. If this could not be accepted, negotiations would be brought to an end. On the fourteenth the American acceptance of this proposal was delivered to the British commissioners. That it had taken six days of intensive drafting was not due to any lack of unanimity on the decision, but to a failure to agree on the wording of the agreement. All the British notes had stated, with varying degrees of asperity, disapproval of American territorial aspirations and refusal to recognize the legality of the Louisiana Purchase or the annexation of Florida. These statements, supported by copies of the bombastic proclamations issued by Hull and Smyth when they attempted to invade Canada, stung John Quincy Adams to draft replies which injudiciously, and at great length, attempted to refute the accusations. His interminable defense of his country's morality was no more appealing to his colleagues than it was convincing to anyone but himself. Most of the American notes were drafted separately by Adams and Gallatin and then criticized and amended by Clay, Bayard, and Russell. Adams retreated further into the bitter solitude of one who thinks himself misunderstood; Russell, who resented his imagined patronage by the others, followed Clay in all he did; Gallatin, Clay, and Bayard, irritated beyond measure by Adams' high moral tone, which was not confined to his diplomatic activities, tried to stifle their personal and political differences to achieve results by compromise. It was uphill work, and they were not helped by the knowledge that their capital had been sacked and their northern frontiers invaded.

The British Cabinet nevertheless sought to obtain peace. The news of Washington gave them temporary strength, but Wellington's dispatches from Paris were gloomy. The government restored under Louis XVIII was feeble and unstable, and there were disturbing signs of a revival of Napoleonic spirit. It was also undeniable that both France and Russia, already unfavorably disposed toward Britain's increasingly aggressive actions against the United States, would have further cause for complaint if the earlier British terms for a peaceful settlement were published by the American government. The arrival on October 17 of the news of Ross' death at Baltimore followed on the heels of Prevost's dispatch reporting failure and retreat. The British government, seeing its hopes of acquiring negotiable territory in the North shattered, became more than ever determined to acquire it elsewhere. Bathurst dispatched an urgent note to Ghent demanding that all territorial settlements in the treaty should be made on the basis of *uti possidetis** and confidently pinned his faith upon the conquest of New Orleans.

An expedition against New Orleans had been planned before the end of the war in Europe. The British had cast envious eyes upon New Orleans during the eighteenth century when it was owned by France, and the Secretary of War had received many suggestions for the capture of the city and of the Floridas. In November, 1812, Admiral Sir John Borlase Warren had proposed a diversion against New Orleans to reduce pressure on the Canadian frontier.[87] His plan to seize the city with his fleet and 3,000 troops and to hold it thereafter with black regiments recruited from the area was, understandably, not considered practical, and troops for this adventure could not be spared from

---

*Signatories to retain territory held at the cessation of hostilities.

Europe or Canada; but the temptation to close the Mississippi River remained.

Cochrane, who replaced Warren in April, 1814, had certainly seen Warren's report before he left London to take over his command and had been present at planning conferences for a powerful expedition against New Orleans. The enormous quantities of stores known to be piling up in the city were enough to attract naval officers much less scrupulous than Cochrane, and he wasted no time in investigating the possibilities. Within a month Captain Hugh Pigot, in the frigate *Orpheus,* was at anchor in the mouth of the Appalachicola conducting negotiations with Creek chiefs. He reported[88] to Cochrane that feeling against the Americans was strong and that about 2,800 Creek warriors were ready to help a British invasion. In addition, he believed that a similar number of Choctaw and almost 1,000 Indians dispersed in the woods might be recruited and that the slaves of Georgia would join if victory seemed likely. With adequate supplies of arms, a small force of regulars, with such powerful help from the Indians, could take possession of Mobile and Baton Rouge. From either, the conquest of New Orleans would follow. Enclosed with Pigot's report was an encouraging letter from the Creek chiefs confirming their resolve to support a British landing designed to drive the Americans from the Gulf territories. The report was written little more than two months after the Creeks had suffered the disastrous defeat at Horseshoe Bend and two months before their chiefs signed away 23,000,000 acres of Indian territory by the treaty of peace imposed by "Sharp Knife," Andrew Jackson.

Cochrane transmitted Pigot's report to London, endorsing his recommendation and adding his own appreciation of the situation. Three thousand British troops, he estimated, would be enough to raise all the Indians and disaffected French and Spaniards against the Americans and to drive them from Louisiana and the Floridas. Without waiting for a reply, he sent Major Edward Nicholls, promoted to the local rank of lieutenant colonel, with 4 officers and 108 marines and supplies of arms and ammunition to start training the Indians. Two naval vessels, the *Hermes* and *Carron,* accompanied this small force.

Cochrane based his assessment on the assumption that a substantial part of the local population would rise against the Americans. His estimate of 3,000 British troops has been described as "a piece of folly so childish that it ought to have warned British Ministers against listening to any of his projects,"[89] but it was his reliance on assurances of powerful local support that was at fault more than his underestimate of the number of troops required. Had such a force been landed at Mobile and received the assistance he had been promised, the defense of New Orleans would have presented Andrew Jackson with problems at least as great as those he overcame against a larger force of regular soldiers in the following December and January. Cochrane asked to be supplied with shallow-draft vessels to navigate the shoal waters (Mississippi Sound) between Mobile and Lake Borgne and to carry heavy guns through into Lake Pontchartrain, immediately to the north of New Orleans. Such a movement would have threatened simultaneously both New Orleans and Baton Rouge and confronted Jackson with a situation similar to that which had defeated Winder. To dismiss Cochrane's plan as "childish folly," based entirely on a "desire for prize money," is to ignore Cochrane's undoubted experience and ability; the competence of the British Cabinet, which was strongly influenced by his advice; and the American appreciation of the situation made by Jackson, who remained convinced, almost until it was too late, that the British attack would be made through Mobile.

By the time Cochrane's report reached London plans for an attack on New Orleans were already far advanced. It was to be made by a powerful army under command of Lieutenant General Sir John Hope. When Hope was wounded in the siege of Bayonne, Bathurst wrote to Wellington asking if Lieutenant General Sir Rowland Hill would be "inclined to accept" the command.[90] Hill, awarded a barony for services in the Peninsula, accepted the appointment and began to gather his staff. To command his engineers, he chose Lieutenant Colonel John Fox Burgoyne, illegitimate son of the General John Burgoyne who had surrendered at Saratoga in 1777. Colonel Burgoyne had served with Sir John Moore's expedition and with Wellington throughout the Peninsular campaign. Lord Hill wrote to him[91] on August 9 urging him to travel at once to London to supervise the allocation of engineers' stores for the expedition and added, "I am sure you will be glad to find that Dickson is going out with us." Lieutenant Colonel Alexander Dickson had directed Wellington's artillery at Vitoria and was regarded as the most capable gunner officer of his day. He had been promoted to a command more properly a general's, over the heads of two senior officers and at Wellington's express wish, and had gained golden opinions from senior and junior officers alike. The appointments of Wellington's second-in-command, "Daddy" Hill, to lead the expedition and of Wellington's most respected artillery and engineer officers were ample evidence of the importance of the original plan.

By the tenth, the day after Hill wrote to Burgoyne, the plan had been revised. Bathurst wrote to Cochrane[92] that circumstances did not permit the release of sufficient troops from Europe to justify the appointment of a senior lieutenant general: Ross' division would be increased to 6,000 and he would be directed to join Cochrane and the reinforcements at Negril Bay, on the west coast of Jamaica, not later than November 20. The objectives of the expedition were explicitly stated: "First to obtain command of the embouchure of the Mississippi, so as to deprive the back settlements of America of their communication with the sea; and, secondly, to occupy some important and valuable possession, by the restoration of which the conditions of peace might be improved, or which we might be entitled to exact the cession of, as the price of peace." The second objective is significant, coinciding with instructions to the British commissioners at Ghent to deny the legality of the Louisiana Purchase.

In his letter to Ross, written on the same day, Bathurst was less explicit, but further instructions sent[93] on September 6 detailed the reinforcements sailing from Plymouth within ten days under Major General John Keane and gave Ross necessary political guidance:

> If you shall find in the inhabitants a general and decided disposition to withdraw from their recent connection with the United States, either with the view of establishing themselves as an independent people or of returning under the dominion of the Spanish Crown, you will give them every support in your power; you will furnish them with arms and clothing, and assist in forming and disciplining the several levies, provided you are fully satisfied of the loyalty of their intentions, which will be best evinced by their committing themselves in some act of decided hostility against the United States. . . . You will discountenance any proposition of the inhabitants to place themselves under the dominion of Great Britain; and you will direct their disposition toward returning under the protection of the Spanish Crown rather than to the attempting to maintain what it will be much more difficult to secure substantially,—their independence as a separate State; and you must give them clearly to understand that Great Britain cannot pledge herself to make the independence of Louisiana, or its restoration to the Spanish Crown, a *sine qua non* of peace with the United States.

This document has been cited as evidence that the British had no permanent territorial ambitions in Louisiana, and the British refusal to recognize the legality of the Louisiana Purchase has been represented as a genuine, but not entirely altruistic, desire to see the territory returned to Spain. It is a charitable view of British armed diplomacy, studiously presented by British historians, and generously admitted by a few objective Americans, but it does not withstand close examination. Spain had been devastated by the Peninsular War and was in political chaos. It is doubtful that a Spanish administration of any competence could have been found for the Louisiana Territory even if it had been regained, and it is inconceivable that Spain could have resisted, by force of arms, any attempt by the British to retain whatever part of it could be conquered. British insistence on the illegality of the Louisiana Purchase was in direct conflict with the instructions to Cochrane and Ross to "occupy some important and valuable possession, by the restoration of which the conditions of peace might be improved or which we might be entitled to exact the cession of, as the price of peace." If the Louisiana Purchase were deemed illegal, Britain could neither restore captured Louisiana Territory to the United States, to which it did not belong, nor exact cession of that territory from any country but Spain. It was diplomatically essential that Ross should support any desire of the population to return to Spain, giving no opportunity for an accusation of permanent conquest, but the declared absence of any pledge to return the territory to Spain or to guarantee its independence as a *sine qua non* of peace signified the equivocal nature of British intentions.

The news of Ross' success at Washington persuaded the government, which had reduced the size of the expedition and withdrawn Hill from its command, to increase the force by another brigade 2,200 strong under Major General John Lambert. Ross' death at Baltimore necessitated more changes. Command of the entire expedition was given to Major General Sir Edward Pakenham, and Major General Samuel Gibbs was ordered to sail with him to command one of the three brigades. Pakenham's army, once assembled, would number more than 8,000, but there was an obvious danger that the three brigades would arrive piecemeal. There was a much more serious danger that the campaign would be set in motion by Cochrane before Pakenham, Gibbs, or Lambert's brigade could arrive.

Cochrane had been ordered to agree with Ross on the tactical operation of the plan for a descent on the Gulf, but Ross' death before he could receive the detailed instructions dated September 6 probably prevented any communication about the campaign between the two commanders. Cochrane still favored a preliminary attack on Mobile, followed by a land assault on New Orleans, supported by shallow-draft naval vessels and heavy guns brought through Mississippi Sound and Lake Borgne to Lake Pontchartrain. This route would offer the army the maximum chance of recruiting help from the Indians and dissident

Spanish and French settlers before the attack on the main objective, New Orleans. While he waited for Ross' division to join him from Chesapeake and for the reinforcements under Major General John Keane to arrive from England, Cochrane probed the areas he considered most vulnerable.

Colonel Nicholls had arrived at the mouth of the Apalachicola in mid-August, and finding that the British Indian agent had left for Pensacola to rouse the Creek who had taken refuge there, Nicholls followed him. The Spanish still held Pensacola and lived in constant fear of an American attack. The British were therefore made welcome, and marines from Captain Percy's small squadron, which had been strengthened by two smaller frigates, occupied the fort. On August 29, Nicholls issued a bombastic proclamation to the people of Louisiana urging them to take up arms to assist in "liberating from a faithless imbecile government, your paternal soil."[94] Two weeks later, Captain Percy set sail to attack Fort Bowyer, at the entrance to Mobile Bay. The fort was little more than a redoubt built on a bare sandbar. It was armed with 20 cannon, of which only 2 were larger than 12-pounders, and the defenses had been allowed to fall into disrepair. Major General Andrew Jackson, commander of the Seventh Military District, did not need any inspiration to divine the British intentions; they had been broadcast by Colonel Nicholls in Havana, a month earlier. Jackson sent Major William Lawrence with 160 regulars to occupy and strengthen Fort Bowyer. By the time the British arrived the fort was in a fair state of defense. On September 12 Nicholls was landed with 60 marines, 130 Indians, and 12 guns, nine miles east of the fort. Contrary winds held back the frigates until the fifteenth, but that afternoon Percy succeeded in bringing the *Hermes* and *Sophie* within range of the fort. Heavy cannonading continued for three hours, but the guns of the fort were more accurate than those of Percy's ships, which were maneuvering under veering winds. The *Hermes* was crippled and ran aground. Her crew were taken off in ships' boats, and the *Hermes* later blew up. British casualties were 32 killed and 37 wounded. Colonel Nicholls, who had been taken ill and was aboard the *Hermes,* served on deck during the action, being wounded in the leg and blinded in one eye. American losses were 4 killed and 5 wounded.

This repulse at Fort Bowyer was a severe setback to Cochrane's plans for the capture of Mobile as a preliminary to the assault on New Orleans. Although this remained a possible approach for the powerful force assembling in Jamaica, the enemy had been alerted, and the withdrawal of Captain Percy's squadron after failure to capture the fort would not encourage the Creek to believe in British invincibility. There was one source of assistance which appeared certain to provide powerful cooperation and essential local knowledge. On the island of Grande Terre, commanding the entrance to Lake Barataria,* lay the headquarters of the notorious pirates and smugglers Jean and Pierre Laffite. Cochrane was a shrewd tactician and not unduly sensitive about the morals or legal standing of his allies. The Laffites commanded a useful force of buccaneers: well-armed, experienced sailors, skilled in gunnery, and permanently at war with the American government in general and revenue officers in particular. To them Cochrane turned for help in the British conquest of New Orleans.

*Also known as Barataria Bay.

XIII

Crescent City

On January 10, 1722, Pierre François Xavier de Charlevoix, Jesuit priest and indomitable traveler, wrote of New Orleans:[95] "This savage and deserted place, which the canebrake and trees cover almost entirely will one day, and perhaps that day will not be distant, be a wealthy city and the metropolis of a great and rich colony." It was a remarkable prophecy. When he saw it, the town comprised "a hundred huts of wood, two or three houses which would not embellish a village in France" and "half a wretched warehouse." The population did not exceed 250, including troops. Fifty years later Du Pratz wrote,[96] "They who are possessed of the Mississippi River, will in time command that continent," and Jefferson, who was responsible for the purchase of the Louisiana Territory from France in 1803, predicted that New Orleans would become "the greatest city the world has ever seen." By 1815 a population of about 20,000 was settled in a crowded, prosperous, and unsanitary city which had become one of the great trading centers of the world.

Travelers had passed by the future site of New Orleans in the sixteenth and seventeenth centuries, but the town owes its foundation to a Scottish murderer and the son of a French colonist in Canada. John Law, a descendant of an archbishop of Glasgow, was sentenced to death in 1694 for the murder, in a duel, of the celebrated dandy Edward "Beau" Wilson. Escaping from prison, Law fled to Holland, later moving to France, where he established the Banque Générale, the first bank in France. A year later, in 1717, his Company of the West received a charter for the exclusive trade of Louisiana, previously granted by Louis XIV to Antoine Crozat, marquis du Châtel, and decided to build a town on the banks of the Mississippi, "thirty leagues up river." It was named for Law's patron, the dissolute Regent of France, Philippe, duc d'Orléans. Law's company, which authorized land grants, brought out settlers, and introduced slavery, proved a disastrous failure and, as Controller General of Finance, he brought France to the verge of bankruptcy. He fled from France in 1720 and died nine years later in Venice. The site of New Orleans was chosen by Jean Baptiste Lemoyne, Sieur de Bienville. The sixth son of Charles Lemoyne, who was ennobled by Louis XIV, and brother to the governor of Montreal, the governor of Guiana, and the founder of the colony of Louisiana, Bienville was born in Montreal. Regarded as the true founder of New Orleans, he established the seat of government there when he became governor of the territory.

By 1760 the "savage and deserted place" had been transformed. The first colonists, for the most part criminals deported from France, had been joined by enterprising merchants and about 1,000 German immigrants, who formed their own settlement known as *La Côte des Allemands* or simply *Aux Allemands* some 40 miles upriver on both banks. With the appointment, in 1743, of the aristocratic Marquis de Vaudreuil* to be governor of Louisiana, New Orleans social life achieved an altogether different sophistication. The town already possessed some fine buildings, designed by French royal architects and military engineers working to the town plan conceived about 1720 by Leblond de la Tour. These set a standard of some elegance, successfully adapting the prevailing French styles to subtropical living conditions without loss of proportion. *Le grand marquis* brought to New Orleans some of the customs of French society, and the balls, levees, soirees, and banquets held during the decade of his governorship introduced a new awareness of social order and bred new aspirations and ambitions among those who could afford to cultivate them.

A second important influence arrived with Spanish government in 1766. By secret treaty Louis XV had given "the Isle of Orleans" and all territory west of the Mississippi to his cousin Charles III of Spain on November 3, 1762; but the French governor was not notified until October, 1764, and the Spanish administration did not arrive until two years later. By this time, under the treaty ending the Seven Years' War, France had ceded all territory east of the Mississippi, with the impor-

---

*Last French governor-general of New France (Canada). He escaped from Quebec after the successful British siege of 1759 but surrendered Canada to the British in 1760.

tant exception of the Isle of Orleans, to Britain. A powerful internal influence was simultaneously removed by the expulsion (by a decree of Pope Clement XIII affecting all the dominions of France, Spain, and Naples) of the Jesuits, who had been among the earliest settlers in New Orleans. Bienville had granted them an extensive property on which they had cultivated myrtle, figs, indigo, oranges, and probably sugar-cane. This land was seized and sold in 1763,* and the Jesuits did not return to the city until 1857.

The change in government was not welcomed in New Orleans, and petitions of protest were sent to France, where they were prevented from reaching the King. In 1768, two years after the arrival of the first Spanish administrator, Antonio de Ulloa, a naval officer and scientist without experience of government, revolution broke out in New Orleans. This was quickly suppressed by General Alexander O'Reilly, an Irishman employed in the Spanish Army, who arrived with 2,600 troops and established order under the rule and laws of Spain. The French flag was hauled down and replaced by that of the Spanish Bourbons, the Place d'Armes† was renamed Plaza de Armas, and eleven of the revolutionary leaders, having failed to prove "the allegations set up in their defense," were executed or imprisoned. In spite of this violent beginning, Spanish rule gave New Orleans thirty-four years of benevolent, though inert, government under which the town prospered.** Trade increased, the first theater was established on the corner of St. Peter and Chartres, and in 1794, the first issue of a New Orleans newspaper, *Le Moniteur de Louisiane,* appeared on the streets.

Among the greatest benefits derived from Spanish government were the buildings given to New Orleans by Spanish benefactors. The cathedral and the two fine flanking buildings, the Cabildo (seat of the Spanish government) and Presbytere (intended as the rectory for the

---

*The Jesuit lands were bounded roughly by the present streets of Felicity, Common, Tchoupitoulas, and Terpsichore. They were sold for $180,000.

†Now Jackson Square.

**"In spite of the assertions of some old colonists who are not greatly satisfied with the new regime, and according to all those among them without feeling and bias, that government, although clothed with great power, does not exercise an abusive authority in this colony, and even has always been very moderate, if one excepts the first years of the Spanish regime [under Ulloa and O'Reilly], which were marked by arbitrary, tyrannical, and cruel acts, and some stormy occurrences, in which on one side the imprudent conduct of various colonists, and on the other, the extreme distrust of the governor-general gave rise to troubles, occasioned the abuse of authority, and compelled that governor to take violent measures, which, fortunately were only on paper and not carried out, thanks to the prudence and firmness of some citizens. From that resulted a solution favorable to the public tranquillity and to colonial safety, and a sincere or political relationship between the governor-general and the colonists." F. Berquin-Duvallon, *Vue de la colonie espagnole. . . .* (Paris, 1803), pp. 166–67.

Cathedral but rented and then sold to the city for use as a courthouse), all owe their existence to the generosity of Don Andrés Almonaster y Rojas. Designed by Gilberto Guillemard, they occupy the north side of the square, which the French population continued to call the Place d'Armes, and the twin rows of brick buildings flanking the square were later given to the city by Almonaster's daughter, the Baroness Pontalba. Many of the finest houses in the city were built during the period of Spanish rule to replace French colonial buildings destroyed in the catastrophic fires of 1788 and 1794. In the fire which began in New Orleans on Good Friday, 1788, nineteen squares were devastated and more than 800 houses razed to the ground, and six years later a second fire caused damage then estimated at $2,500,000.

New Orleans was also threatened by floods and hurricanes. Built on the one relatively dry spit of land near the mouth of the Mississippi, the town lay several feet below the level of the river at high tide and had to be protected by high banks of earth, often more than 50 feet thick, known as levees. These were thrown up to extend about 140 miles above and 60 miles below the town.*

The treaty of Paris in 1783 confirmed Spanish possession of the Louisiana Territory and granted free and open navigation of the Mississippi to all subjects of Great Britain and the United States of America. Twelve years later, New Orleans was opened to American traders for three years as a port of deposit, which enabled them to use the port without payment of duties and subject only to a reasonable charge for storage. Under the terms of this second treaty the port could be closed to American traders at the end of the three-year agreement, but Spain was obliged to offer them an "equivalent establishment" on another part of the banks of the Mississippi. These treaties greatly benefited the trade of New Orleans, which began to attract both investment and a large merchant population.

Napoleon's colonial ambitions, which included Egypt, India, and the West Indies and had prompted a French scientific expedition to Australia, had turned his eyes toward the great Louisiana Territory ceded to Spain. In 1795 he had tried to regain the province by blackmail, but the feeble Spanish King had been prevented from capitulation by his minister, Manuel de Godoy. In 1800 Charles IV agreed to exchange Louisiana for Tuscany, which he wished to present to his

---

*The first levee at New Orleans was completed, on the orders of Governor Périer, on November 15, 1727. It was 1,800 yards long and 18 feet wide at the summit. It was extended approximately 18 miles above and below the town. Levees are as important to the protection of New Orleans today as they were 200 years ago.

recently acquired son-in-law, Louis de Bourbon, heir to the dukedom of Parma. The treaty of retrocession was secret.

Dated October 1, 1800, the Treaty of Ildefonso was accompanied by a clear stipulation that France would not sell or otherwise alienate the territory without first offering to return it to Spain. This was formally confirmed by the French ambassador in Madrid in a note dated July 22, 1802, which was both official and explicit.[97] Within ten months Napoleon had sold the territory to the United States for 60,000,000 francs ($15,000,000), a transaction partly underwritten by the banking house led by Alexander Baring in London.

Rumors of the secret retrocession of the Louisiana Territory to France had reached Jefferson in 1801, and the news had forced from him, the most Francophile of American Presidents, the admission that when Napoleon's troops arrived in New Orleans, "we must marry ourselves to the British fleet and nation." In October, 1802, the Spanish intendant in New Orleans, in direct repudiation of the 1795 agreement, closed the port to American vessels preparatory to handing over the territory to France. Jefferson hastily persuaded Congress to pass a secret appropriation of $2,000,000 for use in "the intercourse between the United States and foreign nations" and dispatched Monroe to Paris with instructions to offer 50,000,000 francs for New Orleans and the Floridas. If the French refused to accept even the free navigation of the Mississippi by American ships, Monroe was to move to London and negotiate an alliance with Britain.

To Monroe's astonishment he found, on his arrival in Paris, that Napoleon's ambitions in Louisiana had already waned. The prospect of an Anglo-American alliance, the disasters which had overtaken French possessions in the West Indies and, in particular, in Santo Domingo, and the apparent indefensibility of New Orleans against Britain decided Napoleon to abandon his plans for the occupation of New Orleans. The astounded Americans found themselves offered the greatest land purchase in history, and at a derisory price. On April 30, 1803, ignoring his previous agreement with Spain, Napoleon sold the Louisiana Territory to the United States. This vast province, which Napoleon rightly declared would strengthen the United States forever, doubled American possessions and made possible the unification of the country. As Napoleon also predicted, and Americans were to discover by bitter experience, unification is not synonymous with unity, but the acquisition of the great Mississippi waterway made unity an evident essential of power which could not be ignored.

The return of French government to New Orleans had been welcomed with public rejoicing. The population had remained obstinately French in speech, thought, and affiliation. The almost immediate sale of Louisiana to the United States aroused very different emotions. New Orleans had grown into a city where, despite insanitary conditions and a reputation for moral depravity, the people prided themselves on their European culture, a commodity not then generally apparent in American cities. The rough, crude, uncouth Americans of their acquaintance, mostly the drunken and quarrelsome flatboatmen from the territories to the north, had failed to impress them favorably. The people of New Orleans looked backward with regret to a France which, under Napoleon, did not exist.

The outraged protests of Spain against the violation, by both France and the United States, of the agreement pendant to the Treaty of Ildefonso, were heard in New Orleans, and the American government thought it prudent to issue a proclamation to the people. It welcomed them to the Union "not as provincials or subjects, but as brothers and beloved fellow citizens" but warned them, "we shall compel our laws to be respected." The tone of the proclamation was not soothing. On December 20 the unfamiliar Stars and Stripes were raised for the first time in the Place d'Armes.

During the first quarter of the nineteenth century many European travelers visited New Orleans and recorded their impressions. Incorporated as a city in 1805, it had become the bustling center of an enormous trade. Before the introduction of sugarcane, in about 1762, the staple crop of southern Louisiana was indigo, but the caterpillar plagues of 1793–95 caused such extensive damage that its cultivation was abandoned. The same plague attacked the Louisiana cotton crops, which also suffered from excessive rain. The area immediately surrounding New Orleans was not suitable for the cultivation of cotton, and on the higher ground above Baton Rouge and in the Attakapas and Opelousas better drainage did not entirely compensate for the severity of the winters, which, though short, necessitated replanting every year. The cotton harvest began in August and ended in December. The cotton crop of Louisiana rose from 3,000 bales in 1800 to 8,000 in 1810 and increased steadily until the Civil War.

The first successful sugar plantation was started in 1795 by Jean Étienne Boré, who was mayor of New Orleans at the time of the Louisiana Purchase. He had succeeded in producing granulated sugar, and the opening of the port of New Orleans to American traders in 1795 made available an extensive market for his products, although his customers frequently complained that the hot weather turned the sugar to molasses. In 1802 sugar production was estimated at 5,000,000 pounds, of which about a third was imported into the United States. Twenty years later it had grown to 15,400 tons. But it was not for its produce that New Orleans had become essential to the United States. As the old frontiers were pushed farther west across the great Appalachian barrier, as Indian trails became mountain passes open to the pack animals, carts, and wagons of the new settlers, as pioneers fought and bartered their way into the scarcely charted areas of Illinois for the fur trade, so new towns, new states, and new commercial opportunities opened up behind them. Kentucky became a state in 1792, Tennessee in 1796, and Ohio in 1803. Boatloads of grain, flour, whiskey, hides, cotton, and an ever-increasing variety of manufactured goods from Cincinnati, Louisville, Nashville, Natchez, and Pittsburgh were floated down the Ohio and Mississippi to New Orleans on the first part of their journey to Europe, the West Indies, or the Eastern states of America.

The rafts and flatboats were broken up at New Orleans, for the current prevented their being returned upriver. The bargemen journeyed by sea to Philadelphia or Baltimore and continued their journey home by land. According to the traveler François André Michaux, writing in 1804,[98] "They prefer this 20 or 30 day passage from New Orleans to one of these two ports and the 300 mile journey by land. This way is not so difficult as the route by land alone, a matter of 1,400 or 1,500 miles from New Orleans to Pittsburgh."

Knowledge of the Ohio and Mississippi rivers was so greatly improved that the distance from Pittsburgh to New Orleans could be computed at 2,100 miles. In spring the barges took between forty and fifty days for a passage which, says Michaux, could be accomplished by two men in a pirogue* in twenty-five.

New Orleans had become the geographical focus of the entire developing Mississippi Valley, the essential outlet for goods from the trans-Appalachian territory. As the French prefect Pierre Clément de Laussat reported to the Duc Decrés just twelve days before the Louisiana Purchase was concluded, "If New Orleans has been peopled and has acquired importance and capital, it is due neither to Spain nor to the Louisianians properly so-called. It is due to three hundred thousand planters who in twenty years have swarmed over the eastern plains of the Mississippi, and have cultivated them, and who have no other outlet than this river and no other port than New Orleans."[99]

*Long, narrow canoe used by Indians and made from a single tree trunk.

From Europe and the West Indies, and from all over the United States, people poured into New Orleans in search of wealth. The population tripled in seven years. In 1804 the Territory of Orleans was created from part of the ill-defined lands acquired by purchase from France, and in 1812 it was admitted to the Union as the State of Louisiana.

The city, twice devastated by fire and governed within a century by three nations of different customs and languages, achieved a character which has remained unique. By 1812 the population had become a gallimaufry of colors and nationalities. The word "Creole," now generally used to describe descendants of the original French or Spanish settlers, was used until late in the nineteenth century to denote people born in the city. There were, therefore, in New Orleans Creoles who were Anglo-American, Irish, German, French, or Spanish, in addition to the whites, mulattoes, and slaves from Cuba, Santo Domingo, and the West Indies, and the Indians from tribes in the area. There were also *gens de couleur,* free people of color who, not infrequently, kept their own slaves.

Houses in the faubourgs close to the river were generally of brick construction from ground level to the first floor, with one wooden story above. The water-saturated soil prevented the digging of cellars, and for some years it was thought that it would not support houses of more than two stories. By the end of the eighteenth century, three-story buildings had been constructed, but the floors at ground level were invariably used for storage, shops, or offices. Heavy local cypress beams were used as frames for the "brick between posts" construction, which was stuccoed with clay, painted white or yellow, from the riverbed, and the same termite-resistant cypress was used for walls, ceilings, and floors of the living quarters above.

From the living rooms, floor-length windows, provided with shutters or jalousies, gave onto outside galleries which served as corridors between rooms and as extra space for sitting, eating, and sleeping in hot weather. Rooftops were flat, providing areas used as European backyards and a drier thoroughfare between houses than the muddy open-guttered streets. Constructed of cypress beams supporting light planks, and thickly covered by a mixture of tar, lime, earth, and oystershells which set like a rock, these roofs "never leaked a drop."

The lack of local stone to pave or cobble the streets left them thick with dust in summer and sluggish with mud in winter. The wooden banquettes, as sidewalks were called, were made from rough planks which were replaced, as they rotted, with wood from flatboats discarded in the river. Through the open gutters ran the sewage of the town, carried by rainwater through canals and bayous to Lake Pontchartrain. Paul Alliot, writing in 1803 shortly after the Americans acquired New Orleans,[100] described the conditions: "... during the rainy season, the streets are in a frightful state. The citizen who lives opposite his neighbor cannot go to see him because of the water which remains there, the dung of horses and cows thrown there by their owners, which is never removed, and by a putrid slime *(une boue pourie)* a foot deep, which when everything is half dry give rise to a stench that occasions diseases fatal to the inhabitants." Alliot's description is in marked contrast with Robert Livingston's. Writing to Talleyrand in the same year, as United States agent in France, Livingston reported on the American appearance of New Orleans "as the regularity of our pavements, our night watch, our city lamps, etc. already testify, in streets where only mud and darkness and danger formerly prevailed." It is possible that Livingston's desire to show that French efforts to retain New Orleans would be unavailing, led him into some exaggeration of the city's amenities. Fifteen years later De Montlezun reported: "The American is still a stranger in the land ... and I do not think that he can reasonably flatter himself with the hope that Louisiana will ever be truly American."[101]

The filth of the frequently flooded streets was not alone in being blamed for the unhealthy conditions of the city. New Orleans was bounded on all sides by water: on the south lay the Mississippi; to the east and north, Lakes Borgne and Pontchartrain; to the west and southwest the region of flooding bayou and cypress swamp leading into Lake Barataria and the Gulf of Mexico. Much of the land above and below the city, and stretching to Lake Borgne, was waterlogged swamp, overgrown by cypress trees, and a breeding ground for snakes, alligators, and mosquitoes. Close to the riverbank much of the land had been reclaimed. Canals cut at regular intervals drained surplus water into the river, leaving well-irrigated and exceptionally fertile soil for cultivation. These areas were divided into plantations, and the houses of brick and cypress, approached by broad avenues and embellished with neoclassical pediments, pillars, and porticoes, reflected, in their European grandeur of style and rich furnishings, the wealth and aspirations of their owners.

The stagnant waters of the swamps nourished mosquitoes carrying yellow fever, which appeared for the first time in New Orleans in 1767. During the following years there were frequent epidemics. The blacks appeared to be almost immune from infection, and the French and Spanish Creoles were less susceptible than visitors to the city. Believing the disease to have been introduced by Americans, the citizens of New Orleans were not greatly disturbed when American visitors died of it, attributing the mischance to "the too lively excitement of passion and intemperance."[102] This was a fault of which, unlike their visitors and contrary to their reputation, they apparently considered themselves incapable. Epidemics of smallpox were rare, but the dangers were magnified by the opposition of the Catholic Church to vaccination, which was forbidden. In the epidemic of 1802, 1,500 children died.

In spite of fires, flood, disease, and frequently unwelcome changes of government, the people of New Orleans were lively and pleasure-loving. By most accounts they were also dissipated, vicious, and immoral. Berquin-Duvallon, who described New Orleans as "one of the gloomiest and most disagreeable places in the world," was no more favorably impressed by its inhabitants. He declared that many of the women had lively eyes, pretty throats, and magnificent hair, but added that he could find scarcely one beauty among twenty, and described their voices as "shrill and piercing." Both sexes were thickset and fairly well built, but their faces, frequently showing signs of "eruptions, gall, and even leprosy," displayed "more simplicity than goodness, more conceit than haughtiness, more cunning than penetration" and an early loss of teeth. Apart from those few born or educated in Europe the Creoles were "gross, envious, selfish, greedy, presumptuous, scoffers, hardhearted, insincere, caustic, talkative, and, above all that, ignorant to the last degree (they cannot even read or write), and are quite satisfied with their ignorance."[103]

This jaundiced view was not shared by all travelers. Others described the Creole women as elegant and beautiful and commented on their appreciation of music, fine furnishings, and fashionable clothes. The men, on the other hand, were generally admitted to have few social graces, preferring the saddle to the salon, and a gun to a book, and making little effort to disguise their boredom at social gatherings. They took their city pleasures at the gaming table and at balls where they could meet women whose colored antecedents made them less socially acceptable but more attractive.

The mingling of nationalities and of races had produced a substantial population of mixed blood—mulattoes, quadroons, or octaroons, depending on their ancestry—and the Quadroon Balls, to which white men, but not their ladies, were admitted, became famous as one of the great mistress markets of the world. These were less formal than the subscription balls given exclusively for white people, which were grand affairs conducted with all the propriety possible in a city where the smallest disagreement provoked a duel. The fencing academies were well patronized. Sunday, as in France, was a day of pleasure. The shops and markets remained open, the theaters played to enthusiastic audiences, and people danced into the small hours. De Montlezun noted: "The balls are attended with an inconceivable avidity. The passion for dancing is at its height. . . . It is a time for dressing up, for games, for love."[104] Berquin-Duvallon ascribed the passion of women for dancing to "revenge" for their lack of talent in music, drawing, or embroidery. "During the winter," he reported, "that passion is at its height. Then they dance in the city, they dance innnin the country, they dance everywhere, if not with much grace, at least with great ardor. . . . There is the eternal quadrille, which is given without ceasing. . . ."[105] It is remarkable that the general absence of carriages obliged the women to walk barefoot through the mud to reach a formal dance, their shoes borne by slaves following at a respectful distance in their train.

There was no official police force, and the preservation of order in the city was the responsibility of patrols of soldiers and citizens. Taverns, open night and day, existed on the corners of almost every street, and gaming houses, billiard halls, brothels, and dance halls abounded throughout the city.

Two factors, above all, contributed to a general disorder: an abundance of alcohol and a continuing surplus of women. Taffia, a type of rum distilled from the juice of sugarcane, provided the stimulus for quarrels between sailors and landsmen, Americans and Creoles, Spanish and French. The permutations of discordant factions ready for a brawl were endless. In the early days of the city there had been a shortage of white women which had inspired Bienville to send out from France, in 1727, a consignment of *Filles à la cassette:* "young ladies of good character, provided with a chest of clothes or linen which gave them their collective name, who were placed in the care of the Ursuline nuns until their marriages to settlers." By 1803 the situation had changed. Berquin-Duvallon[106] observed that girls greatly exceeded boys in number, and the ease with which men could satisfy their sexual appetites without incurring the cost of a wife made marriage a rare celebration. He noticed also a growing tendency toward "a state of celibacy, a monkish life" among the young men of the city. It was as well for the growth of the population that the women were "very fertile, and that early and for a long time."[107]

French, which European visitors reported as fluent but mutilated, was spoken by the majority of the population, with Spanish or English as subsidiary languages. At the single public school in the city, maintained by the government, French and Spanish were taught, with reading, writing, and arithmetic. There was also a boarding school for girls, which failed because the wealthy merchants refused to pay reasonable fees, and the Ursuline convent, which housed, in the beautifully proportioned building designed by Ignace François Broutin in 1745, a small boarding school, day classes, and an orphanage. This inadequate provision for education left its inevitable legacy: "The children of Louisiana," wrote one visitor, "like those of every other part of America, are absolute masters of their fates. The authority of the parents is no restraint at all."[108] There was no college, no public or private library, and no bookstore—"and for good reasons, for a bookseller would die of hunger in the midst of his books . . . whether in city or country there is found no collection of a few assorted books except among a few Frenchmen settled in the colony."

Contemporary descriptions of New Orleans at the time of the Louisiana Purchase were not flattering: ignorance, disease, depravity, and violence were the characteristics of the city and its people most often reported by travelers, but there was also an attractive vitality and a firm foundation of European culture. A few years later a visitor less censorious and perhaps more realistic than some of his predecessors wrote, "To all men whose desire only is to be rich, and to live a short life but a merry one, I have no hesitation in recommending New Orleans."[109]

This was the city to which Governor William Charles Coles Claiborne came toward the end of 1803. He reported to Madison, on December 20, "The Standard of my Country was, this day unfurled here, amidst the re-iterated acclamations of thousands."[110] This, no doubt, would reassure the President that his new governor was being made welcome, but a visitor, who witnessed the scene, left a different account:

> I saw the French flag slowly descending and that of the United States gradually rising at the same time. Soon a French officer took the first to wrap it up and bear it silently into the rear. The American flag remained stuck for a long time, in spite of the efforts to raise it as if it were confused at taking the place of that to which it owed its

glorious independence. An anxious silence reigned at that moment among all the spectators who flooded the plaza, who crowded against the galleries, balconies, and windows; and it was not until the flag had been quite hoisted up that suddenly piercing cries of "Huzza" burst from the midst of one particular group, who waved their hats at the same time. These cries and that movement made more gloomy the silence and quietness of the rest of the crowd of spectators scattered far and wide—they were French and Spanish and were all moved and confounded their sighs and tears.[111]

A Virginian-born lawyer and brother to Brigadier General Ferdinand Claiborne who conducted a campaign against the Creek in 1813, William Claiborne had become governor of the Mississippi Territory at the age of twenty-six. His legal training and administrative experience seemed to fit him for the governorship of the new Territory of New Orleans, but it was a formidable task requiring personal qualities which he lacked. An able administrator, he attempted, by a pompous manner and public demonstrations of authority, to disguise his lack of self-confidence and the private fears which crippled his powers of decision. The city and its people were foreign to him, and he was a stranger among them. He was surrounded by older and more experienced men, at least two of whom had hoped to be governor and might be expected to resent his appointment. Nor can he have been unaware that Andrew Jackson, whose vacated seat in Congress had been filled by the youthful William Claiborne in 1797, had also been among the disappointed contenders.

Claiborne's early letters to Madison overflow with problems, explanations, and anxieties, leaving the impression of a fussy clerk, consumed with detail and fearful of every shadow, but this impression is less than fair to his efforts or his achievements. As an American, accustomed to American ways, his position was one of unusual difficulty. In the later years of their regime, the Spanish had paid little attention to law or its enforcement. The Cabildo, the governing body, had been both incompetent and venal and had been rightly disbanded by Laussat, the last French prefect, but there had been insufficient time to replace it. Claiborne took control of a city which had become substantially lawless and was still occupied by French and Spanish administrators and their soldiers. It required both firmness and tact to deal with an unwelcoming population and the antagonisms of French, Spanish, and American soldiers and sailors, among whom there existed, as Claiborne mournfully explained to Madison, "no cordiality."

During the first nine years of his administration he guided the territory toward admission to the Union with a dedicated competence which won him few friends but gave him a lasting sense of achievement. Though recognition of statehood depended less on suitability than size of population, when, in 1812, Claiborne was rewarded by his appointment to be first governor of the newly created State of Louisiana, there were few who would not have agreed that the reward was deserved.

Rear Admiral Sir George Cockburn. In the background, the city of Washington in flames. Painted by J. J. Halls, 1853.

British Museum

"The Fall of Washington—or Maddy in Full Flight." British political satire published October 4, 1814.

Le Baiser de Judas, ou las bonne foie Anglaise. French political satire published August 24, 1814.

British Museum

William C. C. Claiborne, governor of Louisiana. From an engraving.

Town plan of New Orleans, 1815. Drawn by Jacques Tanesse, engra

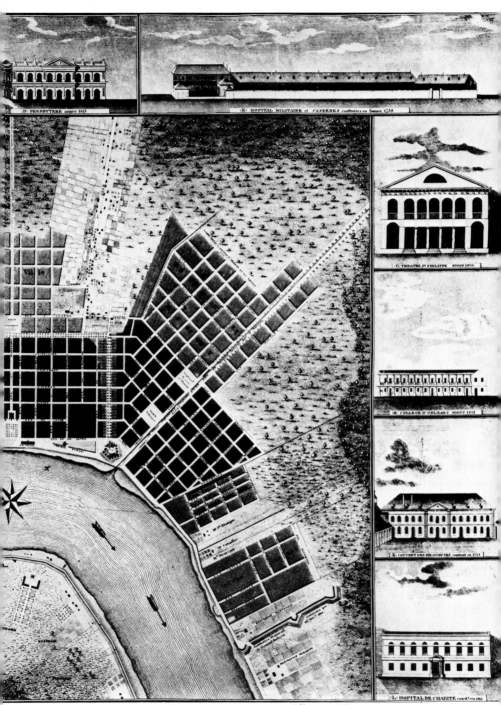

Library of Congress

Rollinson, and published by Del Vecchio and Mospero, 1817.

View of New Orleans from the plantation of Marigny, November, 1803. Painted by J. L. Boqueto de Woieserie.

The Battle on Lake Borgne, 1814. Painted by T. L. Hornbrook.

The signing of the Treaty of Ghent, 1814. (From left to right: Anthony St. John Baker, Henry Goulburn, William Adams, Lord Gambier, John Quincy Adams, Albert Gallatin, Christopher Hughes, James Bayard, Henry Clay, Jonathan Russell, unidentified.)

Major General Andrew Jackson. Painted by Samuel Lovett
Waldo, 1817.

Major General Sir Edward Michael Pakenham in the uniform of colonel of the 7th Regiment, the Royal Fusiliers. Engraving after the portrait in the collection of His Grace the Duke of Wellington.

Major General William Carroll.

Major General John Coffee.
Painted by Ralph E. W. Earl.

Commodore Daniel T. Patterson.
Painted by John Wesley Jarvis.

Major General Sir Edward Pakenham and Major General Sir Samuel Gibbs. Monument by Westmacott in St. Paul's Cathedral.

Photograph: Courtesy of the Warburg Institute

Lieutenant General Lord Keane. Detail from a colored engraving by F. Bromley after the "Peninsular Heroes" group painting by J. P. Knight.

British Museum

General Sir John Lambert. Sketch by W. Sadler for his "Waterloo Banquet" painting.

National Portrait Gallery, London

Admiral Sir Alexander Cochrane. Engraving after the painting by Sir W. Beechey.

The National Maritime Museum, London

The National Maritime Museum, London

Vice Admiral Sir Pulteney Malcolm. Engraving after the painting by S. Lane.

The National Maritime Museum, London

Admiral Sir Edward Codrington. Mezzotint after the portrait by Sir T. Lawrence.

Colonel Alexander Dickson. Physionotrace engraving, 1815.

Lieutenant Colonel John Fox Burgoyne. Watercolor sketch by T. Heaphy, 1814.

Major General Sir Harry Smith, Bt. Portrait by an unknown artist, *c.* 1846.

Private
(Marching Order)

Plate VIII.

Field-Officer
(shewing epaulettes over wings.)

— 1812 – 1816. —
(Service)

Colour-Sergeant.

Museum of the Royal Regiment of Fusiliers, H. M. Tower of London

Uniforms of the 7th Regiment, the Royal Fusiliers, 1812–1816.
Watercolor by J. Percy Groves.

A Private of the 95th Regiment, the Rifle Brigade, 1810. Engraving.
Royal Green Jacket Museum

A Private of the 5th West India Regiment, 1815. Acquatint.
National Army Museum, London

The Battle of New Orleans, January 8, 1815. Painted by Hyacinthe Laclotte, 1815.

XIV

The Baratarian Dilemma

Governor William Claiborne did not exaggerate the difficulties which he poured, in an unending stream, into his letters to Washington. The lawless state of his territory, the absence of formal administration, the "heterogeneous mixture" of races, and the venality of many of the most respected, and outwardly respectable, citizens filled him with dismay. The lack of any unity among the population, unless it was in opposition to the law, gave him endless and unexpected opportunities to offend sectional interests. Whatever his actions or decisions, he seemed obliged to antagonize some influential race, class, denomination, or family, and he often imagined himself surrounded by enemies.

Claiborne was not a brilliant administrator or a man to whom decisions came easily, but he had a valuable and necessary obstinacy. He was determined to govern. He gained strength from a genuine affection for the city and a resolve to make it fine and great. In return New Orleans treated him, at first, like an unwelcome suitor. His first wife, Eliza Lewis of Nashville, fell victim, with their daughter, to yellow fever; his second, a New Orleans Creole, Clarisse Duralde, bore him a son before yellow fever claimed her too; and his brother-in-law, Micajah Lewis, was killed in a duel with a journalist who, he believed, had libeled his dead sister. Claiborne took as his third wife a beautiful Spanish Creole, Sophronie Bosque, who brought him a fortune and bore him two sons.

Not least among Claiborne's more serious problems in his attempts to impose the rule of United States law were the pirate-smugglers of

Barataria. As early as 1794 the Baron Francisco de Carondelet, Spanish governor of Louisiana, had recognized the importance of the island of Grande Terre, at the entrance of the Bay of Barataria, and recommended the mounting of a permanent battery there "to guard the pass or channel entering the Mississippi a league above New Orleans."[112] Eleven years later a band of smugglers held their first formal meeting on the island. It became the headquarters of an organization which controlled as many as thirty privateer vessels and probably not less than 5,000 men. Their leader was Jean Laffite.

It was the early French settlers, not their Spanish successors, who named the area of bayou and cypress swamp south and west of New Orleans after Sancho Panza's insubstantial island. To them it must have seemed as inaccessible. To Laffite and his men it provided a perfect sanctuary. The bay could be approached from the Gulf of Mexico through three narrow channels, of which the widest, and the only one suitable for any but shallow-draft vessels, was a bare quarter of a mile wide and passed between Grande Terre and Grand Isle. Both islands mounted batteries of guns, and the privateers' schooners were armed and manned by seamen skilled in gunnery. From the north and east, the area was approachable only down the bayous or by narrow paths through heavily wooded swamp.

Jean Laffite was born in 1782 at Port-au-Prince, capital of Haiti. The youngest of eight children, he was brought up to hate the Spanish, who had driven his family from their home in Spain and killed his grandfather. With his elder brother, Pierre, he was educated at a private school on Martinique and later received military training. Their eldest brother, Alexandre Frédéric, was already a privateer, preying upon Spanish and British shipping, his true identity hidden, following the common practice of the period, under an alias. As Dominique You, Alexandre acquired a reputation as a brilliant gunner, while Pierre and Jean trained under their kinsman, the experienced seaman, smuggler, and cannoneer Renato Beluche.*

It was the British conquest of the French islands in the Caribbean which drove the privateers to the Gulf of Mexico. During the first years of the Napoleonic Wars, the French were not disinclined to offer commissions to any of the island inhabitants who wished to turn privateer. The involuntary entry of Spain into the struggle increased

*Probably a cousin to the Laffites, though they addressed him as *Oncle*. He was born in 1780 at 632 Dumaine Street, perhaps the earliest house in the Mississippi Valley. The original house was destroyed in the fire of 1788. The site is now occupied by Madam John's Legacy, one of the oldest surviving houses in New Orleans and part of the Louisiana State Museum.

and enriched the prizes. Until 1803 the privateers were brilliantly successful. Commissioned by France and not infrequently financed by respectable citizens of New England, they were not fastidious in their identification of their enemy or scrupulous in their interpretation of maritime law. They buccaneered cheerfully along the main shipping routes, acquiring a reputation for piracy which, however often it may be denied, was well deserved. The French islands offered them refuge and a market for their prizes, and they made easy fortunes. Between 1803 and 1810 the British captured all the French possessions in the West Indies, denying to the privateers the use of their safe harbors. By the time Guadeloupe fell in February, 1810, the privateers were already established in their new sanctuary in the Bay of Barataria.

Pierre Laffite made his first appearance in New Orleans in 1803, when he sailed an armed privateer in company with two unarmed brigs up the Mississippi. The privateer was fired upon from Fort St. Philip, at the Plaquemines Bend, and obliged to heave to. The brigs, displaying the flags of France and Spain, were allowed to proceed. Laffite declared that he had put in for urgent repairs, claiming the right of a ship in distress. Reports later submitted to Governor Claiborne provided evidence that Laffite's shortage of crew, described as caused by desertion, was the result of sales of slaves below Plaquemines; that the unarmed French merchantmen *Hector* was a captured British vessel sailing under forged papers; that the Spanish merchantman, also sailing under forged papers, was almost certainly carrying contraband; and that a captured American brig had been beached and burned by Laffite near Cat Island.* Claiborne seized the "French" merchantman but allowed Laffite to make repairs and depart. It was Claiborne's first experience of the Laffite family, and the court hearings taught him that evidence in New Orleans courts was as easily purchased as taffia.

In June, 1805, Jean, the youngest Laffite, sailed up the Mississippi to New Orleans to meet his brother Dominique You. He brought with him the spoils of his own successful privateering—prize goods and 12,600 pounds in British sterling. Resistance to Claiborne's decision to open a bank in New Orleans, which the Creoles believed would issue worthless paper money, and the depreciation of French and Spanish currency made Jean's fortune in hard cash doubly valuable but difficult to negotiate. This latter problem was surmounted for him by

---

*In the bay west of Bayou La Fourche. Not to be confused with Cat Island in the Mississippi Sound.

Joseph Sauvinet, a French businessman in New Orleans. When the brothers left New Orleans, they had acquired a new depot, below the bend in the river known as English Turn, where they could unload cargoes of slaves and contraband without interference from the American customs, and a new partner with warehouses and a respectable business to store and distribute their goods. Two years later, Jean bought his own warehouse in New Orleans and, in 1808, one in the village of Barataria. His first consignment of contraband to be landed on Grande Terre was put ashore there later in the year and transported by pirogues and flat-bottomed bayou craft to the head of Barataria Bayou and then by mule to the river and the city. The three brothers, joined by Beluche and other privateer captains, had made a promising start.

During the following five years, the Laffites gained wealth and power. They carried refugees to New Orleans from Haiti and the captured French islands, swelling the French and free black population of the city and arousing the enmity of the Spanish and part of the American population; they carried cargoes of slaves; they imported, free of customs dues, coffee, linens, silks, spices, wines, iron, mahogany—anything they captured; and they acquired, through the years, a powerful fleet of armed schooners and brigs and great stores of ammunition. The brothers had become well known in the city, where their wealth and the useful contraband trade they organized brought them more friends than enemies, and many of their friends were influential citizens. Jean Laffite, tall, elegant, and well mannered, was accepted by many of the best Creole families as a gentleman, which, in his own unconventional way, he was. The Laffites' organization was notorious, and its activities were a flagrant affront to the law; but Claiborne was to discover that it was not easy to take effective action against them.

The first attempt was made by Captain David Porter of the United States Navy, in 1810. Three Spanish vessels, reported as taken by pirates, appeared at the Balize, a pilot station at the southeast pass at the mouth of the Mississippi. All were carrying French papers and commissions, and one was listed as the property of Joseph Sauvinet. Porter went downriver with a group of gunboats and forced their surrender. The subsequent proceedings in the courts, in which Porter was represented by the astute Edward Livingston, were complicated and prolonged, and it appears that the district attorney was not indefatigable in his efforts to obtain a conviction. In due course, according to Porter's account, all three prizes were condemned, and they should have been sold and the proceeds delivered to the state. Porter should have received a quarter of the sum raised by the sale. It was presumably no great surprise to anyone but Porter when two of the three vessels slipped quietly away, without customs' clearance and still carrying their privateer crews. One of them later turned up again, escorting a prize which, when seized by the navy, was found to carry slaves subsequently sold for $45,000.

By 1811 Jean Laffite had become the acknowledged leader of all the privateers using Grand Terre and the Bay of Barataria. He supplied slaves and European manufactured goods to many of the wealthy planters and merchants of the district, and it was said that orders for the privateers' goods were received from as far away as New York and Philadelphia. Early in 1812 Laffite decided to make his business more accessible to the good citizens of New Orleans. He held an auction of goods at the Temple, an ancient memorial mound of shells built by the Indians, conveniently situated about halfway between New Orleans and Grande Terre. The auction was an enormous success. As merchants in the city openly canvassed for orders for Baratarian goods, the auctions at the Temple became occasions for fashionable gatherings where society ladies mingled with the motley collection of buccaneers of different colors and nations assembled by the gentleman-pirate, Jean Laffite. Claiborne, who had at first taken a lenient view of the Laffites' irregular activities because they helped refugees, came to look upon them as a public scandal which it was his responsibility to crush. He was encouraged in this view by the continuous stream of complaints he received from the Spanish consul alleging capture of Spanish merchantmen and illegal confiscation of their cargoes.

The State of Louisiana was created just six weeks before the United States declared war on Britain. Under the authority of the President six privateers were commissioned in New Orleans. One of them, the *Spy*, was commanded by "Oncle Renato" Beluche. In November Beluche captured a British vessel and took her, as his first legal prize, into New Orleans. After brief court proceedings he was awarded the ship and cargo. This success within the law proved to be small encouragement to the Baratarians to change their ways. Even if their captains had commanded all the authorized privateers, this would have provided an occupation for less than a quarter of their number, and the disappointing failure of the United States to include Britain's ally, Spain, in the declaration of war excluded the most numerous and profitable prizes from legal capture. Laffite and his men no doubt found it useful to have one of their captains in government employ, but their own business offered them more freedom, more variety, more action, and infinitely more attractive rewards.

In November, 1812, provoked by the endless complaints of the Spanish consul, Claiborne sent Captain Andrew Holmes with a party of almost forty regular soldiers to assist the revenue officers in the area of Lake Barataria. After a brief skirmish, Holmes succeeded, on the night of the sixteenth, in capturing three small vessels carrying contraband. Their crews included both Pierre and Jean Laffite. The brothers obtained their immediate release on bail by the good offices of their counsel, the ubiquitous Edward Livingston. When the district attorney at last filed a petition against them, in April, for more than $12,000, the Laffites were not, of course, anywhere to be found. Claiborne, in a moment of unbalance, caused a notice to be posted in the city offering a reward of $500 "to any person delivering John Laffite to the Sheriff of the Parish of Orleans." In reply, Jean Laffite printed a handbill offering a reward of *$5,000* "to any person delivering Governor Claiborne" to him. The governor, who was not famous for his sense of humor, did not find Laffite's impertinence amusing. He became more than ever determined to destroy the Laffites' organization, but he was uncomfortably aware that a great majority of the citizens of New Orleans were not with him. A number of the city's most prominent men, including Livingston, District Attorney John Randolph Grymes, United States Marshal Pierre Le Breton Duplessis, and Captain Henry Perry, ordnance officer in New Orleans, were involved in the New Orleans Association, an organization formed to supply Mexican patriots with arms and ammunition. This profitable trade was conducted by the eldest Laffite brother, Dominique You, and carried in his ships. Meanwhile, Renato Beluche, sailing under the flag of the rebel republic of Cartagena, had waged war against the Spaniards. In the three years before he took command of the *Spy* he was estimated to have captured or destroyed Spanish vessels to the value of $1,000,000.[113]

British shipping had not escaped the notice of the Baratarian privateers, and the Royal Navy was well informed of their activities. According to Jean Laffite,[114] a British warship appeared at Grande Terre in 1813 and tried to obtain the privateers' cooperation and a route through the hinterland to New Orleans but was driven away by the false information that warships of the United States were in the vicinity. This story is apparently unsupported by any evidence from naval records and is probably a fabrication. The United States Navy was known to be skillful but small, and the British, conscious of their superiority, invited action on every occasion.

In July, 1814, Claiborne scored his first success against the Baratarians. Pierre Laffite, against whom writs were still out, showed himself too brazenly in New Orleans and was arrested by the city marshal. In spite of the efforts of his counsel, Pierre was denied bail and charged as an accessory to piracy. He was consigned to jail, where although sick, he was kept shackled to prevent a second escape. This was a significant victory for the governor, demonstrating for the first time that the law could be invoked and enforced against the Laffites in spite of their wealth and influence.

On September 3, 1814, the British sloop *Sophia* anchored at the mouth of the channel to the Bay of Barataria, firing a signal gun to ask for a parley. Captain Nicholas Lockyer, commander of the sloop, put off in a ship's boat, flying a flag of truce and accompanied by Captain John McWilliam of the Marines. He was met by a boat, rowed from the shore with Jean Laffite in the bows, and conducted ashore. At Laffite's headquarters Lockyer presented him with two documents. The first, Colonel Nicholls' proclamation issued at Pensacola on Augest 29, was an example of the high-flown rhetoric commonly used at the period for such compositions. Its condemnation of the enemy government, sympathy for suppressed peoples, assurances of disinterested aid, and declarations of strength were neither more nor less pompous or convincing than many others written by both British and American commanders during the war and it does not merit the constant repetition it has been accorded. It was accompanied by a letter from Nicholls inviting Laffite and his men to "enter into the service of Great Britain."

The second document, a letter from Captain Percy to Laffite, was more revealing of British demands and intentions. Percy authorized Lockyer to "inquire into the circumstances" of the capture of certain British merchantmen, alleged to have been taken and sold by the Baratarians, and "to demand instant restitution, and, in the case of refusal, to destroy to his utmost every vessel there as well as to carry destruction over the whole place." In this Lockyer was assured of the support of the entire naval force "on this station." Percy was presumably counting on Laffite's being unaware that his naval force "on this station" amounted to four ships, none larger than a frigate. He went on to trust that such extreme measures would prove unnecessary. On the other hand, should the Baratarians be "inclined to assist Great

Britain in her just and unprovoked war against the United States, the security of their property, the blessings of the British Constitution —and should they be inclined to settle on this continent, lands will, at the conclusion of the war be allotted to them in His Majesty's colonies in America." In return, Percy demanded to have handed over to him command of all privateer vessels (for which he offered "remuneration"), the "instant cessation of hostilities against the Spanish government, and the restitution of any undisposed property of that nation." Lockyer was also authorized to offer Laffite a reward of $30,000, a captaincy in the Royal Navy, and his brother's freedom.[115] He handed Laffite a copy of his own instructions from Percy.

Laffite asked for time to consult and persuade his men. The British officers were dined well and invited to spend the night ashore, an invitation they were obliged to accept as Laffite showed no sign of releasing them. The next morning, amid threatening demonstrations from his men, Jean Laffite returned the British to the *Sophia*. Shortly afterward he sent out to them his reply, written in French. Giving as his excuse for delay the presence at his headquarters of three troublemakers, whom he blamed for the "disturbance" when the British officers were ashore, and the need to put his affairs in order, he required two weeks to make a formal answer to the demands. He invited Lockyer to send a boat to the eastern point of the pass in two weeks' time. He assured Lockyer of his personal confidence in him and added, "with you alone I wish to deal, and from you also I will claim, in due time, the reward for the services which I may render to you."[116]

That day, September 4, Laffite wrote another letter. It was addressed to Jean Blanque, a lawyer, banker, and merchant in New Orleans and cousin of the last French prefect of the city, Pierre Clément Laussat. He was a respected member of the New Orleans legislature and also, incidentally, the owner of a number of the vessels sailed by the Baratarians and believed to have a more than casual interest in the illegal importation of slaves. In the hands of Raymond Ranchier, conveyed through the lakes by courier pirogues, the letter covered a journey which normally took three days in a bare twenty-four hours. With the letter were the documents received from the British.

Laffite's letter, often quoted in part, is far more revealing of his real motives if read in full. There cannot be much doubt that he intended it to be seen by Claiborne. It may, however, be doubted whether he had, at the time of writing, made a final decision. To Blanque he wrote[117] on September 4:

Though proscribed by my adoptive country I will never let slip any occasion of serving her or of proving that she has never ceased to be dear to me. Of this you will see here a convincing proof. Yesterday, September 3, there appeared here, under a flag of truce, a boat coming from an English brig, at anchor about two leagues from the pass. Mr. Nicholas Lockyer, a British officer of high rank, delivered to me the following papers, two directed to me, a proclamation, and the admiral's instructions to that officer, all enclosed.

You will see from their contents the advantages I might have derived from that kind of association. I may have evaded the payment of duties to the Custom House, but I have never ceased to be a good citizen and all the offenses I have committed, I was forced to by certain vices in our laws.

In short, monsieur, I make you the depository of the secret on which perhaps depends the tranquillity of our country. Please to make such use of it as your judgment may direct. I might expatiate on this proof of patriotism, but I let the fact speak for itself.

I presume, however, to hope that such proceedings may obtain amelioration of the situation of my unhappy brother—with which view I recommend him particularly to your influence. It is in the bosom of a just man, of a true American, endowed with all other qualities that are honored in society, that I think I am depositing the interests of our common country, and what particularly concerns myself.

Our enemies have endeavored to work on me by a motive which few men would have resisted. They represented to me a brother in irons, a brother who is to me very dear! whose deliverer I might become, and I declined the proposal. Well persuaded of his innocence, I am free from apprehension as to the issue of a trial, but he is sick and not in a place where he can receive the assistance his condition requires. I recommend him to you, in the name of humanity!

As to the flag of truce, I have done with regard to it every thing that prudence suggested to me at the time. I have asked for fifteen days to determine, assigning such plausible pretexts that I hope the term will be granted. I am waiting for the British officer's answer, and for yours to this.

Be so good as to assist me with your judicious counsel in so weighty an affair.

This letter has been accepted as proof positive of Laffite's loyalty, but there is some reason to suppose that Laffite had not then made up his mind to throw in his lot with the United States. It is significant that he began at once, without waiting for any reply from Blanque, to pack up his headquarters and to move from Grande Terre and the Bay of

Barataria. It is probable that he already knew of Claiborne's intention to send a combined naval and military force against him, but he may have hoped to persuade the governor to cancel the expedition and to release Pierre from prison. He had little to fear from the British. The narrow pass into the lake, commanded by the batteries on Grande Terre and Grand Isle, made the Baratarian territory a stronghold proof against any sea assault likely to be mounted by the fleet. From the land, however, the territory could be vulnerable to an attack by regulars accustomed to the country and guided by local knowledge. It is safe to assume that when Laffite left Barataria, it was the Americans he feared more than the British. At that moment he was in some danger of being attacked by both. In those circumstances there was nothing to be lost by revealing to the Americans the offers and demands made by their enemies. That Laffite had already decided not to join the British is not in doubt; to do so would have involved the loss of his privateer fleet, an end to his plunder of Spanish shipping, and a secondhand alliance with Spain. All of Laffite's actions at the time indicate an intention, far more in character than a sudden conversion to patriotism, to retain his independence by moving his entire organization to a new headquarters. It is evident that he hoped to achieve the release of his brother in return for a demonstration of loyalty, but it may be doubted that he intended anything more than a gesture for which Pierre's freedom would be a suitable reward.

Blanque, as anticipated, gave Laffite's letter to Claiborne, who called a meeting of the committee of the legislature to discuss it. He required the committee to pronounce on two questions: were the British letters enclosed with Laffite's genuine, and would it be proper for the governor of Louisiana to enter into discussions or correspondence with the Baratarians? Meanwhile, he sent, through Blanque, a message to Laffite asking him to take no action until a council could be called. The council's decision, strongly voiced by Commodore Daniel T. Patterson, U.S. Navy, Colonel George T. Ross, commanding the 44th U.S. Infantry, and Pierre F. Dubourg, collector of customs, was that the letters were a trick to obtain the release of Pierre Laffite and that the governor should have no dealings with Jean Laffite or his associates. Major General Jacques Villeré, commander of the Louisiana militia, dissented from this decision and advocated enlisting the help of the privateers in the defense of the state. Claiborne, who presided over the meeting and did not vote, also gave it as his opinion that the letters were genuine and regretted the decision not to employ the Laffites and their men. It was determined, instead, that Patterson and Ross should carry out the instructions already received to attack and disperse the Baratarian organization.

It seems probable that the committee's attitude to Laffite's overtures, if not the decision to attack his headquarters, was strongly suspected by Blanque, for on the night of September 6 Pierre escaped from jail. It is scarcely possible that this escape would have been planned at a time when his release might be anticipated. Blanque would have pressed the governor for some indication of his reply to Laffite's letter, and the evasiveness of his verbal message would have given Blanque sufficient reason to set in motion the plan to remove Pierre from his shackles.

At Grande Terre, a letter had come into Jean's hands, written from Havana on August 8. It described the arrival there of the small expedition under Captain Percy and Colonel Nicholls, destined for Pensacola, and related their plan to raise the Indians, secure Mobile, and march against New Orleans. The anonymous writer was persuaded that "the whole [Creek] nation are ready to join the British troops" and added that although the force was small, strong reinforcements were expected from Bermuda. This letter, too, Laffite forwarded to Blanque in New Orleans, and on the tenth he wrote a personal letter to Claiborne in which he again offered his services in return for "an act of oblivion for all that has been done hereto."

Claiborne could not be blamed if he had some doubts about the sincerity of Laffite's profession of loyalty. "I am the stray sheep wishing to return to the flock" came strangely from the pen of one who lived outside the law as leader of a band of cutthroat buccaneers and smugglers. Laffite asserted that his ships sailed under the flag of Cartagena and that his vessels were "perfectly regular in that respect," declaring, somewhat ingenuously, that "if I could have brought my lawful prizes into the ports of the state, I should not have employed the illicit means that have caused me to be proscribed."[118] If Laffite wished to claim the rights of United States citizenship, he could not use the flag of Cartagena to legalize his plunder of Spanish shipping. As a United States citizen he was engaged in piracy, but as a stateless individual, sailing under a flag of convenience, he could not bring Spanish prizes into the ports of his adopted country, which was not at war with Spain. To Claiborne he revealed his intention to leave Grande Terre "so as not to be held to have co-operated with an invasion at this point." By the time his letter reached the governor, Patterson and Colonel Ross were already on their way to attack Grande Terre.

Laffite moved the greater part of his stores of arms and ammunition inland. Ships were loaded with the most valuable merchandise and sailed with him to Isle Dernière some 40 miles to the west. Pierre, who was ill, was sent by pirogue to a hideout on Bayou La Fourche. Their eldest brother, Dominique You, was left in command of about 500 men at Grande Terre. If the British arrived in overwhelming strength, he was to defend the island for as long as he could before burning the vessels in the bay and escaping into the hinterland of swamp where the British would not be able to follow.

On the morning of September 16, Patterson's flotilla of six gunboats, carrying a strong detachment of the 44th Regiment and led by the schooner *Carolina*, arrived off Grande Terre. Dominique You, prepared for the British, could not fire upon the flag of the United States at a time when his brother, and leader, was protesting to the governor his loyalty to that flag. He directed his men to set fire to ships and warehouses and disperse. Patterson and Ross took eighty of them prisoner, including You, and loaded twenty-six captured vessels with merchandise which subsequently became the subject of a prolonged lawsuit. You and his men, who had surrendered without firing a shot, were taken to New Orleans and imprisoned in chains. Patterson filed a suit for prize money, the customs authority filed for possession of all contraband, and the Baratarians, charged with piracy, filed for restitution of the property of Cartagena.

Captain Lockyer, of the British sloop *Sophia*, kept his appointment at the eastern point of the pass into the Bay of Barataria two weeks after his meeting with Laffite, and immediately after taking part in the abortive attack on Fort Bowyer, but found Grande Terre deserted. He returned to report to Captain Percy that his mission had not been successful. It is unlikely that anyone anticipated the cost to the British of this failure.

XV

Jackson in New Orleans

In September, 1813, Claiborne had written to Lieutenant Colonel Michel Fortier expressing his fears of an attack on New Orleans by reunited Creek and Choctaw. Jackson's campaigns and the crippling treaty he had imposed on the Creek nation had dispersed that threat, but it had been succeeded by another, even more dangerous, of a British invasion. On August 8, Claiborne wrote to Major General Jacques Villeré, "The aspect of Affairs is menacing, and we must unite hand and heart in making every preparation for the defence of the State."[119] By the middle of September he was obsessed by a new fear: a slave insurrection. His directive to commanders of militia regiments[120] showed that his apprehension was augmented by imagination:

> Having every reason to believe that there are Agents of the Enemy busily engaged in exciting our Negroes to insurrection, you are hereby required to cause regular Patrol service to be performed within the limits of your command ... to take care that all negro Cabins and other places where arms are most likely to be concealed be closely examined, and that the greatest vigilance and activity be exerted in arresting and carrying before some Judge or Justice of the Peace for examination, all & every person whose conduct, and character, should form reasonable ground of suspicion of his intrigues with the Negroes, or being in any manner connected with the Enemy.

Claiborne hastened to send Jackson the Laffite documents, and kept him informed of the proposed attack on the Baratarian headquarters, a measure of which Jackson approved as thoroughly as he disapproved

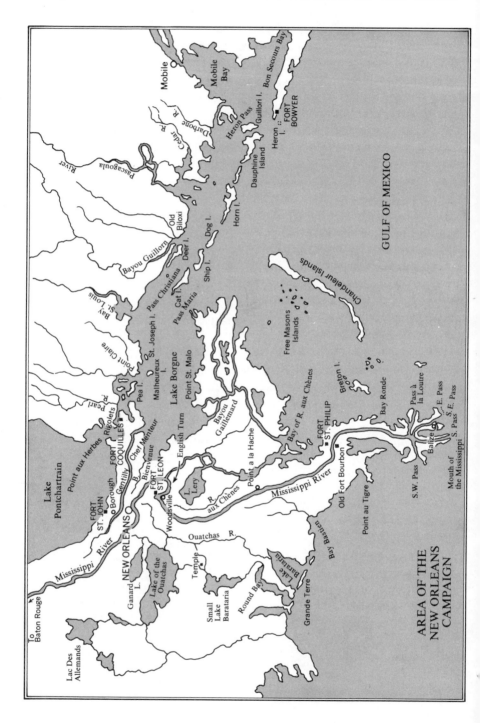

AREA OF THE
NEW ORLEANS
CAMPAIGN

of the Laffites. To Claiborne's mournful complaint that he found[121] "in this city a much *greater Spirit of Disaffection* than I had anticipated, and among the faithful Louisianians there is a *Despondency* which palsies all my preparations.... Laffite and his associates might probably be made useful to us," Jackson replied,[122] declaring his disgust that "those wretches, the refugees from Barataria ... should find an asylum in your city," and added forcefully, "Cause them to be arrested." Jackson's attitude to the Baratarians was made public in his proclamation,[123] posted in New Orleans and elsewhere in the state in answer to Colonel Nicholls' effusion at Pensacola. This composition had at least the forceful style of his personality. His reference to "the base, perfidious Britons ... with their incongruous horde of Indians and negro assassins" is authentically Jacksonian. He ended with a fine, but in the circumstances unfortunate, flourish: "I ask you, Louisianians, can we place any confidence in the honor of men who have courted an alliance with pirates and robbers? ... Have they not made offers to the pirates of Barataria to join them, and their holy cause? And have they not dared to insult you by calling on you to associate, as brethren with them, and this hellish banditti?" Claiborne meekly and untruthfully reported to Jackson that his address had been "well received." It was left to Edward Livingston, who combined the shrewdness of the lawyer with the ambition of the politician, to change the climate of Jackson's opinion. As the Laffites' lawyer, the chairman of the Committee of Public Safety for New Orleans, and an old friend of Jackson's from the days when they had served together in the House of Representatives, he was in a unique position to do so.

On September 25, Monroe wrote to Governor Blount of Tennessee of his belief that the British intended to attack "thro the mobile." Blount forwarded a copy of this letter to Jackson, who had arrived at Mobile on August 22. His analysis of the situation bears a startling resemblance to Cochrane's. Of Mobile he wrote:[124] "A real military man, with full knowledge of the geography of . . . this country, would first possess himself of that point, draw to his standard the Indians, and march direct to the walnut Hills* . . . and being able to forrage on the country, support himself, cut off all supplies from above and make this country an easy conquest." Though this was not written until February, 1815, it was the assumption which guided all his actions until circumstances forced him to change his plan. It was not, however, in Jackson's nature to fight a purely defensive war. He began his

---

*Site of the Battle of Vicksburg in 1863.

defense of New Orleans by attacking the last Spanish possession in the Floridas, Pensacola. After the failure of the British attempt on Fort Bowyer, the Spanish governor of Pensacola had asked for assistance against a threatened American attack. Captain Percy, with Colonel Nicholls and his troops aboard, arrived there on October 31, but they found Fort Barrancas, the single strongpoint, in ruins and no inclination on the part of the Spanish to put it into a state of defense. When Jackson arrived on November 6 with more than 3,000 men, the British blew up Fort Barrancas and withdrew, taking with them a number of friendly Creek and about 200 Spanish troops who preferred to leave.

Jackson was deprived of the victory he had anticipated, and he had deliberately violated the neutrality of Spain. He had, it is true, written to Monroe to inform him of his intentions and admitted that he acted without orders from the government, but his letter, dated October 26, left no time for any reply from the Secretary of War to stop the attack. The government in Washington viewed the escapade with pained disbelief. It appeared to have left all the most vulnerable points of attack unguarded while Jackson satisfied a personal ambition which achieved nothing and caused violent diplomatic repercussions. In fact, Jackson moved his army with Napoleonic speed (he and his army were back in the Mobile area in three and a half days), and his lightning capture of Pensacola and the hurried withdrawal of the British had dealt a deathblow to British prestige among the Creek. It had also given John Coffee's Tennesseans an encouraging first sight of redcoats, in retreat.

Jackson was not deaf to the cries for help he received constantly from New Orleans. Claiborne's anxieties depressed and irritated him. Even in his most sanguine moods the governor was a prey to fears for the future. "The Legislature has not as yet done anything to damp the public ardor . . ." he wrote. "But I fear, I much fear, they will not act with the promptitude and the energy which the crisis demands." Livingston's letters were calmer, but he too urged Jackson to visit New Orleans to "overawe disaffection." Jackson remained convinced that the British would attack through Mobile, and he would not move from there until that approach was satisfactorily covered. Fort Bowyer was strengthened until the general was convinced that "ten thousand troops cannot take it," and regiments of regulars and militia were posted north of the town, as reserves to be hurried to any point of attack. Command of the area was given to Brigadier General James Winchester,* an old friend of Jackson's from his Cumberland militia

*See p. 96.

days before the war. Taken prisoner in January, 1813, and later exchanged, Winchester had not forgotten that his wounded had been massacred at the Raisin River. In giving him command of the station he considered the key to New Orleans, Jackson told him it "must be maintained," but he would be taking no risk; wherever the British chose to attack, Jackson intended to be there to command the defenses.

Jackson left Mobile for New Orleans on November 22. He spent eleven days on the journey, taking a leisurely but necessary and detailed look at the terrain and noting the possible points of attack on the way. He'had sent for his wife, Rachel, to join him in the city, and he was expecting strong reinforcements. Taking advantage of the dislocation of the government in Washington, he had sent out urgent demands for troops from Mississippi, Tennessee, and Kentucky, characteristically disregarding the inconvenient fact that Kentucky was outside his military jurisdiction. His trusted friend of the Creek campaigns John Coffee was already in the field, and William Carroll was raising the Tennessee militia to join him. Jackson showed signs of fatigue but seemed confident. He believed he knew the British plan and that he had taken the right steps to counter it. The troops assembling under his command should be sufficient, behind fortifications and in a mobile defensive role, to repel an invasion by an army unaccustomed to the climate and ignorant of the terrain. Monroe had miraculously raised $100,000 from the bankrupt Treasury to pay for Jackson's army and its supplies. The greatest cause for anxiety was the serious lack of ammunition.

On November 14 at Nashville, Brigadier General William Carroll issued a proclamation calling for volunteers. It was a well-judged composition appealing to self-interest:[125] "The exigency of the times require [*sic*] our immediate march to the lower country there to protect that section of our union which is so important to the people westward of the Alleghany [*sic*] mountains. The City of New Orleans is the grand depot of the products of our country and every one of us ought to feel a strong interest in defending this great Mart of trade and source of Wealth to the upper country." When he issued the proclamation, the river was too low to float the boats, but within a few days "the clouds thickened, the rains descended, and the waters rushed down their channel with rapidity." Young William Priestley, attached to Carroll's staff, kept a diary[126] of the expedition, his florid style underlining his belief in the importance of the events he witnessed. Carroll had received orders from Jackson to march overland, but he disobeyed them. The river route, though longer, was faster, and Carroll was convinced that the situation demanded the exercise of his initiative. It is a notable indication of Jackson's gift for leadership that his closest and most trusted lieutenants respected him but were not in awe of him. They trusted his military judgment but did not believe him infallible, and their own powers of decision and command were not emasculated by serving with him. For all his authority, Jackson had no more use for servile compliance than for interference or obstruction. He chose his subordinates for their ability to act in his absence.

On November 24, just ten days after his proclamation was issued, Carroll embarked with his staff. Two regiments had already departed downriver, to meet him with stores at Clarksville, Tennessee. His departure created some interest: "A numerous concourse of citizens of all ages had assembled on the margin of the river; the scene at every moment grew more solemn. The ties which had so closely cemented friends were about to be severed. . . . Adieus were heard on all sides, and heaven was invoked to shower blessings on those who were leaving their firesides, their Country and their friends."[127] Priestley's use of "their Country" is an interesting indication of the devotion of Americans to their state, a parochial loyalty that seldom extended far beyond its borders. At dawn on the twenty-eighth Priestley was admiring the country along the winding Cumberland River, "wild in a high degree . . . rugged cliffs rear aloft their tree-clad summits . . . miniature mountains sink into extensive plains." As the flotilla reached the mouth of the river at its junction with "the grand, the beautiful, the celebrated Ohio," the course became straighter and the country more level. On the opposite bank they could see in the moonlight the camp of Kentucky militia, who, Priestley noted with disapproval, "were far from being in a state of preparation to descend the river." On the thirtieth Carroll's boats reached the Mississippi, where the banks were "in some places fringed with rushes and in others decorated with the verdant [sugar] cane which flourished in profusion." Several of the boats stuck on a sandbar for two days, waiting for the waters to rise and float them off, and on December 4, Carroll's boat, caught in the turbulent currents of "The Devil's Race Paths" below the magnificent Chickasaw Bluffs, narrowly escaped being wrecked against "majestic trees [which] . . . reared their formidable heads above the stream threatening destruction to all who dared approach."

On the night of the thirteenth "The Invincible Band"—as Carroll and his volunteer company were known—reached Natchez, and some time was spent ashore the following day establishing a hospital for the sick and giving the men time for "putting their clothes in order, as their duties had hitherto been fatiguing." On the fifteenth the flotilla set out again, but strong headwinds reduced progress to about 20 miles, and they did not reach the Pointe Coupee settlements until the following day. There Priestley was inspired to indulge his descriptive powers: "as far as the eye could reach, Art had displayed her unwearied assiduity; numerous cottages, humble, but neat, peeped with their whitened fronts from behind the orange-trees, or the jasmin and multiflora climbed to the eaves, wandering with flowerless but luxuriant tendrils over their snow-white walls. . . ." This idyllic mood was shattered the following day. Carroll received a letter, confirmed on the eighteenth by an express from Andrew Jackson: the British had "appeared off Cat Island and were moving in the direction of New Orleans." Oars were manned to speed the progress of the boats, and all serviceable arms were issued to the men. Carroll sent on a message to Baton Rouge asking for all available arms. In spite of headwinds, which drove the boats ashore, Carroll pushed forward. Oars were broken, boats were towed, boats ran aground and were manhandled into deeper water, but Carroll would allow nothing to obstruct his progress. At four o'clock on the afternoon of December 20 he disembarked his men 4 miles above New Orleans, where he joined John Coffee's troops coming in by forced marches from Baton Rouge in response to Jackson's urgent order. Carroll had brought his men 1,300 miles in less than a month.

Major General Andrew Jackson had ridden into New Orleans early in the morning of December 1. After a brief breakfast at a private house north of the city, he was conveyed in a carriage to his allotted headquarters at 106 rue Royale.* Among the immaculately dressed leading citizens assembled to receive him, Jackson, tired and wasted by recurrent dysentery, cut an unimpressive figure. "His dress was simple and nearly threadbare. A small leather cap protected his head, and a short blue Spanish cloak his body. . . . [He wore] high dragoon boots long innocent of polishing or blacking . . . his complexion was sallow and unhealthy; his hair iron grey, and his body thin and emaciated." Many, however, noticed and reported the fierceness of his expression and the "hawk-like" eyes. Jackson's reception was warm, in spite of torrential rain which soaked the onlookers. Speeches of welcome were made by Claiborne and Mayor Nicholas Girod. Jackson replied briefly and his speech was translated into French by Edward Livingston. He

---

*Frequent renumbering of New Orleans streets since 1814 has created some confusion in the identification of the site of Jackson's city headquarters. The house he occupied was variously numbered 104–6, 92, and 412–14 during the nineteenth century and faced the old Banque de la Louisiane. The site is now occupied by the Civil Courts building (built 1907–9).

gave his pledge to "drive their enemies into the sea, or perish in the effort." If he was not to perish, there was much to do.

The lamentable state of unpreparedness in which Jackson found New Orleans was due less to Claiborne's failure than to the unique character of the population. The "heterogeneous mixture" which Claiborne had described some years earlier had not bred unity. The members of the legislature bickered among themselves, the Committee of Public Safety competed with the Committee of Defense, Claiborne's mobilization of the militia was openly ignored by anyone who did not wish to serve, and in the companies which had been assembled men took leave, changed regiments, or went home at will. The citizens of New Orleans appeared to be simultaneously in the grip of two conflicting influences—fear and apathy—and in the majority it was apathy which was the stronger. Claiborne, with the aid of Lieutenant Colonel William McRae and Colonel Arthur P. Hayne, sent to New Orleans by Jackson in October, had disposed such troops as he had at Barataria, English Turn, Fort St. Philip, and Terre aux Boeufs, but the detachments were pathetically small. General Villeré's letters displayed an acceptance of inadequacy bordering on despair. "Vous savez," he wrote, "tout ce que nous avons à craindre de *l'ennemi domestique*, et vous imaginez bien l'insuffisance de nos moyens en cas d'invasion."* This attitude, which was not uncommon, was anathema to Jackson. He soon identified his allies. Livingston, who offered his services as the general's aide, was appointed colonel; Commodore Patterson's naval resources were small, but he was able and determined; Colonel Ross of the 44th Regiment reported well of his 500 regulars; and Arsène Lacarrière Latour, an experienced engineer recommended by Livingston, was appointed major and principal engineer to the Seventh Military District. With Major Howell Tatum, Jackson's engineer, and his own assistants Bonneval Latrobe and Lewis Livingstone, Latour accompanied Jackson on his inspection of the city's defenses.

On December 3, Jackson reviewed the uniformed Battalion of New Orleans Volunteers in the Place d'Armes. Commanded by Major Jean Baptiste Plauché, the five companies—Carabiniers d'Orleans, Dragons à Pied, Francs, Chasseurs, and Louisiana Blues—were predominantly Creoles. Young men of good family served in their ranks beside veterans of Napoleon's armies in Europe. The exception was the

---

*"You know how much we have to fear from *the enemy within,* and you can well imagine the inadequacy of our resources in the event of invasion."

Louisiana Blues, a regiment containing a number of Irishmen and commanded by an Irish expatriate, Maunsel White, who had married the daughter of the wealthy Pierre Denis de La Ronde. The companies made a brave show in their colorful uniforms, bought, as were their weapons, from subscriptions, but their numbers were pitifully small, less than 100 to each company. In October, Philogène Favrot had written from Nashville to his mother at Baton Rouge:

> You appear to fear the invasion of our country by the English and the Indians; you are forgetting that General Jackson, who is at Mobile, has under his command five regiments of regular troops. . . . Tennessee has provided four thousand five hundred militia and the territory of Mississippi will provide five thousand; a regiment of 1000 cavalry will be raised in Kentucky . . . in the space of one month Jackson will have twelve or fourteen thousand men under his command without counting the Louisiana militia.[128]

It was evident that this overoptimistic reliance on help from other states was also the prevailing mood of the citizens of New Orleans. Until Jackson's arrival they made small attempt to help themselves. Favrot reported to his wife that Jackson's presence revived the spirits of the New Orleanians and "resuscitated Clabo [Claiborne] the very day he entered the town."

Jackson's presence in fact revived and resuscitated everyone he met. His boundless energy and apparent confidence and his ruthless removal of obstacles and obstructionists commanded respect and immediate obedience. He spent the better part of two days in the saddle inspecting, planning, encouraging, and issuing a steady stream of precise and succinct orders. Within twenty-four hours of his arrival he was familiar with the few existing maps of the area; within forty-eight he had given the necessary orders to cover approaches to the city from Bayou La Fourche on the west to Lake Borgne on the east. On December 4 he set out to reconnoiter the river.

Jackson's defensive plan was based on the obstruction of as many as possible of the approaches so that his limited resources could be concentrated. To the west, Bayou La Fourche, in reality a branch of the Mississippi starting from a point midway between New Orleans and Baton Rouge and debouching into the Gulf some 80 miles west of the delta, and Barataria Bay, 10 miles to the east, offered indirect and complex routes to the city. To the east of the river, Lake Borgne provided a number of practicable approaches: by the ascent of Bayou Chef Menteur to the Gentilly Plain; by Bayou Bienvenue to the plan-

tations along the straight stretch of the river below the city; by Bayou
Terre aux Boeufs to the river at English Turn; or through the Rigolets,
narrow and treacherous straits from Lake Borgne into Lake
Pontchartrain, and into the city by the Bayou St. John road. Last,
there was the great highway of the river itself.

There was little chance, in the time available, that any of these
approaches could be permanently sealed, and the forces at Jackson's
disposal did not permit him to guard them with troops in sufficient
strength to do more than create a temporary delay. To be effective,
Jackson's army had to be concentrated and preserved for a decisive
battle. He also had to have warning of the enemy's advance and gain
time to draw the British onto ground of his choosing. One of his first
actions was to give orders for the obstruction of the bayous and their
subsidiary creeks, or coulees, and to post small detachments at strategic
points to give the alarm. On Lake Borgne Commodore Patterson
posted five gunboats, with the schooner *Sea Horse* and a tender, the
Alligator, under the command of Lieutenant Thomas ap Catesby Jones.
These were to be the eyes and ears of Jackson's defense of the eastern
routes to the city.

Jackson had decided not to attempt any defense of the river below
Fort St. Philip, midway between the delta and English Turn. This fort,
which had to be the first and main defense of the river, was built on a
spit of land almost surrounded by the Mississippi and impassable
swamp and commanding a long stretch of the river downstream. The
turn of the river and the enclosing quagmire made this a natural
strongpoint. Jackson inspected the ramparts, which were in a fair state
of repair, and the twenty-eight 24-pounder cannon. On his orders the
inflammable wooden barracks were demolished, the guns augmented
by a 32-pounder, and two new batteries were erected, one across the
river at the ruined Spanish Fort Bourbon, and a second half a mile
upstream. The garrison was reinforced. At English Turn the old Fort
St. Leon had decayed. Jackson ordered the immediate construction of
batteries protected by earthworks, and another battery was mounted
at a point covering part of Bayou Terre aux Boeufs.

Jackson was out of the city for six days, but he sent back a stream of
orders to his engineers, demands to the governor, and requisitions for
troops and stores. On his instructions the slaves of the riverside plantations were called in to throw up earthworks and erect batteries. He
accepted Pierre Jugeat's offer to raise a battalion of friendly Choctaw
and approved the request of Jean Baptiste Savary to form a battalion
of free men of color from among the refugees from Santo Domingo.

Command of the latter was given to Major Jean Daquin. To the assistant paymaster who questioned Jackson's authority to employ black men in the army, the general replied with acerbity:[129] "Be pleased to keep to yourself your opinions. . . . It is enough for you to receive my order for the payment of the troops with the necessary muster rolls without inquiring whether the troops are white, black, or tea." This was the second black battalion in New Orleans. The employment of free blacks in military service had been known in New Orleans since 1729. "Le Grand Marquis" Vaudreuil had listed a force of between 200 and 300 black soldiers "to be relied upon," and the Spanish governors had employed them in militia units to preserve law and order. The arrival of American government and American attitudes to blacks, had given Claiborne, who was in favor of recommissioning the black battalion in United States service, severe problems. In spite of the vociferous protests of many of the citizens who believed that the loyalty of the blacks was unreliable, Claiborne's wish to employ them was approved by Congress, and in 1811 the two companies were used with surprising success to put down a slave insurrection. In 1812 Claiborne commissioned two of their number as second lieutenants, and in August, 1814, the battalion was one of the few units of militia to carry out regular training. It is to Claiborne's credit that the battalion existed, but public opinion had prevented his enrolling the numbers he could have obtained. Colonel Michel Fortier, who armed and equipped his men at his own cost, was appointed to overall command of the two battalions of free "men of color."

Jackson returned to the city on December 10. He has been much criticized for spending so much time on personal reconnaissance, and his behavior has been compared with that of Winder before Washington.[130] This is grossly unjust. Winder's frenetic gallops produced no constructive result whatever. (On the contrary, having made himself thoroughly familiar with the countryside, he spent four vital days sitting in his office dealing with papers and then made a series of decisions which would have disgraced a recruit who had not been trained to read a map.) In contrast, the results of Jackson's reconnaissance, which he made with the senior naval officer and his engineers, were visible in the strengthening of fortifications, the erection of batteries, the obstruction of the approaches to the city, and the placing of outposts. The suggestion that had he been "better acquainted with military history" he would have remained in the city, forming "entrenched camps," invites the conclusion that such an acquaintance would have been confined to the history and ignored its lessons.

Without prior knowledge of which of the many available routes to the city the British would choose, Jackson would have been obliged to form his "entrenched camps" close to the city. Exposed to a siege by troops which had stormed Badajoz, New Orleans would have fallen to the British. The final answer to the comparison is that Washington was sacked.

Jackson returned to the city on the tenth but set out again two days later to inspect the routes from the head of Lake Borgne. The waterways through from Lake Borgne to Lake Pontchartrain were well named the Rigolets. By a seaman's standard they were little more than trenches or gutters, winding through to the pass at Petites Coquilles, where a sandbar prevented the passage of any vessel with a draft of five feet or more. The pass was commanded by a small fort, unfinished but providing some protection for the batteries mounted there. The Chef Menteur road, winding beside the bayou from its mouth at the north of Lake Borgne, through the Plain of Gentilly to Bayou St. John, afforded a 20-mile approach on firm ground. Jackson ordered a battery to be mounted on the road, and Fort St. John, at the mouth of the bayou extending from Lake Pontchartrain to the outskirts of the city, was strengthened and reinforced.

Had Jackson remained in the city he could not have accomplished much for its defense, but his time would have been fully occupied with politics. He had brought from Pensacola an introduction from Don Juan Ventura Morales, who had been Spanish intendant at New Orleans, to his son-in-law, Bernard de Marigny de Mandeville. According to Marigny,[131] Jackson had written to him from Fort St. John indicating that he would be glad to use the Marigny house as his headquarters. It was a remarkable suggestion, for Jackson must have been aware that Don Juan had been expelled from New Orleans by Claiborne for plotting against the American government. If Jackson did consider using the Marigny residence, he had certainly thought better of it by the time his official reception was over. Marigny was not even invited to take part in this celebration, and watched it with other rain-drenched citizens from the street. When the general made his headquarters at 106 rue Royale, Marigny could not conceal his mortification. At twenty-nine he was a leader of the Creole aristocracy, stiff-necked, formidably rich, and a member of the Committee of Defense. As he saw Jackson falling, as it seemed to him, under the influence of the Americans—Claiborne, Livingston, Patterson, Ross—he resented the slight to Creole society and power. Swallowing the insult, he had called on the general, before the latter set out on his

reconnaissance, to counsel the release of the Baratarians, but Jackson
had rejected his advice without spending time on discussion. Marigny
was not deflected from his purpose. While Jackson was out of the city,
Marigny conferred with Judge Dominick Hall at whose suggestion the
legislature was persuaded to pass a resolution demanding the suspension of all charges against the Baratarians for a period of four months.
The judge ordered the district attorney to suspend prosecution. Where
Livingston and General Villeré, both of whom advocated the release
and employment of the Baratarians, had failed, Marigny succeeded.
When Jackson returned from his second reconnaissance, the prisoners
were set free, though the charges against them remained on the lists for
hearing at an unspecified date in the future.

During his brief stay in New Orleans between inspections Jackson
was able to see a new spirit among the citizens. Volunteers were
pouring in. There remained the acute problem of providing arms and
ammunition for them. Stands of arms were known to be on their way
from Pittsburgh, but there was no sign of them. On the eleventh
unexpected help arrived in the unfamiliar form of the steamboat
Enterprise, skippered by Henry Miller Shreve.* Jackson immediately
realized the value of this rare power-driven vessel, impervious to tide
and headwinds, and dispatched it upriver to bring in the ammunition
barges he so desperately needed. That day he had received a report
from Patterson which made the need for arms more urgent than ever.
Lieutenant Thomas ap Catesby Jones had sighted the British fleet off
the mouth of Lake Borgne. To John Coffee, 135 miles away at Baton
Rouge with 2,000 Tennesseans, Jackson wrote: "I expect this is a faint
[*sic*]to draw my attention to that point when they mean to strike at
another—however I will look for them there and provide for their
reception else where."[132]

---

*The first steamboat on the Mississippi, built by Nicholas Roosevelt, had visited New Orleans
in 1812. Robert Livingston (brother of Edward) formed a partnership with the inventor, Robert
Fulton, to claim a monopoly of river traffic. This was successfully challenged by Shreve, who
opened up the Mississippi to free enterprise. Shreveport, Louisiana, is named after him.

XVI

The British Expedition

Major Harry Smith, who returned to London with dispatches after the burning of Washington, had married in 1812 a fourteen-year-old Spanish girl, Juanita, brought to him for protection after the siege of Badajoz. She had shared with him the dangers and privations of two years' campaigning in the Peninsula but had been obliged to stay in England when her husband joined Ross' expedition to the Chesapeake. Juanita was a girl of great beauty and courage, and Smith was anxious to see her again after their first separation. Their reunion was brief. Harry Smith was appointed assistant adjutant general to Pakenham and ordered to sail with him on November 1. On October 31 he set out from London by post chaise, accompanied by John Robb, surgeon of the 95th Regiment, who had been promoted inspector general of hospitals. They arrived at Portsmouth at midnight.

Major General Sir Edward Pakenham was staying in London at Warren's Hotel, Charles Street, St. James's Square, and it was there that his chief engineer, Lieutenant Colonel John Fox Burgoyne, and chief artillery officer, Lieutenant Colonel Alexander Dickson, reported to him. On November 1 the general and his staff sailed from Spithead aboard the frigate *Statira*. With them went Major General Samuel Gibbs and about thirty passengers. They were cramped in their quarters. Pakenham, Gibbs, Burgoyne, Dickson, and Robb shared a cabin with the ship's commanding officer, Captain Spelman Swaine, and the rest, "Oh, so crowded! . . . slept in cots in the steerage."[133]

Pakenham's appointment to lead the expedition had been earned. It was true that the great Duke of Wellington, having married Kitty

Pakenham, was his brother-in-law, and Edward Pakenham had friends in high places; but his military experience and proved ability amply qualified him for an independent command. Edward Michael Pakenham was the second son and sixth child of the second Baron Longford and his wife, Catherine. Longford, a captain in the Royal Navy, was described by one of his closest friends, the author Richard Lovell Edgeworth,* as "shrewd humoured . . . good and kind-hearted without parade," and it is evident that these qualities were inherited by his second son. In May, 1794, at the age of sixteen, Edward Pakenham was gazetted lieutenant in the 92nd Regiment of Foot.† By December 6, 1797, before he was twenty, he had purchased his promotions to captain in the same regiment and major in the 23d Ulster Dragoons. In September, 1798, he saw active service for the first time when the French landed an invasion force in County Mayo commanded by General Jean Marie Humbert. Seventeen years later Pakenham and Humbert were to find themselves once more on opposing sides of a battlefield. The French invasion was repelled. Major Pakenham was mentioned in General Gerard Lake's dispatches for distinguished service at the Battle of Ballinamuck and rewarded with the lieutenant colonelcy of the 64th Regiment.**

In February, 1801, Pakenham sailed for the first time to America, reaching Halifax after an uncomfortable fifty-three days at sea. There he met the governor, Sir George Prevost, with whom he discussed how the "hatred of Jefferson against England" might "mislead the ignorant and unprincipled multitude of the great Southern towns."[134] He spent more than two years in the West Indies before, in June, 1803, he joined the attack on St. Lucia, first of the islands in the West Indies to be captured in the British campaign to drive the French from their colonies in the region. Pakenham was shot in the neck in the assault and invalided home. He obtained a brevet colonelcy in 1805 and as colonel of the 7th, the Royal Fusiliers, attended the wedding in 1806 of his sister, Kitty, to Major General Sir Arthur Wellesley, K.B., "handsome, very brown, quite bald and a hooked nose."[135]

In August of the following year he was present, with Wellesley, at the bombardment and surrender of Copenhagen. In April, 1808, he was once more in America, and on February 1, 1809, he was shot, again in the neck, in the successful attack on Martinique. Wellesley's great

---

*Father of the novelist Maria Edgeworth (1767–1849). His son, Michael Pakenham Edgeworth, was a well-known botanist.
†The Gordon Highlanders.
**2d Staffordshire Regiment.

victory at Talavera in August, 1809, encouraged Pakenham to try for an appointment with his brother-in-law's army. In November he succeeded, becoming deputy adjutant general to the newly created Marquess of Wellington. His position on Wellington's staff, responsible for discipline, supplies, and the execution of the commander in chief's orders, gave him an unrivaled opportunity for observing at close quarters the methods of the greatest British general since Marlborough. Pakenham was intelligent and conscientious, and he longed for a command of his own. Until that opportunity came, he was obliged to be content to observe and learn, though he referred to his job as "this damned clerking business." In August, 1810, he was given a brigade which, to his delight, included his old regiment, the Royal Fusiliers, but his command was short-lived. Having led the brigade in the retreat to the lines of Tôrres Vedras, turning to give the pursuing Masséna an admonitory defeat at Busaco, Pakenham was withdrawn to his "clerking" while Sir Charles Stewart went on leave. On May 16, while Ned Pakenham was, on Wellington's orders, with Sir Brent Spencer in the northern sector, his Fusiliers were sadly mauled at La Albuera. Three months later he obtained his promotion to brigadier general and, once more, commanded a brigade, but again his period of command was brief. After distinguishing himself in a sharp engagement against Auguste Marmont at Aldea da Ponte in September, he succumbed, as did many others, to a violent fever from which he nearly died. He and Charles Napier were sent home to convalesce.

In January, 1812, Ned Pakenham was promoted major general. He celebrated by falling in love. The object of his affections, Annabella Milbanke, was attractive, not only in her person, but also in her prospects. Fifteen years younger than Ned Pakenham, she was the heiress of her uncle Lord Wentworth. Pakenham proposed to her but was rejected. She gave as her reason "that all the Pakenham family have a strong family tendency to insanity."* She subsequently refused Lord Jocelyn for the same reasons and compounded the error by marrying Lord Byron.

In April Pakenham was back in Lisbon, but a recurrence of fever prevented his joining the army before Badajoz, where his brother, Hercules, was severely wounded. When, in June, he was at last fit for active service, the illness of Sir Thomas Picton gave him command of

---

*There does not appear to have been any foundation for this remark, and Miss Milbanke was clearly no judge of normality. Kitty Pakenham was a nervous, unhappy creature, and a younger brother, an invalid who died young, appears to have suffered from acute depression. The rest of the family was not, it seems, any more eccentric than other Irish families of the period.

the 3d Division in time for the Battle of Salamanca. His behavior in this command led Wellington to acknowledge, in his official dispatch,[136] "Pakenham may not be the greatest genius but my partiality for him does not lead me astray when I tell you he is one of the best we have." From the most critical soldier then living this was praise indeed.

At the end of the year the arrival of a more senior general deprived Pakenham of command of the 3d, but he took over the 6th Division in the absence of Sir Henry Clinton, remaining in that command through the campaign of Vitoria, though, to his chagrin, his division was left to guard the rear of the army. Soon afterward Clinton returned, and Ned Pakenham was appointed adjutant general. He remained in this arduous and uninspiring job for the rest of the war in the Peninsula and was rewarded with a knighthood of the Most Honourable Order of the Bath.

Pakenham had hoped that he had "escaped America." When he received his orders, in October, 1814, to command the expedition originally entrusted to Ross, he revealed his true feelings in a letter to his mother:[137] "The Affairs in America have gone ill—staff officers have become necessary, and I have been called on by the Ministers to proceed to the other side of the Atlantic. I confess to you that there is nothing that makes this employment desirable—but under the circumstances of my improved health, I cannot resist a National call or the feelings of my Personal Duty." According to George Napier, whom he saw the day before he sailed, he remarked that he "much doubted the policy of the expedition or the correctness of the information upon which the Government had decided to make an attempt on that place."[138]

Three days out from Spithead, Captain Swaine opened his sealed orders and announced that his destination was Jamaica. Harry Smith records that this news "startled not a little several of our Passengers." Pakenham made a point of talking a great deal about Charleston, and Dickson began to copy a manuscript plan of the siege in the American Revolution. Burgoyne, less easily led astray, wrote,[139] "I can't believe we are going there with such a trifling force and equipment." Either he was unaware of the size of the force assembling at Negril Bay or he had a poor opinion of the defenses of New Orleans. It is hard to believe that any of the senior officers can have been in much doubt about their destination. Officially a secret, it had been reported in newspapers on both sides of the Atlantic. As Burgoyne wrote to his sister, "I take it for granted that we are going to seize upon Louisiana."

Harry Smith, Pakenham's assistant adjutant general, described the

Statira as "a noble frigate" with "a full complement of men," and Burgoyne wrote of fair winds; but progress was slow. Swaine was new to the captaincy of the *Statira* and unfamiliar with his crew. He was "of the old school, and made everything snug at night by shortening sail, to the great amusement of [the] crew, accustomed to carry on night and day."[140] There was some criticism of this apparent lack of a sense of urgency, and Swaine's navigation was not beyond reproach. Nevertheless, the general's party remained "lively and good natured" in spite of their seasickness. Dickson, who seems to have suffered particularly, made notes of winds, weather, and the ship's position, though Swaine discouraged any copying of his charts or log. The monotony of the voyage is revealed in Dickson's journal, in which he noted minutiae of such stifling tedium that the fall of one of the crew from the rigging assumes a positively festive air. Burgoyne later told his son-in-law[141] that "Pakenham . . . showed great anxiety on the voyage to arrive at the scene of operations before the troops had been put on shore."

It was December 6 before the *Statira* passed St. Lucia, and Pakenham's fears were aggravated by a meeting with Lieutenant Alexander Sandilands, commander of the brig *Swaggerer,* who told him that a fleet carrying part of the expedition and including the reinforcements under Keane had taken on troops at Guadeloupe on the way to Jamaica a month earlier. Dickson made some lengthy and complex calculations to show, as it happened overoptimistically, that Cochrane's fleet would have left Jamaica seven days before Pakenham could arrive. A week later the *Statira* reached the rendezvous at Negril Point, just twenty-four days after the date appointed for Cochrane to meet there the army from Chesapeake Bay. Cochrane had sailed about two weeks earlier, but waiting at the rendezvous was Major General John Lambert with 2,000 troops who had sailed from England a week before Pakenham. The three generals—Pakenham, Gibbs, and Lambert—conferred aboard the *Statira.* Lambert's troops, just arrived, needed to take on water and provisions before they could move. Pakenham in *Statira* hurried on, without landing on Jamaica, though Dickson noted gloomily, "I fear . . . we shall not arrive in time to partake of the operation."

Major General John Keane had arrived at Negril Bay on November 25. The force he was to command has been so grossly exaggerated* that

---

*The most recent American historian of the campaign puts Keane's troops at 8,000 and the total force, including sailors, at 20,000.

it is necessary to list it in detail. He had brought with him the 93d Regiment (Argyll and Sutherland Highlanders, 907), six companies of the 95th (Rifle Brigade, 488), a squadron of the 14th Light Dragoons, dismounted (160), the 5th West India Regiment and a company of the 1st West India Regiment (708), a company of artillery, a company of engineers, and a detachment of the Rocket Brigade. To these were added the brigade under Colonel Brooke from Chesapeake Bay: the 85th (King's Shropshire Light Infantry, 460), the 4th (The King's Own, 893), the 21st (Royal Scots Fusiliers, 995), and the 44th (Essex Regiment, 647). The total, including sappers, miners, and artillery, amounted to 5,498 officers and men.* The remainder of the 1st West India Regiment was expected to join the division in a few days. It was a formidable enough division to require no exaggeration. Cochrane had originally estimated that New Orleans could be captured from Mobile with little more than half the strength given to Keane.

Keane's position as commander was delicate. His orders indicated that he was to cooperate with Cochrane and to "pay every deference" to his views. Keane had never held an independent command in action. He had served in Egypt, at the capture of Martinique in 1809 when Pakenham was wounded, and he had led a brigade of Wellington's famous 3d Division at Vitoria. He had continued to serve with Wellington through the Peninsula, being promoted major general in 1814. Thirty-three years old, tall, and black-whiskered, he had acquired a reputation for recklessness. Harry Smith, who was one of the most experienced campaigners in the army and recognized quality in his leaders, wrote that he was "as noble a soldier as our country ever produced."[142] Cochrane, prematurely white-haired, was accustomed to independent command. Thirty-six years of naval service, of which thirty-two had been spent in command of a ship and the past ten as an admiral, had also accustomed him to giving orders and having them obeyed. In conference with Keane, he also enjoyed the inestimable advantages of having the confidence of the government at home and of knowing the coast against which they were to operate. It has been generally accepted that Cochrane browbeat Keane into an ill-advised and premature attack, but there is no evidence to support this theory. On the contrary, Keane's reputation for recklessness would not accord with any reluctance to seek action. It is safe to assume that the choice of the point of attack was Cochrane's. With Keane, he sailed in advance

*The figures are those given in Keane's *Journal*, sent to the Duke of Wellington *(Supplementary Dispatches,* Vol. X, pp. 394–95). Other estimates disregard Ross' casualties and regiments below strength.

of the army on the twenty-sixth to make a personal reconnaissance. The rest of the fleet, carrying Keane's division, followed on the twenty-seventh.[143]

"It is impossible," wrote Gleig, "to conceive a finer sea-view than this general stir presented. Our fleet amounted now to upwards of fifty sail, many of them vessels of war, which shaking loose their topsails, and lifting their anchors at the same moment, gave to Negril Bay an appearance of bustle such as it has seldom been able to present. In half an hour all the canvas was set, and the ships moved slowly and proudly from their anchorage, till having cleared the headland, and caught the fair breeze . . . they bounded over the water with the speed of eagles."

It is evident that Cochrane had already abandoned his plan to attack through Mobile. Captain Percy's unsuccessful assault on Fort Bowyer and the presence of Jackson's army in the vicinity probably helped convince him that a more direct approach could be attempted, but it is clear that he still hoped for assistance from the Indians. On board the *Tonnant,* Cochrane and Keane composed yet another proclamation to "The Great and illustrious Chiefs of the Creek and Other Indian Nations," offering the restoration of their lands in return for aid. The *Tonnant* put in at the Apalachicola and at Pensacola to distribute this exhortation and took on board some Indians. Rear Admiral Edward Codrington, aboard the *Tonnant* as Cochrane's "Captain of the Fleet," recorded his impressions of them in a letter dated December 14 to his wife:[144]

> I find I have not yet . . . mentioned to you the arrival of our magnanimous allies King Capichi and Hopsy (or Perriman), with their upper and second warriors, the Prophet Francis,* Helis Hadjo, the ambassador from the Big Warrior, &c., &c. We had the honour of these *Majestic Beasts* dining with us two days in the "Tonnant"; and we are to be disgusted with a similar honour here today. All the bodyclothes they get they put on one over the other, except trowsers, which they consider as encumbrances it should seem in our way of using them, and they therefore tie them round their waists for the present, in order to convert them into *leggins* hereafter. Some of them appeared in their own picturesque dresses at first, with the skin of a handsome plumed bird on the head and arms; the bird's beak pointing down the forehead, the wings over the ears, and the tail down the poll. But they are now all in hats (some cocked gold-laced ones), and in jackets such as are worn by sergeants in the Guards, and they have now the appearance of dressed-up apes.

*Taken home by the British after the Battle of New Orleans and subsequently returned in the full splendor of a brigadier general's uniform. He was captured by Jackson and hanged in 1818.

On December 1, Codrington had noted an agreeable drop in temperature from 84° to 70°, but by the eighth, when the *Tonnant* anchored between Ship Island and the Chandeleur Islands, the weather had "come on very dirty, and the Admiral did not think it advisable to send the boats after the five American gun-vessels." The "gun-vessels" were the flotilla commanded by Lieutenant "Tac" Jones, U.S. Navy. They carried twenty-three small guns, distributed among the seven boats. From the decks of the massive eighty-gun *Tonnant* the American naval force guarding the entrance to Lake Borgne must have appeared agreeably small.

Commodore Daniel Patterson's orders to Lieutenant Jones were brief and explicit: he was to proceed to Pass Christiana for reconnaissance, and if the enemy tried to cut off the gunboats, retreat to the Rigolets. There, with the protection and help of Fort Petites Coquilles, he had to sink the enemy or be sunk. Jones took station with his flotilla, as ordered, in Pass Christiana at the mouth of Lake Borgne, sending forward Sailing Master George Ulrick and Lieutenant Isaac McKeever in their gunboats to scout the Gulf. On the eighth they watched at a safe distance as the *Tonnant,* with four smaller men-of-war in attendance, anchored off Ship Island. On the ninth, after a brief reconnaissance to make sure that the enemy fleet had not been increased during the night, Jones took his flotilla into Bay St. Louis, where the boats were provisioned from the small fortified storehouse and magazine, and sent a message to Patterson warning him of the British arrival.

The entrance to Lake Borgne was too shallow over the bar to permit the passage of men-of-war, and the British fleet, which began to arrive on December 10, anchored to transfer the army from the heavy transports into lighter vessels. These, escorted by such gun brigs and sloops as could negotiate the shallow waters, made toward the lake, but it was clear that before any landing could be made, the American flotilla of gunboats had to be destroyed. Forty-five launches and barges were unslung and floated. Manned by 1,000 seamen and marines and commanded by Captain Nicholas Lockyer of the *Sophia,* the flotilla was rowed from the fleet at three o'clock on the afternoon of the twelfth. All through the cold night they rowed toward the American gunboats, pausing only when the combination of wind and tide obliged them to anchor. Each of the British boats carried one gun, mostly 12- or 24-caliber carronades. Lockyer divided his force into three divisions, commanded by himself and Captains Henry Montressor and John Roberts. At ten thirty on the thirteenth they were almost within range of the Americans, but Jones, who had at first thought that the British barges were aiming for land to disembark troops, realized that their objective was his own flotilla and began to withdraw. The *Alligator* had already been sent to report to Patterson the movement of the British fleet toward Lake Borgne, and Jones was left with his five gunboats and the schooner *Seahorse*. He sent the schooner to Bay St. Louis to remove stores.

Lockyer's flotilla was greatly superior in numbers but reliant upon the efforts of rowers and therefore vulnerable to the broadsides of the more maneuverable ships under sail. He was determined, as far as possible, to destroy the American force piecemeal. The detachment of the schooner *Seahorse* gave him his first opportunity. Cut off, it was attacked by the division of seven barges under Captain Roberts. Sailing Master Johnson took *Seahorse* under the guns on the shore and held off the British for thirty minutes but finally blew up both his schooner and the stores at Bay St. Louis. Lockyer's remaining two divisions rowed on toward the Americans.

To Jones' dismay he found that three of his gunboats, including his own, were grounded. Desperately the crews tried to float them, throwing overboard everything not required for battle. At three thirty in the afternoon, as the British seamen strained at their oars in an attempt to bring their barges within range, the flood tide began, and the Americans slipped away toward the Rigolets. At eight o'clock that evening Lockyer rested his exhausted men on their oars. The next morning at four o'clock he roused them again to their task and, after more than five hours, rested them, just out of range of the Americans, to eat breakfast. Jones had tried to take his flotilla into the Rigolets and under the guns of the fort at Petites Coquilles, but the wind died and a strong ebb tide prevented their movement beyond the western end of Malheureux Island. Calling his commanders on board his gunboat, he gave them orders to form close line abreast across the passage between the island and the mainland, anchored by the stern with springs on the cables to enable them to turn both broadsides to the enemy. With boarding nets spread, they waited for the British to come within range. As they watched, the little *Alligator* tender, which had carried reports to Patterson in New Orleans, appeared to the southeast and was quickly cut off by Captain Roberts' division. Armed with one 4-pounder, the *Alligator* could not put up more than a token resistance and was surrendered after firing a couple of harmless shots.

The ebb tide, which had prevented Jones from taking his boats into the Rigolets, dragged his own vessel and the gunboat commanded by Ulrick ahead of the line, breaking the regular formation and destroying their mutually defensive crossfire. It was even more hampering to Lockyer's barges. By ten thirty on December 14, when he began his attack, his seamen had been rowing for a period of forty-one hours, spending their rest periods at their oars and with no protection from the weather, which, at night, became uncomfortably cold. Seeing the enemy at anchor and ready to make a stand put new heart into the oarsmen. The Americans opened fire at extreme range, doing no damage. Lockyer reserved his fire until almost ten fifty,[145] when the engagement became general and destructive. An hour later Lockyer's division had concentrated on Jones' gunboat and began to board her while Montressor and Roberts assaulted the second vessel forward of the line, under Ulrick. Two of Lockyer's barges were sunk, and he was wounded twice before he and his marines succeeded in cutting their way through the nets and boarding the first gunboat. Jones, severely wounded, had crawled below, but his men fought a desperate battle on deck before they were finally overwhelmed. Ulrick's gunboat fell to the combined divisions of Roberts and Montressor, who turned the guns on the remaining American boats. Lieutenant Robert Spedden commanded his gunboat after both his arms had been shattered, John Ferris surrendered after his largest gun was dismounted and his boat boarded, and McKeever fought on until his decks became the target of all four captured American gunboats. At twelve forty the action was over, the British having 17 killed and 77 wounded. American losses were 10 killed, 35 wounded, and the whole of their crews taken prisoner.

The Battle of Lake Borgne reflects the greatest credit on both sides. The British enjoyed an overwhelming superiority in numbers; but their guns were small, and the long haul from the fleet to the enemy position, the last part under heavy and accurate fire and against a strong tide, required endurance and courage. The American gunboats were denied their greatest advantage, the ability to maneuver under sail and to draw the enemy under the guns of Fort Petites Coquilles, by wind and tide. Gallantly, they had gained precious time for Jackson and Patterson. No more could have been expected of them. Nevertheless, the news of their capture was a severe blow to Jackson. Though it had been anticipated, no provision had been made to replace the flotilla as the eyes and ears of Jackson's defense. No detachments or scouts from his army were anywhere near the lake. For ten days Jackson was without intelligence of the enemy's movements. It was an oversight which might have lost him the campaign.

Rear Admiral Codrington wrote of the battle:[146] "It is a most brilliant affair, and brilliant consequences may attach to this success. For, besides that we have already forwarded to the advance nearly one thousand troops in these five gun-vessels, we expect by their means to take a fort which guards an important pass. . . . These gun-vessels will probably give *us* the command on Lake Pontchartrain." This letter, written on the sixteenth by Cochrane's fleet captain, who acted as his chief of staff, indicates that it was still Cochrane's intention to move through the Rigolets into Lake Pontchartrain. There is no evidence to show when Cochrane and Keane abandoned this plan. It is certain that Colonel Nicholls had strongly advised the route through Lake Pontchartrain, and this advice was supported by some of Cochrane's naval staff working from maps which proved to be inaccurate.[147] The narrow passes of Chef Menteur and the Rigolets proved, on examination, to prevent the passage of any vessel drawing eight feet, and the advantages of striking from above the city appeared to be outweighed by the ample warning which would be given to the defenders.

While Keane and Cochrane questioned their prisoners and some local fishermen, the army was transported to the mouth of the Pearl River to be landed on Pea Island. This intermediate base was 60 miles from Cat Island, where the fleet lay at anchor, and it was soon found that the greater part of this journey had to be undertaken in ships' boats rowed by seamen. Battleships and large transports could not enter Lake Borgne, but every effort was made to bring lighter vessels part of the way to Pea Island. Codrington records the orders he gave to ships' captains:[148] "Keep on under sail after the smaller vessels ahead until your ship sticks fast in the mud; then find out deeper water, and go forward as far as you can get your ship by any means of lightening her." The flotilla of shallow-draft barges could not carry more than 2,000 men at one time so the sailors were obliged to make the round trip of at least 60 miles three times to row the army to Pea Island, and several more journeys were required to bring up equipment and stores.

Pea Island was not the most attractive of sites for an army encampment. After confinement for ten hours in cramped positions in the boats, the soldiers were turned out on "a swamp, containing a small space of firm ground at one end, and almost wholly unadorned with trees of any sort or description. There were, indeed a few stunted firs upon the very edge of the water, but these were so diminutive in size as hardly to deserve a higher classification than among the meanest of shrubs. The interior was the resort of wild ducks and other water-fowl; and the pools and creeks . . . abounded in dormant alligators. Upon this miserable desert the army was assembled, without tents or huts, or any covering to shelter them from the inclemency of the weather."[149] To add to their miseries, the torrential rain "such as an inhabitant of England cannot dream of, and against which no cloak could furnish protection," which accompanied the landings during the day, were succeeded by bitter frost at night. Many of the blacks of the West India regiments "to whom frost and cold were altogether new fell fast asleep and perished before morning." Dependent for provisions on the barges rowed from the fleet, the army was reduced to salt meat and ship's biscuit moistened with rum. Lieutenant Gleig philosophically accepted that this diet was "no doubt very wholesome."

If the sufferings of the army were severe, those of the sailors manning the barges were all but intolerable. Straining at the heavy oars for four or five days and nights on end, drenched by subtropical rains and chilled by night frosts, they fought hunger, physical exhaustion, and lack of sleep. "Yet in spite of all this, not a murmur nor a whisper of complaint could be heard." All, according to Gleig, "from the General down to the youngest drum-boy" seemed supremely confident of the expedition's success, and this was enough to compensate for whatever rigors the campaign might bring. By the evening of December 19, Keane's army was assembled on Pea Island.

On the sixteenth, two days after the capture of the American flotilla on Lake Borgne, two officers set out on a reconnaissance. They were accompanied by "an intelligent guide," presumably one of the fishermen living on the shores of Lake Borgne. The two officers were Lieutenant John Peddie, deputy assistant quartermaster general to the army, and Captain Robert Spencer from the navy. Their objective was Bayou Bienvenue,[150] and it is evident that in directing this reconnaissance Cochrane and Keane were acting on information obtained from local inhabitants. The Bayou Bienvenue, formerly known as the St. Francis River, drained an area of about 80 square miles into Lake Borgne, receiving the waters of innumerable smaller bayous and creeks. Its breadth varied between 100 and 150 yards with 6 feet of water over the bar rising to 9 feet during the spring tides. The principal branch of the bayou, running southwest toward the Mississippi and draining the canals from the Villeré, Lacoste, and De la Ronde plantations, was known as Bayou Mazant. The firm ground of the plantations, protected from the river by a 4-foot levee, was only 9 miles from the city. Peddie and Spencer sailed across Lake Borgne from Pea Island to the mouth of Bayou Bienvenue. About half a mile from there they found a village of huts where their guide obtained for them fishermen's hats and blue shirts as disguises, and they sailed on up the bayou. The land on each side was swamp and covered with reeds up to 10 feet in height. Turning southwest into Bayou Mazant to avoid the more open marshland of the upper reaches of Bayou Bienvenue, they soon found themselves in cypress swamp and then in the canal leading through the De la Ronde plantation to the river. Peddie and Spencer returned the way they had come, taking with them to Pea Island all the Spanish fishermen from the village except one who was sick. They reported to Cochrane and Keane that the route was practicable and concealed. If the army could be ferried across to the bayou and led secretly along the course of the Mazant to the road running beside the Mississippi, it could be drawn up a short march from New Orleans. On December 21, Keane issued orders for the advance.

Patterson received news of the defeat of his gunboats on Lake Borgne on the fifteenth. He immediately sent a courier with the news to Jackson, who was reconnoitering the Gentilly-Chef Menteur district, and shortly afterward dispatched purser Thomas Shields and surgeon Robert Morrell to the British fleet under a flag of truce. Shields was to negotiate the return of prisoners on parole, and Morrell would attend the wounded. Taken before Cochrane on Pea Island, they were informed that although their flag of truce would be respected, they could not be allowed to return to New Orleans until the British attack had taken place. They were sent aboard the *Gorgon*, where they found the American wounded well cared for. This story, which is supported by contemporary evidence, has been inflated and exaggerated to demonstrate the "outrageous spirit" of the British. Cochrane's refusal to allow Shields and Morrell to depart with all the information they had gained of British movements and intentions—a refusal made with perfect frankness from the first and totally justifiable in the circumstances—has been described as "duplicity unworthy of his high rank." This view, expressed by the earliest historian of the campaign, Lacarrière Latour, has been repeated too often to be allowed to go unchallenged. It is not to be supposed that any commander about to launch an attack by a secret route would permit enemy officers to return to their headquarters with valuable intelligence of his plans. It is all the more remarkable that this accusation has been accepted from a man who subsequently became a spy in the pay of Spain. There appears to be as little foundation for the equally popular story that Cochrane, noticing that Shields was deaf, placed him and Morrell in a cabin from which their conversation could be heard and was thus misled by their deliberately loud talk of the 20,000 troops under Jackson's command at New Orleans. Cochrane and Keane already had a sufficient number of conflicting reports about the state of the city's defenses not to be influenced by such exaggerations from officers they had already questioned. Nothing in the actions of the British commanders indicates that they believed, at this time, that they were faced by superior numbers.

Jackson galloped back to the city as soon as he heard the news of the battle on Lake Borgne. Still weak from dysentery, he issued a stream of orders to deal with the crisis. He sent a courier to William Carroll, urging him to hasten to his aid. To John Coffee at Baton Rouge he wrote, "You must not sleep until you reach me." The panic-stricken citizens of New Orleans felt, for the first time, the iron hand he reserved for an emergency. On December 16, Jackson declared martial law.

XVII

The First Battle

"The major-general commanding, has, with astonishment and regret, learned that great consternation and alarm pervade your city. It is true the enemy is on our coast and threatens an invasion of our territory, but it is equally true, with union, energy, and the approbation of Heaven, we will beat him at every point." Jackson's proclamation, issued on December 15, recorded his "still greater astonishment" at the reports of sedition. There were, it appeared, substantial numbers of citizens who welcomed the opportunity of a return to Spanish rule. Jackson was quick to undeceive them. Denying the truth of suggestions that the British would return the territory to Spain and denouncing Britain as "the common enemy of mankind, the highway robber of the world," Jackson added a message of undisguised menace:

> The safety of the district entrusted to the protection of the general, must and will be maintained with the best blood of the country; and he is confident all good citizens will be found at their posts, with their arms in their hands, determined to dispute every inch of ground with the enemy: that unanimity will pervade the country generally: but should the general be disappointed in this expectation, he will separate our enemies from our friends—those who are not for us are against us, and will be dealt with accordingly.[151]

The following day he declared martial law. "No persons will be permitted to leave the city. . . . Street lamps shall be extinguished at the hour of nine at night, after which time persons of every description found in the streets, or not in their respective houses . . . shall be apprehended as spies."[152] Under a safe-conduct obtained, probably by the good offices of Marigny, from Judge Hall, Jean Laffite called at 106 rue Royale and asked to see General Jackson. There is no authentic record of their conversation, and Latour, who knew Laffite well, is unusually laconic in his description of the meeting. Laffite offered his services, and those of all the Baratarians, in the defense of New Orleans. Jackson, subduing his prejudices against the "hellish banditti," accepted them. There can be little doubt that Laffite's offer was prompted as much by self-interest as by any feeling of patriotism. His eldest brother, Dominique You, with many of his most trusted captains, was under suspended notice of prosecution, and twenty-six vessels and goods conservatively estimated at half a million dollars had been confiscated by the state. There was good reason for Laffite to hope that his intervention at this time of crisis and the wholehearted cooperation of his men in the city's defense would be suitably rewarded with a general pardon and the restitution of his property. Jackson accepted his offer because he was able to do so without making any promises which might later prove embarrassing and because he needed all the help he could get. In addition to their value as artillerymen, Laffite and his men could provide Jackson with all the ammunition he needed from stores hidden in Barataria. Beluche and You immediately formed three companies of artillery while Jean Laffite, on Jackson's instructions, joined Major Michael Reynolds at the Temple, where he was supervising the obstruction of bayous west of the city. Laffite directed the removal of arms and ammunition to Jackson's magazine and returned to the general's headquarters. Having decided to accept his offer of help, Jackson intended to keep Laffite beside him and make the maximum use of his experience and intimate knowledge of local geography.

The defeat and capture of the five gunboats on Lake Borgne had deprived Commodore Daniel Patterson of most of his ships and all but a few of his regular sailors, but he believed that the navy still had an important duty to perform in the defense of New Orleans. He retained in the river the 14-gun schooner *Carolina,* the *Louisiana,* a merchant vessel which could be converted into an armed sloop, and three gunboats. One of the latter he dispatched to Fort St. Philip. With the help of the Baratarians he could furnish his vessels with the guns, powder, and shot they needed, but he desperately needed crews. Every day he saw seamen of different states or nationalities, idling in the streets of the city or along the levees, deprived of employment but unwilling to volunteer for service. Patterson urged Jackson to obtain powers to

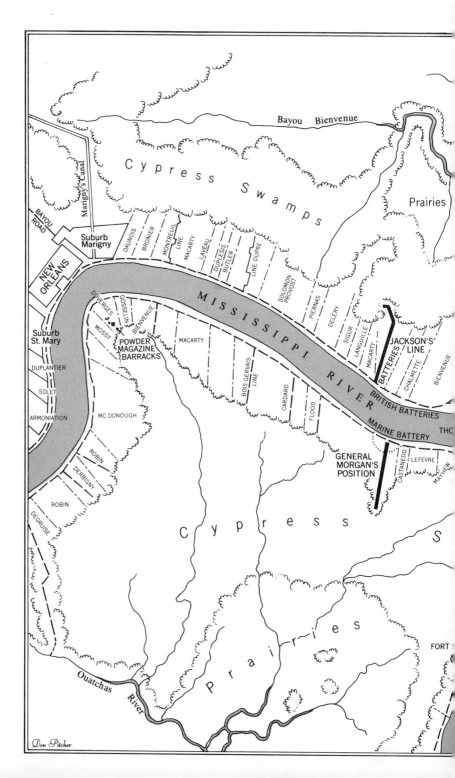

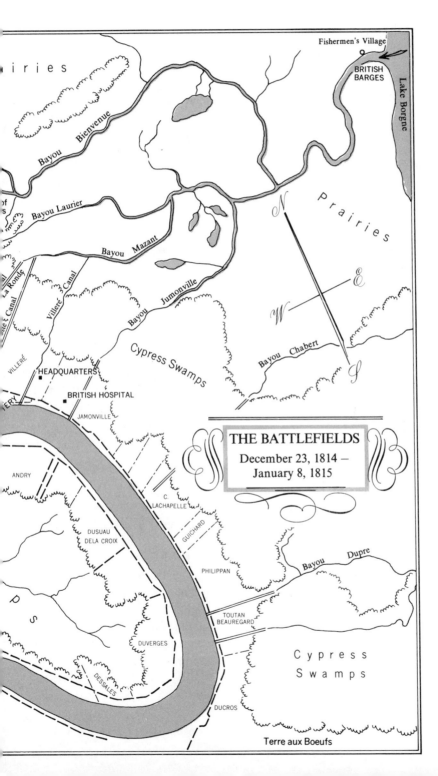

THE BATTLEFIELDS
December 23, 1814 —
January 8, 1815

impress these men. Claiborne approved the suggestion and asked the legislature for an immediate suspension of habeas corpus. Philip Louaillier, who was no friend to either Claiborne or Jackson and was not conspicuous for his energetic support of any emergency measures, rallied the legislature to declare such a suspension inexpedient. On purely legal grounds there can be no doubt that Louaillier's attitude was proper, and it was strongly sustained by Judge Dominick Hall. Claiborne's attempt to adjourn the legislature "for fifteen or twenty days" was also rejected. Sixteen thousand dollars were, however, allocated for the purchase of supplies for the militia, and Patterson was authorized to offer bounties to any sailors willing to volunteer for temporary service. Jackson's proclamation of martial law in the city freed Patterson to impress the men he chose.

On the eighteenth Jackson reviewed his troops in the Place d'Armes. It was the last Sunday before they were dispersed to their allotted defensive positions, and there was good reason to suppose that for many of them it would be their last day with their families. The numbers, though still pathetically small and inadequate, had more than doubled since Jackson's arrival sixteen days earlier. Two regiments of Louisiana militia were led by their honorary commander, Governor William Claiborne. The militia were under strength and poorly armed, but their lack of regimental uniform, at least, was redeemed by the finery of the governor, who had chosen a tightly buttoned tunic with heavy gold epaulets and a collar so stiff and high that his vision must have been restricted to the area immediately to his front. Plauché's battalion of Orleans Volunteers had attracted many new recruits. There was a prestige attached to service in those five companies which overcame the scruples of the least enthusiastic volunteers. Even the prosperous merchant Vincent Nolte found that a partially crippled arm would not exempt him from "malicious remarks" and suspicions that he entertained "a secret preference for the English" which would damage his interests.[153] Resplendent in their bright uniforms, they marched past with the precision and military bearing of regulars. These were troops accustomed to discipline, as Jackson noted with approval, and could be relied upon in any emergency. Lacoste's battalion of Free Men of Color, though less splendidly accoutered, looked well drilled and purposeful, and the general knew that Daquin's second battalion would be ready in a few days although it was not on parade. Last in order came Thomas Beale's Volunteer Rifles. Formed only two days earlier, this company mustered sixty-eight men, most of them merchants and lawyers past middle age but reputed to be fine marksmen. The total army on parade numbered less than 1,500.

To these troops drawn up in the square Livingston read out in French the addresses prepared by Jackson. He had been careful to compose three: one to the militia; one to the battalion of New Orleans Volunteers; and the third specially directed to the Free Men of Color. They were received with genuine enthusiasm by the large crowd and probably had a stimulating effect on recruiting, for several new volunteer units were formed during the following five days. After the parade the men dispersed to their homes for the rest of the day.

Jackson set about posting his troops. Until the arrival of Coffee and Carroll he could not hope to do more than cover the main approaches with troops that could report the enemy's movements and cause some delay, but he still made no attempt to post scouts near the shore of Lake Borgne at points where a landing might be made. A third militia regiment was raised and the command given to Colonel Denis de la Ronde, and a fourth, mustering in the Acadia district, was waiting to be brought to the city by Major General Villeré. To Fort St. John, guarding the approach from Lake Pontchartrain, Jackson sent the best of Laffite's gunners, including Dominique You and Renato Beluche. With them went Plauché's battalion of New Orleans Volunteers. Colonel Alexandre Declouet was already at English Turn with a regiment of militia. This was reinforced, and command of the area given to Major General David B. Morgan. The Gentilly road was guarded by a regiment of militia and Lacoste's battalion.

Major General John Coffee received Jackson's urgent order on the evening of the sixteenth. At four the next morning he wrote that he would be ready to move at sunup and expected to be in New Orleans by the evening of the twentieth. He was better than his word. With 800 of his men he rode 135 miles in three days, camping 4 miles above the city on the morning of the twentieth. Three hundred sick men had been left behind at the camp at Sandy Creek, and 450 more, who could not keep up with him, followed behind. On the same day Thomas Hinds brought in his Mississippi Dragoons, 150 strong. Jackson's army was assembling fast. He still looked for Carroll, on his way down the Mississippi with 3,000 Tennessee militia, and for Major General John Thomas, who followed him with 2,300 Kentuckians demanded by Jackson from a state outside his military jurisdiction.

Coffee's arrival, indeed his physical presence, put new heart into Jackson, whose sickly body was sustained only by his dauntless spirit. Coffee was built in the heroic mold--handsome, tall, powerful, courageous, and gentle—as thoroughbred as the splendid horse he rode, and he led some of the toughest soldiers in the country. Their appearance was startlingly unmilitary to the eyes of the New Orleanians accustomed to the brilliance of their Uniformed Volunteers. They wore "woolen hunting-shirts, of dark or dingy color, and copperas*-dyed pantaloons, made, both cloth and garment, at home by their wives, mothers and sisters, with slouching wool hats, some composed of skins of raccoons and foxes, the spoils of the chase ... with belts of untanned deer-skin, in which were stuck hunting-knives and tomohawks—with their long unkempt hair and unshorn faces."[154] They were, however, "remarkable for their endurance and possessing that admirable quality of being able to look after themselves."

With Hinds' battalion of Mississippi Dragoons came Captain Jedediah Smith's Feliciana Troop of Horse, which included, as troopers, Samuel and Reuben Kemper, famous for their part in the revolution in the Spanish Floridas in 1810. Jackson sent the Feliciana Troop to join Lacoste watching the Gentilly road.

At four o'clock that afternoon Carroll arrived,[155] bringing with him 1,100 muskets overtaken on the way and 50,000 cartridges made by blacksmiths on board one of his boats. The remainder of Coffee's troops, outdistanced in his dash to New Orleans, were in camp by nightfall. Apart from the Kentuckians, Jackson's army was complete. The Tennesseans made camp and settled down to cleaning their arms and equipment, mending clothes, and drilling by companies.

On December 17, Jackson had issued specific orders for the obstruction of Bayou Bienvenue. These orders were acknowledged[156] on the eighteenth by Major Gabriel Villeré, son of General Jacques Villeré, who had been given command of a detachment of militia guarding the approaches from the bayou through his father's plantation. Three days later, on the twenty-first, a detachment of the 3d Regiment of militia, "consisting of eight white men and a serjeant, two mulattoes and one negro, with a single boat," was sent by Major Gabriel Villeré to "the village of the Spanish fishermen, on the left bank of the Bayou Bienveneu, a mile and a half from its entrance into Lake Borgne, for the purpose of discovering whether the enemy might try to penetrate that way, and to give notice of such attempt."[157] When they arrived, they found all but one of the fishermen were absent. The sick man, left behind by Peddie and Spencer, told the Americans that his friends were away fishing. The detachment settled into the fisher-

*A ferrous sulphate, also known as melanterite or green vitriol, used for making ink and dyes.

men's cabins, posting a single sentry. That day and the next, three men were sent out to look for the enemy but returned without having seen any sign of the British. On the night of the twenty-second a single sentry was again posted while the remainder of the detachment slept soundly in the cabins.

At Pea Island General Keane detailed his plan in orders for the advance. There being insufficient boats to carry the whole of his force, he divided it into three brigades. The first, under Colonel William Thornton, was composed of the 85th Light Infantry and 95th Rifles, with part of the 4th Light Infantry, a detachment of rockets, and two light 3-pounders, the last described by Gleig as "convenient enough . . . but of very little real utility in the field." While this force was carried to the mouth of the bayou and as far up its waters as possible to Bayou Mazant, the second brigade, under Colonel Francis Brooke, would be embarked in gunboats and light transports and taken as far across Lake Borgne as the depth of water would allow. This apparently cumbersome maneuver would ensure the reinforcement of the vanguard by Brooke's brigade with the shortest possible delay. The third brigade would not move until the gunboats returned for them at Pea Island. The plan was daring and hazardous. Pea Island lay a full 60 miles from the mouth of Bayou Bienvenue, and the weather could not be relied upon to produce a flat calm on the lake. The first brigade, in flat-bottomed barges, could not be sailed or rowed across that distance in less than twelve hours, and rough weather would certainly take some toll of the heavily laden open boats. Having once landed, this brigade would be exposed to any attack the Americans might be able to launch against it for several hours before any reinforcement could reach it. Keane and Cochrane would watch the arrival of Thornton's brigade and then join it in the advance toward the De la Ronde plantation.

Much has been written, particularly during the past fifteen years, about the making of this plan. It is said, with repeated emphasis, that Keane was forced to act against his better judgment by Cochrane's hectoring and dominant demands. Keane is represented as a timid and indecisive commander who, throughout his campaign, allowed himself to be bullied into issuing orders he was too fearful to initiate.[158] None of the sources quoted by the authors concerned provides any evidence to support this theory. Cochrane's formidable strength of personality is well recorded, but there is nothing in Keane's earlier or subsequent career to indicate that he was fearful, timid, or indecisive. On the contrary, he had earned in the Peninsula a reputation for a certain recklessness as "a young and dashing officer,"[159] and his later career was one of considerable distinction. The criticism, made twenty-five years later, that he relied more on luck than considered judgment does not suggest that he was noted for his caution. There is no record to show whose plan it was to advance through Bayou Bienvenue. The statements that it was Cochrane's, followed unwillingly by Keane, are suppositions based apparently on the unsubstantiated assumption that it was timidity which prevented Keane from fully exploiting his first advance.

On the evening of the twenty-first, Brooke's brigade embarked aboard the gunboats captured from the Americans on Lake Borgne and other small vessels, remaining in them overnight. The next morning Thornton's advance guard of 1,600 men scrambled into their cramped open boats and set out across the lake to the western shore. Soon afterward heavy rain fell and continued throughout the day. It was succeeded, toward nightfall, by sharp frost, and the soldiers, cramped in one position without cover in the boats, became numbed with cold. Charcoal fires were lighted in the stern of each boat, but as dusk gathered, these had to be extinguished to avoid advertising the presence of the flotilla to any watchers on the shore. At midnight the troops arrived off the mouth of the bayou, where they cast anchor and hoisted the boats' awnings. Three barges went ahead to deal with the American picket. Accounts of this minor emgagement differ. Gleig states that the entire American detachment was found asleep, without a sentry, and was captured without resistance. Latour, who was not there and must be presumed to have accepted the accounts given by members of the detachment, states that the sentry allowed three barges to pass and ran to waken the rest of the picket who snatched up their arms and hid. Five more barges appeared and were also allowed to pass before the party ran for their own boat and tried to escape. All but four were captured. Three "wandered a whole day in the prairies and . . . happened to fall into the hands of the enemy, at the very village from which they had fled." One escaped. Difficult as it may be to accept the story given by the members of the detachment, the escape of one of their number, the fact of which appears to be established, is sufficient evidence that Gleig's account is inaccurate. Quartermaster William Surtees of the Rifle Brigade confirms[160] that one or two of the picket escaped.

According to Latour, one of the prisoners, a Mr. Ducros, was taken to Cochrane and Keane and questioned about the numbers of Jackson's army. His estimate of 15,000 was confirmed by other prisoners. Whether the British commanders believed this estimate is not known, but it accorded nearly enough with the information given by Shields and Morrell to be disquieting. Other reports, from American deserters* who might be considered more reliable, spoke of the confusion everywhere in New Orleans and the presence of no more than 5,000 troops at most. Keane ordered the advance guided by Lieutenant Peddie to continue and joined it himself.

The boats, which had been able to carry canvas across the lake, had to be rowed up the bayou. It was heavy work, and the noise they made would have disclosed their advance to any pickets or scouts posted in the area; but there were none. Nor was Bayou Bienvenue or its narrower branch, Bayou Mazant, obstructed in any way. Jackson's orders had been disobeyed by Gabriel Villeré, and the conclusion appears to be inescapable that his disobedience was deliberate. The route from Lake Borgne through Bienvenue and Mazant to the Villeré plantation was ideal for the passage of contraband, and there is no reason to suppose that the Villerés were immune to the temptations to which other plantation owners are known to have yielded.

At daylight the advance brigade, accompanied by Keane, had reached a part of Bayou Mazant too shallow to allow the boats to proceed. The depth of water had fallen by a foot since Peddie's first reconnaissance and there was nothing for it but to land the brigade close to the canal leading to the Villeré plantation. The boats were drawn up bow to stern and used as a bridge by the troops who formed in column behind a detachment of engineers. The land was soft and thick with reeds taller than a man which provided excellent cover. Led by Captain Robert Blanchard, the sappers cleared a way for the brigade, throwing reed and branch bridges over the ditches and streams too wide to be jumped by the soldiers. By ten o'clock the 85th and 95th were landed, and a strong detachment was sent forward to occupy a cypress swamp a mile ahead. At midday the 4th Regiment arrived, and the whole brigade advanced through the wood. The leading company of the Rifle Brigade scouted forward and reported that the Villeré mansion was occupied by troops. Leaving the rest of Thornton's brigade halted under cover, the 95th rushed the mansion and outbuildings, capturing the entire detachment of thirty militia commanded by Major Gabriel Villeré. While British troops searched the other buildings, Villeré was put under guard with his young brother and the rest of his detachment in his own house. Villeré's captors were already exhausted by twenty-six hours in open boats or

*Gleig's description. It is more probable that the informers were Spanish Creoles.

struggling through swamps, and their weariness made them careless. Choosing his moment, when the guards appeared to be less watchful, Villeré sprang for the window, leaped through it, and ran to the paling fence, which he vaulted into the open fields beyond. The riflemen fired at him as he ran, but he was not hit. Breathless but triumphant he reached De la Ronde's plantation, grandly called Versailles, where he found the colonel. Together they rowed across the river, borrowed horses, and galloped to the city.

In the evening of the twenty-second Colonel de la Ronde had reported several sails seen off the point of the three bayous behind Terre aux Boeufs. Jackson believed this news to be doubtful and sent Major Howell Tatum with Lacarrière Latour to investigate. They left the city at eleven o'clock on the twenty-third. Arriving at the boundary of De la Ronde's plantation and Bienvenue's, closer to New Orleans, they met a number of people escaping to the city who told them that the British were at Villeré's, and that Gabriel Villeré was captured. Tatum immediately returned to inform Jackson, while Latour went cautiously forward. Finding the reports to be true, he galloped back to the city.

Keane established his headquarters at the Villeré mansion while the 4th, 85th, and 95th regiments advanced to Lacoste's plantation, about half a mile upriver, and formed three columns between the cypress swamp and the river. A detachment of 100 men was sent to secure the rear, where a party of American militia stationed on Jumonville's plantation retreated before them.

The British position was precarious. Sixteen hundred troops had been landed and brought to within eight miles of New Orleans before their presence was detected, but their situation was weak. Their artillery consisted of two guns so small as to be almost valueless and a few rockets; the troops were in a state of total exhaustion from weariness, hunger, and lack of sleep; the river flank was unsecured against any vessels the Americans might have under sail, and the security of the right flank depended upon a swamp which the Americans might know how to cross; the rear was guarded by a detachment of 100 men against American forces downriver the strength of which was not known; no reinforcements could be expected for several hours; and, worst of all, Keane's lines of communication to Cochrane's fleet lay through swamp and bayou and across 90 miles of water. The greatest weakness undoubtedly lay in the absence of naval support. The strong current of the Mississippi and the shallow entrance over the bar at Balize prevented Cochrane from sending battleships into the river, and it was believed that the strength of Fort St. Philip at English Turn would prevent smaller vessels, dependent on favorable winds to take them through the sharp bend, from forcing a passage. Later Cochrane was to put this to the test, and without success, but by that time the defenses of the fort had been considerably strengthened. It is surprising that no attempt was made to support the British landing immediately after it was made. Although Fort St. Philip might not have been reduced, it might have been engaged while sloops and schooners slipped past into the river above. Through this failure the river, the great highway to the center of the city, became one of Jackson's greatest unchallenged assets in defense.

Keane deployed his advance guard and sent out parties to reconnoiter. They returned without seeing any enemy troops, and orders were therefore given to pile arms and light fires for a hot meal. It was the first hot food that any of Thornton's brigade had eaten since they embarked from Pea Island on the morning of the twenty-second, and after it those who were not on picket duty lay down beside their fires to rest. A few of the troops stripped off their clothes and bathed in the canal.

Between three and four in the afternoon a bugle called them to arms; but the American mounted scouts who had caused the alarm galloped away as soon as they were fired upon, and while daylight lasted, there were no further incidents to disturb the resting troops.

At 6 rue Royale Jackson received the report from Colonel de la Ronde, who had sighted sails in the vicinity of Terre aux Boeufs, and sent Latour to investigate. He was deliberately uncommitted to any line of defense, and only the local militia and artillery were posted. The Tennesseans under Coffee and Carroll, forming the real strength of Jackson's army, were in camp four miles above New Orleans and ready for action at short notice wherever they were required. The general was satisfied that the obstruction of all bayous and creeks, the strengthening of Fort St. Philip, and the posting of detachments at Terre aux Boeufs and on the Gentilly Plain, where the militia were commanded by the governor, would provide warning of any enemy advance and buy sufficient time for him to concentrate his main force. On the morning of the twenty-third Jackson wrote[161] to Colonel Robert Hays, Rachel's brother-in-law, that since the capture of the gunboats the British had made no move of any importance and concluded, "All well." This assurance was shattered by the arrival, about noon, of Augustin Rousseau, who had galloped through the British forward troops as they surprised a picket on De la Ronde's plantation. As

Jackson listened to his story, the panting and mud-stained figures of Colonel de la Ronde and Gabriel Villeré burst into the room. Hard on their heels, Major Howell Tatum confirmed their reports and told the general that Latour had gone forward to reconnoiter.[162] Before two o'clock Jackson had Latour's report. He estimated the British force at 1,600 to 1,800 and was able to give their precise position. An alarm gun was fired in the city, and Jackson sent couriers to his subordinate commanders. It was characteristic of him that he made the decision to attack the British that night.

Jackson's immediate command of the situation has tended to obscure the extent of the crisis which faced him. Henry Adams, in what remains the best history of the United States, wrote:[163] "The record of American generalship offered many examples of misfortune, but none so complete as this. Neither Hull nor Harrison, Winder nor Samuel Smith, had allowed a large British army, heralded long in advance, to arrive within seven miles unseen and unsuspected, and without so much as an earthwork, a man, or a gun between them and their object. The disaster was unprecedented." The comparison is militarily invalid. The record of American generalship in fact offered many examples of incompetence but few of misfortune. Nor can the unseen landing of British troops be justly described as misfortune, for it was due to Jackson's failure to post adequate forward pickets in an area which he knew to be threatened. He was betrayed by the neglect or deliberate disobedience of Gabriel Villeré, but the final responsibility was his own. Nevertheless, the problems which faced him in organizing the defense of New Orleans were very different from those which had confronted Hull, Harrison, Winder, or Smith. Not only were the possible approaches to the city too many, too varied, and too widespread to permit any effective defensive positions to be constructed, but the main body of Jackson's army did not come in until December 20. In these circumstances his only course was to keep his defense flexible, relying on the essential principles of concentration and mobility. The effectiveness of this course depended on early warning. It was the failure of his warning system which allowed the British to achieve some measure of local surprise although their intentions in general outline had been broadcast several months earlier.

The immediate crisis arose from the proximity of the British force to the city. Jackson had expected a landing and believed that he would have time to oppose the invaders before they came within striking distance of their objective. The arrival of the enemy less than eight miles from New Orleans confronted him with a dilemma to which immediate and effective answer had to be found if the city was to be saved. From Latour's professionally reliable report Jackson knew that the British force at Villeré's was no more than a part, possibly a small part, of the army sent against New Orleans. He was obliged, therefore, to decide whether it represented the vanguard of the army, a feint attack to draw him away from a stronger assault elsewhere, or the left prong of a forked attack. Jackson believed that the attack was a feint[164] but decided to strike at the enemy on Villeré's plantation with the intention of mauling the army while it was divided. It was a situation typical of Wellington's early defensive campaign in the Peninsula, and Jackson's tactics were suitably Wellingtonian: commanding an inferior army under attack, he waited until his enemy was divided or overextended and concentrated his strength against a vulnerable division. He chose a night attack because the terrain, difficult enough in daylight to an enemy unfamiliar with it, would favor his troops, and the cover of darkness would disguise his numbers and create the maximum confusion.

The decision made, he issued his orders. Carroll was to bring his Tennessee division into the city and remain under arms ready to move at once to any point under attack. His troops would form the reserve. Coffee's division, Hinds' Mississippi Dragoons, Jugeat's Choctaw, and Plauché's battalion at Fort St. John were to join the 7th and 44th U.S. Infantry, Beale's Rifles, and Daquin's Haitian Colored with a small detachment of artillery and two 6-pounders just below the city at Fort St. Charles,* where they would be given their orders for the attack. Patterson would go on board the *Carolina,* which would float silently down with the tide and anchor within range of the British camp. Jackson's troops for the attack numbered 2,131.[165]

As soon as he had issued his orders, Jackson lay down and fell instantly asleep.[166] By four o'clock he was in the saddle at Fort St. Charles. Livingston joined Patterson aboard the *Carolina.* As Jackson's troops assembled, the Feliciana Dragoons went forward to reconnoiter the enemy position. They returned, having been fired upon by pickets, to report that the British force did not exceed 2,000 and that they had not moved since the morning. Plauché's battalion came in at the double, having run most of the 10 miles from Fort St. John, their splendid uniforms dusty and dark with sweat. As dusk fell, Jackson moved his division forward toward the De la Ronde plantation and

*The site of this Spanish fort, erected in 1792, is now occupied by the old United States Mint building (400 Esplanade Avenue).

formed his battle line, separated from Keane's position by the Lacoste plantation. Only 500 yards divided the two armies, but so silently had Jackson's troops moved that the British pickets were unaware of their presence.

In the British camp, fires blazed as the soldiers cooked their evening meal. Lieutenant Gleig pronounced his dinner "excellent with claret to it" and prepared to lie down by his fire to sleep. At seven thirty lookouts on the levee sighted a large vessel on the river. The darkness made recognition of the ship impossible. As she anchored and the sails were furled, the British lookouts came to the conclusion that the vessel must be one of Cochrane's squadron which had succeeded in moving up the river to assist Keane's advance guard. They hailed her repeatedly but, receiving no reply, spread the alarm through the bivouacked division and fired several rifle shots at her. The gun flashes and deadly hail of grapeshot which answered them were also Patterson's signal to Jackson. As the British troops scrambled from their fires to take cover behind the levee, Jackson's troops began their advance across Lacoste's plantation. Coffee's Tennesseans, with Beale's Rifles and Hinds' Dragoons, guided by De la Ronde and Pierre Laffite, moved off toward the cypress swamp on their left to turn the exposed British flank. The artillery and marines were posted on the levee road, and the rest of the troops extended from the river toward Coffee's brigade near the swamp.

The fire from the *Carolina,* whose 7-gun broadside* was served by skilled Baratarian gunners, created havoc in the British camp. Blazing logs of wood were scattered among the troops, kettles were overturned, officers threw down knives and forks to snatch up their swords, soldiers ran for their arms, bugles sounded, and the artillery detachment discharged a few inaccurate rockets which were ineffective but "made a beautiful appearance in the air." As the troops lay under the inadequate cover of the levee, firing was heard from the pickets. Colonel Thornton succeeded in creating some order out of the general confusion, sending the 95th to support the pickets along the river road and the 85th to extend along the line toward the right flank. The 4th was withdrawn to the Villeré mansion in reserve.

The engagement which followed was general, chaotic, and desperate. "All order, all discipline were lost. Each officer, as he suc-

---

*Five 6-pounders on port and starboard broadsides and two long 12-pounders swivel-mounted fore and aft.

ceeded in collecting twenty or thirty men about him, plunged into the midst of the enemy's ranks, where it was fought hand to hand, bayonet to bayonet, and sabre to sabre."[167] Jackson's line, forced inward upon itself by a bend of the river, disintegrated into detachments. Near the river the Rifle Brigade came near to capturing the American guns, which were rescued by part of the 7th U.S. Infantry. The 44th, hard pressed, were saved by Plauché's battalion and Daquin's Haitians. On the land flank, Coffee's Tennesseans dismounted and began, with Beale's Rifles, a steady sweep in toward the river intended to roll up the British right. The 85th Regiment retreated, rallied and charged, and was driven back again. At this critical moment they were unexpectedly reinforced by the arrival of four companies of the 21st Regiment which led Brooke's second brigade. Coffee's attack was diverted. Beale's Riflemen became separated, and 24 of their 64 men were taken prisoner.[168] Two of their number had already been killed. Coffee's Tennesseans had fought their way almost to the levee, where they would be exposed to the fire of the *Carolina,* when Jackson's message reached Coffee ordering a withdrawal to his original position on the left flank. At English Turn General David B. Morgan's 350 Louisiana militia were in the rear of the British position, but Morgan refused to move without orders from Jackson. When his men could no longer be restrained, he led them to Jumonville's plantation, immediately below Villeré's, where they were fired on by the rearguard outposts. At three o'clock, after several hours in a muddy field, Morgan withdrew to English Turn. At four o'clock Jackson also withdrew. It was evident that British reinforcements were arriving, and there was a danger that he would become too heavily committed. He gathered his troops behind the Rodriguez canal between the Macarty and Chalmette plantations about two miles upriver. His casualties were 213, of which 24 were killed and 74 missing.

Keane's army was in no state to attempt pursuit. He had lost 276 officers and men, including 46 killed and 64 missing, and his camp was a shambles of dead and wounded. As Brooke's brigade arrived, the division reorganized and began to clear the battlefield. Gleig wandered over the muddied stubble looking for his friend Captain Grey among the dead. Hardened as he was to war, he was shaken by the evidence of the ferocity of the night's fighting. "The most shocking and disgusting spectacles everywhere met my eyes ... wounds more disfiguring or more horrible I certainly never witnessed ... many had met their deaths from bayonet wounds, sabre cuts, or heavy blows from the butt ends of muskets; and the consequence was, that not only were the wounds themselves exceedingly frightful, but the very countenances of the dead exhibited the most savage and ghastly expressions." He found Grey lying by the cane stack where he had last seen him soon after the battle began. Lieutenant George Robert Gleig of the 85th Regiment, veteran of Wellington's Peninsular army, and of Bladensburg and Baltimore, but not yet nineteen years old, threw himself down beside the body of his friend and wept.[169]

XVIII

Christmas Eve Treaty

While Pakenham followed Keane toward Jamaica and New Orleans, the British and American delegations at Ghent wrestled with instructions, reports, memoranda, proposals, and counterproposals. By the middle of October agreement had been reached that the Indians should be restored to the rights and possessions they had held in 1811. This represented a British retreat from the unacceptable proposition for a buffer state, and the shadow of Plattsburg hung over the Cabinet's stipulation of the principle of *uti possidetis.* This principle, which had yet to be accepted by the Americans, was intended to be flexible to the extent of allowing a revision favorable to the British of the frontiers of New Brunswick and Quebec, and the continued possession of Fort Niagara and the island of Michilimackinac. There was also to be an interchange of boundary forts captured by both sides. Bathurst's instructions to the British commissioners were clouded by limited knowledge of Canadian geography, but it was clear that he hoped to exchange sufficient territory to provide direct land communication between Halifax and Quebec. Prevost's failure, however, had watered down the government's demands to pallid proposals, and even these, Bathurst conceded, might be renounced if they proved to be an obstacle to peace. Lord Liverpool continued to growl threats of blockade and devastation but admitted that "the contest is a contest only for terms of peace."

As a last resort it was contemplated that Wellington might be persuaded to accept the command in Canada. The duke, who had never approved of the American war and was charitably disinclined to

247

blame Prevost for his palsied campaign, showed little enthusiasm for the duty. Bathurst promised him every support if he chose to go to America, but Wellington believed and insisted that his presence was required in Europe. Fear was growing in Paris that there would be a rising to overthrow Louis XVIII.

The British commissioners, confident that the Americans would accept, without argument, the principle of *uti possidetis* as proof of reason and moderation and a genuine desire for peace, hurriedly converted Bathurst's instructions into a formal proposal. The Americans, with unaccustomed speed and unanimity, rejected it. On the evening of October 24 this disagreeable news was on its way by special courier to London, where it was received by Liverpool and Bathurst with stunned disbelief. They were accustomed to the concept that Britain proposed and Britain alone disposed. The American rejection of a principle which was intended to appear mild and conciliatory made them tremble alternately with rage and anxiety.

The war in America was proving both wasteful and expensive. The failure to achieve a decisive victory on territory which might be retained had blunted British authority at the conference table, and there was an unnerving possibility that the troops engaged in America might be required again in Europe. Liverpool publicly accepted the possibility that the war might be prolonged, but both he and Bathurst were agreed that it must be brought to an end. Bathurst wrote a note to Goulburn instructing him to play for time. Goulburn, Gambier, and Adams, as confused and dismayed as their masters in London, composed a note, outwardly clear, but of such masterly diplomatic opacity that delay was inevitable. The British commissioners were, as they stated, empowered to sign a treaty without further delay on the terms already specified in their last note, but the Americans were invited to submit counterproposals. This gave no hint of British intentions, nor did it disclose on what point, if any, negotiations might be continued.

To the Americans the concept of *uti possidetis* was synonymous with the cession of territory. Lacking instructions from Washington, and dependent on a series of increasingly perplexing and contradictory reports from Reuben Beasley in London, they had no comprehension of the effect the news of Plattsburg and the brittle state of France had produced on the British government. Nothing the British commissioners might have devised could more certainly have guaranteed delay than the suggestion that the Americans produce counterproposals. The loneliness, responsibility, and anxieties of their task had exacerbated all the differences, as much personal as political, existing between Adams, Gallatin, Clay, Bayard, and Russell. The right to dry fish on Canadian shores, a privilege acquired by the Treaty of 1783 but repeatedly claimed in British notes to have ended with the American declaration of war, was a New England, therefore a Federalist, interest. British navigation of the Mississippi, guaranteed by the same treaty, might be restored in return for the fisheries right, but the Kentuckian Henry Clay refused to sign any treaty which exchanged the navigation of one of the greatest commerical waterways in the world for "drying fish upon a desert."

Adams had been prepared to refer the matter of impressment to a commission to be appointed after the treaty was signed. Clay insisted that it should be included in the treaty. When the commission voted on this, Adams reversed his attitude and voted with Clay and Russell. While their political differences divided them during the working day, their personal antipathies kept them apart during their hours of leisure. Adams took long and solitary walks because, as he wrote to his wife, he could find no one to accompany him. Clay's uninhibited pleasures, which included cards, wine, cigars, and—it was rumored—chambermaids, kept him late from his bed and made him unpunctual at meetings. Adams, who occupied the room next to Clay's and rose at five every morning to read his Bible, was unable to disguise his contempt for such behavior. Nor were their many dissensions their only obstacle to finding agreement: Clay, Bayard, and Russell were habitually late for meetings, arriving on occasion barely in time to bid the rest good-night. Adams' meticulous draft proposals were hacked to pieces by his four colleagues, but he was undaunted in his determination to produce a series of proposals which the British must either accept or, by their rejection, show to Europe their desire to prolong the war for gain.

The document which was at last agreed and delivered to Goulburn late in the evening of November 10 was nothing less than a draft treaty of fifteen articles accompanied by a note substituting the principle of *status quo ante bellum* for that of *uti possidetis*. The draft made no mention of Mississippi navigation and assumed the preservation of the fisheries right as if it had never been denied. Provision was made for an immediate end to hostilities, the restoration of territory and property, and the appointment of commissions to deal with outstanding boundary disputes. The northwest frontier, however, was drawn deliberately to exclude the British from direct communication with the upper Mississippi. The Indian solution was already agreed, but Adams added a rider committing both nations to restraining the Indians living within their territories from hostilities and prohibiting their employment in any future war.

These subjects, covered in the first ten articles, might have been acceptable with little amendment. The following three articles might have been drafted with the deliberate intention of demonstrating the contempt of the American commissioners for all the previous negotiations. Impressment was to be temporarily prohibited, the British use of blockades was to be severely restricted, and indemnity was demanded for all losses and damage sustained by citizens of the United States, both during the war and prior to it, by reason of any British action "contrary to the known and established rules of the law of nations." Amnesty was proposed for all those of either nation who had given aid to the enemy, and rules for ratification were outlined. While the American commissioners congratulated themselves on the satisfactory outcome of their unusual accord, Henry Goulburn read through their proposals with astonishment and disgust. Whatever the views of his government, it was clear to him, at least, that these extravagant pretensions must be instantly rejected. It was time the recalcitrant colonials were shown the whip.

Goulburn was not in such a position of confidence that he was able fully to appreciate his government's predicament, but he was a shrewd and able negotiator. In the letter he sent to Bathurst enclosing the American proposals he did not neglect to draw attention to the question of Louisiana: "to accede to the proposition the Americans have made of discussing the boundary of Louisiana might be considered as a recognition by us of their right to occupy the country."[170] This fact was not lost on Bathurst. He had also in front of him the Duke of Wellington's considered but unpalatable opinion:

> In regard to your present negotiations, I confess that I think you have no right *from the state of war** to demand any concession of territory from America ... from particular circumstances, such as the want of the naval superiority on the Lakes, you have not been able to carry it [the war] into the enemy's territory, notwithstanding your military success, and now undoubted military superiority, and have not even cleared your own territory of the enemy.... You cannot then, on any principle of equality in negotiation, claim a cession of territory excepting in exchange for other advantages which you have in your power. ... Then if this reasoning be true, why stipulate for the uti possidetis? You can get no territory; indeed the state of your military operations, however creditable, does not entitle you to

*Author's italics.

demand any. . . . If you had territory, as I hope you will soon have New Orleans, I should prefer to insist upon the cession of that province as a separate article than upon the uti possidetis as a principle of negotiation.[171]

As to the suggestion that he should command in America, the duke, whose life was threatened by an assassination plot,[172] declared, "I feel no objection to going to America, though I don't promise to myself much success there." This lack of objection was more than counterbalanced by the firm assertion "You cannot, in my opinion, at this moment decide upon sending me to America. In case of the occurrence of anything in Europe, there is nobody but myself in whom either yourselves or the country, or your Allies, would feel any confidence."[173] False modesty was not one of the duke's vices.

The Cabinet's plan to remove Wellington from physical danger in France to expose him to the threat of having his military reputation ruined in a doomed campaign in America clearly found no favor with the duke, whose trenchant observations on the conduct of the peace negotiations were as unwelcome as they were self-evidently true. Affairs in Europe, moreover, strongly supported his contention that he could not be spared. Castlereagh's attempts to wrest Poland from the grasp of Russia had been rebuffed by the Czar Alexander, whose enormous army was still marching belligerently about eastern Europe. Supported by Metternich, Castlereagh had brought the victorious alliance to disintegration and the brink of war. For Lords Liverpool and Bathurst the last straw was supplied by the publication in America, and afterward in England, of all the records of the peace negotiations. It was useless to denounce Madison's behavior in releasing these documents as scandalous. Had the British part in the negotiations been uniformly reasonable and honorable, Madison's action would have been both ineffective and unobjectionable. Publication of the British terms—with simultaneous publication of the emasculated proposals offered in October, which were made too late for inclusion—made them appear minatory and absurd. The American people were inflamed, and their determination to fight was stimulated. The British people, already grumbling over the tax burden imposed by a war they no longer favored, applauded the attacks made daily in the newspapers against the government which had designed these discreditable transactions.

Lord Liverpool was obliged to retreat. He wrote to Wellington accepting his objections to the American command but urging him to suggest a publicly agreeable reason for his removal from Paris. In

December a suitable solution was found. Castlereagh was brought home, returning to his seat as Leader of the House, and Wellington was assigned to his place at the Congress of Vienna. The solution to the problems at Ghent was neither so simple nor so satisfactory. Bathurst, as usual, conveyed the necessary instructions to Henry Goulburn. The principle of *status quo ante bellum* was accepted, and the dispute over the fisheries right was not considered of sufficient importance to merit the continuance of the war. The list of reasons given for this retreat from the principle of *uti possidetis* was long and detailed, but nothing Bathurst could manufacture obscured the admission, as inadmissible as it was clearly implied, that Britain lacked the essential power to compel the Americans to submit. Some crumb of comfort might be found in the demonstration of British sincerity and moderation. If the Americans refused the new terms, they would have some difficulty in explaining their refusal. No mention was made of Louisiana.

These new instructions did not reach Goulburn until November 25. By that time the American commission had also received three dispatches from Monroe, the latest of them dated October 19. These were determinedly cheerful, expressing "nothing of alarm or apprehension," but they introduced a realism into the American government's instructions which had been lacking in previous communications. In effect they authorized the commissioners to negotiate on the basis of the *status quo ante bellum.* This was comforting news to John Quincy Adams, who had been primarily responsible for proposing this basis to the British. His note informing his own government of this proposal had not even arrived in Washington at the time he received Monroe's dispatches vindicating his decision.

On November 27 the British reply to the draft treaty was delivered to the American commissioners. Some amendments had been made to the first nine articles, the most important being the revision of the proposed northwestern frontier to give the British access to the Mississippi and free navigation of the river. The remainder were "inadmissible" but could be resubmitted in different form. The principle of *uti possidetis* was finally abandoned. In spite of the rejection of five articles and the high tone of the reply, the Americans were optimistic. Their most important object had been achieved, and the British had demonstrated, by the withdrawal of their most offensive demand, their urgent desire for peace. The articles dealing with impressment, rights to blockade, amnesty, and the restraint of the Indians could all be discarded if necessary. None of the five commissioners had ever seriously contemplated the possibility of their being accepted. It was the supreme irony that the British abandoned with such reluctance territorial gains which they had not ever considered in 1812, while the Americans were prepared to discard, with the utmost cheerfulness, three of the causes for which they had declared war, at the same time recognizing that the fourth was unattainable.

Buoyed up by their satisfaction and enthusiasm, the American commissioners settled to their customary composition and editing of drafts with renewed vigor. Within twenty-four hours Gallatin had produced his first draft, which was amended by the rest from dawn until eleven on the morning of the twenty-eighth. When they met at noon, they began at once to divide into factions. The British insistence on navigation of the Mississippi had to be countered, so Gallatin contended, by an equivalent insistence on the fisheries right, which had not been mentioned. This was fiercely denied by Henry Clay. The news of the impending Hartford Convention, which had arrived the previous week, persuaded both Gallatin and Adams that the renunciation of the fisheries right would be acutely damaging to the Union, but Clay foresaw even more disastrous consequences attaching to a permanent British presence on the Mississippi. A compromise, limiting British access to the river, was at length agreed. A new note was dispatched on November 30, and a session of both commissioners arranged for the following day.

The American commissioners were right in thinking that peace was within their grasp for the first time since negotiations had begun. The long and lonely task to which they had devoted themselves with such courage and tenacity was nearing completion, but certain obstacles remained. The worst of these was the British commissioners, whose persistent belief in British superiority engendered a reluctance to accept their instructions at face value. Goulburn, in particular, constantly sought to maneuver for an advantage and seldom yielded any point without specific instructions to do so. His behavior cannot be faulted on this score, for it arose from the proximity of Ghent to London. The American commissioners were obliged, by distance from Washington, to take responsibility for their own decisions. The British negotiations were conducted, in fact, from London, and the negotiators took no decision on which their instructions were not clear beyond doubt. Bathurst's capacity for stating a firm position and then retreating from it in the same letter of instruction was responsible for delays while his intentions were clarified.

A second problem, for which no easy solution presented itself, concerned possession of the Passamaquoddy Islands off the coast of Maine.

Moose Island had been captured and occupied by the British in June, 1814, seizing control of the Passamaquoddy Bay region. Moose Island, in particular, was considered by the British Cabinet as having been "always a part of New Brunswick," and there was little sign of any intention to relinquish it. Much depended on the first article of the draft treaty which, as amended by the British, stipulated the return of all territory "belonging to one part and taken by the other." The wording was significant and its interpretation open-ended. If Britain contended, after ratification of the treaty, that Moose Island was part of Canada, it would not be easy for America to regain possession. Far more serious, though this does not appear to have been fully apprehended either in Washington or by the American commissioners at Ghent, was the uncertain position of Louisiana. The British could contend, as they had done since 1803 and with considerable justification in law, that the whole of the Louisiana Territory rightfully belonged to Spain. If, by that time, a powerful army of Peninsular veterans occupied New Orleans, supported by Cochrane's fleet, it might prove impossible to dislodge them.

The joint session of the two commissions on December 1 was not a success. After discussion, the British agreed to leave the disputed Passamaquoddy Islands to be settled by a commission after the treaty was signed, but there could be no question of an evacuation from Moose Island in the meantime. There was agreement on the constitution of the commissions, which would be composed of one member nominated by each nation with a "friendly sovereign," whose neutrality was accepted by both sides, acting as referee. John Quincy Adams then raised the dual problem of the Mississippi and fisheries right. He asked if he was to assume that British silence on the matter of the fisheries right should be interpreted as agreement that this was to be confirmed. It was, as he recalled, part of the same Treaty of 1783 which guaranteed British navigation of the Mississippi, a matter on which the British had made their demands abundantly clear. The calm, almost somnolent atmosphere of the meeting was changed instantly by a vehement British chorus of dissent. Adams continued in his silkiest tones. Either there should be articles dealing with both these matters or they both should be omitted. It must also be understood that British access to the river had to be restricted to one point where there would be proper customs control and payment of duties. He was seconded by Gallatin.

The British commissioners were aghast at this resuscitation of matters which they had congratulated themselves on having buried. Into the acrimonious arguments which followed, John Quincy Adams interjected the American agreement to waive all indemnity claims except those arising from the first six months of the war. The English Dr. Adams, presumably attempting to justify his appointment to the commission—an attempt doomed by his irascible temperament and lack of judgment to abject failure—launched into a diatribe as irrational as it was offensive. Gambier and Goulburn, embarrassed by the outburst, did not support him, and his arguments, easily refuted by the Americans, died away in incoherent rumblings. The meeting broke up. The problem of the Passamaquoddy Islands had been shelved, and the composition of the subsequent commissions agreed; but the fisheries and Mississippi rights remained undetermined, and feelings of mutual hostility had been revived. The best hope for the future of the negotiations lay in the belief of both parties that peace, however elusive, was attainable.

Another joint session on the tenth was spent in discussion of terms altered little by correspondence with Bathurst, apart from the British proposal for a new article "for the more effective Abolition of the Slave Trade." This was not welcomed by the Americans, who considered that it impugned their ability to frame and enforce their own laws. They retired to confer among themselves. By Monday, December 12, the political chasm which emphasized the personal differences between John Quincy Adams and Henry Clay had brought them again into open conflict. Adams, representing the interests of New England, was the only one of the five to feel that the Passamaquoddy Islands and fisheries right were worth prolonging negotiations for when agreement was so near. Even the Federalist Bayard could not support this contention though he favored one last attempt to retrieve the fisheries. Gallatin pressed strongly for immediate settlement. Clay, followed by the bewildered Russell, alternated between fulminations against the lunacy of fighting to preserve the rights of treacherous New England and assertions that the preservation of American honor demanded the continuation of the war. After a long and furious argument it was agreed to try again at the next joint session the following morning.

The Americans were not in the best of tempers, and they lost no time in making the British lose theirs. Adams' flat announcement that the Passamaquoddy Islands would not be ceded under any circumstances, however temporary, was sufficient to induce Goulburn to abandon all control. Lord Gambier, imposing and not a little pompous in his admiral's uniform but undeniably sincere, restored some temporary

order by suggesting that the commissioners move on to another subject. John Quincy Adams stated that the British proposals regarding
Mississippi navigation and the fisheries right were unacceptable. He
proposed, instead, that both problems should be left, with other
"unadjusted" obstacles, for consideration and solution after the treaty
had been ratified. He produced a draft article to this effect, which was
immediately rejected. Gallatin amended it, and it was again rejected.
Each of the eight commissioners then settled down to drafting his own
article and rejecting those drafted by others until, in a moment of
infuriated aberration, Goulburn found himself denouncing one of his
own. At length, under pressure, the British commissioners admitted
that they could not reach any agreement until their government had
been consulted. The article dealing with the slave trade was briefly
discussed, and the meeting was adjourned.

For two days the American commissioners argued bitterly among
themselves. They agreed to allow the problems of the Passamaquoddy
Islands and Mississippi navigation to be omitted from the treaty and
shelved for decision after it had been signed, but Adams was isolated
and immovable in his refusal to allow the fisheries right to be shelved in
the same way. On the afternoon of Wednesday December 14 they sent
a last note to the British. Adams, who threatened to refuse to sign the
note or any treaty arising from it, added his signature to a proposal
excluding the Passamaquoddy Islands, Mississippi navigation, and the
right to dry fish from the treaty. Clay and Gallatin were no more
satisfied with the final draft treaty than was Adams, but all were
agreed that the war had to be ended at once or prolonged for several
years. The alternative to an unsatisfactory peace was an intolerable
war.

On the afternoon of Thursday the twenty-second the British
Cabinet's reply arrived in Ghent, and it was not long before the
American commissioners heard that their proposals had been accepted. They met to examine the British note and make a final draft of the
treaty incorporating the most recent changes. To the astonishment and
dismay of the other four, Henry Clay chose this moment to unleash all
his frustration and anger against the terms they were about to accept.
Now that the treaty was within twenty-four hours of being signed and
peace with Britain was practically an accomplished fact, Clay
remembered the fine speeches that he and his supporters had made in
the Twelfth Congress. "What," he had demanded, "are we not to lose
by Peace?—commerce, character, a nation's best treasure, honor!"
Three years later, after two and a half years of war which had, it

seemed, achieved nothing, he was asking the same question. He could see only the hopes forgotten, the ambitions annihilated, the causes deserted. And yet, although he was unable to comprehend it at the time, the cause which he had personally made his own had been preserved and vindicated. In spite of military incompetence, internal dissension, and financial ruin, his country's honor was held in greater respect in Europe than at any time since the Revolution.

It was, as always, Gallatin who calmed him. Throughout the five months of tedious negotiation it had been Gallatin who brought the commissioners together. His moderation, tact, and diplomacy had repeatedly kept his colleagues from an irreparable division. For the first time he lost his temper. He turned on Clay all the repressed fury which had festered in his mind and silenced him. In the lull which followed his outburst he surveyed his shattered colleagues and quietly proposed a meeting with the British commission for the following day.

The session on the twenty-third was brief and the atmosphere restrained. The commissioners parted, having agreed that each side should produce three copies of the treaty to be signed the following day. From all points of view it was an extraordinary document when examined in the light of the ambitions of the two nations for whom the commissioners were to be signatories. British hopes of territorial gains were dashed or, at best, postponed, and their military reputation was sadly tarnished. Of the stated reasons for America's declaration of war, impressment and maritime rights were not so much as mentioned, the conquest of Canada had been demonstrated to be impossible, and the Indian problem was only partly solved. There was no provision for indemnities, and the disputes over the fisheries right, the navigation of the Mississippi, and the possession of the Passamaquoddy Islands remained unsolved.

At four o'clock in the afternoon of Christmas Eve, 1814, the two commissions met. Two hours later they signed a Treaty of Peace Between His Britannic Majesty and the United States of America. A few hours later, Major General Sir Edward Pakenham arrived to take command of the British army before New Orleans.

XIX

Pakenham Takes Command

Throughout December 24, troops continued to arrive at Keane's lines on the Villeré plantation, and by nightfall the whole of the available British force had been landed. The 1st and 5th West India regiments were sadly reduced in numbers. No attempt appears to have been made to supply these troops with warm clothing, and "during the voyage the regiment had been much scattered in small craft, where the soldiers were obliged to sleep on deck, exposed to the torrents of rain which fell by day and the frosts that came on at night; and being unaccustomed to the severity of an American winter, large numbers of them died from cold and exposure, the 5th West India Regiment suffering equally with the 1st."[174] About 200 men from these regiments died of cold, and many others were too ill to be sent forward from Pea Island. With the casualties suffered and prisoners taken by the Americans during the attack on the night of the twenty-third, Keane had already lost approximately one-tenth of his total army.

Most historians of the campaign have stated that Colonel William Thornton pressed upon General Keane his recommendation for an advance upon New Orleans immediately after their arrival on the twenty-third. The origin of these statements, which accord with all that is known about Thornton's character and reputation, appears to be Alexander Walker, who published the story in *Jackson and New Orleans* in 1856. Although Walker was in New Orleans at the time and may have had the opportunity of talking to British prisoners (who included Major Samuel Mitchell of the Rifle Brigade, captured on the night of the twenty-third), he cites no authorities for the story. No evidence to support it has been uncovered in any of the contemporary British accounts. It is on the evidence of Keane's decision not to advance on the twenty-third that the otherwise unsupported accusation of timidity and excessive caution is based. Since the leading regiment of Brooke's brigade, the 21st, did not arrive at Villeré's until late on the night of the twenty-third, Keane's assault on New Orleans would have had to be made with Thornton's brigade alone. This comprised three regiments with a maximum total of 1,841 men* with small detachments of artillery and engineers and two light 3-pounder guns. These men were already exhausted after an advance made under appalling conditions and lasting twenty-six hours. During this period they had been soaked and frozen and without sleep or food. Keane is criticized for not marching troops in this state against a city, eight miles away, through unfamiliar terrain, and defended by enemy troops whose numbers were unknown but might be as great as 15,000.

The British military historian Sir John Fortescue wrote:[175]

> It was not much past noon, and five hours of daylight would suffice for the work in hand. Had Keane realised, as he ought, that he was engaged not upon a military operation but upon a mere buccaneering adventure, he would have acted on this advice. The troops, set down as they were in the midst of chilly, unhealthy swamps after their long and miserable exposure in the boats, were sure to become sickly; and delay would permit his enemies to improve their earthworks and collect fresh levies. At best he might achieve a daring and striking success; at worst he would sacrifice no more than a small detachment, whose defeat would indeed mean the ruin of the expedition—in itself no misfortune—but could hardly be reckoned a great disgrace. However, treating affairs seriously as he did, he pointed to his men still out of condition after a long voyage, to his supports, supplies, and means of retreat, all of them eighty miles away, and declined, in spite of the remonstrances of Admiral Cochrane and Colonel Thornton, to take the risk.

This criticism has been generally accepted as definitive.

There was, in fact, no reason for Keane to believe that the expedition he led was anything other than a military operation, and it is abundantly clear that the British government designed it as such. The forces employed, the geographical importance of New Orleans as the chosen objective, and the officially expressed desire to "occupy some important and valuable possession ... which may entitle us to exact its

---

*This figure is the total number on the strength of these regiments when they left Jamaica and makes no allowance for the sick left behind aboard the fleet or on Pea Island.

cession as the price of peace" are sufficient evidence that the expedition was never intended to be "mere buccaneering" as Fortescue suggests. Nor is it possible, on the evidence, to assign to Cochrane any of the praise or blame for advocating an immediate advance. Cochrane was at the Spanish fishermen's village throughout the landing of the whole force and until after Pakenham's arrival[176] and can therefore have expressed no opinion, one way or the other, unless he did so from a distance and without ever seeing the ground. The senior naval representative with the advance was Rear Admiral Pulteney Malcolm.

To suggest that Keane would be risking only "a small detachment" is to ignore the fact that it represented more than a third of his finest troops. That the ruin of the expedition was "in itself no misfortune" is not readily acceptable to a British historian today, and it is inconceivable that Keane or any man in the expedition would have accepted any such suggestion.

In the circumstances as they were known to Keane, any attempt to attack New Orleans on the twenty-third would have been reckless to the point of lunacy. With no useful artillery, an unguarded rear, a long and also unguarded line of communications, and his nearest reinforcements nine hours away and coming in one regiment at a time, it is scarcely possible that such an advance would have achieved anything but the total annihilation of his forward brigade and the piecemeal destruction of Brooke's brigade when it followed. Had Jackson had a larger and more resolutely led division guarding Terre aux Boeufs, in the British rear, it is possible that Keane's advance brigade would have been decisively defeated in the attack on the night of the twenty-third. But for the mauling his army received from Jackson's night attack and the guns of the *Carolina*, Keane might have considered an advance on the twenty-fourth and an attack on the twenty-fifth. By that time he had been superseded in command by the arrival of Pakenham.

During the hours of daylight on the twenty-fourth Keane's army, gradually augmented by the arrival of the second and third brigades, was under continuous bombardment from the river. The *Carolina*, supported by two gunboats,[177] had been joined by the converted sloop *Louisiana,* which anchored at noon about a mile above the schooner. The *Louisiana* carried 16 guns,[178] all of them heavier than anything the British had in the field or available to them unless they were brought from the fleet, and large stores of powder. To avoid unnecessary casualties, Keane drew back his left wing from the bank of the Mississippi, placing his flanks on the Villeré and Lacoste canals; but this change could not be effected until nightfall, and during the whole of the twenty-fourth the men of the 85th and 95th were obliged to shelter behind the levee. At night the road running beside the river was abandoned to pickets.

While the British consolidated a position which was, of necessity, defensive, Jackson began to entrench his army behind the Rodriguez canal. This was a dry, grass-covered ditch about 12 feet wide and 4 to 8 feet deep. Originally a millrace, it extended from the levee to a thickly wooded swamp some 900 yards inland from the river.[179] There, behind the ditch, Jackson made his line for the defense of New Orleans. Wooden stakes and fence rails were driven into the ground, and earth was piled behind them. The earth was too soggy to permit digging to sufficient depth to provide an adequate embankment, and much of the soil had to be excavated and brought from the rear. Jackson had the city ransacked for entrenching tools and brought forward slaves to help with the digging. By the night of the twenty-fourth the entrenchment was taking shape.

That morning Captain Swaine brought the frigate *Statira* to anchor, and Pakenham, with Gibbs, Swaine, Dickson, Burgoyne, and Captain Alexander Campbell Wylly, one of the general's aides, put off in the captain's gig to be rowed to the inner anchorage of the fleet. At ten o'clock that night they went on board the brig *Anaconda*, where Captain Sir Thomas Hardy* informed them of the landing made the previous morning and of the battle on Lake Borgne on the fourteenth. While a second boat was made ready, Pakenham and his staff had a meal before moving on toward the entrance to the Bayou Bienvenue. The night was clear but bitterly cold, and the freezing wind was against the boats until early morning, when it became possible to hoist a sail. From the entrance to the bayou Cochrane's red ensign, flying from the top of a tree, was clearly visible, marking his headquarters at the fishermen's village. At eight o'clock on the morning of Christmas Day Pakenham arrived to find Cochrane "just going into Breakfast and [we] made a very hearty one."[180] Codrington was also there, supervising the transport, by the navy, of guns, stores, and ammunition from the fleet to the forward positions, and working from "a new shed, thatched and made altogether of reeds, neither wind-tight nor water-tight . . . situated on a part of a mud bank, rather less wet than the surrounding swamp."[181] Fires were kept burning day and night at the camp and at the mouth of

---

*Sir Thomas Masterman Hardy (1769–1839), Nelson's flag captain aboard the *Victory* at Trafalgar in 1805.

the bayou to guide boats coming from the fleet and also to keep off alligators "or some other brute [who] might make a meal of us."[182]

Cochrane was able to give Pakenham detailed information of the landing and also news of the American attack on the night of the twenty-third. Pakenham, more than ever anxious to reach his army, left immediately after breakfast with Gibbs, Burgoyne, Dickson, and Wylly in two gigs which were alternately sailed or rowed, according to the wind. Dickson's description of the bayou is the most detailed to survive and gives an accurate picture of the route covered by the army and all the guns, stores, and equipment:

> The creek has a great many turns and reaches in it, and the whole way up is covered on each side by high reeds, it is of a good breadth for four or five miles, and then narrows so much, and is so shallow, that the boats cannot row for want of room, and are pushed through the mud by means of the oars shoving against the bank. About a mile above the Huts [Cochrane's headquarters] there are two broad creeks, one running away into the Marsh to the right [Upper Bienvenue], and the other to the left [Mazant], and all the way up there are on both sides a number of little Channels or inlets, full of water, which would render moving along the bank impossible, even where it is hard enough. From the landing place to [Keane's] Head Quarters is about 2½ Miles, the road being nothing more than a very bad and boggy path along the bank of a little Canal . . . which extends from the Creek nearly to the Mississippi, and is navigable for Canoes to within 1000 yards of the river, this is named the Bayoue Villaré [sic], being for the use of that plantation. The Road for the distance of ¾ of a mile from the landing place is through Reeds and the ground Consequently very boggy, it then enters a thick wood about 1¼ miles across . . . the wood is generally of Cypress trees growing closely together, and full of thick Brush and Palmettos, the bottom being swampy with deep holes interspersed, full of water, it is therefore in every respect impracticable. From the edge of the wood to Villaré's [sic] plantation the distance is about half a Mile of tolerably good and broad road, and from the Plantation to the bank of the river is about 300 yards. A party is employed in improving this road.[183]

Over this route of bayou and bog the navy had, by the time of Dickson's arrival, hauled twelve field pieces and three brass howitzers from the marine artillery. Pakenham and his party reached the landing place soon after eleven o'clock and continued on foot along the muddy tracks to Keane's headquarters.

Later accounts of the campaign have stated that Pakenham was horrified to find his command in such a vulnerable position and that at a conference in the Villeré mansion on the evening of the twenty-fifth he proposed to withdraw his army but was shamed by Cochrane into agreeing to stay. These statements, once again, rest on the account given by Alexander Walker, who quotes the conversation verbatim in which Cochrane is supposed to have asserted that if the army could not take New Orleans, his sailors would do the job and the army could then bring up the baggage. Walker was not in any position to know what passed between the senior British commanders that evening, nor is it recorded that he ever met anyone who was present at the conference, if it took place. More significantly, it is not recorded in any of the British journals that Cochrane ever came forward to Pakenham's headquarters that evening, and it is unlikely that Dickson, whose journal is exceptionally accurate and detailed, would have omitted to make a note of such a visit. Nor was Pakenham the man to take orders from the fleet commander. Sufficient is known of his character to make it certain beyond reasonable doubt that Cochrane, if he had so far forgotten himself, would have been given a quick and far from gentle reminder that Pakenham was commander in chief. The conversation, as given by Walker, must be regarded as a fabrication, produced forty years after the event, to support the charge that Cochrane's special interest in the campaign was the booty, in prize money, to be expected from the capture of New Orleans.

The accusation that booty was the main purpose of the expedition has been leveled at almost everyone who took part in it from the British government to the humblest deckhand or drummer boy. As usual, it was Latour's and Alexander Walker's work which set the course followed by later historians, and the story has gained strength and decoration in the telling. Little attempt appears ever to have been made to examine or challenge it, and even Sir John Fortescue accepted the charge as proved and added a totally untenable (but often repeated) prejudice of his own.

Walker stated flatly, "The charge against . . . the projectors of the expedition to New Orleans, as one for plunder and spoils, is too well established now to be questioned."[184] Against "the projectors"—the British government—there can, in fact, be no charge whatever. The evidence is overwhelming that the government's objective was territorial and diplomatic. Bathurst's orders to Pakenham,[185] dated October 24, 1814, gave specific instructions that all booty must be condemned officially and disposed of under the direction and authority of the Admiralty courts. Under the rules then prevailing this method of distribution would allow the government no share, but the whole, after proper assessment and the calculation of shares by rank, would be distributed among the victorious army and navy. It was Pakenham's responsibility to prevent, as far as possible, looting and theft by individuals and to ensure that accurate assessments of value were made on the spot. The whole of the cost of the expedition was borne by the government, but no share of the spoils could accrue to the Treasury. This disposes altogether of Walker's charge, so often slavishly repeated, against the government, the "projectors" of the expedition.

That the charge against Cochrane and the navy, in general, has some substance is beyond doubt, and there can be little doubt, either, that the army was at least well aware of the bounties to be gained by the conquest of New Orleans. It was estimated at the time that goods stored in the city included a hundred thousand 320-pound bales of cotton valued at $14,250,000 (excluding 10,000 bales in planters' stores); $1,250,000 worth of sugar; approximately $500,000 of shipping; and produce of Kentucky—whiskey, flour, pork, cordage, hempen yarn, and cotton bagging—and other commodities such as pig lead, pig copper, mahogany, and log wood—producing a total value of not less than $20,000,000.[186] Fortescue states:[187] "Prize-money had for nearly two centuries been the motive for all amphibious operations recommended by the Navy; and this of New Orleans was no exception. If any naval officers had shown stronger lust of prize than others, they were the Scots; and all three of the Admirals engaged in this expedition —excellent men in their own profession—were by a singular coincidence Scotsmen, Cochrane, Cockburn and Malcolm." In this, Fortescue has allowed prejudice to subvert accuracy: Cockburn was not at any time employed in the New Orleans expedition but was sent to carry out a diversionary attack against Cumberland Island, off the coast of Georgia. This attack was made successfully on January 12, 1815, though it had been scheduled for November.

No direct evidence exists to support the charge against Sir Alexander Cochrane, but it is clear that some of his contemporaries believed it. Writing to Pakenham's brother in May, 1815, the Duke of Wellington stated bluntly that the expedition originated with Cochrane and that his object was plunder.[188] Colonel Burgoyne, later Field Marshal Sir John Burgoyne, told his biographer and son-in-law,[189] that "the operation had originated with the admiral on the station, who anticipated a large amount of prize money from its success. . . . Pakenham, who distrusted the proceedings of Sir Alexander Cochrane, showed great anxiety on the voyage to arrive at the scene of operations before his troops had been put on shore." It is scarcely possible to believe that either Wellington or Burgoyne would have made this charge unless it was well substantiated. Burgoyne's opinion was not published until forty years after Cochrane's death, but Wellington's letter contained a libel which he would have been unlikely to publish, even in a letter to Lord Longford, without confidence in his ability to prove justification. It is only fair to add, however, that none of the contemporary journals reveals any suspicion of Cochrane's motives, and no such charge appears to have been made against him until the time came to apportion blame for defeat.

Gleig's account, of which there are several versions and altered editions, mentions the stories of rich booty waiting in New Orleans told by American deserters. Neither he nor any of the other diarists includes any evidence to support the charge that either the army or navy considered the prospect of booty as any more than a bonus to be drawn from victory. Even Latour, who allowed his prejudices to destroy any semblance of accuracy in his account, shows some hesitancy in accepting the story that the British army's parole and countersign "on the memorable 8th February* . . . were *beauty and booty.*" He adds:[190] "Although this report is generally believed in the United States . . . I have not thought it sufficiently authenticated to record it as an historical fact," but goes on to say that the failure of the British government to deny it officially and to produce proof to refute the charge indicates that "the report must be considered true." It may well be true that this slogan circulated freely among the army, though there is no evidence to support even this theory. That the words were used as the official password and countersign is inconceivable. There can scarcely be any question of Pakenham, who was a man of unimpeachable honor, deep religious beliefs, and impeccable behavior, allowing such a password; the similarity between the pronunciation of the two words would make them utterly unsuitable for use as password and countersign; and there is no mention of any such use in the private journals or regimental records. It is not possible to believe that both Gleig and Dickson, whose journals are so meticulous and detailed, should have omitted anything of such significance, particularly in view of Gleig's pronounced tendency to denigrate British successes and criticize British behavior.

Following the publication of the *Memoirs* of Major Eaton and James Stuart's *Three Years in America,* Major General John Lambert wrote a denial and refutation, signed by other officers present at the battle on January 8, which was passed to the President on July 14, 1833.[191] This denial has been consistently overlooked or ignored by later historians, who have been content to repeat the story without producing a single piece of evidence to support it. In the absence of such evidence, there is no longer any reason to believe that "Beauty and Booty" ever existed as

_____
*An error for January.

anything more than a slogan in the ranks, if it originally existed at all outside Latour's account.

Pakenham left no record of his thoughts or actions after his arrival in New Orleans, but it is unlikely that his first impressions of the position occupied by his army were favorable. He was too experienced an officer, and had observed Wellington's tactics too closely, not to understand the vulnerability of an army divorced from its supplies and obliged to rely on lines of communication stretched to breaking point. Keane's achievement in bringing the army unobserved to within nine miles of New Orleans had been vitiated by his inability to land sufficient numbers of men, and in fit condition, to carry New Orleans by a *coup de main*. Jackson's deliberately flexible defensive plan had enabled him to attack the invaders while he could take the field with a temporary superiority in numbers, and Patterson's control and good use of the river gave the Americans a superiority in artillery which they maintained throughout the campaign.

Pakenham inspected his troops, in their lines out of range of the *Carolina* and her attendant gunboats, and then surveyed the position. Colonel Dickson was conducted over the ground by Admiral Malcolm. He found the twelve pieces of artillery, of which the heaviest were two 9-pounders, supplied with sufficient ammunition for little more than one day's expenditure. Major Alexander Munro, commanding the artillery prior to Dickson's arrival, had sent to the fleet for substantial supplies, but these would take several days to arrive. Pakenham decided that little could be achieved while the *Carolina* and the two gunboats remained at anchor enfilading his line and seconded by the heavily armed *Louisiana* a mile upstream. Dickson believed that he could reach the *Carolina*, 800 yards off, with his guns, and that night he had embrasures cut in the levee to accommodate the two 9-pounders, the four 6-pounders, and both 5½-inch howitzers, the whole of the artillery at his disposal except the four light 3-pounders which could be of no use at that range. Pakenham ordered that they should not be used until morning and then postponed the order to open fire in the hope that two 18-pounders ordered from the fleet might have arrived.

On the night of the twenty-fifth, according to Latour, the Americans cut the levee "on the foreground of Chalmette's plantation, for the purpose of overflowing the ground in front of our lines" (forward of the British position). The orders had been given by Jackson to Latour, but it appears from Latour's account that he did not accompany the troops detached to carry them out. He states that the "temporary swell of the river" subsided and the water drained away. Dickson, however, gives a different version which is evidently correct:

> ...a party of the Enemy either came across the water, or up by land from Detour des Anglois, and made a cut in the Levee, not more than 151 or 200 Yards distance from our piquet on the great road below Head Quarters. By this Cut which was very deep, the Water was admitted from the river into the plain and it was rushing in very strongly, when discovered by Genl. Keane this morning, and a strong working party being immediately sent, the Gap was filled up. This was so great a Neglect on the part of the piquet, which had been ordered to Patrole along the Levee every hour during the night, that the officer Commanding A Captain MacLean of the 21st regt. has been put in arrest by order of Sir Edward Packenham.[192]

Dickson's account makes it clear that the cut was made *below* the British forward positions instead of on Chalmette's plantation in front of the British lines and dividing them from Jackson's defenses on the Rodriguez canal. If a second cut was made in this area, it was evidently insignificant, for Dickson does not even mention it. Had Jackson's orders been carried out as he intended, the British route for an advance against New Orleans would have been made impassable and Pakenham's immediate retreat would have been inevitable.

Before daylight on the twenty-sixth Dickson had his guns in the shelter of the levee and covered with "cane trash." The embrasures had been cut some way above the *Carolina*'s position so that fire could be continued if she tried to make way upriver. Pakenham was still doubtful of the ability of small field pieces to reach the target and, in spite of Dickson's assurances of success, deferred the decision to open fire. This failure to take the advice of his artillery commander, whom Pakenham knew to be one of the ablest gunners in the British army, was a serious error. While Jackson was building his defenses, every delay lessened the British chances of success, and no attack could be launched along the river under the flanking artillery of the *Carolina* and *Louisiana*.

Pakenham reorganized his force. Major General Sam Gibbs was appointed to command the brigade on the right, consisting of the 4th, 44th, 21st, and the 1st West India Regiment, and Major General John Keane took the left brigade of the 85th, 93d, and 95th with the 5th West India Regiment. Sam Gibbs was a veteran soldier who had particularly distinguished himself during the storming of the defenses of Java in 1811. Unlike Pakenham, Keane, and Lambert, he was not one of Wellington's Peninsular commanders, but he had acquired a reputation for rugged determination and courage. He was to need both qualities in full measure during the fifteen days following his arrival.

The forward posts of the army, visited by Pakenham, accompanied by Dickson, on the twenty-sixth, were held by Colonel Thornton with the light infantry. They had thrown up a defensive rampart at Lacoste's plantation house about half a mile ahead of Pakenham's headquarters. Advanced pickets were in a wooden barn and a small house 300 yards farther forward, from which Pakenham and Dickson were able to obtain a fair view of the plain toward Jackson's defensive lines, hidden by a turn in the river. While they were there, a body of American cavalry appeared and "set fire to the Cane trash in the fields in front of their piquets [sic], which being very high and thick made a great blaze, but this will be to our advantage, as it clears the ground for advancing."[193] Dickson describes them as wearing "a kind of Blanket dress" and armed with "long Musquets or Rifles" which indicates, as he assumed, that they were Tennesseans, though it is possible that they were the Feliciana Dragoons, who had been ordered by Jackson to scout in front of his line.

During the day the *Carolina* opened fire on the house used as a hospital and so marked by a flag. Dickson reports that "Sir Edward was extremely enraged at this fireing [sic] upon our wounded, and wished the battery [Dickson's guns on the levee] to begin, but I recommended him to defer it to the morning early, when we shall take the Enemy by Surprise." Fortunately the fire of the schooner did no damage. A little ammunition for the artillery arrived, but Dickson confessed that he found "our prospect of supply is very disheartening." He added, "we must be Economical in our expenditure upon the Schooner, as otherwise I fear we shall have no Gun Ammunition when the Army advances."[194] This anxiety was to be his preoccupation throughout the rest of the campaign. As the lack of sufficient shallow-draft boats had dictated the place of landing and prevented the transport of an adequate force in time to make an assault before Pakenham arrived, the want of heavy artillery and the continuing shortage of ammunition for the guns available deprived Pakenham of the strength necessary to success. Early nineteenth-century artillery was too inaccurate to be effective unless it was used in mass. It was employed in preparation for an attack, to breach defenses, and to disorganize and demoralize the enemy. Its effectiveness depended more on weight, mass, and ample supplies of ammunition than upon accuracy, though at short range against advancing columns of troops it could cause havoc.

Sir Thomas Troubridge* took command of sixty seamen who were

*Sir Edward Thomas Troubridge, son of Rear Admiral Sir Thomas Troubridge (1758–1807) who led the British lines at the Battle of Cape St. Vincent. Like Sir Thomas Hardy, Edward Thomas Troubridge had served aboard the *Victory*.

put at Dickson's disposal to help with manhandling the guns, since few horses had been captured, and orders were given to bring the batteries into action against the *Carolina* at dawn on the twenty-seventh. The troops made themselves as comfortable as morning fog, torrential rain, and bitter night frosts, accompanied by intermittent bombardment from the ships on the river, would allow. Food was acquired from local inhabitants—mostly from slaves who had remained on the plantations deserted by their owners—and carefully paid for, and the oranges found on the trees were made, with the abundant sugar in store in all the plantation buildings, into "good wholesome marmalade."[195]

At about two o'clock on the morning of the twenty-seventh the gunners lit fires to heat shot for the bombardment. Red-hot shot was a weapon particularly favored by Dickson, whose use of it at Salamanca had set fire to the garrison's stores and magazines and been instrumental in forcing the surrender of the town. Shortly before eight o'clock the guns opened fire, the 9-pounders with hot shot and the 6-pounders and heavy howitzers with cold shot and shells. The guns found the range almost at once, and the crew of the *Carolina,* after returning "Four Shot at Random," took to the boats and rowed ashore on the far bank of the river. The British guns kept up their fire until flames and smoke spread over the schooner. At half past ten the *Carolina* blew up, "exploding beautifully," and sank. Dickson turned his guns on the *Louisiana,* at extreme range about a mile upriver, but she was saved by her crew who leaped into the boats and warped her upriver to safety. From his post in the rear of Jackson's lines some days later young William Johnson wrote a breathlessly unpunctuated and misspelled letter to his father[196] informing him that Commodore Patterson and Captain Henley "lost all their effects on board the schooner nothing was saved." The *Louisiana,* he added, came near to sharing the same fate, "they fired three or four bums at her which broke over her quarter deck." In the same letter William Johnson mentions the arrival of British deserters: "we are put to mind this post through which some deserters have came and some papers have been found which shows they know the way up here the deserters say that many would desert but are afraid of Jacksons Indians so they cale the Teneseans from their black appearance and Whooping."

Dickson had used nearly a third of his ammunition; but the army was freed to move without the threat of bombardment, and Pakenham made plans to advance. No mention is made of the two gunboats which had been at anchor close to the *Carolina,* and it must be assumed that these escaped up the river out of range since gunboats were later noted in support of the *Louisiana.* Dickson withdrew his guns from the levee and moved them forward to advance with the rest of the army the following day. The 1st West India Regiment, of which only forty-six men had been fit to join the rest of the troops at Villeré's, were detached from General Gibbs' brigade and put under command of the artillery officers to manhandle the guns. Dickson, confirming other accounts, wrote of them:[197] "It is difficult to express how much the Black troops here suffered from the excessive Cold, which they are so little accustomed to, and also so unprovided with warm clothing . . . several here died from mere Cold, and the whole appear quite Torpid and Unequal to any exertion; I am Convinced little or no benefit will be derived from these troops whilst exposed to such cold." The white troops also suffered, although they were accustomed to cold weather and better provided with warm clothing. Admiral Codrington wrote [198] that he was "clothed in two pair of trowsers and two coats, three waistcoats, and so forth," and he was at Cochrane's relatively sheltered headquarters near the mouth of the bayou where fires were kept burning day and night.

Dickson has been criticized for not dividing the fire of his guns between the *Carolina* and the *Louisiana* in the hope of destroying both. He was faced with a difficult choice: he could concentrate on the *Carolina* with some certainty of destroying her, or by dividing his guns between the two targets, he could hope to destroy both and accept the risk of failure. The siting of his guns made it unlikely that the *Carolina* could be warped upriver in time to escape, but she might be allowed to run with the current and beach downriver, where her guns could be saved. Dickson was technically an excellent gunner whose reputation had been built upon knowledge, experience, and reliability, but he was cautious. The *Louisiana* lay at the extreme range of the heavy howitzers, and he was uncertain of their ability to do enough damage, before she was moved, to justify risking the escape of the *Carolina.* The part subsequently played by the *Louisiana* in the course of the campaign has underlined Dickson's failure to destroy her while he had some chance of doing so, but this does nothing to invalidate his decision.

While the British, having disposed of the *Carolina,* prepared to advance, Jackson supervised the construction of his defenses. The line, following the dry ditch of the Rodriguez canal, stretched from the river to the wood on the left flank. On the right, by the levee and blocking the river road, an advance redoubt was constructed flanking the ground immediately in front of the canal. From there the line extended straight to within 150 yards of the wood, where an inverted redan provided crossfire on the vulnerable left. It was there that Jean Laffite pointed out to Livingston, who reported at once to Jackson, that the line had to be extended through the wood as far as the impenetrable cypress swamp and then bent back to protect the flank.[199] Latour, who had designed the works, makes no mention of this defect in his plan which Jackson immediately gave orders to correct. News came that the British had landed troops which were advancing across the Plain of Gentilly. Jackson sent Latour with 200 Tennesseans to reinforce Claiborne, whom he had left in command there. That he took no more urgent action indicated that he believed the information false, as it proved to be. By Christmas Day he was already convinced that the British attack would be made along the ground by the Mississippi. He planned, if he was given enough time, to throw up earthworks for two defensive lines before the city. If he were driven from these, he would fight in the city or above it as circumstances dictated. He brought in troops from all but a few of his outposts elsewhere and called forward part of Carroll's division to help with the works. As a precaution Jackson transferred large stores of powder to a vessel lying close to the city and gave her captain orders to prepare to take her upstream.

News of these preparations, and the rumor that Jackson was ready to burn New Orleans rather than see its rich stores fall a prize to the British[200] reached the ears of the New Orleans legislature. Citizens who rode out to view the defenses in course of construction reported that they were pitifully inadequate. It seemed to them impossible that a mud rampart would hold back a powerful and determined army, and they returned to the city to spread alarm and gloomy predictions of imminent disaster. On the twenty-seventh Colonel Declouet spent an evening's leave at the house of Magloire Guichard, speaker of the lower house of the state legislature. The substance of their conversation was later investigated by a committee of the legislature which exonerated Guichard and other members from treasonable intentions. Whether this verdict was justifiable must remain in doubt. When Declouet left Guichard in the morning, he was under the firm impression that a strong faction in the legislature was prepared to negotiate with the British in order to save New Orleans from destruction. The refusal of the legislature to adjourn during the crisis made this a practicable possibility, and there was no doubt in Declouet's mind that if Jackson suffered a reverse, the city would be given up to the enemy. As he set spurs to his horse to inform Jackson, the British army began to advance toward the American position.

XX

Reconnaissance and Failure

At daylight on the twenty-eighth Pakenham advanced his army in a reconnaissance in strength. It was later asserted that the word "reconnaissance" was used to disguise an attack which failed, but all the evidence is against this assumption. Pakenham clearly intended the move as a probe to discover the strength of the enemy position, the troops employed, and the weight of the enemy's artillery. If the probe had revealed weakness which could be exploited, there can be little doubt that the reconnaissance would immediately have been converted into an assault. Harry Smith, who was, as Pakenham's assistant adjutant general, in a position to know the general's intentions, wrote that the movement was made "to reconnoitre the enemy's position, or to attack if we saw it practicable."[201]

It was a clear frosty morning. The mist had lifted, and the sun shone brightly on the two columns. On the left, using the road by the levee, Keane's brigade of light infantry was screened by the Rifle Brigade, sent forward in extended line to join with the skirmishers of Gibbs' brigade on the right. Dickson accompanied Keane with the light mortars and half the rocket equipment under Captain Lane. The 3-pounders and the other half of the rocket equipment were attached to Gibbs' brigade, which moved along the edge of the swamp. The two 9-pounders under Major John Michell and two of the four 6-pounders were held in reserve moving at the rear of Keane's brigade.

The two columns advanced steadily, using 3-pounders and rockets to clear the enemy pickets and cavalry scouts from De la Ronde's plantation house and then from the Bienvenue plantation buildings,

272

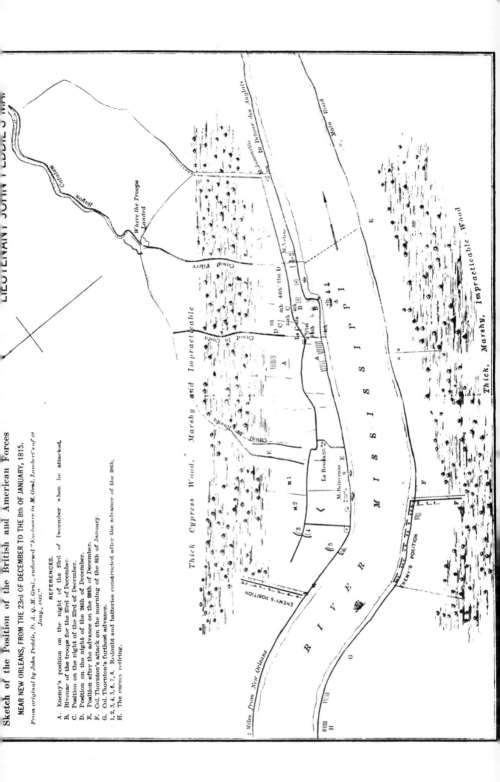

Sketch of the Position of the British and American Forces

NEAR NEW ORLEANS, FROM THE 23rd OF DECEMBER TO THE 8th OF JANUARY, 1815.

From original by John Peddie, D. A. Q. M. Genl., enclosed "Enclosure in M. Genl. Lambert's of 28 Jany., 1815."

REFERENCES.

A. Enemy's position on the night of the 23rd of December when he attacked.
B. Bivouac of the troops for the 23rd of December.
C. Position on the night of the 23rd of December.
D. Position on the night of the 24th of December.
E. Position after the advance on the 28th of December.
F. Col. Thornton's attack on the morning of the 8th of January.
G. Col. Thornton's furthest advance.
1, 2, 3, 4, 5, 6, 7, 8. Redoubts and batteries constructed after the advance of the 28th.
H. The enemy retiring.

which the Americans set on fire as they retreated. It was the forward troops of Gibbs' column on the right who first sighted Jackson's line, hidden from Keane's brigade by houses at the bend in the river. Passing through the turn of the road, Keane found his brigade only 700 yards from the American defenses. Captain Lane's rockets were brought into action as Jackson's guns opened fire. His line mounted four batteries which included two 24-pounders. Dominique You and Renato Beluche, hurried from Fort St. John with a crew of Baratarians, served one of them, and a Baratarian crew from the *Carolina* under Lieutenant Otho Norris, the other.[202] The *Louisiana,* commanded by Lieutenant Charles Thompson, had been allowed to float some yards downriver so that her heavy broadside enfiladed the ground in front of Jackson's line.

As Keane's brigade appeared, the *Louisiana*'s 12- and 24-pounders poured a deadly fire into its flank. "Scarce a ball passed over or fell short of its mark, but all striking full into the midst of our ranks, occasioned terrible havoc. The shrieks of the wounded, therefore, the crash of firelocks, and the fall of such as were killed, caused at first some little confusion; and what added to the panic was, that from the houses beside which we stood bright flames suddenly burst out. . . . The scene was altogether very sublime. A tremendous cannonade moved down our ranks, and deafened us with its roar; whilst two large chateaux and their outbuildings almost scorched us with the flames, and blinded us with the smoke which they emitted."[203] Though there was evidently some confusion and the brigade on the road took some punishment, Gleig's description creates an exaggerated picture of the start of an action which, according to Keane's report, caused "casualties not exceeding 60 men."[204] The brigade was ordered to deploy in line over the stubble fields and take cover while Dickson ordered up Michell's 9-pounders and two 6-pounders under Captain Lewis Carmichael. One of the 9-pounders and a heavy howitzer were turned on *Louisiana* while the rest of the guns were brought into action against the American line.[205]

Sir Edward Pakenham galloped to the left and spoke to Keane and Dickson, ordering the artillery to keep up their fire and the brigade to hold fast while he reconnoitered the enemy defenses. With Dickson he rode over to Gibbs' brigade and, dismounting, went forward on foot while Lieutenant Peter Wright of the Engineers climbed a tree to examine the American position. He reported to Pakenham that the ditch in front of it was filled with water[206] and that the cypress swamp would foil any attempt to turn the flank opposed to the British right.

Pakenham ordered troops from Gibbs' brigade to throw up earthworks to protect advanced batteries and sent Dickson back to bring up his guns.

It appears that Pakenham was, at that stage, considering an attempt to engage Jackson's right while he assaulted his left, out of range of fire from the *Louisiana*. Gibbs' brigade had made good progress, and it seemed possible that Jackson's flank could be turned. When Dickson reached the road, he found both 6-pounders out of action, their wheels or axles shot away, and the 9-pounders forced to withdraw to cover. Carmichael was sent back to bring up the two remaining 6-pounders, but by the time he returned with them, Pakenham had decided against making an attack. Sir Thomas Troubridge led a party of seamen and artillerymen to manhandle the two dismounted 6-pounders out of range of the enemy guns, and these were then returned to Villeré's for repair. Pakenham withdrew both brigades to a position about halfway between Jackson's line and Villeré's plantation. There he decided to wait until heavy guns could be brought from the fleet

For the next three days Pakenham concentrated on the construction of batteries, and there is good reason to suppose that it was during that period that he lost his first opportunity of victory. At the time of the reconnaissance on the twenty-eighth Jackson's line was little more than a mudbank behind a ditch. In places it was waist high, and the left, where the defenses ran into the wood, was particularly vulnerable. Pakenham's right wing, commanded by Gibbs, was scarcely visible to the gunners on the *Louisiana* and at extreme range for their guns. There were, therefore, strong arguments in favor of a concentrated and de-termined infantry assault with rocket and light artillery support against Jackson's ill-protected left, while the remainder of the artillery and rockets created as much confusion as possible on his right. The risks of such an assault would have been great, but every delay made them greater. Pakenham had in the field double the number of troops available to Keane on the twenty-third; twelve field pieces including two 9-pounders; and an army comparatively fresh after four days at Villeré's, eager to take revenge for Jackson's night attack and the frequent incursions of snipers. It is strange that historians of the cam-paign, so ready to castigate Keane for his timorous failure to attack with one exhausted brigade, make no criticism of Pakenham's decision to spend three days waiting for heavy artillery while Jackson completed his defenses on both sides of the river. By this decision Pakenham entrusted the whole responsibility for success to artillery which had to be brought 80 miles from the fleet.

Dickson did his best, and Cochrane's sailors achieved one of the most remarkable feats of transportation in modern history; but Pakenham's army remained, as it had been from the beginning, hopelessly outgunned. The accuracy of the American artillery had already been proved. The ability of the navy, whatever its exertions, to bring forward a sufficient number of 18-pounders to defeat the 24- and 32-pounders on the *Louisiana* and in the American line must always have been doubtful. The Americans, indeed, thought it little less than a miracle that the British were able to bring 18-pounders across Lake Borgne and up the bayou. They had assumed that the route was impassable for any but light field guns. Dickson was faced by another serious problem: that of protection for his batteries. It was useless to dig, for water flooded any hole deeper than eight inches, so all cover for the guns had to be constructed aboveground from any materials available.

By the evening of the twenty-eighth two 18-pounders had arrived, and orders were immediately sent to the fleet to hasten the arrival of eight more. Dickson erected his first battery of two 18-pounders by the main picket on the left of the army's position. The guns were dragged up during the night of the twenty-ninth, and Lieutenant Robert Speer, appointed to command them, was supplied with the materials necessary for heating up shot to fire at the *Louisiana* should she move downriver within range. During the next two days and nights the navy brought forward no less than eight 18-pounders and four 24-pounder carronades. The labor involved in this operation baffles description. The journey across Lake Borgne in boats lying dangerously low in the water was hazardous. The greater part of the journey across the lake and up the bayou had to be made by sailors at the oars, for changing winds upset the balance of the overloaded boats if sails were hoisted. Where the bayou narrowed, the guns had to be lifted and dragged through a morass of mud and reeds to the road leading to Villeré's plantation. Officers of the navy shared with their men the labor of manhandling the guns, and they worked night and day without rest.

Dickson's difficulties in mounting the guns were hardly less severe. All but Speer's battery were to be pushed forward to within 800 yards of the American line, and the batteries could not, therefore, be constructed or the guns put in position until the night before the bombardment was to begin. Lacking gins,* he was obliged to mount his guns by placing "the carriage over the gun upside down, and after

*Hoisting apparatus consisting of three poles and a windlass used for mounting heavy guns on their carriages.

keying the Capsquares upon the Trunnions, it was turned over upon its trucks by the Strength of Men."[207] All were moved on improvised carts found on the plantations. The 24-pounder carronades were brought forward along the road on their own carriages, but "near two kegs of grease" had to be used to prevent the friction from setting them on fire. For protection of the batteries Dickson obtained sugar casks, which were filled with earth and supported by soil heaped on either side, but the cover provided could not be greater than the height of one cask which left the gunners exposed, from the lower ribs upward, to the fire of the enemy. Dickson was also anxious that the platforms, to be constructed with the rest of the battery, in darkness, would be neither firm nor level enough to enable the guns to be fired with accuracy. The carriages of the guns from the fleet were unwieldy and unsuited to fieldwork. Lastly, there was the continuing problem of ammunition. He set up a "laboratory" for the manufacture of cartridges and ransacked the plantation houses for "Hangings, Bed Curtains, Sheeting etc., that would answer, and a Detachment of Tailors, part from the Artillery, and part from the line, were set to work to make Cartridge bags."[208]

By evening on the thirty-first Dickson had surmounted the obstacles, insofar as they were surmountable, and as darkness fell, Burgoyne's engineers and Dickson's artillerymen, with strong detachments of sailors and marines and 500 infantry, assembled to construct the batteries. On the left, on the road, Captain Wolfram Lempriere was to command a battery of two 18-pounders to fire upon Jackson's right; to the right of him Captain Willaim H. Lawrence took charge of three 5½-inch mortars, and forward of his position Captain Henry Lane commanded a rocket battery;* to his right a 7-gun battery under Major Michell consisted of two 9-pounders, three 6-pounders, and two 5½-inch howitzers; and in the center, straddling a road, a powerful battery of six 18-pounders with four 24-pound carronades under Captains Peter Crawford and James Money of the Royal Navy were to try to silence the enemy artillery and then batter a breach in the defenses. All were dangerously short of ammunition, and none of the heavy guns was supplied with sufficient for a single day's firing.

---

*Sir William Congreve (1772–1828) developed the rocket missile, which he described in *The Details of the Rocket System,* published in 1814. The smallest—6- and 9-pounders—were about 18 inches long and mounted on 7-foot sticks. All were fitted with external fuse paper, ignited from a vent, which could be set for any length less than twenty-five seconds. Rockets were fired from the ground on flat or elevated trajectories or from special tripod stands. They were notoriously inaccurate but made a fearsome noise and acted as incendiary bombs where they fell. Wellington tried them in the Peninsula, not entirely without success, but wrote: "I don't want to set fire to any town and I don't know any other use of rockets."

From eight thirty on the evening of December 31 until five forty-five the next morning the gunners, engineers, and sailors labored to complete their task, the infantry being dismissed at two o'clock to be rested before the attack. Dickson, who supervised all the work himself, reported that the gun platforms were "ill laid, uneven, and unsteady, but in finding these faults, it is but justice to add, that under existing circumstances no more could possibly have been done in the time."[209] By daylight all the batteries were ready for action.

During the three days' respite provided by the British preparations Jackson was able to strengthen his line and to add important defenses on the right bank of the river.

As Jackson watched the British columns advancing against his line on the twenty-eighth, he realized the danger to his left wing, where the Tennesseans held a low mud rampart providing little cover. Gibbs' column, unaffected by the flanking artillery fire from the *Louisiana,* advanced with determination along the side of the wood, and Lieutenant Colonel Robert Rennie of the 21st Regiment led skirmishers into the swamp, where they routed the Tennessean pickets. Jackson hurriedly dispatched Jugeat's Choctaw to hold the swamp and galloped toward the left to take personal command. He was halted on the way by one of his volunteer aides, Abner Duncan, who yelled through the thunder of gunfire that he had an urgent messsage from Governor Claiborne. The legislature, he said, was about to give up the country to the enemy. Jackson questioned him briefly and, finding that the message came in fact from Colonel Declouet, told Duncan to ride at once to Claiborne. The governor was to be instructed to make immediate inquiries. "If he finds this is true, tell him to blow up the legislature," Jackson shouted, and spurred on his horse to join his Tennesseans. As he reached them, the British halted and, soon afterward, began to withdraw. The skill of Jackson's gunners, for the most part Laffite's "hellish banditti," had persuaded Pakenham not to risk turning the armed reconnaissance into an assault.

The American guns kept up their bombardment of the British columns for seven hours, pinning Keane's troops to whatever ground cover they could find until he was able to extricate them. Jackson rode back to his field headquarters at Macarty's plantation house. He found waiting for him Senator Bernard Marigny, who demanded to know Jackson's reasons and authority for closing the state legislature. The general was dismayed by the speed of events in the city. In answer to his questions, Marigny made an impassioned speech in defense of the legislature and the loyalty of its members. Abner Duncan, a prominent New Orleans lawyer, had taken upon himself the responsibility for interpreting Jackson's orders to Claiborne as a firm instruction to the governor to close the doors of the legislature's chambers and prevent that assembly from sitting. Jackson patiently explained to Marigny that his instructions had been misunderstood, but Marigny still wanted to know what were Jackson's plans for the city if he was forced to retreat. The general's reply was deliberately ambiguous. He told Marigny to return to the legislature "and say to them from me, that if I was so unfortunate to be beaten from they [*sic*] lines . . . and compelled to retreat through New Orleans, they would have a *warm session.*"[210] This might be interpreted as indicating a determination to defend the city at all costs, a message intended to stiffen the resolution of the legislature. Jackson's explanation, given when the campaign was over, showed that he intended to burn the city with everything in it which could be of use to the enemy and compel them to withdraw by cutting off their supplies.[211] Marigny, whose account[212] makes Jackson's words sound more apologetic and less ominous, was reassured by the conversation and by the British withdrawal he had witnessed. He returned to the city to comfort the anxious members of the legislature, only four of whom were serving in Jackson's army.[213]

The second line of defense, on Dupré's plantation about two miles upriver, was taking shape, and Jackson ordered a third to be started a mile below the city. Nine hundred slaves were employed on the construction of these two lines. It was already clear to him that the artillery would play a crucial part in any coming battle, and he concentrated on completing and strengthening his line, particularly on the vulnerable left flank, and mounting his guns. With the help of about 150 bales of cotton requisitioned from a merchant vessel belonging to Vincent Nolte, his engineers and artillerymen were able to construct firm and level platforms for the guns.* By nightfall on December 31, Jackson had seven batteries ready for action on his line. They mounted, according to Latour, one 32-pounder, three 24-pounders, one long brass

---

*Jackson's use of cotton bales became greatly exaggerated in later accounts of the campaign, though contemporary records contain little mention of them. Nolte (*Fifty Years in Both Hemispheres,* pp. 216 and 232) insisted that none but his bales were used and recorded that when he complained of the waste of expensive cotton when cheaper bales might be easily obtained in the city, Livingston replied, "Well, Mr. Nolte, if this is your cotton, you at least will not think it any hardship to defend it." Cotton bales on the main rampart would have been easily set alight by hot shot and rockets, but there can be no doubt that they were used for the gun emplacements, as a base for timber flooring and as firm walls, covered in a thick layer of mud. Latour records their use for "checks of the embrasures of our batteries" (*Historical Memoir of the War in West Florida and Louisiana,* p. 134); they are also mentioned in a British account as being incorporated in the main

18-pounder, three 12-pounders, three 6-pounders, and a 6-inch heavy howitzer. In addition, Patterson had put two 24-pounders under Captain John D. Henley of the *Carolina* in a square redoubt on the right bank of the river and opposite the city. On the twenty-ninth he landed from the *Louisiana* two 12-pounders, which were placed behind the levee on the right bank, and the following night he added a 24-pounder to his battery which commanded the left flank of Pakenham's army across Chalmette's and Bienvenue's plantations. General Morgan's militia, removed from Terre aux Boeufs, had been transferred to the right bank, where a defensive line was under construction to prevent any attempt by the British to turn the American right flank by way of the river.

Each day the *Louisiana* dropped down the river to take station at the anchorage she had occupied on the twenty-eighth, and at night Tennessean sharpshooters scouted through the wood on the left of the line to snipe at British pickets. Dressed in their brown hunting dress, they were difficult to see, and their "hunting parties" scored some successes against forward detachments which were kept in a constant state of anxiety. Jackson's men were still short of arms, though the Baratarians had provided all the ammunition he needed, and he ordered privately owned firearms to be collected in the city and sent to the front. On the morning of the thirtieth Major General Villeré arrived from the Acadian coast with 300 militia and took command of the troops guarding the Piernas canal, which led from the upper reaches of Bayou Bienvenue to Jackson's rear. Deserters from the British lines reported that strong reinforcements were expected there and that heavy guns were being brought up from the fleet. During the night of the thirty-first the Americans, waiting in their line, could hear the British working at their batteries, and it was evident that an attack was planned for the next day.

New Year's Day, 1815, dawned in thick fog. It cleared gradually under showers of rain, which also obscured all vision of enemy positions. The British troops formed in two columns, ready for the assault. At nine o'clock Pakenham's artillery opened fire. The first shots were directed at Macarty's house, where Jackson had his headquarters. The

---

embankment (Aitchison, *Autobiography*, MS., p. 72) and by Pakenham's aide Wylly, who wrote of the strength of the American works "from their solidity and the heavy bales of cotton with which they were lined and protected and in which our shot was immediately buried" *(Pakenham Letters)*. General William Carroll wrote later: "A very general impression prevails that our breast works were of cotton bales. This was not so. The only use we made of cotton was to form embrasures for the cannon on the line" (Tulane University. Special Collections. John Minor Wisdom MSS f.I.B.). Carroll's statement may be accepted as definitive.

general and his staff were in the house, but although it was struck repeatedly, no one was hurt.[214] The Americans ran to their posts and returned fire. The artillery duel continued for more than three hours, at the end of which Dickson's guns had run out of ammunition. Latour states, without revealing the source of his information, that "in about an hour's time, our balls dismounted several of his guns; and when the firing ceased the greater part of his artillery was unfit for service."[215] It must be assumed that he deduced, from the enemy's silence, that the British artillery had been put out of action. He could not have known the desperate straits to which Dickson was reduced by lack of ammunition. Latour added, "Jusice obliges us to acknowledge that the fire of the British was for a long time vigorously kept up and well directed. We had the carriage of a twenty-four pounder broken by one of their balls, at captain Dominique's [You's] battery, and that of the thirty-two pounder, commanded by lieutenant Crawley of the navy, was also damaged by a ball; the fore-train of the twelve-pounder of general Garrigues [Fleaujac] was likewise broken . . . the rockets blew up two artillery caissons, in one of which were a hundred rounds."

In fact, as Dickson noted soberly in his journal (which, unlike Latour's account, was kept every day and was not intended for publication), the British guns "only ceased for want of Ammunition, for we had not one piece of heavy Ordnance disabled, or even struck."[216] The only damage was to the howitzer, which had been hit, and to a few wheels which were broken. The artillerymen had suffered 13 killed, including 1 officer, and 13 wounded, and Dickson added, with his usual attention to accuracy, "even if there had been Sufficient Ammunition, the nature of our Batteries were such the men could not have gone on for many hours longer." Though it was true that the damage to British guns was negligible, it was clear that the gun crews were too exposed to enemy fire. The protection afforded by a single line of sugar barrels filled with mud was slight, and it is a tribute to the British gunners that they served their guns so coolly. The platforms constructed the previous night were "uneven and loose," and the carriages of the 18-pounders, intended for ship service, "were found very Awkward and unmanageable." Dickson admitted that "during the Cannonade, or at least until the latter part of it, our fire did not attain the precision it ought, neither could it be kept up with the rapidity necessary to Silence the Enemies Guns." He believed that the lack of field gun carriages was more serious than the shortage of ammunition. The combination of the two deficiencies proved to be a formula for defeat.

Though he could not have realized it when he wrote his journal,

Dickson was admitting that Pakenham's army was already defeated. Pakenham had delegated to his artillery responsibility for silencing the enemy's guns and breaching his line before his infantry attacked; Dickson had failed to win the artillery battle; and he stated as the most important reason for failure (sea service gun carriages) a factor which could not be changed.

During the cannonade, Lieutenant Colonel Rennie again led men of the 21st Regiment into the swamp on the right, driving in the American pickets and then taking cover to wait for the signal for a general assault. When the firing ceased, he sent back for orders and was withdrawn. In the wood he had found the body of Lieutenant Peter Wright of the Royal Engineers,* who had been missing since he set out on a reconnaissance on the thirtieth.

Pakenham ordered Dickson to withdraw his guns from their vulnerable forward batteries. He had determined to wait for reinforcements. That afternoon it rained unceasingly, and the clay soil of the plain rapidly became a morass. As soon as it was dark, the light guns were brought back without much difficulty. The two 18-pounders of Lempriere's battery proved more troublesome, but they were, at length, dragged to a position behind Speer's. It remained to move the heavy battery of ten guns in the center. The men, dispirited by the failure of the battle, drenched with rain, and sinking to their knees in mud, abandoned the task and stole away in the darkness. The temporary sling carts were broken, and the guns had to be brought out before dawn. Dickson, in desperation, reported the deplorable state of affairs to Pakenham, who was asleep at Lacoste's house. He immediately went to the front and took personal charge. Harry Smith, who had wakened the general with Dickson's report and went with him to the guns, reported that the men of the 21st and 44th regiments were "not distinguished for discipline," and it was only the presence of the commander in chief which persuaded the men to save the guns. Both regiments belonged to the brigade commanded by General Sam Gibbs. Both were to play important parts in the final assault a week later.

According to Harry Smith, "Poor Sir Edward was much mortified at being obliged to retire the army from a second demonstration and disposition to attack, but there was nothing for it."[217] Pakenham's mortification was shared by his men. Gleig's reaction was probably typical:

---

*Described by Keane as "an enterprising and intelligent officer." It was he who had climbed a tree on the twenty-eighth to examine the enemy's line for Pakenham (see p. 275).

For two whole nights and days not a man had closed an eye, except such as were cool enough to sleep amidst showers of cannon-ball; and during the day scarcely a moment had been allowed in which we were able so much as to break our fast. We retired, therefore, not only baffled and disappointed, but in some degree disheartened and discontented. All our plans had as yet proved abortive; even this, upon which so much reliance had been placed, was found to be of no avail; and it must be confessed that something like murmuring began to be heard through the camp.[218]

This was not surprising. Pakenham's troops had suffered great hardship since they left the fleet. On their arrival they had been subjected to heavy fire from the *Carolina,* which they were unable to return, and since the twenty-eighth they had been almost continuously under fire from artillery and from Tennessean "Dirty Shirts" who hunted them like game. Seasoned soldiers will accept almost any hardship or danger, provided they are given action, but Pakenham's army had twice prepared for battle and had been withdrawn on both occasions without being given an opportunity to fight. There can be little doubt that Pakenham's refusal to attack, however justifiable, invited and contributed to a breakdown in discipline.

It is strange that Pakenham's decision has scarcely been questioned. Following the strictures of Admiral Codrington, who was not present but nevertheless described the failure to win the artillery battle as "not to be expected and . . . a blot on the artillery escutcheon,"[219] historians have readily blamed Dickson without examining Pakenham's tactics. It is arguable that he should have attacked on the twenty-eighth while the American batteries and breastworks were incomplete. The argument against his absolute reliance on the use of artillery is even more persuasive. From his first sight of Jackson's hastily constructed ramparts on December 28, Pakenham persisted in regarding them as fortifications requiring reduction by siege, although he had no siege train and the cutting of saps* in such waterlogged ground would be impossible. The American artillery was inferior in numbers and total weight of shot, though the batteries were mounted on solid platforms and included at least one gun heavier than anything the British could muster. It was excellently directed and served; but it could not have engaged both Pakenham's troops and his artillery simultaneously, and the route beside the wood and swamp toward Jackson's left, where Gibbs had made almost unimpeded progress on the twenty-eighth,

*Approach trenches in zigzag patterns dug to cover an advance to a fortified objective.

offered an advance safe from the attentions of a good part of Jackson's artillery. If Pakenham's decision is accepted that no infantry assault should be made until the American guns were silenced and the breastworks breached, he had no choice but to withdraw his army, but that decision was based on a false appraisal of the strength of Jackson's position. Further delay would give Pakenham reinforcements with the arrival of Lambert's brigade, but he might have assumed that Jackson's army might also be reinforced and his line would certainly be strengthened.

The British position was one of extreme difficulty requiring a commander of exceptional ability. Pakenham, for all his personal courage and popularity, had not the steely ruthlessness essential to victory. In common with most of Wellington's generals, he was an excellent subordinate, but he lacked the qualities of imagination, flexibility, and pitiless dedication necessary for independent command.

XXI

Preparation for Battle

On January 3, two days after the artillery battle, Jackson wrote to Monroe:[220] "The enemy occupy their former position and are engaged in strengthening it; our time is spent in the same employment and in exchanging long shot with them. . . . I do not know what may be their further design—Whether to redouble their effort, or apply them elsewhere. . . . I am preparing for either event." While he waited the defenses on the Rodriguez canal were completed, the two reserve lines thrown up, and a solid artillery position was created on the right bank.

Pakenham, having made the decision to wait for the arrival of Lambert's brigade, had formulated a new plan of attack. From Harry Smith's account it appears that Pakenham had earlier recognized the importance of the right bank of the river. The batteries mounted there by Jackson before the abortive attack on January 1 had demonstrated the part they would play in repelling any frontal assault on this position. Pakenham proposed to capture these batteries and to turn them against Jackson's line, and it was Cochrane who devised the method.[221] From January 2 strong working parties were employed in deepening and widening the canal from the landing place to the levee with the object of moving boats from Bayou Bienvenue to the Mississippi. These would be used to transport Colonel Thornton with a force of about 1,100 men across the river at night. Their object would be to capture the enemy's guns before they could be spiked. As soon as they were ready for use against Jackson's flank, a signal rocket would be fired to inform Pakenham that the main assault might go forward. Although the arrival of reinforcements would strengthen British

chances of breaking into Jackson's line, the plan hinged on the ability
to put boats into the river. The army was divided to work in four shifts
day and night until the canal was cut.

Intermittent but heavy rain throughout January 2 hampered the
work, and the American artillery, fired at intervals from both sides of
the river, caused some casualties among the forward troops. Dickson's
guns, brought to the rear during the night, had suffered more damage
in the move than during the action on the first. He was obliged to ask
Cochrane for naval carpenters to repair wheels and carriages, and he
sent an officer to the fleet to supervise the provision and transport of
ammunition and artillery supplies. Previous requisitions had not been
completed, the navy having calculated the army's needs on the basis of
ammunition expenditure in a sea engagement. While the army was
engaged in digging the canal, there was time to bring forward ammunition in the quantities required for artillery in the field.

During the afternoon of the second news came of the arrival of
Lambert's brigade at the main anchorage, and twenty-four hours later
General Lambert arrived at Pakenham's headquarters. During
January 4 his two regiments, the 7th and 43d, were brought forward to
join the rest of the army. An American deserter provided Dickson with
information of the small damage inflicted on the enemy's guns during
the artillery duel. More valuable was the intelligence that they were
preparing to fire hot shot against all the buildings occupied by the
British since they had information that ammunition was stored in
some of them. Throughout the fourth the British artillerymen were
engaged in removing all ammunition and stores from these buildings
to tented dumps distributed over the fields. Hot shot was fired at
Bienvenue's house on the fourth, and on the fifth the slave huts in front
were set on fire.

By the evening of the sixth Dickson had received substantial quantities of ammunition, sufficient for his guns to support Pakenham's
attack. Some of it had been brought forward in the knapsacks of
Lambert's infantry. A boat from the *Statira* turned over on Lake
Borgne, and the seventeen unfortunate Fusiliers, weighed down by
round shot, sank at once without trace. Work on the canal was so far
advanced that it was anticipated that Thornton's brigade could be
sent across the river on the night of the sixth. Pakenham's assault was
planned for daylight on the seventh. Dickson erected batteries of six
18-pounders and two 24-pounder carronades to engage any enemy
vessels floated down the Mississippi and to fire across the river in
support of Thorton's attack. The remainder of the 18-pounders and the

24-pounder carronades were to reoccupy the old forward batteries in the center. Major Michell would accompany Thornton with the two 9-pounders and two heavy howitzers for use against Jackson's line when the American position on the right bank had been captured.

Pakenham regrouped his army into four brigades. The first, under Lambert and comprising the 7th, 43d, and part of the 1st West India Regiment with the dismounted 14th Light Dragoons, was to form his reserve. It was Lambert's role to advance in the center but several hundred yards behind the leading brigades. The second brigade, led by Gibbs, was to make the main assault on Jackson's left. This column, consisting of the 4th, 21st, and 44th regiments, would follow an advance guard of the 44th carrying fascines and ladders to bridge the ditch. Their right flank would be protected from any counterattack through the wood by a battalion of their own light infantry companies. Keane's third brigade, on the left, would advance across the fields along the line of the road and about 125 yards inside the levee behind the light companies of the 43d and 93d regiments led by Colonel Rennie. Rennie's task was to break into the forward redoubt on Jackson's right and spike the guns enfilading the ground in front of the American line. Keane, following close behind, would take advantage of any opportunity created by Rennie's success or move against Jackson's center as circumstances indicated. The fourth brigade was Thornton's. Having captured the enemy's batteries on the right bank of the river and turned the guns on Jackson's lines, he was to march his infantry toward the city and "demonstrate" against it from the far bank. His brigade included a detachment of rockets under Captain Lane which would have made such a demonstration suitably awe-inspiring against a civilian population who could not know how limited was their effect.

On the sixth the canal was not ready for the boats. The attack was postponed until the eighth. Two days earlier, as Lambert's brigade arrived to join Pakenham's army, Jackson was reinforced by 2,368 Kentuckians under Major General John Thomas. Only a third of their number was armed. Jackson could not believe it: "I never in my life," he is reported to have said, "seen a Kentuckian without a gun, a pack of cards and a jug of whiskey."[222] He stripped of their muskets four companies of militia left in the city and armed 400 more Kentuckians, but more than half of Thomas' force had to be left with unarmed Louisiana militia on the second line at Dupré's. Lack of arms was not the Kentuckians' only problem: they were also clothed in rags and would have suffered from the cold and wet weather but for the generosity of the citizens of New Orleans. With a grant from the legislature a total of $16,000 was raised and used for the purchase of blankets which were distributed among the ladies of the city to be made into clothing. Latour recorded[223] that "within one week twelve hundred blanket cloaks, two hundred and seventy-five waistcoats, eleven hundred and twenty-seven pairs of pantaloons, eight hundred shirts, four hundred and ten pairs of shoes, and a great number of mattresses, were made up, or purchased ready made, and distributed among our brethern in arms, who stood in the greatest need of them."

Although Jackson had erected strong batteries on the right bank covering the river and enfilading the ground in front of his line, it appears not to have occurred to him that they might require protection from attack. Latour had supervised the construction of a line behind Boisgervais'[224] canal on the right bank about three miles below the city, but at the main gun position there was a short, untenable trench without a single gun directed to the front. This was occupied by Major General David B. Morgan's Louisiana militia. On January 6, Sailing Master Johnson took three small vessels through the Chef Menteur pass from Lake Pontchartrain into Lake Borgne and intercepted a British transport schooner, which he captured and burned.[224] From the ten prisoners captured he learned that the British were digging out the Villeré canal and extending it to the river. Patterson, who had gone downriver to observe the enemy's movements from the west bank, confirmed this.[225] Jackson could spare few troops from his line and had made no provision for transferring men direct to Morgan's position. He ordered 400 Kentucky militia, of whom less than half were armed, to march back to New Orleans, where they were ferried across the river. This order was not given until seven o'clock on the evening of the seventh. Meanwhile, acting on Patterson's advice, Morgan mounted a 12-pounder and two 6-pounders in the breastworks facing downriver. These defenses covered only 200 yards, little more than a tenth of the distance between the river and the swamp on the west flank.

Jackson still feared a British movement up the Bayou Bienvenue to take his position in the rear from the Piernas canal. On the fifth, Reuben Kemper took eleven men in two canoes down the bayou on a reconnaissance. They penetrated as far as the junction of Bienvenue with Mazant, where the British had made a fortified camp, and Kemper went forward to a point where he could observe the Mazant obstructed by a line of boats. While he was returning to his canoes, they were discovered by British boats under Captain James Laurence of the *Alceste* moving up the Bienvenue. All but one of the men left to guard them escaped into the reeds, and Kemper succeeded in leading his detachment back to camp the following day. The prisoner taken by Laurence gave Pakenham information of the arrival of the Kentuckians in Jackson's line.[226]

Both generals were well informed of each other's movements, but Jackson's information was probably more accurate than Pakenham's. In the period following his night attack on December 24, Jackson had taken more prisoners, and he had also received the help of more deserters. Dickson, the least prejudiced of observers, mentions only one American deserter—a man from the 44th U.S. Infantry who gave warning of the intention to fire hot shot against the buildings housing ammunition—but he records the desertion of three men of the 21st Regiment and one of the 95th, and it seems certain that his record was far from complete.

The two armies were not as ill-matched as the disparity in numbers might suggest. The British were able to put into the field about 5,400 men against Jackson's 4,000, but Jackson's choice of position left his enemy an advance over some 2,000 yards of open ground under fire while his own troops were sheltered by a mud rampart between 14 and 20 feet thick. Pakenham's troops were veterans, but their health and discipline had been eroded by appalling conditions, an evil climate, and the frustration of continued false starts and delays. It is not possible for anyone who has not experienced the irritations and lethargy produced by the damp, lung-constricting climate of Louisiana to imagine its effect upon European troops encumbered by tightly fitting uniforms and heavy equipment. To these discomforts were added accurate and frequent bombardment and the depredations of Tennessean hunting parties. Nothing, however, reduced the morale of Pakenham's troops so much as the denial of an opportunity for action. Jackson's troops, on the other hand, though largely untried and apprehensive, showed a spirit and cheerfulness which warmed his heart. There had been some temporary reaction among the militia regiments against blistering their hands in throwing up ramparts, but Coffee's men, who occupied the position on the extreme left, where they worked, ate, and slept in mud over their ankles, made no complaint.

Dickson's loss of the artillery duel on January 1 was crucial to the outcome of the campaign. It has been suggested that the American guns were better served and directed by their largely Baratarian crews than those of the British, but the actual damage caused to the artillery of each side does not support this theory. In spite of the inadequacy of their platforms and the unwieldy naval carriages, Dickson's guns had registered more direct hits than Jackson's. The disagreeable fact, made plain by the artillery battle, was that Pakenham's belief in the ability of his artillery to silence the enemy's and simultaneously to breach the rampart was unfounded. The wet mud construction of Jackson's rampart made it impervious to the fire of the heaviest guns which could be brought up the bayou, and continuous bombardment required quantities of ammunition which had not been made available. As Pakenham's proposed offensive was founded upon the success of his artillery, no attack could be made. With characteristic honesty Dickson admitted that it was unwise to make the attempt with so little ammunition, but he evidently did not feel able to advise the postponement of the advance. It is certain that neither he nor Pakenham had understood the strength of Jackson's ramparts or the efficiency of his gunners. Pakenham's second plan implies an acceptance that Jackson's line had to be breached and stormed by infantry, though he hoped to reduce the odds against them by the destruction of an important part of the enemy's artillery.

By the evening of the seventh Jackson had reason to believe that the British planned to attack on both sides of the river the following day. He was anxious about the position occupied by General Morgan on the west bank, but he was satisfied that his dispositions along the Rodriguez canal were as strong as he could make them. Shortly after one o'clock on the morning of Sunday January 8 he inspected his line. On the extreme right his forward redoubt commanded the levee road and the front of the line. It contained two 6-pounders served by a detachment of the 44th U.S. Infantry and was guarded by a company of the 7th Regiment. Behind the line, in the rear of the redoubt, Beale's Rifles were stationed. To their left, and 70 feet from the river, Captain Enoch Humphrey of the U.S. Artillery commanded battery No. 1, consisting of two 12-pounders and a 6½-inch heavy howitzer; 90 yards to his left battery No. 2 mounted one 24-pounder; and a farther 50 yards inland Dominique You and Renato Beluche commanded two 24-pounders. The line between these batteries was held by the 7th U.S. Infantry. Between the third and fourth batteries, the latter consisting of the giant 32-pounder, Plauché's battalion of Uniformed Volunteers and Lacoste's battalion of Free Men of Color held a short stretch of 20 yards. Daquin's Haitians and the 44th Regiment were ranged along the 220 yards between the 32-pounders and batteries 5 and 6, two 6-pounders under Captain Henry Perry and a 12-pounder directed by General Garrigues Fleaujac. The rest of the line to the edge of the wood included battery No. 7, a long 18-pounder and a 6-pounder served by regular U.S. artillery crews, a small brass carronade at No. 8, and the inverted redoubt, and was held by General Carroll's Tennesseans supported by Kentucky militia under Brigadier General John Adair. The line running into the wood and turning back in a dogleg from the swamp was defended by the Tennesseans commanded by General Coffee. Latour's map of these dispositions does not accord with his description.[227] Plauché's and Lacoste's battalions are shown as occupying 220 yards of line between batteries 3 and 4, a distance described as being 20 yards. It seems likely that it is the description rather than the map which is at fault. The 7th Regiment, numbering 430, account for 150 yards, whereas Plauché's and Lacoste's, numbering 569, are allotted, in Latour's written account, a mere 20 yards. Hinds' Mississippi Dragoons and detachments of about 250 Louisiana militia were posted in reserve behind the main line.

During the day Jackson had taken a telescope to the upper floor of his field headquarters at Macarty's plantation house. From there he had been able to see a great deal of activity in the British camp, and it appeared that troops were making fascines and "working on pieces of wood, which we concluded must be ladders." Soon after dusk he could distinctly hear the sound of parties at work in the British batteries which had been occupied and evacuated on January 1. Quickly he moved down his line, pausing at each battery and at each company position to have a word with his men.

In the British camp Pakenham had issued his orders for the attack. Forty-two boats from the fleet had been brought up to the Villeré canal, and a dam had been built behind them to raise the water level when the levee was breached and enable the boats to be floated into the river. According to Harry Smith,[228] "Sir Edward went to inspect the bayou, the boats, etc. I heard him say to the engineer, 'Are you satisfied the dam will bear the weight of water which will be upon it when the banks of the river are cut?' He said 'Perfectly.' 'I should be more so if a second dam was constructed.' The engineer was positive." From the tone of the replies it seems most probable that they were made by Colonel Burgoyne, the senior engineer officer with the army, and it is certain that he must have supervised the work. Burgoyne made no mention of the conversation in his memoirs, an understandable omission in view of subsequent events, but neither is there any other evidence to support Smith's record. Having satisfied himself that all necessary preparations had been made to carry out his plan, Pakenham went to bed and to sleep.

While Pakenham slept at his headquarters, the plan began to go wrong. The first boats were dragged into the Mississippi at about nine o'clock; but the river was low, and the labor involved in manhandling them over the cut in the levee was far greater than had been anticipated. Smith attributes this difficulty to the collapse of the dam "as Sir Edward seemed to anticipate"; Burgoyne declares that "the banks of the new cutting" fell in; Codrington told his son that the banks of the cutting were not firm enough, although he had personally suggested that the mud cut from the canal should be formed into a firm path for the seamen to use while dragging the boats; Dickson mentions only the barrier at the levee, where the seamen worked "in a deep Mud into which they frequently sunk up to the Middle." All are agreed that the exertions of the men were "beyond belief." Whatever the cause of the delay, only thirty boats were in the river by three fifteen on the morning of January 8 and at five o'clock Thornton's brigade had still not left the east bank.[229]

While Cochrane's sailors struggled with the boats for Thornton's brigade, Dickson's guns were being hauled forward into the batteries they were to occupy during the forthcoming battle. At half past two Sir Thomas Troubridge reported to him that the men moving the guns intended for the center batteries had been unable to find any direct route to the position and had therefore been obliged to drag them to the levee road and from there to the batteries. He reported also that the batteries themselves were unfinished and he doubted if the 18-pounders could be in position by daylight. Two hours later Lieutenant Benson Earle Hill, sent by Dickson to urge the work forward, reported that the batteries were still "not half finished."[230]

Throughout this period of intense activity and exertion to overcome unforeseen obstacles no one appears to have thought of wakening the commander in chief, although it must have been obvious that the delay in Thornton's crossing, in particular, jeopardized the entire plan of attack.

Pakenham rose at five o'clock. According to Dickson,[231] "he was Surprised on learning that Col. Thornton had not yet put off, and finding it so near daylight he felt doubtful whether to let the Detachment go, as there could not be time for them to get possession of the works on the other side, and bring up Artillery to enfilade the Enemies line in Corroboration of the general attack, which was to take place at daylight, but considering that at all events Col. Thornton's attack on the other side might as a diversion greatly Assist the main attack, he sent to the boats to know the number of men on board, and having been informed in reply that the 85th were on board with Marines, making them up to 460, that there were 9 boats still to get into the river, but that those afloat would take 100 Men more, he ordered these to be embarked, and that the boats should put off, which was done accordingly." Pakenham sent for Harry Smith, seconded to Lambert as military secretary, who found him "greatly agitated." The general said, "The dam, as you heard me say it would, gave way, and Thornton's people will be of no use whatever to the general attack."[232] This was half an hour before daylight.

The disastrous consequences of failing to waken Pakenham now became clear. Had he been informed of the difficulties two hours earlier, he might have sent part of Thornton's brigade ahead in the twenty or more boats already launched. The remainder could have followed as soon as the boats returned, and, as Dickson remarked, "the whole force with Artillery etc. would have been across long before daylight." By that time all the boats would have been on the river, ready to carry reinforcements or withdraw Thornton's brigade according to circumstances. Since the 9-pounders and heavy howitzers had not been loaded, Dickson persuaded Pakenham to keep them on the east bank and sent them forward to support the main advance.

Pakenham had been prepared for Thornton to fail. The orders signed by Major Charles Ramus Forrest and sent to Dickson on the evening of the seventh[233] made it clear that his artillery was not to be sent across the river unless the enemy's position on the west bank could be carried with the bayonet "and the signal of Colonel Thornton's failure will be a *Blue Light* burnt opposite the house of M. Bienvenue." Success was to be signaled by "a Rocket . . . fired directly in a perpendicular direction from the same point on the opposite Shore that the Blue Light is to be Thrown in the Event of failure." Officers on the shore batteries were specially required to look out for either signal. The blue light was to be their cue to open fire against the American batteries on the farther shore. What is not known is how Pakenham proposed to act in the event of Thornton's failure. With forty-two boats on the river it would have been possible for him to reinforce Thornton and carry the American position on the right bank under cover of fire from Dickson's batteries on the levee. He was certainly not prepared for the situation which confronted him on the morning of January 8.

Pakenham was faced by an agonizing decision: he must either make his frontal attack, as planned, exposing his army to fire even more devastating than that experienced a week earlier when he had retreated, or he must, once more, turn aside from the prospect of victory and withdraw an army prepared for battle. There was a third possibility, which does not appear to have been considered: to postpone the attack until Thornton was across the river and had signaled his success. This would necessitate an immediate retreat by the advance guards of both columns from their assault positions which were only about 650 yards from Jackson's line. Had Pakenham done this, the main assault must have been made in daylight and the enemy would have had ample warning of his intentions on both sides of the river. Smith urged Pakenham to withdraw, but the commander in chief replied, "I have twice deferred the attack. We are strong in numbers comparatively. It will cost more men, and the assault must be made." Smith again counseled delay. "While we were talking, the streaks of daylight began to appear, although the morning was dull, close and heavy, the clouds almost touching the ground." Pakenham said,[234] "It is now too late." He had made his decision. At his order the rocket signaling the advance was fired.

XXII

The Eighth of January

At four o'clock on the morning of January 8 the troops of Keane's and Gibbs' brigades moved forward to their assault positions. When daylight came, the advance parties of both columns would be about 650 yards from the American line, within sight and easy range of the enemy's artillery. For this reason it was an essential part of the plan that the leading troops should storm the ditch at first light.

As Pakenham's orders made clear, his main attack was to be conducted by Gibbs. His advance guard was composed of part of the 44th Regiment, carrying ladders and fascines, and part of the Rifle Brigade to act as a firing party covering the approach under the enemy's rampart. As soon as the ladders and fascines were in place, Gibbs' brigade, following on the heels of the advance guard, would cross the ditch and break into the defenses.

The 44th Regiment was commanded by Lieutenant Colonel The Honourable Thomas Mullens, third son of Lord Ventry, a captain holding the local rank of lieutenant colonel in America. His orders from Pakenham were explicit:[235] "The Advance Guard is to carry forward with it, six long Ladders with planks on them & ten small Ladders, as well as the Fascines. The officer commanding the 44th Regt. must ascertain where these requisites are, this evening, so that there may be no delay in taking them forward tomorrow to the old Batteries." When he read these orders, Mullens was heard to say,[236] "It is a forlorn hope, and the Regiment must be sacrificed." The following morning he led his regiment past the redoubt where the ladders and fascines were stored and took up his assault position. It was half an hour before anyone realized this "Most Extraordinary blunder."[237] Mullens took his men back to the redoubt 500 yards to the rear. When they returned to the forward position, the battle had already begun and Mullens was not with them.

Covering the right flank of the 2d brigade were the light infantry companies of the 4th, 21st, and 44th with a detachment of the 1st West India Regiment. Commanded by Lieutenant Colonel Timothy Jones of the 4th Regiment, they were to penetrate the wood and, having protected the brigade against a flank attack during the advance, to try to break into the weak log rampart on Jackson's left.

Close to the levee Keane's brigade was in position for the attack. In front and to his left Rennie's advance guard stood ready to storm the forward redoubt at the extreme right of the American line. Pakenham rode across to Keane and gave him fresh orders.[238] Hoping to preserve the 3d brigade from the worst of the fire from the west bank, which he realized could not be silenced by Thornton before the attack began, Pakenham ordered Keane to advance on a diagonal line and make his assault to the left of Gibbs. Rennie was to storm the redoubt and spike the guns unsupported. It is not clear whether Rennie was intended to hold the redoubt or to attempt to fight his way into the main defenses behind.

Lambert's first brigade formed in the center and to the rear. His troops, the 7th and 43d regiments, were the elite of the army. As Pakenham had told Harry Smith,[239] "Those fellows would storm anything." He added, "but, indeed, so will the others, and when we are in New Orleans, I can depend on Lambert's reserve." The remark is significant. Pakenham had had plenty of opportunities to witness the breakdown of discipline following the storming of a defended town in the Peninsula. It was he who, as commander of the reorganized military police, had gone about "like a raving lion" enforcing Wellington's orders against plunder twelve months earlier. Even if he had not heard rumors from the ranks of "beauty and booty," he was certainly informed about the wealth of New Orleans, and he was prepared to use the two great Peninsular regiments to maintain order after victory.

Dickson's guns were in position, occupying the old center battery; but the platforms and defenses were no better than they had been a week earlier, and the crews were working in muddy water as much as 18 inches deep. Keane's new line of advance would take his brigade across the main field of fire, destroying any possibility of effective artillery support. Unaware of this late change in Pakenham's orders, Dickson rode forward with Burgoyne.

The American pickets, observing the advance of the British columns, withdrew to their line. Before dawn Jackson was aware that his enemy was on the move. Half his troops were resting in the rear. Quickly Jackson gave orders for them to join their comrades at the ramparts. The gun crews stood ready in the batteries. There was no sound of firing from the position on the right bank where General Morgan's militia guarded the great battery of sixteen guns covering the front of Jackson's line. The security of that position, so essential to the main defenses, was the source of acute anxiety to him, but he could spare no more troops from the Rodriguez canal to reinforce Morgan. Jackson had kept his defenses flexible so long as flexibility was required. When, in spite of his precautions, the enemy had made a surprise landing, he had struck at them and halted their advance. His hastily formed line had withstood bombardment, and the British had been persuaded to postpone their attack while he strengthened his defenses and received all the reinforcements he had expected. Though short of arms, he had roused the forces of four states in the defense of New Orleans, and he had deployed them to the best of his ability. There was nothing more that Jackson could do but wait.

On the right bank General Morgan and Commodore Patterson had been informed of the British plan to cross the river; but their defenses were inadequate, and Morgan's deployment of his troops was incompetent. The weakness of the line lay in its extent. Against the advice of Latour, Morgan had chosen to hold Raguet's canal, stretching 2,000 yards from the river to the cypress swamp on the right flank. Along 200 yards of this he had thrown up a strong but uncompleted bastion and a small redan. The remainder of the line consisted of a mud embankment. During the afternoon of the seventh one 12-pounder and two 6-pounders were mounted on the left facing downriver. Morgan's troops comprised Colonel Declouet's Regiment of Louisiana Drafted Militia, the 2d Louisiana Militia under Colonel Zenon Cavallier, and the 1st Louisiana Militia (Colonel J. B. Dejan) with a detachment of the 6th. The effective total was 546 men.[240] To this force was added a company of two hundred Kentuckians under Colonel John Davis.

On Jackson's orders Davis had marched 500 of the Kentucky militia from the Rodriguez canal to New Orleans, but only about a quarter of their number were armed, and no more than seventy rifles could be found in the city. Davis therefore crossed the river with less than half his original force. The Kentuckians reached Morgan's line at four o'clock on the morning of the eighth, after a five-mile march through mud up to their knees, and were immediately ordered to move forward another mile to join Major Pane Arnaud's detachment of 120 of the 6th Louisiana Militia on Mayhew's plantation. Davis' men had eaten little or nothing since noon the previous day. By the time they reached the forward area occupied by Arnaud they were exhausted. Morgan's force, already too small to cover more than a small part of the line he had chosen, was thus improvidently divided between two positions, neither defensible, a mile apart. The troops were inexperienced and ill-armed. Morgan's mismanagement of them was an open invitation to defeat.

It was already dawn when Lieutenant John Crawley of the rocket brigade fired Pakenham's signal for the attack. As the blazing trail of flame rose into the gray clouds, the advance guards on both flanks ran forward toward Jackson's line and the American guns opened fire. They were answered at once by Dickson's batteries, and from across the river, Patterson's guns took up the challenge. Amid the roar of cannonfire could be heard the steady beat of drums from the advancing British columns and, from Keane's brigade on the left, the skirl of the pipes of the 93d Regiment. For the brief moment before men began to die Pakenham's army paraded in proud, colorful, and stirring display. Within five minutes the image was shattered; within ten the parade ground had become a churned field of mud heaped with tangled and bloodied masses of scarlet, tartan, and green.

On the right the second brigade came under heavy fire from the three batteries on Jackson's left. The Rifle Brigade advance guard deployed in skirmishing order and rushed the canal, scrambling into the ditch and attempting to cut their way up the rampart with their bayonets. Contrary to their orders, the firing party of the 44th halted and began to shoot at the enemy position. Answered by a withering volley from Carroll's and Adair's militia and battered by Jackson's guns, they broke and fled. Gibbs' main column, advancing steadily into a hail of artillery fire which plowed great furrows through the ranks, was thrown into disorder by the flight of the advance guard. The fascine carriers of the 44th, who had not reached the head of the column, threw down their burdens and took to their heels with their firing party. Desperately Sam Gibbs tried to rally his crumbling brigade. Major John A. Whittaker led the 21st Regiment in a gallant assault which broke into the crescent redan held by Adair's Kentuckians; but the regiment was cut to pieces by cannon and musket fire, and no one came to exploit their initial success. Whittaker was killed.

Lieutenant John Leavock,[241] one of those who had climbed into the American position on the steps cut by the bayonets of his regiment, later asserted that all but two officers of the Kentuckians were in flight: "Conceive my indignation on looking round to find that the two leading regiments had vanished as if the earth had opened and swallowed them up." He was made prisoner. At this crucial moment in the battle on the British right Major General Sam Gibbs was mortally wounded.

On the left Colonel Rennie had also broken into the American defenses. Leading the light companies of the 21st, 43d and 93d, he had stormed Jackson's forward redoubt and driven out the defenders. Pressing his advantage, Rennie leaped into the ditch and clawed his way to the top of the breastwork. Beale's riflemen, guarding the line behind the redoubt, shot him down, but Rennie's men held the redoubt and began to spike the guns. Had they been supported, Jackson's right flank would have been turned, but they were alone. Obeying Pakenham's last order, Keane's brigade veered across the field toward the right, exposing a flank to the enemy fire. The pipers began to play "Monymusk," the regimental charge of the 93d, and the tartan-trousered* Highlanders broke into a run. Lieutenant Gordon afterward wrote in his diary:[242]

> The enemy ... no sooner got us within 150 yards of their works than a most destructive and murderous fire was opened on our Column of round, grape, musquetry, rifle, and buckshot along the whole course and length of our line in front; as well as on our left flank. Not daunted, however, we continued our advance which in one minute would have carried us into their ditch, when we received a peremptory order to halt—this indeed was the moment of trial. The officers and men being as it were mowed down by ranks, impatient to get at the enemy at all hazards, yet compelled for want of orders to stand still and neither to advance or retire, galled as they were by this murderous fire of an invisible enemy, for a single American soldier we did not see that day, they kept discharging their musquets and rifles without lifting their faces above the ramparts.

Colonel Robert Dale had led the 93d across the field until the head of his column had reached Gibbs' point of assault, expecting to find fascines in the ditch and ladders set ready for his men to scale the ramparts. He found, instead, the remains of the 21st Regiment with

*During the New Orleans campaign the 93d was forbidden to wear the kilt. They wore tartan trousers, with black gaiters and "high-low" shoes and "hummle bonnets" ("humble," plain round forage caps without plumes).

skirmishers of the Rifle Brigade trying to cut steps with their bayonets, and the 44th nowhere to be seen. He heard General Gibbs calling loudly for Colonel Mullens. As Dale halted his men, he was shot dead. Colonel Andrew Creagh ran to the front to take command. Gibbs rode forward, shouting, "Colonel Mullens, if I live till tomorrow you shall be hanged from one of these trees," but almost immediately toppled from his horse mortally wounded.[243] The Highlanders "stood like statues," helplessly waiting for orders. "The ladders and fascines were called for and the rage of men and officers was unbounded . . . most of the men crying from rage and vexation at seeing their comrades fall so fast, with no chance of a fight."[244]

As the battle began, Pakenham had trotted forward with his staff, remarking cheerfully as he passed the first brigade, "That's a terrific fire, Lambert."[245] The field was partly obscured by the smoke of artillery and musket fire, but it was almost immediately apparent to Pakenham that Gibbs' brigade was in serious difficulties. He set spurs to his horse and galloped to the right flank to take command. As he rode, he was heard to exclaim in anger,[246] "Lost from want of courage." One of his staff officers* shouted to the Highlanders,[247] "93rd! Have a little patience and you shall soon have your revenge." Pakenham rallied the column and rode forward to lead the assault. As he did so, grapeshot shattered his knee and a bullet killed his horse. His senior aide-de-camp, Major Duncan Macdougall, dismounted and helped the general to his feet. Pakenham was wounded a second time, in the arm, and he had difficulty in mounting his aide's pony. Macdougall took the bridle and went forward on foot, leading the horse as Pakenham raised his hat high in the air and shouted, "Come on, brave 93rd!" A moment later he was struck in the spine. He fell into Macdougall's arms and died as he was being carried to the rear.[248]

Sir John Tylden galloped to find General Keane, but he looked for him in vain. Keane, too, had been hit by a bullet which penetrated deep into his groin. In the woods on the extreme right Colonel Jones of the 4th Regiment had led the light infantry companies of Gibbs' brigade in a spirited attempt to turn Jackson's left flank. His attack failed, and the light infantry took cover among the trees, carrying with them their mortally wounded colonel.

The loss of Pakenham, Gibbs, and Keane left the assault brigades without any commander. The heavy casualties among the senior

---

*Probably Sir John Tylden, who had taken over from Harry Smith as assistant adjutant general.

officers of the leading regiments left no one to replace them. Among the dead and wounded were Colonel Paterson, Lieutenant Colonel Rennie, and Major Whittaker of the 21st; Lieutenant Colonel Dale of the 93rd; Lieutenant Colonels Francis Brooke, Faunce, and Jones of the 4th; and Lieutenant Colonel Henry Debbieg of the 44th. In the 2d and 3d brigades scarcely a single officer of field rank remained on his feet. Casualties among the junior officers had been as heavy. Deprived of their leaders, many of the men turned and fled. The rest stood helpless, waiting for orders which did not come.

As Pakenham fell he spoke to Macdougall. There is no reliable record of his last words, but it is said[249] that his dying order was for Lambert to throw in the reserve brigade. Nor is it clear whether Pakenham arrived at the head of the assault column before or after Gibbs was wounded, though it is evident that they both were hit almost simultaneously. The story[250] that Gibbs rode back to Pakenham shouting, "The troops will not obey me," may be discounted. Not only is there no evidence to support it, but it is also inconceivable that Gibbs would have ridden away from an attack which was faltering. The consequences of such an action would have been immediate and catastrophic. Gibbs received his fatal wound only fifty paces from Jackson's line,[251] and disaster overwhelmed his brigade within minutes of the advance.

Dickson, who had moved forward shortly before the signal rocket was fired, was only a few yards beyond the 10-gun battery occupied a week earlier—a short ride which he supplies evidence to show could have taken him little more than five minutes—when he heard that Pakenham had been hit. "Immediately afterwards," he wrote, "I met the troops coming back in numbers and in great confusion."[252]

Lambert's reserve brigade continued to advance in good order, but in front of them there was chaos. The British artillery, screened from the enemy by the shattered remnants of Keane's brigade and the mass of retreating soldiers, was powerless to help. The infantry recoiled so fast that Captain Carmichael withdrew his troop of light guns after firing only five shots. General Lambert, at the head of his brigade, which was already suffering casualties from the enemy artillery fire, found himself in command of a beaten army. "In this situation, finding that there had been no impression made,—that though many men had reached the ditch, and were either drowned or obliged to surrender, and that it was impossible to restore order in the regiments where they were," he concluded that the sacrifice of his two remaining regiments in another assault would serve no purpose and might, indeed, result in the annihilation of his remaining force. But Lambert did not immediately decide to withdraw. Leaving his brigade lying behind whatever cover they could find and within easy range of the enemy's artillery fire, he returned to Gibbs' forward headquarters to confer with Admiral Cochrane.

Dickson, on his way to join Lambert, met Harry Smith, ordered to cross the river and recall Thornton's brigade. Dickson proposed that Smith's orders should be countermanded until further information had been obtained. Lambert agreed but asked him to wait until Cochrane had been consulted. There is no record of what passed between Lambert and Cochrane at their council of war, though there has been no lack of accounts based on supposition.[253] That Lambert had left his brigade in a forward position and had ordered no general withdrawal is evidence that he was undecided. After his council with Cochrane he ordered Dickson to cross the river to ascertain whether Thornton's position on the right bank could be held. This does not indicate any immediate intention to retreat. Burgoyne, also ordered to report on the situation, could not be found to accompany Dickson,[254] and it was thought that he had already crossed. Dickson, with Major Robert Ord of the artillery, found a boat and was rowed to the right bank. A thick fog had descended, blanketing both sides of the Mississippi and offering unexpected cover to the wounded and to the troops of Lambert's brigade lying in their exposed forward position on the battlefield. From the sailors in the boats Dickson learned that both Colonel Thornton and Captain Money of the navy had been severely wounded and brought back to the left bank.

Thornton's brigade had landed on the west bank at dawn. His total force, including seamen and artillery, had been reduced by the lack of sufficient boats to 560 men. The current had carried them 1,000 yards below their intended landing place. As they reached the far shore, the sound of heavy gunfire signaled the start of the battle along the Rodriguez canal. Supported by three armed boats on the river, Thornton advanced immediately in an attempt to capture the American batteries enfilading the British attack on Jackson's line. The American troops on Mayhew's plantation were quickly routed, Arnaud's detachment abandoning their position at once and Davis' Kentuckians waiting no longer than necessary to fire two or three volleys. They were heavily outnumbered and occupied a line which they could not have been expected to defend. Their flight, much criticized later, was no less than prudent. The fault lay with Morgan, who should have retained every available man behind his main defenses and pushed forward a picket to warn him of the enemy's arrival. Davis withdrew his men to the vulnerable right flank of Raguet's canal, beyond and separated from the end of the fortified line. To his right was a small detachment of drafted militia commanded by Lieutenant Colonel Philip Caldwell.

Thornton was anxious to make his attack without delay. He was well aware of the importance of the American batteries on the right bank, the urgency of his mission, and the likely consequences of failure. From an orange grove about 700 yards from the American line he made a hasty reconnaissance. He saw that the left, protected at the river's edge by a redoubt, was the strongpoint, while the right could be flanked. He ordered Captain Money with 100 sailors and a company of the 85th to feint at the redoubt while Lieutenant Colonel Richard Gubbins led two companies to turn the right. With the remaining two companies and 100 marines he attacked the center. The threats to the center and left were met by heavy fire from the three guns mounted in the line and from the muskets of the Louisiana militia, but Gubbins quickly drove in the Kentuckians on the right and threw them back in confusion toward the river. Patterson, who had kept his battery in action since dawn against the British advancing against Jackson's line, tried to turn his guns on Thornton's brigade, but he was too late. As Morgan's defenses crumbled and his entire force fell back toward the Boisgervais entrenchments, Patterson was obliged to abandon his guns even before they had been efficiently spiked. Thornton captured 16 guns, including three 24-pounders and a 10-inch howitzer,[255] the latter originally taken from the British and inscribed "Taken at the Surrender of York Town 1781." British casualties were 6 killed and 76 wounded against American losses of 1 killed and 3 wounded, a disparity not entirely attributable to the advance against an entrenched position. Thornton claimed the capture of 30 men, but the Americans reported only 15 missing. The action, which once more gave Thornton the opportunity to demonstrate his dash and resolution, reflected little credit on Morgan or his troops. He was contemptuously described by Jonathan Rees, who had witnessed his timid and indecisive behavior at English Turn on the night of the twenty-third, as "an old woman."[256]

Dickson arrived on the west bank to find that Harry Smith had preceded him and that the orders to withdraw were already being carried out. The pursuit beyond the Raguet canal position had been halted about 1,200 yards ahead[257] and Major Michell was employing his detachment of artillerymen to complete the destruction of Patterson's guns and their carriages. Dickson stopped this work and went forward with Michell and Lieutenant Peddie to examine the forward position occupied by Lieutenant Colonel Gubbins and the 85th Regiment. As the ranking officer on the west bank and Lambert's representative, Dickson took it upon himself to make decisions and give orders. The decisions were not irreversible, nor the orders injudicious, but they were all directed toward a tacit acceptance of retreat. Gubbins and his regiment were withdrawn to the Raguet canal and ordered to fall back farther as soon as the guns had been spiked or destroyed. The armed boats floated with the tide to follow the troops. From the position chosen by Dickson, Gubbins would have a short line to defend and the support of the shore batteries on the other side of the river. Had Thornton not been seriously wounded and returned to the left bank, the orders might have been different.

Dickson returned to Lambert and reported that the position on the west bank could not be held by much less than 2,000 men. After conferring again with Cochrane,[258] Lambert gave orders for all troops to be recalled from the other side of the river. This decision, based on Dickson's military appreciation of the situation, has been much criticized and was evidently resisted by Codrington and Burgoyne. Both gave as their opinion that the position should be held and the main assault renewed. It is probable, though there is no evidence to substantiate the suggestion, that Cochrane also favored another assault. It has been asserted in this connection that "It was not Pakenham, but Sir Alexander Dickson, who lost the third battle of New Orleans."[259] In consequence of his decision to evacuate the west bank, Lambert decided on a general withdrawal. As final proof of his determination not to renew the attack he ordered Dickson to destroy the four 18-pounders and four 24-pounder carronades in the forward batteries as soon as it was dark.

At his line on the Rodriguez canal Jackson viewed his victory with astonishment bordering on incomprehension. His casualties had been negligible, and yet the battlefield was heaped with British dead and wounded. Both the British assault columns had been driven from the field, and he estimated that about 1,500 of the enemy had fallen or been taken prisoner. "Carnage" was the word which a number of his men used to describe the scene, and even Jackson, who yielded to none in his loathing of the British, found his satisfaction in victory tempered by sorrow at the slaughter of so many gallant soldiers. News of Morgan's defeat quickly dispelled any thoughts of celebration. Captain Alan Simpson of the 93d, who was wounded and captured in the first assault on Jackson's line, "had an opportunity of observing the conssternation caused to the enemy by Colonel Thornton's attack on the opposite bank."[260] Jackson wrote:[261] "This unfortunate rout had totally changed the aspect of affairs. The enemy now occupied a position from which they might annoy us without hazard, and by means of which they might have been able to defeat, in a great measure, the effects of our success on this side of the river. It became therefore an object of the first consequence to dislodge him as soon as possible." He sent General Jean Marie Humbert, Pakenham's old adversary in Mayo in 1798,* with 400 men to cross the river and take command. He was instructed to drive the enemy from Patterson's batteries at any cost.

Both Jackson and Patterson subsequently stated that the American guns on the west bank had been spiked, and it is probable that Jackson, at least, believed this to be so. Major Michell's diary, however, makes it clear that the job was not finished since he had "Commenced cleaning enemy's guns to form a battery to enfilade their lines on the left bank" when he "Received orders from general Lambert [delivered by Harry Smith] to destroy everything and retire."[262] Events on the right bank after Humbert's arrival are described by Latour[263] with some acidity and a fusillade of punctuation:

> ... there arose disputes concerning military precedence. Other militia officers [Latour tactfully excludes Morgan] did not think it right that a French general, enjoying the confidence of a large proportion of the troops; known by reputation which he had acquired, not on parade, or at reviews, but by his sword; holding a rank which he owed, not to the commission of a state governor and legislative assembly, but to which he had been raised, step by step, through all the inferior grades, and after having fought in a number of battles—these officers, I say, did not think it becoming that a French general ... should be sent to remedy the faults of others, and repulse invaders, who, perhaps, would not, with impunity, have landed on that bank, had he there commanded. Happily, during this discussion, the enemy ... thought it prudent to retreat.

Jackson expressed his profound relief in his dispatch to Monroe on the ninth: "I need not tell you with how much eagerness I immediately regained possession of the position he had thus happily quitted." The American musket fire had ceased soon after eight o'clock, but their batteries kept up a continuous bombardment for another six hours, by which time Jackson was certain that the west bank was once more in his hands and the assault could not be renewed that day.

*See p. 217.

In the afternoon Harry Smith was sent by Lambert under flag of truce to ask for a suspension of hostilities while the dead were buried and the wounded brought in. He had some difficulty in approaching the American line: "It was a long time before I could induce them to receive me. They fired on me with cannon and musketry, which excited my choler somewhat, for a round shot tore away the ground under my right foot, which it would have been a bore indeed to have lost under such circumstances. However, they did receive me at last and the reply from General Jackson was a very courteous one."[264] Jackson's reply to Lambert was also prudent: he agreed to a temporary cessation of hostilities, on the east bank only, until noon on the ninth; but it was understood that the suspension did not apply to the other side of the river, and it was to be agreed that no reinforcements be sent by either army to the west bank before midnight on the ninth. Since he had already sent 400 troops to reinforce Morgan, he felt confident of the outcome of any further engagement on that side. Lambert asked for time to consider these terms and accepted them at ten o'clock on the morning of the ninth. In the meantime he withdrew all troops from the west bank.

A line of truce was agreed upon 300 yards from Jackson's position. This left to the care of the Americans some 300 British wounded who had fallen under their ramparts, and these were carried into New Orleans and laid in the barracks. The people responded with typical generosity to an appeal by the military commander in the city, providing blankets, mattresses, pillows, lint, and old linen for bandages. British accounts are unanimous in praising American treatment of the wounded.

American casualties in the battle on the left bank had been 6 killed and 7 wounded, though the action at Morgan's position and later sorties from Jackson's line had increased the total killed, wounded and missing to 71. In the series of actions between December 23 and January 8 losses were 333, of whom only 55 had been killed.[265]

British casualties were even larger than Jackson had estimated. In the attack on the Rodriguez canal 285 men had been killed—less than 1 in 10 of those employed in the two assault brigades—but the wounded numbered 1,186 and a further 484 had been taken prisoner.[266] Allowing for a maximum of 150 casualties among the reserve brigade, it is clear that Keane's and Gibbs' brigades lost almost two-thirds of their strength. During the period from December 23 to January 8 total British losses were little less than 2,500, nearly half the effective force which could be put into the field and nearly eight times as many as the Americans.

Analysis of the British casualties on January 8 does much to support claims that it was the American artillery which won the battle and goes some way toward justifying Lambert's precipitate decision to abandon the right bank and order a general retreat. Losses among regiments out of range of rifle or musket fire were disproportionately high—the 44th Regiment, which led Gibbs' column, suffered less than the 4th, which was last in the line of march—and almost every British account stresses the effect of heavy gunfire. It is particularly noticeable that the Rifle Brigade, extended in skirmishing order in front of Gibbs' brigade and offering the most difficult target to artillery, lost only 11 killed, the same number as the 43d Regiment, which was (apart from the light company) in reserve, and less than a quarter the number of any other assault regiment. This does not support the later stories of deadly musket fire from the American breastwork. Indeed, it is clear from all accounts that Coffee's division of excellent marksmen scarcely fired a shot, and according to Latour the battalions of Plauché, Daquin, Lacoste, with three-quarters of the 44th U.S. Infantry did not fire at all. The best-trained men could not load and fire the muskets of the period at much better than two shots a minute, and it is clear from Dickson's account that the British assault brigades were within musket range for little more than five minutes.

In the light of later knowledge of the situation on both sides it is easy to criticize Lambert's decision. Thornton's brigade had captured sixteen American guns in working order, thirteen of which had been employed against the flank of the British attack on Jackson's line. These batteries contained more than half of the total American artillery strength. There can be little doubt that the 85th, led by Gubbins after Thornton was wounded, could have cleared Morgan's militia from their second position and fired rockets upon New Orleans itself. The argument that the *Louisiana* could have been used to threaten the position does not stand examination. The guns of Patterson's captured batteries and the British shore batteries would have blown her out of the water. Dr. Carson Ritchie blames Dickson for the decision:[267] "He could think of nothing but defense." This, however, discounts the weight of the views known to have been expressed by Codrington, Burgoyne, and Macdougall, and undoubtedly supported by others, in favor of renewing the attack. It also ignores the fact that, whatever the weight of conflicting advice, the decision was Lambert's alone.

It should not be forgotten that Lambert had personally witnessed the destruction of Keane's and Gibbs' brigades. The slaughter had appalled the toughest Peninsular veterans, and it had been all the more shocking for being entirely unexpected. But there was another factor, overlooked in accounts of the battle, which must have been a powerful influence: the army had lost the majority of its leaders. Three out of 4 generals and 8 colonels had fallen, and casualties among more junior officers and sergeants had been crippling. The 4th Regiment alone had lost 24 officers, including its colonel, and 12 sergeants. At the moment of decision only two regiments on the left bank, the 7th and 43d, were fit to fight.

Discussion of Lambert's decision therefore resolves itself into the simple question whether Patterson's guns, turned against Jackson's line, would have been sufficiently damaging to compensate for the loss of the greater part of two brigades and to oblige the Americans to fall back on their second line of defense. It is certain that Jackson considered his situation to be dangerous, although he appears to have believed at the time that Patterson's guns had been spiked. Had he known that they required little more than cleaning before use against his line he would have realized that his position was critical. It was not until this stage of the battle, when the British were defeated, that the brilliance of Cochrane's plan to take possession of the west bank batteries was fully comprehended. More than any other action or omission in the entire campaign, it was the failure of Pakenham's staff to wake him when it became clear, during the night of January 7 to 8, that Thornton's brigade could not be ferried across the river before daylight, that cost the British their last battle for New Orleans.

XXIII

Retreat

Lambert's decision to withdraw Thornton's brigade from the west bank was an irrevocable acceptance of final defeat. Although Major Michell had spiked Patterson's guns so that they could not be used against an assault on Jackson's line, there could be no question of renewing the attack without their support. On the contrary, it was going to be difficult enough to remove the army to the safety of the fleet 70 miles away without exposing it to annihilation.

At ten o'clock on January 9, Lambert's reply was handed to Jackson, and hostilities were suspended until midday.[268] During the following two hours both the Americans and the British toiled on the Chalmette plantation carrying in the wounded and digging graves for the dead. Harry Smith went out with the fatigue party, armed only with entrenching tools, and was met by "a rough fellow—a Colonel Butler, Jackson's Adjutant-General. He had a drawn sword and no scabbard." He recorded, however, that "to the credit of the Americans not an article of clothing had been taken from the dead except the shoes. Every body was straightened, and the two great toes tied together with a piece of string."[269] The wounds were horrifying, even to those accustomed to warfare in the Peninsula, "there was not a vital part of man in which I did not observe a mortal wound, in many bodies there were three or four such, some without heads." Young Lieutenant Gleig had ridden out, "prompted by curiosity," but soon turned his horse's head and galloped back to camp: "Of all the sights I ever witnessed, that which met me there was beyond comparison the most shocking and the most humiliating. Within the compass of a few hundred yards were gathered nearly a thousand bodies, all of them arrayed in British uniforms."[270] Working parties gathered the dead and laid them in shallow ditches which soon filled with water. The rains of the following days washed away the mud hastily thrown over them, revealing the hideous sight of contorted limbs pointing to the sky.

At the British camp on De la Ronde's plantation conditions were no less gruesome. General Sam Gibbs had died at ten thirty after a night of agony. His body and Pakenham's were disemboweled and sealed down in casks of rum to be transported to England. Surgeon Inspector General Robb had to deal with three times the number of casualties he had been warned to expect,[271] and the wounds caused by the American guns were ghastly. He and his assistants worked without anesthetics or antiseptics, and surgery, though improving, was primitive. Nothing could be done for chest or abdominal wounds except to stitch the edges together and hope that the patient might recover. For anything worse than a simple fracture or flesh wound on the arms and legs the immediate remedy was amputation performed with a saw. It was a soldier's code to bear pain without complaint, but surgeons carried as part of their regular equipment a canteen of wine or spirits. As a medical handbook of the period stated, "Many men sink beyond recovery for want of a timely cordial before, during and after operations."

Benson Earle Hill described the scene at De la Ronde's: "Almost every room was crowded with the wounded and dying. . . . I was the unwilling spectator of numerous amputations; and on all sides nothing was heard but the piteous cries of my poor countrymen." General Keane was one of those lucky enough to survive. On the eighth he had been wearing "pantaloons of a thick worsted stuff which saved his life. The ball took the waistband of these pantaloons a considerable depth into his groin carrying the pantaloons with it. In the waistband of his drawers it made a large hole, and a still larger in his shirt; but such was the elasticity of the worsted . . . that it not only resisted perforation effectually, but actually jerked the ball out uninjured, leaving a very severe wound of great depth."[272] His sword, which he had left on the field when he was wounded, was later courteously returned, at his request, by Jackson.

After the battle on the eighth Jackson issued an address[273] to his men, complimenting them upon "one of the most brilliant victories in the annals of the war" but expressing "mortification" at "the want of discipline, the want of order, a total disregard of obedience, and a spirit of insubordination, not less destructive than Cowardice" on the west bank. He also commented unfavorably on "private opinions as to the competency of officers [which] must not be indulged, and still less expressed." This was a reference to the treatment of Humbert, and he had sent General William Carroll to take command at Morgan's position. To Monroe he wrote on the ninth, "The enemy having concentrated his forces, may again attempt to drive me from my position by storm." Four days later he still believed that the British might attack again: "Whether, after the severe loss he has sustained, he is preparing to return to his shipping or to make still mightier efforts to attain his first object, I do not pretend to determine . . . it becomes me to act as though the latter were his intention."[274] Some of his officers urged him to follow up his victory and complete the destruction of Pakenham's army, but Jackson, supported by Livingston, refused to be drawn from his entrenchments. It was a wise decision. According to Major Norman Pringle,[275] who was present, "it was the prayer of every soldier" that the Americans would leave their defenses and try to fight in the open. It was one thing to repel an attack over open ground from the protection of strong ramparts and with the support of effective artillery, but Jackson knew that it was quite another to lead a largely untried and amateur army, without the benefit of artillery, in an assault against regular troops. "The British lion had indeed been sorely stricken, but he was the lion still."[276]

While Jackson remained on the defensive, Lambert was preparing his final retreat. This maneuver presented great difficulties and considerable hazards. The shortage of boats made it impossible to transport the army down the bayou, and even when its mouth was reached, only half could be moved across the 70 miles of water to the fleet in one load. The rest would be perilously vulnerable to attack by the Americans in overwhelming numbers. Lambert decided to move his army secretly, at night and by land, to the mouth of the Bienvenue. Once arrived there, half the army would entrench themselves as securely as possible while the other half was loaded into the boats. Large working parties were immediately set to the task of building a road from Villeré's plantation to the mouth of Bayou Bienvenue. The labor involved was as great as any undertaken during the campaign. For long stretches of the route the ground was deep morass, intersected by broad ditches which could only be bridged by branches and bundles of reeds. To Dickson's mortification it became clear that his heavy guns had to spiked and left to the enemy.

On the ninth a flotilla from Cochrane's fleet took the action which should have been taken two weeks earlier and attacked Fort St. Philip.

It is difficult to avoid the conclusion that of the three admirals—Cochrane, Malcolm, and Codrington—onshore, one might have been spared to remain with the fleet and direct operations in the Mississippi. Cochrane's failure to make any attempt to take possession of the river is incomprehensible. The work of his seamen was beyond praise, but his powerful fleet lay off Cat Island, 80 miles away, of no more assistance to the army than a convoy of unarmed merchantmen. At the time of the British landing on December 23 the defenses of Fort St. Philip were feeble and incomplete. There can be little doubt that any resolute attempt to pass the fort would have succeeded. By January 9 the attack was already too late, and circumstances at the fort were much changed.

Since Jackson's visit to Fort St. Philip in December it had been converted into a substantial stronghold, garrisoned by 366 men, of whom the majority were regular soldiers of the 7th U.S. Infantry and companies of artillery, and mounting twenty-nine 24-pounders, two great 32-pounders, and several heavy mortars and howitzers. A gunboat commanded by Lieutenant Thomas Cunningham, used as a scout on the river, was warped up the bayou on the eighth to protect the rear of the fort. The garrison was commanded by Major Walter H. Overton, a thirty-two-year-old Virginian originally gazetted lieutenant in the 7th U.S. Infantry seven years earlier but serving as major in the 3d Rifles. A connection of the brothers Judge John Overton and militia Brigadier General Thomas Overton, both intimate friends of Jackson's in Tennessee, Walter was on leave in New Orleans when the British ships appeared in the Gulf. His offer to serve in defense of the city was accepted with enthusiasm, and Jackson appointed him to one of his most important commands.

At about ten fifteen on the ninth[277] the British flotilla of five small armed vessels hove in sight and anchored about two miles below the fort. From there they sent two barges upriver to take soundings close to the American positions, but they were driven off by fire from Cunningham's gunboat. At three thirty the two British bomb vessels opened fire with four heavy mortars, and Overton found, to his "great mortification," that they were out of effective range of his guns. They kept up this bombardment for the following eight days, throwing more than a thousand heavy shells into the fort and causing some damage but remarkably few casualties. Overton kept his men under cover whenever they were not manning his own batteries, and the majority of the British shells buried themselves deep in the mud before they burst. During the night of the ninth the British ships took advantage of a fair wind to try to pass the fort, but the effort failed and was not attempted again.

Overton's artillery, commanded by Captains Charles Woll-stonecraft and Thomas Murray, kept up a spirited fire throughout the bombardment, their crews exposed to drenching rain and night frosts. Several of the gun carriages were smashed, and one of the 32-pounders was hit five times; but the garrison repaired them and kept the batteries in action. Just before dawn on the eighteenth the British ships ceased firing and made sail downriver. They did not return.

Some idea of the effect in New Orleans of a successful move up the Mississippi earlier in the campaign may be inferred from Dudley Avery's letter to his mother written on January 10: "The enemy have five vessels in the river below fort Plaquemine [St. Philip], we have heard a heavy cannonade today in that direction, if they should pass that fort, all our efforts here I am afraid will be unavailing, there would be but little to prevent them after from coming to New Orleans. . . ."[278] The British action in the Mississippi appeared to have served no useful purpose, but in fact it made a valuable contribution to the escape of Lambert's army. While British ships remained on the offensive in the river, there was every reason to believe that Lambert was planning another assault on land. Jackson had no way of divining the enemy's intentions, but he was taking no chances. He spent the days after the battle strengthening his line and reinforcing the west bank while Patterson reestablished batteries there and prepared hot shot to welcome any ships on the river. Six guns were moved down the right bank to harass the flank of the enemy position, and with maximum elevation the heavy pieces mounted on the Rodriguez canal could reach Lambert's lines.

In the British camp there appeared to be little activity, but out of sight of Americans, work on the road to be used for the evacuation of the army was progressing with feverish haste. Lambert had withdrawn his troops to comparative safety, but he was obliged to maintain forward positions within artillery range to bluff Jackson into believing that he intended to keep his ground while another attack was planned. His troops suffered at least as much after the battle as they had before it was fought. Sheets of subtropical rain fell during the day, drenching the men, who were without shelter of any kind. At night they lay in the mud while their sodden uniforms froze on their bodies. Supplies of food were running out, and the men in the forward areas and on the left flank were continuously harassed by fire from the American artillery. Gleig described the situation:[279]

Of the extreme unpleasantness of our situation it is hardly possible to convey an adequate conception. We never closed our eyes in peace, for we were sure to be awakened before many minutes elapsed, by the splash of a round shot or shell in the mud beside us. Besides all this, heavy rains now set in, accompanied with violent storms of thunder and lightening, which lasting during the entire day, usually ceased towards dark, and gave place, to keen frosts. Thus we were alternately wet and frozen. . . .

There was also constant skirmishing at night with American detachments attacking the pickets.

Nor were these the only evils which tended to lessen our numbers. To our soldiers every inducement was held out by the enemy to desert. Printed papers, offering lands and money as the price for desertion, were thrown into the piquets, whilst individuals made a practice of approaching our posts, and endeavouring to persuade the very sentinels to quit their stations. . . . Many desertions began daily to take place. . . ."[280]

Gradually those of the wounded who could be moved were taken to the boats on the bayou and transferred to the fleet. They were followed by stores and baggage, and all the noncombatants concerned with administration and supplies. On the eleventh news came that the 40th regiment had arrived at the fleet anchorage, and the following day the regiment landed at the mouth of Bayou Bienvenue. Lambert sent orders that the 850 men should be reembarked again immediately and returned to the fleet.[281] Even less agreeable to Dickson was the intelligence that ordnance ships had arrived at the fleet carrying 26 pieces of field artillery, including two invaluable heavy howitzers and two large mortars, an armament which would have produced a different result had it been available to him on January 1. The reinforcement was too late. Dickson was engaged in returning ammunition and arranging to spike all but the light guns.

Harry Smith, appointed Lambert's military secretary on the recommendation made by Sir Edward Pakenham before he was killed, was deputed to negotiate for the exchange of prisoners. Jackson sent Edward Livingston to represent him, and the two men found no obstacle to agreement. Smith described Livingston as "a perfect gentleman, and a very able man" and added, "I never had to deal with a more clear-headed man."[282] It was presumably this ability and clearheadedness which determined Smith to let slip to Livingston a few casual hints that Lambert was planning a night assault on the

American lines. On the seventeenth a formal agreement was signed. Prisoners aboard Cochrane's ships were returned to the Rigolets, where they were exchanged, rank for rank, with an equal number from the American lines. Among the Americans released from the fleet were the irate and vengeful purser Thomas Shields and Dr. Robert Morrell, detained on December 15 after the gunboat battle on Lake Borgne. The British were to have cause to wish that they had detained them a week longer.

A similar exchange took place across the battlefield. The American prisoners returned from the British camp were deliberately led along a route which took them past all the guns left in battery in the hope that they would report on the apparent strength and permanence of the position. As soon as they were gone, however, the remaining 6-pounders were hurried to the boats.[283]

By the time the last of the prisoners had been exchanged on the eighteenth all preparations had been made for retreat from the position before New Orleans and from Louisiana. They had been made with great skill and secrecy, and even the desertion of three men of the 7th Regiment on the seventeenth failed to alert Jackson. The 1st and 5th West India regiments had left four days earlier, and on the fifteenth the 44th Regiment, in disgrace after the battle and taken out of the line to work on the road, followed with the Marines. The 14th Light Dragoons moved two days later, leaving Lambert with his seven regiments of the line to withdraw as soon as it was dark. Dickson, at the landing place, left to Lieutenant Speer the important task of spiking the six 18-pounders in the two batteries along the river. He issued precise instructions to ensure that the guns would be made unserviceable and particularly cautioned Speer against noise. Captain Lane and his rocket detachment were allotted to the rear guard. As a weapon of destruction the Congreve rocket was of little value except for its use in starting fires, but its intimidating noise and trail of flame were capable of striking terror into inexperienced troops who did not realize its limitations.

At five thirty[284] on the evening of the eighteenth the 21st Regiment led the retreat, followed at intervals of an hour between each regiment, by the 4th, 93d, and 85th.

> Trimming the fires, and arranging all things in the same order as if no change were to take place, regiment after regiment stole away, as soon as darkness concealed their motions; leaving the piquets [*sic*] to follow as a rear-guard, but with strict injunctions not to retire till

daylight began to appear. As may be supposed, the most profound silence was maintained; not a man opening his mouth, except to issue necessary orders, and even then speaking in a whisper. Not a cough or any other noise was to be heard from the head to the rear of the column; and even the steps of the soldiers were planted with care, to prevent the slightest stamping or echo.[285]

While the route lay along the line of the river the ground was firm, but as soon as it cut across the swampland to the bayou, the marching troops quickly reduced the makeshift path into a dangerous morass. Gleig describes the conditions when the 85th passed through:

> . . .by the time the rear of the column gained the morass all trace of a way had entirely disappeared. But not only were the reeds torn asunder and sunk by the pressure of those who had gone before, but the bog itself, which at first might have furnished a few spots of firm footing, was trodden into the consistency of mud. The consequence was, that every step sank us to the knees, and frequently higher. Near the ditches, indeed, many spots occurred which we had the utmost difficulty in crossing at all. . . . At one of these places I myself beheld an unfortunate wretch gradually sink until he totally disappeared.[286]

Three regiments—the 95th, 43d and 7th—with the rear guard pickets struggled through this lethal quagmire after Gleig had been saved from drowning in the mud by a canteen strap thrown to him by one of his soldiers. These last troops took more than ten hours to cover the distance of nine miles.

As soon as the rear guard had passed the landing place, Lambert and Admiral Malcolm followed down the bayou by boat. Dickson and Burgoyne were behind them in the armed barge of the *Asia,* which had been left to guard the vulnerable junction of the Mazant with the upper Bienvenue. In the rear of the retreating army, Lieutenant Peddie directed the destruction of all bridges. By about midday on the nineteenth the entire army was miserably encamped in the area of the Spanish fishermen's village. The men were exhausted, cold, covered in mud, and hungry. By the time the last of them were embarked they were nearly starving. Once more, Cochrane's supply lines showed themselves to be stretched to breaking point. For nine days the boats were sailed and rowed between the fleet and the mouth of Bayou Bienvenue. At nine o'clock in the evening of January 27 the last companies of the 7th and 43d regiments reached their transports. There they remained for six days while fierce gales whipped up the sea and cut off all communication between the ships.

Not until dawn on the nineteenth did Jackson realize that the British army had gone. It was, it is said, General Humbert who remarked on the strangeness of enemy sentries standing motionless with birds perching on their heads. A reconnaissance party was sent out to make certain that the move was not a ruse. Shortly afterward a British doctor arrived from Villeré's plantation to deliver a letter from Lambert. In this he informed Jackson that his army had evacuated the position and abandoned, for the time, the campaign against New Orleans. He recommended to Jackson's care some eighty wounded who were too severely injured to be moved. Surgeon General David C. Ker was charged with making the necessary arrangements for the British wounded, who were later taken to New Orleans by steamboat, and Jackson turned his attention to the consolidation of victory. Colonel Hinds was sent with the cavalry to follow Villeré's canal as far as possible toward the British landing place, and Lacoste formed a detachment of expert hunters to scour the woods for stragglers and escaped slaves. Jackson and his staff rode over to inspect the enemy's camp. Colonel Denis de la Ronde, with Reuben Kemper and a detachment of cavalry, exploring the area of the upper Bienvenue, took four prisoners close to the junction with Bayou Mazant but were deterred by the sound of numerous voices from advancing farther.

Jackson made no serious attempt to pursue or harass his defeated enemy. The retreat had been carried out with such skill and secrecy that by the time he was aware of it there was little he could do. He was always aware of the vulnerability of his unseasoned troops if they were caught in the open, and he had no intention of allowing victory to be snatched from him by an injudicious change from defense to attack. Though he believed "Admiral Cochrane is sore, and General Lambert crasy [*sic*]" he still thought it possible that they might "attempt some act of Madness—if their Panic does not prevent it."[287] Jackson had come to New Orleans to defend it against an attack by the strongest British force ever sent against the American coast. That force, although maimed and bloodily repulsed, remained with a powerful fleet offshore. Jackson would not relax his vigilance until that fleet had departed, and until that time his tactics were unchanged: flexible defense based on concentration and mobility. The extent of his victory on January 8 was to prove more of a handicap than an asset in his dealings with the people of New Orleans, who believed that the danger no longer existed.

Robert Morrell and Purser Shields were not satisfied to remain inactive while the British departed. No sooner were they released, in the exchange of prisoners, than they persuaded Patterson to authorize the recruitment of volunteers for an expedition on Lake Borgne. On the nineteenth, with 34 men in four small boats, they put out from Bayou St. John. At Fort Petites Coquilles next morning they were reinforced by two more boats and 19 men. On the twentieth this small force passed into Lake Borgne by the Chef Menteur passage, and that night, rowing with muffled oars, they surprised and boarded a transport carrying 40 dragoons and 14 seamen, whom they captured. By the twenty-second Shields and Morrell had taken six launches, a transport schooner, and more than 60 prisoners. The schooner was set on fire when it was found that she could not be brought over the bar at the Rigolets, and a number of the prisoners were released for lack of sufficient numbers to guard them; but Lambert was obliged to send out boats and soldiers from the fleet to clear the lake. Shields was eventually captured again in February, leading a daring raid on Horn Island after the British fleet had left Lake Borgne. Cochrane was so impressed by the purser's exploits that he invited him to dinner aboard the *Tonnant* to give a personal account of them.[288]

Knowing nothing of the success of the negotiations at Ghent, Lambert was obliged to consider his next move. It was inconceivable that his army should return to England without attempting anything to efface the disaster at New Orleans. His men were despondent: "a sullen carelessness, a sort of indifference as to what might happen"[289] had followed defeat and exhaustion. A successful operation was essential to restore their spirit. On January 28 at a conference on board the *Tonnant* he revealed his intention to land the army on Dauphine Island, at the entrance to Mobile Bay, and take possession of Fort Bowyer. "Then he would consider how far it would be of advantage to attack the Town of Mobile."[290] Contrary to the expansive accounts of later historians,[291] this does not indicate any firm intention to renew the campaign against New Orleans. Nevertheless, the reinforcements of troops and artillery received before he quitted Lake Borgne might have tempted Lambert to make an attempt by the land route if the war had continued.

On February 6, the gales having died down, the fleet left the anchorage. Two days later, while Keane landed the remainder of the army on Dauphine Island, Lambert led the second brigade against Fort Bowyer. The choice of the 4th, 21st, and 44th regiments for this task was clearly a deliberate effort to enable them to regain their confidence and to provide an opportunity for the 44th to redeem its tarnished reputation. By noon on the eighth the three regiments had been put ashore on Mobile Point, a barren sandy spit of land sparsely dotted with pine trees, about 3 miles from Fort Bowyer. Sand hills provided good cover to within 200 yards of the defenses and, after a reconnaissance, Dickson began to land his artillery. Burgoyne set his engineers to dig formal siege works. Lambert intended to take his time, avoid unnecessary casualties, and take no risks of failure. On the morning of the eleventh Dickson had four 18-pounders, two 6-pounders, two heavy howitzers, and eight mortars in position, and Burgoyne had taken his trenches to within 25 yards of the fort.[292] At ten o'clock Harry Smith was sent with a flag of truce to demand the surrender of the fort and garrison. In the event of refusal the women and children were to be allowed to leave under Lambert's personal guarantee of safety.

Colonel William Lawrence asked for two hours to consider the terms. At twelve o'clock he accepted them on the condition that the garrison should not evacuate the fort until noon on the twelfth. During the following twenty-four hours the British remained in their positions with guns manned at the batteries, but at midday the American garrison of 370 men, the majority from the 2d U.S. Infantry, marched out and laid down their arms. Dickson reported "they were very dirty, and both in dress and appearance looked much like Spaniards."[293] Among them were 20 women and 16 children. Dickson took charge of the captured artillery, 22 pieces including three 32-pounders. Later that day a force of about 1,000 Americans was sent from Mobile to relieve the fort but withdrew on learning that it had been surrounded. The following day the frigate *Brazen* arrived from England with news that peace had been signed at Ghent on December 24. Until confirmation arrived that the treaty had been ratified by Congress, the war was not officially ended, but no one doubted that official confirmation would soon follow.

There remained nothing for Lambert to do but to complete his final negotiations with Jackson. These were mainly concerned with the continuing exchange of prisoners but included also an acrimonious argument about the return of slaves who had left with the British. Latour states that the British "carried off all the negroes of the plantations they had occupied. There were doubtless some amongst these, who were very willing to follow them; but by far the greater part, particularly the women, were decoyed, or carried off by force."[294] Like much of Latour's account, this is an invention fabricated to court popularity among Louisianians. Dickson, writing his journal at the fishermen's village on January 19 after watching the rear guard of the army complete its nine-mile march from Villeré's plantation, noted: "A good many Negroes, both Men, Women, and Children have taken the opportunity of the night to accompany the Army down to the Huts, which Genl. Lambert was extremely displeased at."[295] Lambert's displeasure is scarcely surprising. His army assembled at the fishermen's huts was critically short of food. Quite apart from the obvious inconvenience likely to be caused by these unwelcome guests on board the fleet, their transport to the ships would require the navy boats to make additional unnecessary journeys, and there was, meanwhile, no food for them. "For two whole days the only provisions issued to the troops were some crumbs of biscuit and a small allowance of rum."[296] Far from carrying any of them off by force, it was only Lambert's human concern for the plight of the slaves if their masters caught them again that persuaded him to allow them room in the boats. Having done so, he did not feel obliged to return them against their will.

The argument continued through six long weeks, the Americans insisting on the restitution of property and the British declining to force slaves to return to their masters. Latour notwithstanding, it was clear from the start that the British regarded the runaway slaves as a burden which only compassion persuaded them to carry. There was no underlying motive of financial gain to balance the American motive of financial loss. As Lambert wrote in his letter to Jackson dated February 8, "I did all I could to persuade them to return at the time, but none was willing, as will be testified by Mr. Celestin,* a proprietor whom I had detained until the British forces had evacuated their last position: this gentleman saw the slaves that were present, and did all he could to urge them to go back."[297]

Later, when news of the ratification of the Treaty of Ghent had been received and both sides had agreed on a cessation of hostilities, Lambert again refused to concede that the clauses concerning removal of property could be applied to runaway slaves:

> If those negroes belonged to the *territory* or *city* we were *actually* in *occupation* of, I should conceive we had no right to take them away; but by their coming away, they are virtually the same as deserters. . . . I am obliged to say so much in justification of the right; but I have from the first done all I could to prevent, and subsequently, together with Admiral Malcolm, have given every facility, and used every persuasion that they should return to their masters, and many have done so; but I could not reconcile it to myself to abandon any, who, from

*Presumably Celestin Lachiapella, shown in Latour's Appendix LXVIII as having lost 43 slaves out of a total of 199 listed as "taken" by the British.

false reasoning perhaps, joined us during the period of hostilities, and have thus acted in violation of the laws of their country, and besides become obnoxious to their masters.[298]

Latour's accusation that the British "repeatedly declare their intention to restore them to their owners, on their coming to claim them" is demonstrably untrue. The offer, it is clear, applied only to those slaves who were willing to return. When the British sailed, the slaves who had refused to return to their masters went with them. They were landed, at their request, on colonial islands, including Jamaica and Bermuda, where they settled in poverty but freedom.

By that time Jackson was too much engaged in the jealousies, quarrels, and general obloquy which followed victory to concern himself with the dubious rights of plantation owners.

XXIV

Resentment and Ingratitude

On January 19 Andrew Jackson wrote to Abbé Dubourg, administrator apostolic of the diocese of Louisiana, asking that a service of public thanksgiving be held for "the signal interposition of Heaven, in giving success to our arms against the enemy." The same day he informed Monroe of the British retreat and added,[299] "there is very little doubt but his last exertions have been made in this quarter, at any rate, for the present season." The 2d Louisiana Militia were left at Villeré's plantation, and the 7th U.S. Infantry guarded the Rodriguez canal line; but the rest of the army returned to the city. Before the troops left the scene of their great victory, general orders were read at the head of each regiment. They were Jackson's thanks to his men, and he named every corps, every commander, and every officer on his gun batteries. To the Baratarians he gave "warm approbation," mentioning Dominique You and Renato Beluche for "the gallantry with which they have redeemed the pledge they gave . . . to defend the country" and promising "the brothers Laffite [who] have exhibited the same courage and fidelity" that the government should be informed of their conduct. Though no corps was excluded, the special attention given to the artillery shows that Jackson was fully aware of his debt to gunnery. He owed to the Baratarians, also, the vital supplies of ammunition. Altogether, his agreement with the "hellish banditti" had proved to be one of the most crucial decisions of his life.

Those who left the battlefield for the city did so with considerable relief. Heavy rains had washed the shallow covering of mud from the hastily dug graves, and the stench of death was overpowering. The danger of disease was a cogent reason for withdrawing the army as soon as the British retreat was known to be final. On Saturday January 21, New Orleans welcomed the victorious troops. Casualties had been so small that there was scarcely a family whose joy was tempered by the sorrow of bereavement. Curfew suspended, the celebrations went on all night. Pierre Favrot wrote to his wife at eight o'clock the following morning that he had never seen such crowds, "Tomorrow they . . . will crown the General; twelve young girls will strew his path with flowers. . . . They are practising at Mme. Floriant's."[300]

The twenty-third had been set aside for the thanksgiving service, and however Jackson might direct the gratitude of his men toward "the God of Battles," the citizens of New Orleans were determined to honor the gaunt and haggard general from Tennessee. A *Te Deum* was to be sung in St. Louis Cathedral, and the Place d'Armes was decorated for the parade. From the entrance on the riverside the brilliantly uniformed companies of Plauché's New Orleans Volunteers lined the route to a triumphal arch resting on six columns in the center of the square. From the arch to the cathedral the way was marked by "young ladies, representing the different states and territories composing the American union, all dressed in white, covered with transparent veils, and wearing a silver star on their foreheads. Each . . . held in her right hand a flag, inscribed with the name of the state she represented, and in her left a basket trimmed with blue ribands, and full of flowers. Behind each was a shield suspended on a lance stuck in the ground, inscribed with the name of a state or territory."[301] Under the arch, standing on two pedestals, two children held crowns of laurel for the conqueror. Madame Floriant had reason to be satisfied with her pupils.

Jackson and his staff passed through the square to the cathedral. As he reached the arch, he received the laurel crown "and was congratulated in an address spoken by Miss Kerr, who represented the state of Louisiana." The Abbé Dubourg received him with another address of congratulation and yet another laurel crown at the doors of the cathedral and conducted him to a seat near the altar. "*Te Deum* was chaunted with impressive solemnity, and soon after a guard of honour attended the general to his quarters, and in the evening the town, with its suburbs, was splendidly illuminated."[302]

The people of New Orleans had celebrated a great victory. They had thanked God for their deliverance and crowned with laurels the general who had, with the support of the Almighty, smitten the unrighteous. The war, for them, was satisfactorily concluded. It came as a most disagreeable surprise when they awoke on the twenty-fourth to find that this view was not shared by their hero. Jackson reimposed the stringent restrictions of martial law, and the regiments of militia, which had anticipated a speedy disbandment, were marched and drilled with unaccustomed vigor. The long-delayed cargo of arms had arrived from Pittsburgh, and there was no shortage of rifles captured from the British on the eighth. With the reserve companies thus supplied, Jackson's army was stronger and better equipped than it had been before the last battle.

The rumors of a peace treaty did not encourage Jackson to relax either his vigilance or his iron discipline. The day before he received his laurel crowns in the Place d'Armes he wrote to General Winchester at Mobile approving sentences of death on six ringleaders of a mutiny among the Tennessee militia. He ordered redoubts to be constructed at strategic points and distributed his troops above and below New Orleans while parties of cavalry reconnoitered the British positions so long as they occupied any part of the Bayou Bienvenue.

These measures were not popular. Nor were his relations with Governor Claiborne improved by his actions immediately after the battle. He had given the governor command of the troops on the west bank but had removed Morgan and 600 men for other duties. Claiborne, who considered himself second only to Jackson in the military hierarchy in the state, was offended by the reduction of his force and retired in high dudgeon to the statehouse. His part in the defense of New Orleans had been small and lacked the luster suitable to his status as governor and the impressive uniform he had designed. He was bitterly disappointed that he had been given no opportunity to distinguish himself, and the stories spread in the city of the governor's cowardice and incompetence during the campaign increased his resentment.

Jackson did nothing to alleviate the tension. He was too busy to play politics or attend to wounded feelings. To the New Orleanians, and to the militia who had left their homes in other states to defend the city, it seemed that Jackson was not improved by victory. A proposal approved by the lower house of the state legislature to present the general with a ceremonial sword was voted down by the Senate. Worse was to follow. A resolution of the General Assembly expressing at great length the thanks of the legislature, on behalf of the people of Louisiana, reads like a roll call of the participants in the battle, but Andrew Jackson's name does not appear in it. This extraordinary document was enclosed by Claiborne with his own personal letters to Major Generals John Thomas of Kentucky, William Carroll and John

Coffee of Tennessee, Brigadier General John Adair, and Colonel Thomas Hinds. Alone among them, John Coffee could not forbear to comment on the exclusion of Jackson's name from the resolution. In his reply to Claiborne he wrote:

> While we indulge the pleasing emotions that are thus produced, we should be guilty of great injustice, as well to merit as to our own feelings, if we withheld from the commander-in-chief, to whose wisdom and exertions we are so much indebted for our successes, the expression of our highest admiration and applause. To his firmness, his skill, his gallantry—to that confidence and unanimity among all ranks produced by these qualities, we must chiefly ascribe the splendid victories in which we esteem it a happiness and an honour to have borne a part.[303]

News had arrived on February 19, in a dispatch from General Winchester, of the fall of Fort Bowyer. Jackson was furious, not only at the surrender of this strategic point guarding Mobile but also at the indifference to its loss shown by the population of New Orleans. Livingston had returned from a visit to the British fleet, conducting negotiations for the further exchange of prisoners and, less successfully, for the removal to their owners of runaway slaves, bringing with him strong rumors of peace. On February 21 a British launch brought a note from Cochrane enclosing a copy of a Foreign Office bulletin announcing the signing of the treaty, which awaited ratification. Congratulatory notes passed between Jackson, Lambert, and Cochrane, but although handbills issued by the *Louisiana Gazette* released the news to the city, Jackson published a retraction, proclaimed a warning that the reports might be a "stratagem" devised by "an artful enemy," announced his intention to recapture Fort Bowyer without delay, and ordered the *Gazette* to destroy every copy of its "unauthorized and improper" notice. In spite of these restraining actions, ships were loaded with merchandise and made ready to sail, and the price of cotton tripled overnight.

The militia began to desert. Claiborne pressed Jackson to disband the regiments, and the Abbé Dubourg pleaded with him on behalf of "unfortunate half starved women of Terre Aux Boeufs," but he remained steadfast in his determination to keep his army intact until official news of ratification was received. The Tennesseans and Kentuckians caught yellow fever, and nearly 1,000 who had survived the British attack on January 8 died miserably in hospital tents two months later. To avoid further service, French citizens in the militia, encouraged by the French consul, Louis de Tousard,* registered their nationality and were discharged. Jackson, realizing the danger to his army if this practice should be extended, through the accommodating Tousard, to all citizens of French extraction, banished him and all those to whom he had issued discharge papers to Baton Rouge.

This high-handed action was criticized at length in *La Courrière de la Louisiane* on March 3. The article reminded Jackson how much he owed his victory to the French Creoles. There was a mutiny among the troops at Chef Menteur, and a company of militia refused to obey orders to march from the city to take their place. Discovering that the article had been written by Philip Louaillier, a member of the legislature, Jackson had him arrested on the fifth. Federal Judge Dominick Hall, who granted a writ of habeas corpus, was promptly arrested also for "abetting and exciting mutiny" and consigned to a cell in the barracks with Louaillier.

Into this tempestuous situation sailed the stout and homely figure of Rachel Jackson. At forty-seven she had retained her youthful energy; but she had never seen any town larger than Nashville, and her dowdy clothes, inelegant shape, and healthily tanned complexion would have created much sophisticated amusement had she not been Jackson's wife. Livingston, who had opened his home to the general, had married a young Creole widow, Louise Davezac. Rachel Jackson found herself the center of attention and the recipient of innumerable invitations to "balls Concerts Plays theatres &c &c but we Dont attend the half of them." Louise Livingston applied herself with enthusiasm to the task of dressing the general's lady suitably for these occasions. The results made up in good taste and fashion what was fundamentally lacking in grace of contour, and any deficiencies were eclipsed by Rachel's unaffected charm. She was wide-eyed in wonder at the dinner and ball held to celebrate Washington's birthday, describing,[304] "The Splendor, the brilliant assemblage the Magnificence of the Supper and orniments of the room with all our greate Characters in Large Letters of Gold on a long Sheet of Glass about four Inches wide with Lamps behind that they might be read as we Sat at Supper I was placed opposit the Motto Jackson and Victory." The "orniments and Supper" excited her comment a second time, and she added in childlike amazement, "ther was a gold ham on the table."

Where a haughty elegance and sophistication might have exacer-

---

*Chevalier Anne Louis de Tousard (1749–1817), a French-born colonel in the United States Army, provided the first organization of the garrison of West Point as a military school.

bated the bitterness against Jackson, Rachel's engaging simplicity brought warmth to the stoniest heart. As Vincent Nolte noted,[305] "To see these two figures, the general a long, haggard man, with limbs like a skeleton, and Madame le Generale, a short, fat dumpling, bobbing opposite each other . . . to the wild melody of *Possum up de Gum Tree* . . . was very remarkable." It was also very charming, and if the smart society of New Orleans laughed at the bizarre spectacle, the laughter was without malice.

News of Jackson's victory was received in Washington on February 4. A copy of the Treaty of Ghent arrived ten days later, and ratifications were formally exchanged on the seventeenth. Not until March 6 did a sweat-stained officer gallop to Jackson's city headquarters at 6 rue Royale and deliver to him a sealed packet which a covering letter described as official notification of the end of hostilities. When the package was opened, it was found to contain papers from Washington but nothing about the ratification of the treaty. Accustomed to the blunders of ministers, officials, and clerks, Jackson privately accepted the unexciting bundle of letters as if they had been the news for which the whole city was waiting. He wrote at once to Lambert informing him that he was confident that the treaty had been ratified. The following day he disbanded the local militia, retaining only the volunteer companies, and authorized Tousard and his "registered" Frenchmen to return to the city.

Louaillier was tried by court-martial presided over by Brigadier General Edmund P. Gaines. Accused under seven formidable charges which included spying and mutiny, Louaillier was in court for two days, at the end of which the court acquitted him of spying and dismissed all other charges as being outside the jurisdiction of a military court. Jackson, in fury, set aside the findings and returned Louaillier to the barracks. Judge Hall was escorted out of the city and instructed not to return until official notification of peace had been received. Two days later the firing of minute guns informed the city that this notice had arrived. Martial law was revoked, Judge Hall returned, and Louaillier was released with other prisoners. The militia regiments of Tennessee, Kentucky, and Mississippi were ordered to return to their homes, and the last of the Louisiana irregulars were dismissed.

On March 15, in a city whose population appeared to have forgotten instantly any feelings of resentment against him, Andrew Jackson celebrated his forty-eighth birthday. Six days later he received a summons, signed by Judge Hall, charging him with contempt of court for his refusal to recognize the writ of habeas corpus issued for Louaillier. As Jackson's counsel, Edward Livingston disputed the court's juris-diction over the commander in chief's actions while martial law was imposed on the city, but Hall rejected this defense and ordered Jackson to appear.

On March 31, 1815, Judge Hall heard the case of the *United States vs Andrew Jackson*. The courthouse was packed with the general's sup-porters, including about fifty Baratarians led by Dominique You and Renato Beluche. They greeted Jackson, immaculate in civil dress, with roars of approval, and Dominique shouted to him, "General, say the word and we pitch the judge and the bloody courthouse in the river."[306] Jackson silenced them, and the trial began. Refusing to answer to interrogation, he was sentenced to a fine of $1,000. In passing sentence, Hall remarked on the defendant's important services to his country but added: "The only question is whether the Law should bend to the General or the General to the Law."[307] Led by cheering Baratarians, the crowd unhitched the horses from Jackson's carriage and dragged it in triumphant procession through the streets to the Exchange Coffee House. There, standing on the seat of the carriage, Jackson addressed them: "I have during the invasion exerted every one of my faculties for the defense and preservation of the constitution and the laws. On this day, I have been called on to submit to their operation under circum-stances which many persons might have thought sufficient to justify resistance. Considering obedience to the laws, even when we think them unjustly applied, as the first duty of a citizen, I did not hesitate to comply with the sentence you heard pronounced, and I entreat you to remember the example I have given you of respectful submission to the administration of justice."[308]

Before he left New Orleans, Jackson's fine was collected by public subscription, but he refused to accept the money and asked that it should be distributed, instead, to the needy families of men killed during the campaign. By the middle of May he and Rachel were once more home in Nashville. Congress voted him the nation's thanks and a gold medal, and there was soon talk of running him for the Presidency. Meanwhile, he retained his military command in the South, and his aide, John Reid, began to sort through Jackson's papers to write his biography.[309]

The war on land was ended; but ships at sea remained in ignorance of the ratification of the treaty of peace, and for some of them the fighting continued until the end of June. Stephen Decatur slipped out of New York in the *President* but was intercepted by the British frigate *Endymion* on January 15. After an action lasting more than two hours the arrival of two more frigates from the blockading squadron forced Decatur to surrender. Captain Charles Stewart escaped from Boston in the *Constitution* in December. In a three-month cruise, he successfully evaded the heavy British ships sent after him and, off Madeira in February, defeated and captured the sloops *Cyrene* and *Levant*. The American sloops *Peacock* and *Hornet* took part in the last engagement of the war. The *Hornet* defeated the sloop *Penguin*, which was too damaged to be taken as a prize, but was chased into the harbor of San Salvador by a British battleship. The *Peacock* captured four small vessels and, approached by a fifth with news of peace, ordered the British captain to strike his colors. When he refused, Captain Lewis Warrington of the *Peacock* poured a broadside into the British ship. This disreputable action, which took place on June 30, was the last between British and American arms.

It was not until a month later that the last of 6,000 American prisoners, transported from Canada or captured at sea during the war, left the disease-ridden prison on Dartmoor. Several hundred had died of pneumonia and smallpox, and in April, when the survivors complained of appalling conditions in the prison and a shortage of bread, the commandant ordered the guards to open fire. The 7 prisoners killed and 54 wounded were the last casualties of the war. They were victims, three months after the signing of the peace treaty and six weeks after its ratification, of one of the most tragic and unnecessary actions in a tragic and unnecessary war.

From New Orleans on April 3 a young naval officer wrote to friends in Charleston:

> What a vast difference there is in the appearance of this City at present to what it was about five months ago—then you could see nothing but armed men in the Streets, Stores, houses, &c. all shut up not a female ever to be seen—Every place deserters—and nothing to be seen but the Sentinel pacing the solitary rounds—nothing to be heard but the roaring of Cannon down at the Lines—Now Everyone is in bustle and commotion the Wharves crowded with merchantmen continually pouring in carts rattling through the streets—& beautiful Girls to be seen in all Directions.[310]

The starved cotton markets were greedy for goods from New Orleans, and the warehouses, bursting with valuable merchandise at the end of the war, were quickly emptied. Commerce flowed through New

Orleans, and the city prospered as if the war had never happened: but the controversies of the war were not forgotten. Major Villeré, tried by court-martial on March 15, was honorably acquitted on all charges of negligence or responsibility for the loss of his picket. He offered no testimony on his own behalf, and his failure to obstruct the Bayou Bienvenue as ordered was not mentioned.[311]

Major General William Carroll presided over the court of inquiry into the reasons for the retreat on the right bank after Thornton's landing. The court came to conclusions which most satisfactorily exonerated all the senior officers—Colonels Davis, Dejan, Cavallier, and Declouet—and attributed "the causes of the defeat . . . to the shameful flight of the command of major Arnaud, sent to oppose the landing of the enemy;—the retreat of the Kentucky militia, which, considering their position, the deficiency of their arms, and other causes, may be excusable;—and the panic and confusion introduced in every part of the line, thereby occasioning the retreat and confusion of the Orleans and Louisiana drafted militia." [312] The unfortunate Arnaud became the scapegoat for the incompetence of General Morgan, whose name was not mentioned in the court's findings. The Kentuckians were also dissatisfied with this result. Two years later, extracts from *A History of the Late War in the Western Country* appeared in the *Kentucky Reporter*. These contained a grossly exaggerated account of the resistance made by the Kentucky militia and cast doubt on the behavior of the Louisiana militia and their commander. Morgan hastily wrote to David Rees[313] asking for his help in obtaining certificates from officers who were present to refute the aspersions against him. He evidently feared that Declouet might have little enthusiasm for this project: "he don't like me much . . . *however,* I am not asking him to say anything in my favour without he thinks I merit it." The controversy continued and remained unresolved. Morgan, who should have borne the responsibility, escaped censure.

On Jackson's recommendation the Baratarians received a free pardon, and all indictments outstanding against them were discounted. Most of them returned to piracy. Vincent Gambie was captured and tried in May, 1815, but succeeded in obtaining an acquittal. Some years later he attacked a privateer commanded by his old commander, Jean Laffite. After a long fight Gambie went down with his ship. Renato Beluche joined Simón Bolívar and became his most distinguished admiral. Dominique You sailed for a time with his brothers; but his health was poor, and he retired to settle in New Orleans, where he became proprietor of a seedy tavern. He died in penury in 1830, and the city which had neglected him for fifteen years turned out in force to attend his funeral. He was buried with full military honors in St. Louis Cemetery No. 2 after a service in the cathedral. Business houses closed for the day, flags were flown at half-mast, and the *Louisiana Courier* and *L'Abeille* published glowing obituaries of the hero they chose to remember only in death.

The younger brothers, Pierre and Jean Laffite, like Dominique, found patriotism a poor investment. They had lost almost everything in the raid carried out by Patterson and Ross, and their first action had to be to succeed in their defense against the official claim to the ships and merchandise taken from Barataria Bay. Already represented by advocate Pierre Morel, the Laffites persuaded Edward Livingston to appear for them. An even greater coup was achieved when they drew to their side John Randolph Grymes, the brilliant district attorney who had been one of Jackson's aides during the campaign. The case, *United States vs Certain Goods & Merchandise taken at Barataria by Comm. Patterson & Others,* was fought with all the bitterness and malice common to suits involving great sums of money. Grymes, accused by his successor as district attorney, John Dick, of dishonorable conduct, shattered his adversary's hip in a duel. The British letters to Jean Laffite were adduced in evidence of his loyalty to his adopted country. A private and undated letter from Jackson to Pierre was also produced in which he paid tribute to his courage and good judgment, and added, "considering you, Sir, as one of those to whom the country is most indebted on the late trying occasion, I feel great pleasure in giving this my testimony of your worth, and to add the sincere assurance of my private friendship and high esteem."[314]

The case dragged on, and it became evident to the Laffites that no quantity of testimonials or Presidential pardons would be likely to effect the restoration of their property. Seven weeks after the battle they published an advertisement calling on any remaining creditors to make and submit their accounts. The Laffites were bankrupt. In December, Jean was in Washington, addressing himself in unfamiliar English to the President in a last attempt to obtain "the restitution of at least that part of my property which will not deprive the treasury of the U.S. of any of its own funs [*sic*]." Although he signed himself "your Excellency's very respectful and very humble & obedeant savant" [*sic*] he was more astute than scholarly. He was already in the pay of Spain.

Three men who had played significant parts in the New Orleans campaign became, sometime during the course of 1815, spies in the service of the Spanish government. They were Pierre **and** Jean Laffite and John Williams. The last was better known to the citizens of New Orleans as Jackson's engineer and the author of a long history of the campaign, filled with patriotic fervor and laudatory remarks about prominent Louisianians. "John Williams" was the alias of Arsène Lacarrière Latour. Many historians on both sides distorted or misrepresented their recollections of the campaign, though few at such length as Latour; for obsequious sycophancy and hypocrisy Latour had no rival. For some years he supplied the Spanish authorities with maps and topographical reports, and it appears that he settled in Cuba, dying in France in 1839. But for his *Historical Memoir* he would have left no mark on history, for he receives little attention in other contemporary accounts. His part in the campaign was, nevertheless, of some importance. His single work of history is at the same time the most detailed, the most interesting, and in parts the most prejudiced and mendacious account of the New Orleans campaign to survive.[315]

The Laffites, finally disillusioned and defeated in the courts, enjoyed for five years a life of glorious complexity while they double- and triple-crossed the Spanish and American governments and the Mexican patriots who were aiming to form a new republic. Employed to destroy the privateers operating against Spanish shipping, the Laffites seized Galveston, claimed simultaneously by Spain and the United States, and created a pirate organization there more powerful, more damaging, and more profitable than Barataria at its zenith. Repeated attempts to dislodge them peacefully were met by reproachful assurances of innocence, integrity, and loyalty to whichever government happened to lodge the complaint. Not until March 3, 1821, did the United States finally succeed in putting an end to these activities. Given two months' notice by the American Navy to pack up and leave, the Laffites bowed to superior force and obeyed. For eleven years Jean Laffite escaped from history. He reappears in June, 1832, in Charleston, where he married for the second time, under the name of John Lafflin. Ten years later he was trading as a manufacturer of gunpowder in St. Louis, and in 1847 he made a prolonged visit to Europe, where he met and became an intimate friend and patron of Karl Marx and Friedrich Engels. He died seven years later at the age of seventy-two. His brother Pierre, also retired under the name of Lafflin, had died at the age of sixty-five ten years earlier.

In 1816 Jackson was again in New Orleans, where he made his peace with Judge Hall. Five years later, on his way to take up his appointment as governor of Florida—an appointment neatly maneuvered by

President Monroe to avoid the terrifying prospect of having Jackson at the head of the United States Army—he arrived in New Orleans with Rachel. Amid the honors paid to the general, she found time to comment on "the wickedness, the idolatry of this place! unspeakable riches and splendor."[316] Of the latest of her husband's decorations she remarked tartly, ". . . they crowned him with laurel. The Lord has promised his humble followers a crown that fadeth not away; the present one is already withered the leaves falling off. . . . Pray for your sister in a heathen land."

Seven years later Andrew Jackson was elected seventh President of the United States in succession to John Quincy Adams, and in 1832 he was reelected for a second term. For a man of his intemperance of speech and action, whose genius for creating uproar and dissension was matched by his intolerance of fools, cowards, and incompetents, it was a remarkable achievement. That he owed it to his conduct of the New Orleans campaign is scarcely doubted. It is curious to reflect that to a significant extent Andrew Jackson owed his election as President of the United States to the aid of the Laffites and their band of Baratarian pirates.

Other reputations were enhanced by the New Orleans campaign. William Carroll was twice governor of Tennessee; John Adair was governor of Kentucky; and Jean Baptiste Plauché became lieutenant governor of Louisiana. Adair, Hinds, and Overton served in Congress, as did Edward Livingston, who, in Jackson's administration, became Secretary of State. Perhaps alone among the most senior participants, Governor Claiborne ended the campaign with his reputation diminished. Although there seems to have been little foundation for them, malicious rumors abounded in New Orleans after the battle of January 8. The governor was unpopular and the legislature suspect. The Creoles of New Orleans, conscious of their own part in victory, were not above taking their revenge on Claiborne by inventing and spreading vivid stories of his incompetence and cowardice. He spent much of his remaining two years attempting to obtain detailed certificates in refutation of these calumnies. Clairborne died on November 23, 1817, at the early age of forty, still burdened by the great problems of reconciling disparate nationalities, a disappointed and generally underrated servant of the state.

The richest beneficiary of the campaign was the city of New Orleans. The British attack had drawn the attention of the Western world to the importance of the Mississippi trade through New Orleans. The Gulf of

Mexico filled with the white canvas of merchantmen, and the people of the city grew rich. The British failed to capture New Orleans; the United States took possession of the city but also failed to capture it. After 170 years of American rule New Orleans remains obstinately independent and cosmopolitan: beautiful and squalid; vicious and welcoming; a place of extremes of gaiety and misery; a city for many to love or for a few to hate, but a city where life is as highly spiced as Creole food—rich, aromatic, and never dull.

XXV

An End and a Beginning

On Dauphine Island, where all but the second brigade, which was engaged in capturing Fort Bowyer, had encamped, the traditional resilience of the British Army began to assert itself. Even the Highlanders, whose regiment had been decimated on January 8, found that the consolations of rest, shelter, regular food, and recreation revived their spirit. Gradually the grief for comrades lost in battle was supplanted by relief at having survived.

The island, about 12 miles in length and varying between 1 and 3 miles in breadth, was dry, sandy, and wooded with groves of pine, cedar, oak, and laurel. It was inhabited only by a Mr. Rooney, a midshipman in the United States Navy, who had been banished there to atone for some misdeed during his service, and his wife. They lived in a house among the ruins of a fort. The climate of the island was considered so healthy that it was used as a convalescent center for the sick of the American Army, and it was stocked with cattle.

It was evident to the troops that the war was at an end. News had arrived of the treaty signed at Ghent, and it was thought to be a foregone conclusion that ratification would follow without delay. They settled down to make themselves as comfortable as possible in their tents and amused themselves with fishing and shooting. Their quarry included wild fowl, pigs, and cattle, even the latter being considered wild enough to provide some sport. A theater was erected and the officers performed *The Honeymoon* and *The Mayor of Garratt*.* Dickson

*This play, also performed on board the *Royal Oak* the previous July during the voyage to Bermuda, was a favorite since most of the parts required no costumes more complicated than regimental uniform.

pronounced both to be "admirably acted and the scenery and dresses were excellent." A performance by noncommissioned officers of *The Mountaineers*, however, was less successful, and the artillery commander thought the play "completely murdered." Lieutenant Benson Earle Hill, who later wrote a picturesque and highly imaginative account of the campaign, excited some admiration for his lively female impersonations, but most of the women's parts were taken by wives who had been put ashore from the fleet while the transports were scrubbed out.

Armed with fir cones the officers of the 7th and 43d regiments and the 14th Light Dragoons conducted a spirited campaign lasting several days against those of the 85th, 93d, and 95th. This was watched by "the whole army, not even excepting the Generals." It may seem a strange and juvenile occupation for the officers of any army bloodily defeated in battle two months earlier, but it was a symptom of relief and recovery which, in similar circumstances, a modern psychologist would both understand and welcome. With the coming of warmer spring weather the island became alive with snakes and alligators, and hunting parties were organized to clear them from the camp. Harry Smith devised an ingenious method for constructing baking ovens from mortar made from burned oystershells, and this enabled the cooks to produce fresh bread. Supplies were short, and the offer of some bullocks from Mobile to feed the sick was gratefully accepted. American visitors came and went, carrying dispatches between Jackson and Lambert and arranging for the final exchange of prisoners. Edward Livingston, who led the delegation from New Orleans, and his son, "Captain Livingstone [*sic*] . . . a gentlemanly young man," were particularly popular with the British officers, and the negotiations, in spite of the dispute over runaway slaves, were conducted with remarkable cordiality.

On March 14 a frigate arrived bearing the news of the cessation of hostilities, and the following day the troops began to embark. The fleet put in at Havana and did not reach the English Channel until May. On the seventh, passing Brest, those on deck were astonished to see the tricolor flying from the flagship on the citadel. Two days later, anchoring off Spithead, Lambert's army learned that, for some of the regiments, there would soon be an opportunity to wipe away the disgrace of the New Orleans campaign. On February 26, Napoleon had escaped from Elba.

At the Congress of Vienna the glittering assembly of representatives of the allies waited confidently for Napoleon to be brought to Paris in an iron cage as Marshal Michel Ney had promised. Instead, troops flocked to the eagle standard raised at Fréjus, and Ney rejoined his old master. On March 13 the Congress proclaimed the returned Emperor an outlaw, but a week later he entered Paris in triumph. Not a single shot had been fired in protest. Louis XVIII fled in undignified haste to Ghent, and the allies made urgent arrangements to raise money to support an adequate army. The Duke of Wellington, appointed commander in chief, was doubtful of the wisdom of attempting to buttress the crumbling Bourbon dynasty, but he was informed by Castlereagh that this must be the policy for the time being.

Wellington was dissatisfied with his army. Many of his best commanders and veteran regiments had been dispersed, and he narrowly avoided being lumbered with the dukes of Cumberland and Richmond. After numerous arguments he wrote, at the beginning of May,[317] "I have got an infamous army, very weak and ill-equipped, and a very inexperienced Staff." Repeated complaints in this vein at length obtained for him a formidable array of Peninsular generals. Among them was Major General Sir John Lambert, recently knighted for his services in Spain. Also from Lambert's New Orleans army came Dickson, Colonel Francis Brooke, Harry Smith, and the 4th, 7th, 40th, and 43d regiments. To Creevey, Wellington confided,[318] "I think Blücher and I can do the business."

By June 14, Napoleon, who had left Paris in great secrecy two days earlier, had gathered an army of 122,000 with powerful artillery in the area of Beaumont. The combined forces of the allies outnumbered the French by 90,000, but the Emperor was accustomed to using concentration and speed of movement to compensate for lack of numbers. Politically divided, the allies should be separated also in the field and defeated in detail. Outwitting Wellington, who was saved only by the flexibility of his strategy, Napoleon succeeded in separating and defeating Blücher's Prussian army at Ligny, while an indecisive but bloody engagement at Quatre Bras prevented Wellington's Anglo-Dutch force from moving to help Blücher. Both commanders had narrowly escaped capture, and the gallant old marshal had been seriously trampled by cavalry; but both remained cool and sure in their movements. They withdrew, regaining the communication and cooperation between their two armies which Napoleon had determined to break.

On June 18, 1815, the third anniversary of President Madison's declaration of war against Britain, Napoleon was decisively defeated at Waterloo.

The second battalion of the 44th Regiment, decimated in the battles of Quatre Bras and Waterloo, redeemed the regiment's reputation, but in Dublin ten days later Lieutenant Colonel Thomas Mullens was tried by court-martial and dismissed from the Army for having "shamefully neglected and disobeyed" the orders given to him by General Gibbs, for "scandalous and infamous misbehaviour" and for "scandalous conduct."[319] Harry Smith believed: "It was all very well to victimize old Mullins [sic]; the fascines, ladders, etc., could have been supplied by one word which I will not name."[320] He was evidently thinking of Pakenham's words "Lost from want of courage."

At Quatre Bras and Waterloo Wellington showed, once again, what the British Army was capable of achieving when it was well led, but he admitted that "the soldiers think what they have to do the most important since I am there . . . and they will do for me what perhaps no one else can make them do."[321] Charles Napier agreed:[322] "He feels that he owes all to his own abilities, and he feels that justly;—but he should not shew it, for his soldiers stood by him manfully." It was evident throughout the Peninsular campaigns that Wellington's presence was essential to victory. Even his most experienced and reliable subordinates revealed serious weaknesses and a frightening capacity for failure in independent command. Some, indeed, deliberately avoided such responsibility, acknowledging their incapacity to bear it. Wellington's self-confidence gave him authority, and this, in turn, inspired confidence in his men. No other British commander produced such an effect, by his presence, upon the spirit of an army. The campaigns in America, above all, demonstrated both to the British and the Americans that dynamic leadership alone could wrest victory from the most unfavorable circumstances, and a flaccid commander could secure defeat unaided. No single factor contributed so greatly to the destruction of American ambitions in Canada or British expeditions in America as the inadequacy of their generals.

Wellington had never favored an attack on New Orleans. Although the maps available were not sufficiently detailed or accurate to enable a stranger to make a definitive judgment, the duke laid his finger unerringly on the weakness inherent in any amphibious expedition against the city. "Was there navigation?" he is reported to have asked, and when told that there was none, he said that "it would never do." In a letter to his brother-in-law, Lord Longford,* in May, 1815, he stated[323] that he had inquired the previous July how it was proposed to land an adequate army with artillery, supplies and stores, "and after-

*Sir Edward Pakenham's brother.

wards communicate with them." The entire concept of the campaign transgressed one of his inviolable laws of military strategy: the preservation of secure communication between an army and its base. It was for this principle that he refused, whatever the temptation of victory, to relinquish his hold on a safe approach to the coast—and thus to the British Navy, which provided his base—during the Peninsular campaign. It was also the reason for his misinterpretation of Napoleon's intentions before Quatre Bras.

In justice to Cochrane it must be repeated that he originally planned an attack from Mobile and had assumed the provision of a sufficient number of shallow-draft vessels to give support to the army from Lake Pontchartrain, but the responsibility for landing the army without satisfactory communications with the fleet rests largely with him. Having made this decision, for which Keane, as the acting army commander, must also bear a share of the blame, Cochrane failed to attempt the one movement which might have repaired the chain. Not until January 9, twenty-four hours after Pakenham's army had been repulsed and seventeen days after the first landing, did Cochrane send a small flotilla to force the Mississippi past Fort St. Philip. The delay is incomprehensible, and the effect of Cochrane's failure was decisive. Without the support of the *Carolina* and *Louisiana* and with British command of the river allowing his enemies free access to the west bank, Jackson could not have held any line below the city.

Keane, on whom later historians have heaped opprobrium for his alleged timidity, was, on the contrary, guilty of recklessness which was probably compounded by an error of judgment. The landing and advance, in widely separated brigades, over unfamiliar and arduous terrain, exposed his army to defeat before it could be concentrated. This was a move which required great strength of nerve and which, had Jackson's orders been obeyed and his warning posts better positioned, might have ended in disaster. If Keane believed that he would be able to continue the advance, without pause, and make his assault on New Orleans on the twenty-third, experience was to prove him sadly mistaken. Sixteen hundred exhausted troops and two guns scarcely larger than toys did not make up a force which even the most optimistic commander would have led in an 8-mile advance against a defended city. The lunacy of such an attempt is underlined by the success of Jackson's hastily formed attack during the night of the twenty-third. News of Pakenham's arrival at the fleet anchorage on the morning of the twenty-fourth precluded any further attempt by Keane to snatch a victory while he retained command of the army.

Pakenham was confronted by a situation which was both complex and dangerous. He found his army precariously encamped 8 miles from its objective and 90 miles from its supply base, its left flank resting on a river controlled by the enemy and its right extending toward unknown swampland. The Americans, whose strength had not been ascertained, were throwing up defenses to the front and were known to be posted in the rear. His artillery was inadequate, unsuitable for field work, and poorly supplied with ammunition. His lines of communication and supply, stretched to the limit, might at any time be severed. Under these circumstances the choice lay between an immediate assault, which might be suicidal, or immediate withdrawal, which would be humiliating. Any delay which allowed the enemy to complete a defensive line was an invitation to defeat.

Pakenham's actions were both indecisive and cautious, indicating an overestimate of American strength and a hesitancy to commit his force. Though Dickson had his guns in position on the morning of the twenty-sixth, Pakenham did not order them into action against the *Carolina* until the twenty-seventh, and it was not until the twenty-eighth that the first "reconnaissance in strength" probed Jackson's line. This minor action convinced him that nothing could be undertaken without the support of heavy guns from the fleet, which would take three days to arrive. This series of delays gained Jackson six vital days, and it is surprising that Pakenham's decisions have not been more severely challenged. There are numerous contemporary witnesses to the destruction and casualties caused by the guns of the *Carolina*, but it is open to doubt whether it was necessary to destroy her, or the *Louisiana*, before an assault could be launched. The fact that Pakenham was able to review his army, immediately after his arrival, on the right of his position and out of range of either ship, suggests that Jackson's weak left flank might have been stormed without serious interference from the river. The advancing troops would soon have been out of the rage of the *Carolina*, which could not have been brought back into the action without being warped upriver against the tide. Even if it was thought essential to destroy one or both of these vessels, there appears to be no unassailable reason for not engaging them, as Dickson suggested, on the twenty-sixth in concert with an assault along the line of the cypress swamp against Jackson's left.

Having committed himself to an artillery battle, Pakenham was also committed to accept that victory hinged on its result. If Dickson's guns could not destroy, or at least breach, the defenses which these delays had allowed Jackson to build, all hope of a successful frontal attack without support from the river was irretrievably lost. The construction of Patterson's batteries on the west bank, completed on the thirtieth, more than compensated Jackson for the loss of the *Carolina*. The failure of his artillery either to silence the enemy's guns or to make any impression on the defenses left Pakenham with no thought but to wait for reinforcements—a further delay which was likely to benefit the enemy at least as much as himself. It was, indeed, the execrated Cochrane who devised the one plan which might then have gained a British victory.

The plan of attack for January 8 suffered from its complexity. Its success depended on a series of difficult movements each of which was vulnerable to unforeseen obstacles or human error. Pakenham's experience on the night of January 1, when he had been obliged to take personal command of the working parties ordered to withdraw Dickson's artillery, had shown him the uncertain mood of his troops and the failure of his subordinate commanders to exact obedience from them, and yet he was content to leave the crucial and complicated arrangements of the night of the seventh–eighth to those subordinates, without appointing any senior officer to act in overall command, while he slept. The failure of his staff either to act with decision in his name or to wake him when the plan began to fail cast away the last chance of success. Pakenham died heroically, performing the last ritual function of a defeated general. Two and a half years earlier, at the time of Salamanca, the zenith of his military career, he wrote to his mother: "Recollect, Woman, that you are the Mother of Soldiers, and you must meet our Circumstances with good Countenance as they come."[324] It is not recorded that she found any consolation in these words when her son's mutilated body was returned to Ireland.

Pakenham was not, as Wellington had observed, a commander of "the highest genius," and he lacked the essential gift of all successful commanders: good fortune. The prime responsibility for failure at New Orleans was his, and he shouldered it by taking sacrificial command of his leading troops in the moment of failure.

There were many who believed that Lambert should have renewed the attack when he found himself in command after Pakenham, Gibbs, and Keane had been carried from the field. Though it is possible that the capture of Patterson's enfilading batteries on the west bank might have enabled him to drive Jackson from the Rodriguez canal position, it is difficult to believe that Lambert could have achieved more, and the cost to his already decimated army must have been grievous. Had his attack failed, the remnants of his army would have been annihilated or taken prisoner. His decision to withdraw was more courageous than any order to advance. It made him a ready target for accusations of caution and timidity. By offering himself as a scapegoat for the errors of others, Lambert salvaged all that remained to be saved. The retreat was conducted with unusual skill. It is significant that the decision was never criticized by the government, by Wellington, or indeed by any but junior officers. Lambert died thirty-two years later, holding the rank of general, after an honorable, if not particularly brilliant, military career.

Keane's later command of the Army of the Indus at the storming of Ghuznee and capture of Kabul in 1839 confirmed his reputation for recklessness and good fortune. Accepting risks that could only be justified in victory, he fought a much-criticized, probably underrated, and certainly successful campaign in Afghanistan which gained for him a barony, the thanks of Parliament, and a pension of 2,000 pounds a year.

Colonel William Thornton rose to the rank of lieutenant general and was knighted in 1836. Probably as the result of his wounds, he later suffered from brain damage and delusions. He shot himself on April 6, 1840.

Cochrane remained unemployed from 1815 to 1821, perhaps a reflection on his part in the New Orleans campaign, but he was promoted in the Order of the Bath to Knight Grand Cross in 1815 and to the rank of admiral four years later. Pulteney Malcolm and Codrington were both knighted on January 2, 1815, for services prior to the campaign, but both received further honors and promotion in later years. Codrington's controversial destruction of the Turkish fleet at Navarino in 1827, though severely criticized, failed to impede his promotion or stem the tide of decorations bestowed on him.

Of all of Pakenham's army none had a more distinguished and exciting career than Harry Smith. His autobiography fills two volumes which rival in romance and adventure any work of fiction, and his exploits in South Africa and India reveal him as an heroic commander whose courage, dash, and enterprise were equal to any soldier's of his time. He died in 1860, loaded with honors which included a baronetcy and the recipient of the thanks of both houses of Parliament, the East India Company, and the Duke of Wellington. His beautiful wife, Juanita, who shared so many of his dangers, is commemorated in the name of the town of Ladysmith, Natal.

Of the many disputed theories relating to the New Orleans campaign, none is more interesting than those which concern British intentions. The most industrious researches undertaken over a period of 150 years have failed to reveal any direct evidence of an intention to annex New Orleans, the State of Louisiana, or, as it has been alleged, the entire Louisiana Territory, but there is evidence from which it is possible to make important deductions. It is not disputed that the British had noted the potential importance of New Orleans at least half a century before they attempted to capture it, and numerous proposals were made to acquire it by purchase, by diplomacy, or by force. Nor is it any secret that the British disputed—and, in law, correctly—the legality of the Louisiana Purchase of 1803. That this purchase, whether legal or not, could not by any stretch of the imagination be said to be British business (though it might affect British commerce) does not appear to have inhibited the Cabinet in the forming of policy or the publication of dogmatic pronouncements upon the subject. In the negotiations at Ghent, in particular, it was made abundantly clear that no agreement could be construed as assuming British acquiescence in the substance, principle, or conditions of the purchase.

The precise wording of the Treaty of Ghent thus becomes particularly significant. Article I, the broad principle of which was not affected by any later clause in the treaty, made the terms clear: "All territory, places, and possessions whatsoever, taken by either party from the other during the war, or which may be taken after the signing of this Treaty, excepting only the islands hereinafter mentioned [Passamaquoddy], shall be restored without delay." The words "taken by either party from the other" tacitly excluded, by definition, any part of the Louisiana Territory, which, by the Treaty of Ildefonso, must be considered to belong to Spain.

In this connection, the wording of Bathurst's instructions to Cochrane and Ross* take on a special emphasis. The order to "occupy some important and valuable possession . . . which we might be entitled to exact the cession of " may be examined in conjunction with the instruction, written on the same day, that although the population of Louisiana was to be directed "toward returning under the protection of the Spanish Crown" no pledge could be given "to make the independence of Louisiana, or its restoration to the Spanish Crown, a *sine qua non* of peace." It is clear that the retention by Britain of conquests in Louisiana, though not, perhaps, a formally stated intention, was at least a proposal which the Cabinet had considered and an option which was to be kept open.

*See p. 173.

Historians of the campaign have made much of the tenuous evidence that the invading army brought to New Orleans the full machinery of government. Pakenham, it is said, "carried in his pocket" the promise of an earldom and his appointment as governor. To lend color to this otherwise unsubstantiated story it has even been written that his wife, "Mrs. Pakenham, waiting on one of Cochrane's ships for the signal to enter New Orleans as the governor's wife, instead saw with horror her husband's body loaded aboard the ship preserved in a barrel of rum."[325] It is necessary only to add that Pakenham was not married.

That there were, with the army, some civil administrators is neither denied nor surprising. There would, indeed, have been little excuse for organizing an expedition to capture one of the greatest commercial centers of the Western world without including a nucleus of the necessary civil administration. Nor is it remarkable that a large number of women was present on board the fleet. It was common practice for a regulated number of wives to accompany their husbands on campaigns. The presence, however, of no less than 104 children embarked with one regiment[326] (the 93d Highlanders) is not so easily explained. Even the most liberal allowance for Scottish fecundity would leave Pakenham with some 600 soldiers' children from among the ten regiments aboard the transports, an uncomfortable burden for any army but more acceptable to one which proposed to settle in the territory it conquered.

On the evidence it seems clear that the British government intended to garrison New Orleans and to set up at once a limited administration. This much could have been done without causing any great offense either to Spain or to the European allies represented at Vienna. Beyond that point the future of New Orleans would have depended upon negotiations between Britain, Spain, and the United States, but possession of the city would have given the British an incomparable advantage in the conduct of these discussions.

On February 28 the Earl of Liverpool wrote to the Duke of Wellington: "It is very desirable that the American war should terminate with a brilliant success on our part."[327] By the time the news of the disaster at New Orleans reached London, the greater threat of Napoleon's return had, once more, banished the war in America to the hinterland of interest it had occupied before Napoleon's defeat and abdication. It had ended in a massacre more terrible than any of the war, but to a government once more engaged in a critical struggle in Europe it was easily dismissed and forgotten. An unpopular war—costly, commercially damaging, unnecessary, and inconclusive—was thankfully ended. Beside this and the escape of Napoleon, a humiliating reverse and the loss of 2,000 men faded into obscurity. It could even be argued that the war had ended in victory at Ghent. No territory had been lost and no right abdicated. There had been, it was true, some loss of prestige in Europe, but this was regained and magnified by the Battle of Waterloo.

The Americans had gained peace without victory. Jackson's splendid achievement at New Orleans set him on the road to the White House but came too late to have any effect on the conduct of the war or the conditions of peace. The effects lay deeper, and they can be recognized only in the perspective of history.

Battles are not fought in isolation. They are inseparable parts of a broad canvas, highlighted for their dramatic impact but often less important to the effect of the whole than the quieter passages of diplomacy and negotiation. The spirit of the composition gains emphasis from these highlights but exists independently of them. The New Orleans campaign, often dismissed as of no importance because the decisive battle was fought after the treaty of peace had been signed, was a campaign of lasting influence.

The causes of the war remain indefinable. The declared reasons for which Americans went to war are recorded to a degree seldom discoverable among wars in history. What cannot be computed is the relative importance of those reasons. An extraordinary amount of research has been dedicated to the aim of proving that one or another reason was preeminent. No exercise in research is altogether valueless, however sterile the ultimate object, and this well-excavated ground has yielded valuable evidence and valid argument; but it is inescapable that no single grievance caused the War of 1812. It was the lamentable, but inevitable, conclusion of a steadily rising tide of unsatisfied and deeply felt grievances which had their source in the years preceding the Revolution.

None of the published aims of the war was achieved. Only those few who believe that the war was fought for honor can be satisfied with its conclusion. To the Americans, honor was not Falstaff's "mere scutcheon"; it was resentment and a spirited resistance against the contemptuous attitude of the British toward colonial peoples. This attitude, little affected by the reverses of Yorktown and Saratoga, was savagely mutilated at New Orleans. The British belief in their own superiority over the peoples of other nations remains. It is an impenetrable armor against disaster, an essential part of the national character which, however unlikable, has formed the cornerstone of survival. Other nations might have survived Dunkirk, but no other people possess the arrogance to persist in regarding it as a victory. The catastrophe at New Orleans lacks the ingredients of victory or even of a triumphant defeat. In British history it is therefore ignored. The one lesson to be learned from the battle of January 8, and from the war, was neither ignored nor forgotten. Contempt for the American colonists—a contempt which Napoleon made clear was not confined to Britain— died with Sir Edward Pakenham and the best of his army on the banks of the Mississippi. Subsequent history has denied it any possibility of resurrection.

The war cannot be said to have cemented bonds of loyalty between states of the American Union, but it provided valuable lessons in cooperation and in the dangers inherent in disunion. The astonishing victory at New Orleans was the outcome of a combination of good generalship and the cooperation, through intelligent self-interest, of four states. Following the almost unbroken succession of failures owing to incompetence and discord, it provided an inspiring and unassailable argument against those who favored secession. The argument was not proved until fifty years later. It had been overlooked, but it was not forgotten.

Probably no more divided or less competent administration ever entered into war, but the United States emerged from it with the first awakening knowledge of nationhood. In Europe, too, it was understood for the first time that a new and potentially powerful force had entered international affairs, no longer a poor relation of dubiously mixed parentage but a nation capable of defending its rights and commanding respect. The distrust existing between the peoples of the United States and Great Britain before the war and the bitterness generated by it were not dispelled by peace, but from the ashes of their conflict there rose a friendship which has endured through 150 years. If it may be accepted that self-confidence is born in victory, humility in defeat, and respect in battle, it must be acknowledged that this enduring friendship was founded on the field of Chalmette.

Notes and References

Chapter I   War in Europe 1803–1807

1. *Annals of the Congress of the United States 1789–1824* (especially Twelfth Congress, First Session), Washington, 1834–1856.

2. *Morning Post,* April 16, 1803. Wordsworth's *Poems Dedicated to National Independence and Liberty* XVI ("It is not to be thought of that the Flood . . .").

3. Quoted by Sir Arthur Bryant, *Years of Victory, 1802–1812* (London, 1944), p. 85.

Chapter II   Blockade and Impressment

4. *American State Papers, Foreign Relations,* Vol. III, p. 98, Washington, 1832–1833.

5. *Ibid.,* p. 111.

6. John Marshall had stated this principle of blockade as Secretary of State in 1800, and it was repeated by William Pinckney in his letter to the British Foreign Secretary dated January 14, 1811. Neither, however, made any attempt to insist on it. (See *American State Papers, Foreign Relations,* Vol. II, p. 488, and Vol. III, p. 410.)

7. *Annals of Congress,* 1814.

8. *American State Papers, Foreign Relations,* Vol. II, p. 148.

9. Jefferson to Pinckney, June 11, 1792.

10. J. F. Zimmerman, *Impressment of American Seamen* (New York, 1925), pp. 260–63.

11. *American State Papers, Foreign Relations,* Vol. III, p. 188.

12. *Private Correspondence of Granville Leveson-Gower, Earl Granville* (London, 1916), Vol. II, pp. 236–37.

13. Jefferson to Gallatin, August 11, 1808.

14. New York *Evening Post,* February 28, 1809.

15. *Ibid.,* September 21, 1808.

Chapter III   Drift to War

16. See Paul L. Ford, ed., *The Writings of Thomas Jefferson* (New York, 1892–99), especially Vols. IV and V.

17. See New York *Evening Post,* especially June–August, 1808; and *Annals of Congress,* 1808, p. 172.

18. Monroe to Jefferson, January 18, 1809.

19. Sergeant Nicol, *With Wellington at Waterloo.*

20. Recorded by Kincaid, Gurwood, Gomm, Charles Napier, George Napier, and many others.

21. Vere Foster, ed., *The Two Duchesses* (London, 1898).

22. *Ibid.*

Chapter IV   Territorial Ambition

23. Jefferson, *Papers* (September 10, 1807), Vol. CLXXI; Madison, *Papers,* Vol. XXXII; Henry Adams, *History of the United States of America, 1801–1817* (New York, 1889–91).

24. F. Brock Tupper, ed., *Life of Sir Isaac Brock* (London, 1847), pp. 106, 130, 181.

25. Prevost's dispatch to Lord Liverpool, May 18, 1812. PRO Co.42/146

26. *Ibid.*

27. *Ibid.*

28. Henry Adams, *op. cit.,* Vol. II, p. 68.

29. *Annals of Congress,* Eleventh Congress, Third Session, pp. 55–64, December 28, 1810.

30. Alexander Baring, *An Inquiry into the Causes and Consequences of the Orders in Council; and an Examination of the Conduct of Great Britain towards the Neutral Commerce of America* (London, 1808).

Chapter V   The Twelfth Congress

31. James D. Richardson, *A Compilation of the Messages and Papers of the Presidents, 1789–1897* (Washington, 1896–99), Vol. I, p. 494.

32. Jackson, *Papers,* Vol. IX. Library of Congress.

33. *Annals of Congress,* Twelfth Congress, First Session. Unless otherwise specified, all speeches in this chapter are quoted from this source.

34. Madison, *Papers,* Vol. XLVI.

35. Grundy to Jackson, February 12, 1812. Jackson, *Papers,* Vol. IX.

36. *Niles' Register,* Vol. II, pp. 101–4.

37. Quoted, *ibid.*

38. A. T. Mahan, *Sea Power in Its Relations to the War of 1812* (London, 1905), Vol. I, p. 273.

39. Russell to Monroe, May 9, 1812. U.S. State Department MSS. Quoted by Mahan, *op. cit.,* Vol. I, p. 275.

40. Richardson, *op. cit.,* Vol. I, pp. 499–505.

41. Madison to Russell, November 15, 1811. U.S. State Department MSS. Quoted by Mahan, *op. cit.,* Vol. I, p. 266.

42. *Annals of Congress.* Twelfth Congress, First Session.

Chapter VI   1812

43. *The Writings of James Madison,* Vol. II, p. 563. Philadelphia 1865.

44. Baynes to Prevost. Canadian Archives C. 377, pp. 27–37.

Chapter VII   The Burning of York

45. See p. 30.

46. All figures for prizes are taken from *Niles' Register.*

47. See *Captains' Letters,* May, 1813, National Archives, Department of the Navy.

48. *Ibid.,* November 5, 1814.

Chapter VIII   The 1813 Campaigns

49. Mahan, *op. cit,* Vol. II, p. 70.

50. John S. Bassett, ed., *Correspondence of Andrew Jackson* (New York, 1926–33), Vol. I, p. 244.

51. *Ibid.,* Vol. I, p. 304.

52. *Ibid.,* Vol. I, p. 416.

Chapter IX America Secures Its Frontiers

53. February 10, 1814. Bassett, *op. cit.*, Vol. I, p. 459.

54. Jackson to Blount, undated. Augustus C. Buell, *History of Andrew Jackson* (New York, 1904), Vol. I, p. 325.

55. Fragment of a private undated letter. Tennessee Historical Society, Nashville. Quoted by Marquis James, *Andrew Jackson: The Border Captain* (Indianapolis, 1933), p. 183.

56. Historical Manuscripts Commission. Bathurst MSS., p. 216.

57. G. C. Moore, ed.,*Autobiography of Lieutenant General Sir Harry Smith* (London, 1901), Vol. I, p. 94.

58. Lord Broughton, *Recollections of a Long Life* (London, 1911), Vol. I, p. 190.

59. Lieutenant Colonel John Gurwood, ed., *Dispatches of Field Marshal The Duke of Wellington . . .* (London, 1838), February 22, 1814, Vol. VII, p. 327.

Chapter X Mission for Peace

60. Goulburn to Bathurst, August 9, 1814. Duke of Wellington, ed., *Supplementary Dispatches . . .* (London, 1862), Vol. IX, p. 177.

Chapter XI The Destruction of Washington

61. April 14, 1814. Wellington, *op. cit.*, Vol. IX, pp. 82–85.

62. Wellington to Bathurst, June 11, 1814. Gurwood, *op. cit.*, Vol. VII, p. 512.

63. Charles Brooks *(The Siege of New Orleans)*, Lady Pakenham *(Major-General Sir Edward M. Pakenham)*, and others identify him as Major General Alexander Ross. The latter, also a general who served in America, was governor of Fort George and died in 1827 at the ripe age of eighty-five.

64. Dalhousie to Ross, May 29, 1814. Wellington, *op. cit.*, Vol. IX, p. 117.

65. Pakenham, June 6, 1814. *Ibid.*, pp. 135–37.

66. *Pakenham Letters,* quoted by Elizabeth Longford, *Wellington: The Years of the Sword* (London, 1969), p. 427.

67. John Hamilton, *Sixty Years as an Irish Landlord* (London, 1894), p. 164.

68. "Nominal Return of General and Other Staff Officers Who Have Embarked in the American Expedition." Bordeaux, June 6, 1814. Wellington, *op. cit.*, Vol. IX, pp. 135–37.

69. G. R. Gleig, *The Campaigns of the British Army at Washington and New Orleans.* At least six editions of this work were published between 1821 and 1847. The original journal is reprinted in part in Barrett's *The 85th King's Light Infantry,* and another altered version appeared, without the author's name, under the title *A Subaltern in America* (Philadelphia, 1826 and 1833). Significant alterations were made in the various editions.

70. Bathurst to Ross, P.R.O. War Office, 1/141-4.

71. Gleig, *op. cit.* (1847 edition), p. 36.

72. Cochrane to Prevost, Canadian Archives, C 684, p. 221.

73. Lady Bourchier, ed. *Memoir of the Life of Admiral Sir Edward Codrington* (London, 1873), Vol. I, p. 313.

74. Cochrane's Orders, July 18, 1814, Canadian Archives, C. 684, p. 204.

75. *The Writings of James Madison,* Gaillard Hunt, ed. (New York, 1900–10), Vol. III, pp. 408–9 and 422–26.

76. Winder's *Narrative, American State Papers, Military Affairs,* Vol. I, pp. 552–60.

77. Monroe to Madison, August 20 and 21, 1814, *American State Papers,* Vol. I, p. 537.

78. Lieutenant Edwards' *Report,* July 25, 1814, *American State Papers, Military Affairs,* Vol. I, p. 545.

79. Henry Adams, *op. cit.,* Vol. VII, p. 136.

80. *Niles' Register,* Vol. VII, Supplement, p. 159.

81. Gleig puts the figure at "upwards of five hundred men," but this was an exaggerated guess which is contradicted by official reports.

82. Moore, *op. cit.,* Vol. I, p. 200–1.

Chapter XII   The Threat to the South

83. Cochrane's Report, September 17, 1814. Quoted by William James, *Naval History,* Vol. II, Appendix 73.

84. Gleig, *op. cit.,* p. 113.

85. Bathurst to Ross, September 29, 1814. P.R.O. War Office, 1/14-4.

86. Bathurst to Commissioners, October 4, 1814. Quoted by Fred L. Engelman, *The Peace of Christmas Eve* (London, 1962), p. 182.

87. Warren to Melville, November 18, 1812. Warren Papers MSS, National Maritime Museum, Greenwich.

88. Pigot to Cochrane, June 8, 1814. P.R.O. Admiralty, 1/506, pp. 394–97.

89. Sir John Fortescue, *History of the British Army* (London, 1911–20), Vol. X, p. 151.

90. Bathurst to Wellington, April 27, 1814, Wellington, *op. cit.,* Vol. IX, p. 42.

91. Hill to Burgoyne, August 9, 1814. George Wrottesley, *Life and Correspondence of Field Marshal Sir John Burgoyne* (London, 1873), p. 298.

92. Admiralty to Cochrane, August 10, 1814. P.R.O. War Office, 1/141, pp. 7–14.

93. Bathurst to Ross, September 6, 1814. P.R.O. War Office, 6/2, pp. 9–12.

94. A. Lacarrière Latour, *Historical Memoir of the War in West Florida and Louisiana* (Philadelphia, 1816), Appendix, pp. VII–VIII.

Chapter XIII   Crescent City

95. P. F. X. de Charlevoix, *History and General Description of New France, with the Historical Journal of a Voyage Made in Northern America* (1744).

96. Le Page du Pratz, *Histoire de la Louisiane* (Paris, 1755).

97. Casa Irujo to Madison, September 4, 1803. Quoted by James A. Robertson, *Louisiana under the Rule of Spain, France, and the United States, 1785–1807* (Cleveland, 1911), Vol. II., p. 78.

98. F. A. Michaux, *Voyage à l'ouest des monts alléghanys, dans les états de l'Ohio, du Kentucky, et de Tennessee* (Paris, 1804). Quoted by Oscar Handlin, *This America* (Cambridge, Mass., 1949).

99. Robertson, *op. cit.,* Vol. II, p. 36.

100. *Ibid.,* Vol. I, p. 71; Paul Alliot, *Historical and Political Reflections on Louisiana* (Louisiana MSS., Library of Congress).

101. De Montlezun, *Voyage fait dans les années 1817 et 1818 de New York à la Nouvelle Orléans* (Paris, 1818).

102. C. C. Robin, *Voyages dans l'intérieur de la Louisiane, de la Floride Occidentale, et dans les Isles de la Martinique et de Saint-Dominque, pendant les années 1802-1806* (Paris, 1807).

103. F. Berquin-Duvallon, *Vue de la colonie espagnole du Mississippi ou des provinces de Louisiane et Floride occidentale* (Paris, 1803), Vol. I, pp. 166–67.

104. De Montlezun, *op. cit.*

105. Berquin-Duvallon, *op. cit.*, Vol. I, pp. 201–8.

106. *Ibid.*

107. *Ibid.*

108. De Montlezun, *op. cit.*

109. Henry Bradshaw Fearon, *Sketches of America* (London, 1818).

110. Claiborne to Madison, December 20, 1803. Quoted by Robertson, *op. cit.*, Vol. II, p. 225.

111. Robin, *op. cit.*

Chapter XIV The Baratarian Dilemma

112. Baron de Carondelet, *Military Report on Louisiana and West Florida.* Quoted and translated by Robertson, *op. cit.*, Vol. I, p. 332.

113. Jane Lucas de Grummond, *The Baratarians and the Battle of New Orleans* (Baton Rouge, 1961), p. 24.

114. *Journal of Jean Laffite* (New York, 1958), pp. 50–51.

115. Bibliotheca Parsoniana. Latin-American MSS., 1024.

116. *Ibid.*, 1031.

117. *Ibid.*, 1022

118. Stanley Clisby Arthur, *Jean Laffite, Gentleman Rover* (New Orleans, 1952), pp. 71–2. (Arthur's translation.)

Chapter XV Jackson in New Orleans

119. De la Vergne Papers, f. 3. Tulane University (Special Collections).

120. Claiborne to Colonel Alexander Declouet. David Rees Papers, f. 165. Tulane University. (Special Collections).

121. Claiborne to Jackson, September, 1814. Library of Congress. Quoted by Marquis James, *op. cit.*, p. 205.

122. September 30, 1814. Bassett *Jackson Correspondence*, Vol. II, p. 63.

123. *Ibid.*, Vol. II, pp. 57–58.

124. Jackson to Monroe, February 18, 1815. *Ibid.*, Vol. II, p. 174.

125. Colonel Andrew Hynes Collection, f. 1. Tulane University (Special Collections).

126. William Priestley, *General Carroll's Expedition to New Orleans and the Occurrences During the Siege and Subsequent to It 1814-15* (dated Monte Bello, 1817). Tulane University (Special Collections).

127. *Ibid.*

128. October 10, 1814. Favrot Papers, Vol. XII, p. 1017. *Transcriptions of MS. Collections of Louisiana.* Tulane University. (Author's translation.)

129. John S. Bassett, *Life of Andrew Jackson* (New York, 1911), Vol. I, p. 157.

130. Henry Adams, *op. cit.*, Vol. VIII, p. 335.

131. Bernard de Marigny, *Réflexions sur la Campagne du Général André Jackson en Louisiane.* (Pamphlet published by J. L. Sollee, New Orleans, 1848.)

132. December 11, 1814. Bassett, *Jackson Correspondence*, Vol. II, p. 112.

Chapter XVI   The British Expedition

133. Moore, *op. cit.*, Vol. I, p. 226.

134. *Pakenham Letters.*

135. A. Hare, ed., *Life and Letters of Maria Edgeworth* (London, 1894), Vol. I, p. 151.

136. September 7, 1812. Gurwood, *op. cit.*, Vol. IX, p. 395.

137. Thomas Pakenham, ed., *Pakenham Letters* (London, 1914).

138. W. Napier, ed., *Passages in the Early Life of General Sir George Napier* (London, 1884).

139. Wrottesley, *op. cit.*, pp. 299–300.

140. Moore, *op. cit.*, Vol. I, p. 228.

141. Wrottesley, *op. cit.*, p. 304.

142. Moore, *op. cit.*, Vol. I, p. 228. Charles Brooks, *The Siege of New Orleans* (Seattle, 1961), p. 66, writes of Keane's Peninsular experience that he "had only moved a regiment doubtfully here and there to carry out orders." Samuel Carter, *Blaze of Glory* (New York, 1971), p. 90, falls into the same error in writing that Keane was "accustomed to obeying orders and not giving them." Both demonstrate strangely uninformed views of the duties of a brigadier general in Wellington's Peninsular army.

143. The dates given are Keane's (Wellington, *op. cit.*, Vol. X, p. 395). Gleig, Surtees, and others give dates varying by as much as two days on either side.

144. Bourchier, *op. cit.*, Vol. I p. 329.

145. Codrington (*ibid.*, p. 330) states that the British barges held their fire until eleven thirty, but Lockyer's account is preferred as Codrington was not present.

146. Bourchier, *op. cit.*, Vol. I p. 330.

147. Cochrane Papers, f. 2328, p. 117. MS. in National Library of Scotland, Edinburgh.

148. Bourchier, *op. cit.*, Vol. I p. 330.

149. Gleig, *op. cit.*, pp. 141–42.

150. Bayou Bienvenue appears in most of the British accounts under the name Bayou Catalan or Cataline, apparently the name by which it was known to the Spanish.

Chapter XVII   The First Battle

151. Quoted by Latour, *op. cit.*, Appendix XXI.

152. James Parton, *Life of Andrew Jackson* (Boston, 1887), Vol. II, p. 60.

153. Vincent Nolte, *Fifty Years in Both Hemispheres* (New York, 1854), p. 205.

154. Alexander Walker, *Jackson and New Orleans* (New York, 1856), pp. 154–55.

155. Carter, *op. cit.*, p. 148, states, "Jackson made no mention of Carroll's tardiness," which he attributes to the latter's decision to move by river. In fact, Carroll had covered 49.6 miles a day, a speed which could not have been matched by cavalry over that terrain. With marching men, though the land route would have been shorter, Carroll could not have hoped to reach New Orleans by the end of December.

156. Villeré Papers, F. 23 and 24. Historic New Orleans Collection.

157. Latour, *op. cit.*, p. 78.

158. Chief among the culprits are Charles Brooks (*The Siege of New Orleans*) and Samuel Carter (*Blaze of Glory*). Both make unsupported character judgments, quote "verbatim" reports of unrecorded conversation, and make statements which are

not substantiated by the cited references. Brooks' character assassination of Mrs. Mullens (whom he repeatedly describes as "Lady Mullins") appears to be the product of his own prejudices and imagination. He quotes no relevant sources or authorities for his descriptions of this lady's behavior or for his extraordinary view of Keane's character.

159. *Dictionary of National Biography.*

160. W. Surtees, *Twenty-five Years in the Rifle Brigade* (Edinburgh, 1833), pp. 340–41.

161. Bassett, *Jackson Correspondence*, Vol. II, p. 123.

162. It is not certain who first brought the news of the British landing to Jackson. Walker, who was in New Orleans at the time, wrote his account thirty-five years after the event. In this (p. 151) he indicates that Rousseau arrived first but gives credit for the first accurate information to Villeré. A private letter, written on the morning of the twenty-fourth and published in the *Columbian Centinel* on the twenty-eighth cites Villeré as the first informant. Other writers have awarded the credit to Tatum, but his own account (*Journal*, Smith College *Studies in History*, Vol. VII, p. 107) modestly states that Jackson received the information "by Major Latour."

163. Henry Adams, *op. cit.*, Vol. VIII, p. 339.

164. William Priestley, *Carroll's Expedition*, pp. 50–51. Tulane University MSS.

165. Latour, *op. cit.*, pp. 103–4. The figures vary in different accounts, but all agree that the total was about 2,000. Latour gives the numbers in detail:

Hinds' Mississippi Mounted Rifles	107
Coffee's Tennessee Mounted Rifles	563
Beale's Rifles	62
Seventh U. S. Infantry	465
Forty-fourth U. S. Infantry	331
Jugeat's Choctaws	18
Daquin's Company Haitian Colored	210
Plauché's Battalion	287
Marines	66
Light Artillery with two 6-pounders	22
	2,131

166. Walker, *op. cit.*, p. 157. Jackson shared with many of the greatest leaders the ability to sleep at his own command immediately before a period of intensive activity. It is acknowledged that acute anxiety or nervousness occasionally produces a soporific effect, the reverse of the restless wakefulness generally experienced. The possible connection between this unusual effect and the ability to make command decisions does not appear to have been explored.

167. Gleig, *op. cit.*, p. 154.

168. Gleig *(Subaltern,* p. 225) states that they were made prisoner "to a man," but the *Diary of Captain Benjamin Story* (Tulane University Library) gives the figures as twenty and four taken prisoner, of whom four were wounded. Two more were killed, and six wounded were not captured.

169. Dr. Carson A. Ritchie, who correctly draws attention to some of the many differences in the various editions of Gleig's account *(Louisiana Historical Quarterly,* Vol. XLIV, No. 1), dismisses Gleig's story of his tears as "excessive use of sentiment ... very

false in comparison with the military memoirists of the day. . . . Gleig would have us believe that he not only stood weeping over his friend's grave, but even collected some soldiers to weep with him!" The story is less surprising when we remember that Wolfe's men wept over his body at Quebec and that the "Iron" Duke of Wellington shed bitter tears over his dead at Badajoz. Latour, *op. cit.* (p. 178), also reports that the British troops wept when they collected Colonel Rennie's body on January 9. There is, in fact, ample evidence to show that the idea of tears being unmanly is a comparatively recent one.

Chapter XVIII Christmas Eve Treaty

170. Goulburn to Bathurst, November 10, 1814. Wellington, *op. cit.*, Vol. IX, p. 427.

171. Wellington to Liverpool, Paris, November 9, 1814. *Ibid.*, Vol. IX, p. 426.

172. "A Loyal Subject" (Secret Agent Francis McGee) to Liverpool, November 28, 1814. *Ibid.*, Vol. IX, p. 458.

173. Wellington to Liverpool, Paris, November 9, 1814. *Ibid.*, Vol. IX, p. 425.

Chapter XIX Pakenham Takes Command

174. A. B. Ellis, *History of the First West India Regiment* (London, 1885).

175. Fortescue, *op. cit.*, Vol. X, p. 155.

176. Dickson, *Journal*, pp. 1–6 (*Dickson Papers*, Royal Artillery Institution, Woolwich).

177. These gunboats do not appear to be mentioned in contemporary American accounts. They are, however, recorded by Keane, Forrest, and Dickson and are also shown on maps produced by Peddie and Captain H. M. Moorsom of the Rifle Brigade. It is not clear when the gunboats arrived, but it seems probable that they floated down with the *Carolina* on the night of the twenty-third. On the maps cited they are shown downriver and in line with the *Carolina*. Latour dismisses them as floating logs.

178. Keane reported that the *Louisiana* was armed with 16 long 24-pounders, but Forrest stated that the 16 guns included 24-pounders and 12-pounders.

179. The most reliable description of Jackson's line at the Rodriguez canal is contained in the report made after the battle (March 30, 1815) by Captain Harry D. Jones, Royal Engineers, who was sent by Burgoyne to make an official survey after the peace was ratified. (Reprinted in Wrottesley, *op. cit.*, pp. 301–4.)

180. Dickson, *op. cit.*, pp. 7–8.

181. Bourchier, *op. cit.*, Vol. I, p. 331.

182. *Autobiography of Admiral R. Aitchison.* MS. Historic New Orleans Collection, 52 - 1 - 1.

183. Dickson, *op. cit.*, pp. 7–8.

184. Walker, *op. cit.*, p. 206.

185. P.R.O. War Office Papers 6/2, pp. 26–29.

186. Letter from a merchant in New Orleans, published New York *Herald*, January 24, 1815.

187. Fortescue, *op. cit.*, Vol. X, p. 151.

188. Wellington to Longford, May 22, 1815. MS. Longford Collection.

189. Wrottesley, *op. cit.,* p. 304.

190. Latour, *op. cit.,* pp. 255–56.

191. A copy of this is in the Dickson MSS. at Woolwich.

192. Dickson, *op. cit.,* p. 11.

193. *Ibid.,* p. 14.

194. *Ibid.,* p. 15.

195. Aitchison, *op. cit.,* p. 71.

196. William Johnson to his father from "Madam Pear Neaufs Beouy" (Piernas Bayou), undated. MS. L 976.31 B. 894 L, Tulane University (Special Collections).

197. Dickson, *op. cit.,* p. 18.

198. Bourchier, *op. cit.,* p. 331.

199. Livingston to Jackson, December 25, 1814. Jackson, *Correspondence,* Vol. II, p. 125.

200. Nolte, *op. cit.,* states that Jackson "openly declared" this intention. This is most unlikely; but such an intention would not have been out of character, and it is probable that Jackson discussed the possibility with some of his officers.

Chapter XX Reconnaissance and Failure

201. Smith, *op. cit.,* Vol. I, p. 228.

202. Accounts of Jackson's artillery strength on the twenty-eighth differ. Keane estimated that the Americans had "two heavy guns on his right, one 32-pounder in his centre, and a small 9 on his left." Latour mentions two 24-pounders (one of which, he asserts, was mounted under fire) but states that the 32-pounder was not mounted until that night.

203. Gleig, *op. cit.,* p. 170.

204. Wellington, *op. cit.,* Vol. X, p. 397.

205. Latour *(op. cit.,* pp. 119–21) states that the British advance was begun on the evening of the twenty-seventh and that the batteries were set up during the night to fire upon the *Louisiana.* This is contradicted by all the British accounts (see especially Dickson, *op. cit.,* p. 21) and is clearly incorrect.

206. British and American accounts are contradictory on this point. When Captain Jones made his survey, the ditch was filled with brambles, but others describe the ditch variously as dry or filled with water. On the twenty-eighth it may have contained water, following the heavy rains of the previous weeks, which later drained away.

207. Dickson, *op. cit.,* p. 28.

208. *Ibid.,* p. 30.

209. *Ibid.,* p. 39.

210. Bassett, *Jackson Correspondence,* Vol. III, p. 240.

211. Parton, *op. cit.,* Vol. II, p. 143.

212. Marigny, *op. cit.,* pp. 5–6.

213. Brigadier General Garrigues Fleaujac, Major Eziel, Sebastian Hiriard, and James Buford.

214. Brooks, *op. cit.,* gives a graphic description of Jackson reviewing his troops, but the sources he cites do not substantiate this. On the contrary the reference he cites in Latour describes Jackson and his staff as being in Macarty's house when the battle began. J. L. de Grummond, *op. cit.,* repeats the story of the parade but quotes no sources. The only contemporary reference appears to be Gleig *(op. cit.,* p. 173), but he states that his regiment, being only 300 yards from Jackson's line, could see the parade. This is certainly false. The British for-

ward batteries were 700 yards from the American line, and anything happening behind the ramparts would have been invisible to the British troops on the ground.

215. Latour, *op. cit.*, pp. 133–34.
216. Dickson, *op. cit.*, pp. 41–42.
217. Smith, *op. cit.*, p. 232.
218. Gleig, *op. cit.*, pp. 174–75.
219. Bourchier, *op. cit.*, Vol. I, p. 335.

Chapter XXI   Preparation for Battle

220. Bassett, *Jackson Correspondence*, Vol. II, p. 130.
221. Lambert (Despatch, quoted Latour, *op. cit.*, Appendix LXVI, No. 4), Burgoyne (Wrottesley, *op. cit.*, pp. 305–9), and Codrington (Bourchier, *op. cit.*, Vol. I, p. 336) all give Cochrane credit for originating this plan.
222. Buell, *op. cit.*, Vol. I, p. 423.
223. Latour, *op. cit.*, pp. 141–42.
224. *Ibid.*, p. 144.
225. Patterson to Secretary of the Navy, January 13, 1815. Latour, *op. cit.*, Appendix XIX, also p. 144.
226. *Ibid.*, pp. 139–40; Dickson, *op. cit.*, p. 55.
227. Latour, *op. cit.*, pp. 147–52.
228. Smith, *op. cit.*, pp. 234–35.
229. Dickson, *op. cit.*, p. 63.
230. *Ibid.*, p. 63.
231. *Ibid.*, pp. 63–64.
232. Smith, *op. cit.*, pp. 235–36.
233. Dickson, *op. cit.*, p. 62.
234. Smith, *op. cit.*, p. 236.

Chapter XXII   The Eighth of January

235. Pakenham's Orders. Major C. R. Forrest MS. *Journal of the Operations Against New Orleans in 1814 and 1815.* R.A. Institute, Woolwich.
236. *General Court Martial for Trial of Brevet Lieutenant-Colonel Thomas Mullens* (Dublin, 1815). It is clear from these proceedings that Mullens also received written orders from General Gibbs reinforcing Pakenham's orders to the army.
237. One report (Cavendish, *op. cit.*, p. 44) asserts that the 44th was in position for three hours before returning for the ladders and fascines, but this does not accord with others, all of which show that the troops moved to their forward positions, in accordance with Pakenham's orders, at 4 A.M. on the eighth.
238. Dickson, *op. cit.*, p. 70. See also Keane's *Journal* (Wellington, *op. cit.*, Vol. X, p. 400).
239. Smith, *op. cit.*, p. 235.
240. Latour, *op. cit.*, pp. 165–66. "A Return of Strength for 16 January 1815" (Louisiana State Museum, f. 15) shows a total of 795 for the three regiments, of which 87 were sick and 134 unarmed.
241. Cavendish, *op. cit.*, p. 45, spells the name Leavach. Variously spelled by Fortescue and Cooke, "Learock" and "Larack." The spelling used is taken from the Army List for 1815.
242. *Ibid.*, p. 44.
243. Maunsel White MS., Ensign Graves' account. Louisiana Planters' Papers. Tulane University (Special Collections).
244. *Ibid.*
245. Smith, *op. cit.*, p. 236.
246. Dickson, *op. cit.*, p. 68. Quoted in later accounts as Pakenham's last words.
247. Lieutenant Gordon's Diary. Cavendish, *op. cit.*, p. 44.
248. Dickson, *op. cit.*, p. 68, states

that Pakenham was being carried to General Gibbs' house; Lieutenant Gordon, Cavendish, *op. cit.;* Pakenham, *op. cit.;* Lambert's Dispatch.

249. This is repeated by both Marquis James, *op. cit.,* and Samuel Carter, *op. cit.,* but neither cites any source.

250. Bassett, *Life of Andrew Jackson,* p. 194.

251. Bourchier, *op. cit.,* Vol. I p. 335.

252. Dickson, *op. cit.,* p. 66.

253. Brooks *(op. cit.,* p. 245) once again produces a piece of dialogue which is not authenticated by the sources he cites and his account is repeated by Carter. According to Brooks, Lambert said, "I do not think it prudent to renew the attack, Admiral." Cochrane is made to reply, "Why not? You saw Rennie make it. Rally the troops and we'll have this battle, General." This "verbatim" report appears to be entirely imaginary.

254. Accounts given by Smith and Burgoyne which appear to refer to this first council of war in fact refer to a second, held after Dickson's return. See note 258.

255. Dickson, *op. cit.,* p. 71, lists the guns taken:

1 10 inch Howitzer ⎫
2 4 Prs. Field Pieces ⎬ Brass
3 24 Prs. ⎫
3 12 Prs. ⎬ Iron
6 9 Prs. ⎭
1 12 Pr. Carronade not mounted

He also shows that the detachment of the 5th West India Regiment intended to accompany Thornton's brigade did not cross the river.

256. David Rees Papers. MS. 165, Box 1. Tulane University (Special Collections).

257. Dickson, *op. cit.,* p. 72. Gleig *(op. cit.,* p. 181) states that the pursuit was carried forward for two miles.

258. At the time of the first conference Burgoyne was absent looking for a boat to take him across the river and Smith was already on his way to the west bank. Wrottesley's statement that "Colonel Burgoyne strongly urged a renewal of the attack" must be considered suspect since he asserts that this was reported to him by Lieutenant Colonel Stovin, "who was assistant adjutant-general to the force and who was present." Stovin (as he shows in his own return of casualties dated January 28) was "severely" wounded in the action on the night of December 23 and had been replaced by Sir John Tylden. It is unlikely that Stovin was present at the council. Codrington, singled out by Smith as having been particularly in favor of renewing the assault, makes no mention of the council.

259. Dr. A. Carson Ritchie, "British Documents on the Louisiana Campaign, 1814–15." *Louisiana Historical Quarterly,* Vol. XLIV No. 2 (1961), p. 113.

260. Cavendish, *op. cit.,* p. 45.

261. Jackson to Monroe, January 9, 1815.

262. Diary of Major J. Michell. R.A. Institute, Woolwich.

263. Latour, *op. cit.,* pp. 175–76.

264. Smith, *op. cit.,* p. 240. Latour *(op. cit.,* p. 163) records with dramatic effect that the British fired on Americans who climbed from their ramparts, while their guns were cannonading the enemy, to help the

wounded—"But with horror I record the atrocity!" etc. This error, which he describes as an "atrocious act," was at least committed under heavy fire and during the battle. The fire directed at Harry Smith's flag of truce—though obviously also an error—evidently left Latour speechless, for he does not mention it.

265. Robert Butler's official report, January 16, 1815. Latour, *op. cit.,* Appendix XXIX.

266. These figures are taken from Lambert's official dispatch dated January 10, 1815, after deduction of Thornton's casualties on the west bank.

267. Ritchie, *op. cit.*.

Chapter XXIII   Retreat

268. Gleig, *op. cit.,* p. 182, states that the suspension was for two days, but this is contradicted by all other accounts and is probably a misprint. Certain other accounts refer to a period of six hours. Jackson's report to Monroe dated January 9 (Latour, Appendix XXIX) clearly states his proposal that the suspension should be until "twelve o'clock of this day." This is confirmed by Dickson (p. 78): "there was a suspension of Arms untill 12 this day [January 9] for the burial of the dead." It is also clear that Lambert's note of acceptance was not delivered until ten o'clock that morning.

269. Smith, *op. cit.,* p. 240.

270. Gleig, *op. cit.,* p. 182.

271. Smith, *op. cit.,* p. 239.

272. Bourchier, *op. cit.,* Vol. I, p. 339. Brooks (*op. cit.,* p. 241) and Carter (*op. cit.,* p. 258) state that Keane "felt a sharp sting in his neck," surely a unique reaction to a wound in the groin.

273. Latour, *op. cit.,* Appendix XXX.

274. Jackson to Monroe, January 13, 1815. Quoted by Latour, *op. cit.,* Appendix, XXIX.

275. Major Norman Pringle, Letters: *Vindicating the Character of the British Army* (Edinburgh, 1834).

276. *Ibid.*

277. Latour, *op. cit.,* p. 190, states "About 12 o'clock" but the report from Major Overton quoted by Latour in Appendix XXXIV gives the time as ten fifteen.

278. Tulane University (Special Collections), MS. L 976.31 A 954L.

279. Gleig, *op. cit.,* pp. 185–86.

280. *Ibid.*

281. This regiment, estimated at a strength of 1,000, appears on Latour's list of Pakenham's army (Appendix LXIV), a piece of guesswork or deliberate misrepresentation which has misled many historians of the campaign.

282. Smith, *op. cit.,* p. 244.

283. Dickson, *op. cit.,* pp. 85–90.

284. Forrest, Ms. *Journal* (Royal Artillery Institution, Woolwich).

285. Gleig, *op. cit.,* p. 187.

286. *Ibid.,* pp. 187–88.

287. Bassett, *Jackson Correspondence,* Vol. II, p. 153.

288. Dickson, *op. cit.,* p. 122.

289. Gleig, *op. cit.,* p. 192.

290. Dickson, *op. cit.,* p. 94.

291. Carter, *op. cit.,* obligingly provides a map showing Lambert's route for a twin-pronged attack on New Orleans and Baton Rouge from Mobile but cites no source. No evidence of such intentions after the

battle appears to exist outside Carter's book.

292. Dickson, *op. cit.*, pp. 106–16.

293. *Ibid.*, p. 117.

294. Latour, *op. cit.*, p. 202.

295. Dickson, *op. cit.*, p. 93.

296. Gleig, *op. cit.*, pp. 189–90.

297. Latour, *op. cit.*, Appendix XXXVIII.

298. *Ibid.*, Appendix LVI.

Chapter XXIV Resentment and Ingratitude

299. Latour, *op. cit.*, Appendix XXXII.

300. Pierre Favrot to his wife, January 21, 1815. Louisiana State Museum MSS.

301. Latr, *op. cit.*, p. 199.

302. *Ibid.*, p. 200.

303. *Ibid.*, Appendix XXXVII.

304. Rachel Jackson to Robert Hays, March 5, 1815. Library of Congress.

305. Nolte, *op. cit.*, p. 238.

306. Charles E. Gayarré, *History of Louisiana: The American Domination* (New York, 1866), Vol. IV, p. 620.

307. Bassett, *Life of Andrew Jackson*, p. 229.

308. Gayarré, *op. cit.*, Vol. IV, p. 625.

309. John Reid and Henry Eaton, *Life of Andrew Jackson* (1817).

310. Tulane University (Special Collections). MS. M 47.

311. Latour, *op. cit.*, Appendix LXI.

312. *Ibid.*, Appendix LXII.

313. D. B. Morgan to David Rees, April 20, 1817. Rees Papers, Tulane University.

314. Arthur, *op. cit.*, p. 131.

315. For a more detailed discussion of Latour see Arthur, *op. cit.;* Latour, *op. cit.* (introduction by Jane L. de Grummond to facsimile edition 1964); and Edwin J. Carpenter, Jr., "Arsène Lacarrière Latour," *The Hispanic American Historical Review*, Vol. XVIII (May, 1938).

316. Quoted by Parton, *op. cit.*, Vol. II, p. 595.

Chapter XXV An End and a Beginning

317. Moore, *op. cit.*, Vol. XII, p. 358.

318. John Gore, ed., *The Creevey Papers*, p. 130.

319. June 29, 1815. P.R.O. War Office, 30/40/43.

320. Smith, *op. cit.*, p. 244.

321. Sir G. Larpent, ed., *The Private Journal of F. Seymour Larpent, Judge-Advocate General* (London, 1853), Vol. I, p. 285.

322. Lieutenant General W. Napier, *The Life and Opinions of General Sir Charles Napier* (London, 1857), Vol. IV, p. 306.

323. Wellington to Longford, May 22, 1815. Quoted by Ritchie, *op. cit.*, p. 43.

324. *Pakenham Letters.* Quoted by Longford, *op. cit.*, p. 465.

325. Harry L. Coles, *The War of 1812* (Chicago, 1965), p. 233.

326. Cavendish, *op. cit.*, p. 149.

327. Wellington, *op. cit.*, Vol. IX, p. 582.

Bibliography

I   MANUSCRIPT MATERIAL
Historic New Orleans Collection
  Villeré Papers.
  Auotbiography of Admiral R. Aitchison
Library of Congress
  Alliot, Paul, *Historical and Political Reflections on Louisiana* (Louisiana MSS.).
Louisiana State Museum
  Favrot Papers.
National Library of Scotland
  Codrington Papers.
National Maritime Museum, Greenwich
  Warren Papers.
Public Archives of Canada, Ottawa
  "C Series" MSS. (Military).
Public Record Office, London
  Admiralty Papers: especially 1/502-508, 2/163, 2/1374-1381, 51/2675, 98/123, 98/228.
  Colonial Office Archives: especially 42/146, 42/151-157, 42/352-355, 43/23, 43/40, 43/49-50.
  War Office Archives: especially 1/96, 1/141-144, 6/2, 71/243.
Royal Artillery Institution, Woolwich
  Dickson Papers.
  Forrest, Charles Ramus, *Journal of the Operations Against New Orleans in 1814 and 1815.*
    Michell, Major John, *Diary.*
Tulane University, New Orleans (Howard Tilton Library: Special Collections)
  Andrew Hynes Collection.
  William Johnson Hapers.
  Louisiana Planters' Papers.
  William Priestley's Diary.

David Rees Papers.
De la Vergne Papers.
John Minor Wisdom Collection.
University of Texas
Bibliotheca Parsoniana: Latin American MSS., 1022, 1024, 1031.

II PUBLISHED SOURCES

Adams, Charles F., ed., *The Works of John Adams.* Boston, 1856. 10 Vols.
———*The Memoirs of John Quincy Adams.* Vols. I–III. Philadelphia, 1874–77. 12 Vols.
Adams, Henry, *History of the United States, 1801–1817.* New York, 1889–91. 9 Vols.
———, *Life of Albert Gallatin.* Philadelphia, 1879.
American State Papers: Class I. Foreign Relations. Washington, 1832–59. Vols. II–V.
American State Papers: Class V. Military Affairs. Washington, 1832. Vol. I.
American State Papers: Class VI. Naval Affairs. Washington, 1834. Vol. I.
Andrew, Charles, *The Prisoners' Memoirs, or, Dartmoor Prison.* New York, 1815.
Annals of the Congress of the United States 1789–1824. Washington, 1834–56.
Arthur, Stanley Clisby, *Jean Laffite, Gentleman Rover.* New Orleans, 1952.
Auchinleck, Gilbert, *A History of the War Between Great Britain and the United States of America During the Years 1812, 1813, and 1814.* Toronto, 1855.
Barbé-Marbois, F. de, *Historie de la Louisiane et de la cession de cette colonie par la France aux États-Unis de l'Amerique Septentrionale.* Paris, 1829.
Baring, Alexander, *An Inquiry into the Causes and Consequences of the Orders in Council; and an Examination of the Conduct of Great Britain Towards the Neutral Commerce of America.* London, 1808.
Barrett, C. R. B., ed., *The 85th King's Light Infantry.* London, 1913.
Bartlett, C. J., *Castlereagh.* London, 1967.
Bassett, John S., *The Life of Andrew Jackson.* New York, 1911. 2 Vols.
———, *The Correspondence of Andrew Jackson.* Washington, 1926–35. 7 Vols.
Bathurst, Earl, *Historical Manuscripts Commission: Report on the Manuscripts of Earl Bathurst, preserved at Cirencester Park.* London, 1923.
Berquin-Duvallon, F., *Vue de la colonie espagnole du Mississippi ou des provinces de Louisiane et Floride occidentale.* Paris, 1803.
Bourchier, Lady, ed., *Memoir of the Life of Admiral Sir Edward Codrington.* London, 1873. 2 Vols.
Brackenridge, H. M., *History of the Late War.* Philadelphia, 1839.
———, *Views of Louisiana Together with a Journal of a Voyage up the Missouri River in 1811.* Pittsburgh, 1814.
Bradbury, John, *Travels in the Interior of America in the Years, 1809–11.* Liverpool, 1817.
Brenton, Edward P., *The Naval History of Great Britain, 1783–1822.* London, 1825.
Brooks, Charles P., *The Siege of New Orleans.* Seattle, 1961.
Broughton, Lord, *Recollections of a Long Life.* London, 1911.
Bryant, Sir Arthur, *The Age of Elegance, 1812–22.* London, 1950.
———, *Years of Victory, 1802–1812.* London, 1944.
Buchan, John, *The History of the Royal Scots Fusiliers, 1678–1918.* London, 1925.
Buell, Augustus C., *History of Andrew Jackson.* New York, 1904. 2 Vols.
Burt, A. L., *The United States, Great Britain and British North America, from the Revolution to the Establishment of Peace After the War of 1812.* New Haven, 1940.

Cable, George, *The Creoles of Louisiana.* New York, 1884.

Carter, Samuel, *Blaze of Glory.* New York, 1971.

Casey, Powell A., *Louisiana in the War of 1812.* Baton Rouge, 1963.

Cavendish, Brigadier General A. E., *The 93rd Sutherland Highlanders, 1799–1927.* Privately printed, 1928.

Charlevoix, P. F. X. de, *History and General Description of New France, with the Historical Journal of a Voyage Made in Northern America.* 1744.

Coles, Harry L., *The War of 1812.* Chicago, 1965.

Cooke, Captain J. H., *A Narrative of Events in the South of France and of the Attack on New Orleans.* London, 1835.

Cooper, John Spencer, *Rough Notes of Seven Campaigns.* Carlisle, 1869.

Cope, Sir William H., *The History of the Rifle Brigade.* London, 1877.

Cowper, Colonel L. I., *The King's Own.* Oxford, 1939.

Cotterill, R. S., *The Old South.* Berkeley, 1936.

Dictionary of American Biography. New York, 1930.

Dictionary of National Biography. London, 1921–22.

Drake, Benjamin, *The Life of Tecumseh, and His Brother the Prophet.* Cincinnati, 1841.

Ellis, A. B., *History of the First West India Regiment.* London, 1885.

Engelman, Fred L., *The Peace of Christmas Eve.* London, 1962.

Fearon, Henry Bradshaw, *Sketches of America.* London, 1818.

Ford, Paul, ed., *The Writings of Thomas Jefferson.* New York, 1892–99.

Ford, Worthington C., ed., *The Writings of John Quincy Adams.* Vols. IV–V. New York, 1915. 12 Vols.

Fortescue, Sir John, *A History of the British Army.* London, 1911–20. Vols. VIII–X.

Fortier, Alcée, *A History of Louisiana.* New York, 1903. 4 Vols.

Foster, Vere, ed., *The Two Duchesses.* London, 1898.

Gallatin, Count, *A Great Peacemaker. The Diary of James Gallatin, Secretary to Albert Gallatin.* London, 1914.

Gayarré, Charles E., *History of Louisiana: The American Domination.* New York, 1866. 3 Vols.

Gilpin, Alec R., *The War of 1812 in the Old Northwest.* Toronto, 1958.

Giraud, Marcel, *Histoire de la Louisiane Française.* Paris, 1953.

Gleig, George Robert, *The Campaigns of the British Army at Washington and New Orleans . . . in the Years 1814–15.* London, 1821. Republished with alterations in 1826, 1833, 1836, and
847.

———, *A Subaltern in America.* Philadelphia, 1826. Published anonymously.

Gore, John, ed., *The Creevey Papers.* London, 1934.

Granville, Countess Castalia, ed., *Lord Granville Leveson-Gower: Private Correspondence, 1781–1821.* London, 1916. 2 Vols.

Grummond, Jane Lucas de, *The Baratarians and the Battle of New Orleans.* Baton Rouge, 1961.

Gurwood, Lieutenant Colonel John, ed., *The Dispatches of Field Marshal the Duke of Wellington During His Various Campaigns. . . .* London, 1838. 12 Vols.

Hamilton, John, *Sixty Years as an Irish Landlord.* London, 1894.

Hamilton, Stanislaus M., ed., *The Writings of James Monroe.* New York, 1901. 7 Vols.

Handlin, Oscar, *This America.* Cambridge, Mass., 1949.

Hare, A., ed., *Life and Letters of Maria Edgeworth.* London, 1894.

Hill, Benson Earle, *Recollections of an Artillery Officer*. London, 1836. 2 Vols.

Hitsman, J. MacKay, *The Incredible War of 1812*. Toronto, 1965.

Hopkins, James F., ed., *The Papers of Henry Clay*. Lexington, Ky., 1959. Vol. II.

Horsman, Reginald, *The Causes of the War of 1812*. Philadelphia, 1962.

———, *The War of 1812*. London, 1969.

Hosmer, James K., *History of the Louisiana Purchase*. New York, 1902.

Hunt, Charles Havens, *Life of Edward Livingston*. New York, 1864.

Hunt, Gaillard, ed., *The Writings of James Madison*. New York, 1900–10.

Ingersoll, C. J., *Historical Sketch of the Second War Between the United States of America and Great Britain*. Philadelphia, 1845. 3 Vols.

James, Marquis, *Andrew Jackson: The Border Captain*. Indianapolis, 1933.

James, William, *Military Occurrences in the American War of 1812*. London, 1818. 2 Vols.

———, *Naval History of Great Britain from . . . 1793 to the Accession of George IV*. 1826. 6 Vols.

King, Grace R., *New Orleans, the Place and the People*. New York, 1895.

———, *Creole Families of New Orleans*. New York, 1921.

Laffite, Jean, *Journal*. New York, 1958.

Landry, Stuart O., *Side Lights on the Battle of New Orleans*. New Orleans, 1965.

Larpent, Sir G., ed., *The Private Journal of F. Seymour Larpent, Judge-Advocate General*. London, 1853. 2 Vols.

Latour, A. Lacarrière. *Historical Memoir of the War in West Florida and Louisiana*, translated by H. P. Nugent. Philadelphia, 1816.

Lewis, Michael, *The History of the British Navy*. London, 1957.

Lipscomb, Andrew A., *The Writings of Thomas Jefferson*. Washington, 1903–4.

Longford, Elizabeth, *Wellington: The Years of the Sword*. London, 1969.

Lossing, Benson J., *The Pictorial Field Book of the War of 1812*. New York, 1868.

[Madison, James], *The Papers of James Madison*. Published by order of Congress. New York, 1864. 4 Vols.

———, *Letters and Other Writings of James Madison*. Philadelphia, 1865. 4 Vols.

Mahan, Captain A. T., *Sea Power in Its Relations to the War of 1812*. London, 1905. 2 Vols.

Marigny, Bernard de, *Réflexions sur la Campagne du Général André Jackson en Louisiane 1814 et 1815*. New York, 1848.

Martin, François-Xavier, *The History of Louisiana*. New Orleans, 1827–29. Reprinted 1882.

Maxwell, Sir Herbert, ed., *The Creevey Papers*. London, 1905.

Michaux, F. A., *Voyage à l'ouest des monts alléghanys, dans les états de l'Ohio, du Kentucky, et de Tennessee*. Paris, 1804.

Montlezun, De, *Voyage fait dans les années 1817 et 1818 de New York à la Nouvelle Orléans*. Paris, 1818.

Moore, G. C., ed., *The Autobiography of Lieutenant-General Sir Harry Smith, Bart., G.C.B.* London, 1901. 2 Vols.

[Mullens, Lieut-Colonel], *General Court Martial for Trial of Brevet Lieutenant-Colonel Thomas Mullens*. Dublin, 1815.

Napier, Lieutenant-General Sir W., *The Life and Opinions of General Sir Charles Napier G.C.B.* London, 1857.

———, ed., *Passages in the Early Life of General Sir George Napier*. London, 1884.

Nolte, Vincent, *Fifty Years in Both Hemispheres*. New York, 1854.

Pakenham, Thomas, ed., *Pakenham Letters 1800–1815*. London, 1914.

Parton, James, *Life of Andrew Jackson*. Boston, 1887. 3 Vols.

Perkins, Bradford, *Prologue to War: England and the United States, 1805-1812*. Los Angeles, 1962.

———, *Castlereagh and Adams: England and the United States 1812-1823*. Los Angeles, 1964.

Pratt, Julius W., *Expansionists of 1812*. New York, 1925.

Pratz, Le Page du, *Histoire de la Louisiane*. Paris, 1755.

Pringle, Major Norman, *Letters: Vindicating the Character of the British Army*. Edinburgh, 1834.

Read, David B., *Life and Times of Major-General Sir Isaac Brock, K.B.* Toronto, 1894.

Reiid, John, and Eaton, Henry, *Life of Andrew Jackson*. 1817.

Richardson, James D. *A Compilation of the Messages and Papers of the Presidents, 1789-1897*. Washington, 1896-99.

Robertson, James A., *Louisiana Under the Rule of Spain, France and the United States, 1785-1807*. Cleveland, 1911. 2 Vols.

Robin, C. C., *Voyages dans l'intérieur de la Louisiane, de la Floride Occidentale, et dans les Isles de Martinique et de Saint-Dominique, pendant les années, 1802-1806*. Paris, 1807.

Rolo, P. J. V., *George Canning*. London, 1965.

Roosevelt, Theodore, *The Naval Wars of 1812*. New York, 1889.

Rowland, Dunbar, *Official Letter Books of W. C. C. Claiborne, 1801-1816*. Jackson, Miss., 1907. 6 Vols.

Schaumann, A. L. F., *On the Road with Wellington: The Diary of a Commissary in the Peninsular Campaigns*, edited and translated by A. M. Ludovici. London, 1924.

Stuart, James, *Three Years in North America*. Edinburgh, 1833. 2 Vols.

Surtees, William, *Twenty-five Years in the Rifle Brigade*. Edinburgh, 1833.

Tatum, Howell, *Major Howell Tatum's Journal*, J. S. Bassett, ed., *Smith College Studies in History* VII. Northampton, Mass., 1921-22.

Taylor, George Rogers, ed., *The War of 1812. Problems in American Civilization*. Lexington, Mass., 1961.

Tupper, Ferdinand Brock, ed., *The Life and Correspondence of Major-General Sir Isaac Brock, K.B.* London, 1847.

Updyke, Frank A., *The Diplomacy of the War of 1812*. Baltimore, 1915.

Van Deusen, G. G., *The Life of Henry Clay*. Boston, 1937.

Vane, Charles, ed., *The Memoirs and Correspondence of Robert, Viscount Castlereagh*. London, 1848-1853.

Walker, Alexander, *Jackson and New Orleans*. New York, 1856.

Walters, Raymond, Jr., *Albert Gallatin*. New York, 1957.

Webster, C. K., *British Diplomacy, 1813-15, Select Documents*. London, 1921.

———, *The Foreign Policy of Castlereagh, 1812-15*. London, 1934.

Wellington, the Duke of, ed., *Supplementary Despatches, Correspondence, and Memoranda of Field Marshal Arthur Duke of Wellington, K.G.* Vols. IX–X. London, 1862. 10 Vols.

Whitaker, Arthur P., *The Mississippi Question, 1795-1803: A Study in Trade Politics, and Diplomacy*. New York, 1934.

Wiltse, Charles M., *The New Nation, 1800-45*. New York, 1965.

Wood, William, ed., *Select British Documents of the Canadian War of 1812*. Toronto, 1928. 3 Vols.

Wrottesley, Lieut-Col. The Hon. George, *Life and Correspondence of Field Marshal Sir John Burgoyne, Bart.* London, 1873. 2 Vols.

Zimmerman, James F., *Impressment of American Seamen*. New York, 1925.

III NEWSPAPERS, PAMPHLETS, AND PERIODICALS

In addition to those cited in the text, the following publications which contain either original material or valuable research by other historians have been consulted:

American Historical Review. Vol. LXI (1956). Latimer, Margaret K., *South Carolina—A Protagonist of the War of 1812.*

Battle of New Orleans Sesquicentennial Historical Booklets

Casey, Powell, *Louisiana at the Battle of New Orleans.*

Christian, Marcus, *Negro Soldiers in the Battle of New Orleans.*

Dixon, Richard R., *The Battle of the West Bank.*

Eler, Admiral E.; Morgan, Dr. W. J.; and Bosoco, Lieut. R., *Sea Power and the Battle of New Orleans.*

Huber, Leonard V., *New Orleans as It Was in 1814–1815.*

Meuse, William E., *The Weapons of the Battle of New Orleans.*

Scott, Valerie McNair (Lady Pakenham), *Major-General Sir Edward Pakenham.*

Watson, Elbert L., *Tennessee at the Battle of New Orleans.*

Wilson, Samuel, Jr., *Plantation Houses on the Battlefields of New Orleans.*

Louisiana Historical Quarterly

Vol. V (1922). Hart, W. O., *Mrs. Louise Livingston, Wife of Edward Livingston.*

Vol. IX (1926). *Report of the Committee of Inquiry on the Military Measures Executed Against the Legislature.*

Vol. IX (1926). *Letter of the Duke of Wellington (May 22, 1815) on the Battle of New Orleans.*

Vol. IX (1926). Dart, Henry P., *Jackson and the Louisiana Legislature.*

Vol. IX (1926). Mayhew, Thaddeus, *A Massachusetts Volunteer at the Battle of New Orleans.*

Vol. X (1927). Hardin, J. Fair, *The First Great River Captain.*

Vol. X (1927). *General David B. Morgan's Defense of the Conduct of the Louisiana Militia in the Battle on the Left [sic] Side of the River.*

Vol. X (1927). Morse, Edward C., *Captain Ogden's Troop of Horse in the Battle of New Orleans.*

Vols. XVI, XVII (1933–34). Adams, Reed McC. B., *New Orleans and the War of 1812.*

Vol. XXIII (1940). Faye, Stanley, *The Great Stroke of Pierre Laffite.*

Vol. XLIV (1961). Ritchie, Dr. Carson A., *British Documents on the Louisiana Campaign, 1814–1815.*

Louisiana History (Louisiana Historical Association)

Vol. III (1962). Nasatir, A. P., *An Opposition to the Sale of Louisiana.*

Vol. V (1964). Holmes, J. D. L., *Robert Ross's Plan for Invasion of Louisiana.*

Vol. VI (1965). Mahon, J. K., *British Command Decisions Relative to the Battle of New Orleans.*

Mississippi Valley Historical Review

Vol. X (1923–24). Hacker, Louis M., *Western Land Hunger and the War of 1812: A Conjecture.*

Vol. XII (1925–26). Pratt, Julius W., *Western War Aims in the War of 1812.*

Vol. XXVIII (1941). Goodman, Warren H., *The Origins of the War of 1812: A Survey of Changing Interpretations.*

Niles' Weekly Register. Baltimore, 1812–15.

Smith College *Studies in History.* Vol. VII, Nos. 1–3 (1922).
    Major Howell Tatum's Journal While Acting Topographical Engineer (1814) to General Jackson Commanding the Seventh Military District, J. S. Bassett, ed.

Times, London, 1812–1815.

Times-Democrat, June 18, 1893. *In Pakenham's Camp: The War Diary of Captain Benjamin Storey, Orleans Rifle Company.*

William and Mary Quarterly. Vol. XVIII (1961). Risjord, Norman J., *1812: Conservatives, War Hawks and the Nation's Honor.*

Index

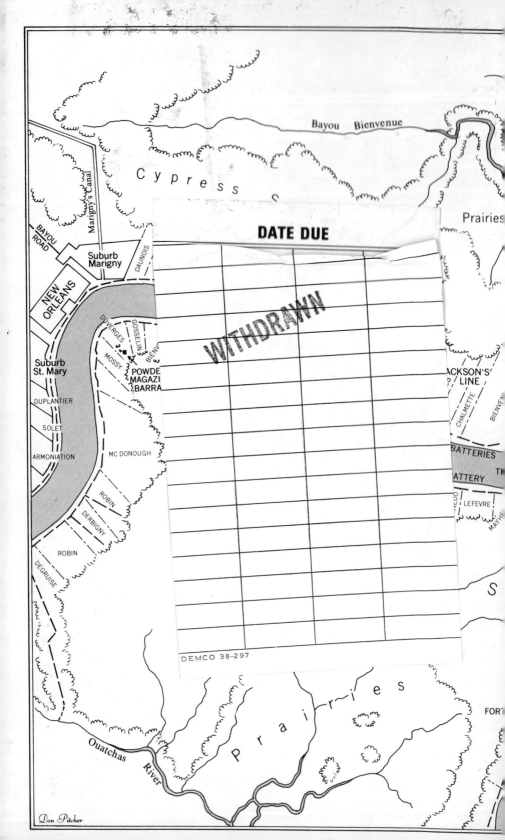

Bayou Bienvenue

Cypress s

Prairies

BAYOU
ROAD

Marigny's Canal

Suburb
Marigny

DAUNOIS

NEW
ORLEANS

DUVERGES

GOSSELIN

MOSSY

BIENV

Suburb
St. Mary

POWDE
MAGAZI
BARRA

DUPLANTIER

SOLET

ARMONIATION

MC DONOUGH

ROBIN

DERBIGNY

ROBIN

DEGRUISE

JACKSON'S
LINE

CHALMETTE

BIENFE

BATTERIES

TH

ATTERY

LEFEVRE

MAYHE

P r a i r i e s

Ouatchas
River

FORT

S

Don Pitcher